A Study of Chinese Characters

As the first volume of a two-volume set on Chinese ancient characters and newly unearthed literature, this book brings together the author's research articles that discuss the development of Chinese characters and the tradition of Chinese palaeography.

The 23 chapters in this book focus on two aspects of Chinese characters. The first 13 chapters centre on the evolution of Chinese characters, analysing the composition system and its transformation, the motivation and mechanisms behind its evolution, as well as the methodology of the study of ancient characters. The subsequent 10 chapters mainly revolve around *Shuowen Jiezi*, one of the oldest character dictionaries in China. The author offers a novel understanding of the core issues related to this most important philological work, such as the version of the dictionary, misunderstandings in previous scholarship, and its relations with other palaeographical materials.

The title will appeal to students and scholars of Sinology, Chinese philology, and palaeography, as well as Chinese characters.

Wang Guiyuan is Professor and Doctoral Supervisor at the School of Literature at Renmin University of China. He is a leading scholar in the field of Chinese palaeography and lexicology.

China Perspectives

The *China Perspectives* series focuses on translating and publishing works by leading Chinese scholars, writing about both global topics and China-related themes. It covers Humanities & Social Sciences, Education, Media and Psychology, as well as many interdisciplinary themes.

This is the first time any of these books have been published in English for international readers. The series aims to put forward a Chinese perspective, give insights into cutting-edge academic thinking in China, and inspire researchers globally.

To submit proposals, please contact the Taylor & Francis Publisher for China Publishing Programme, Lian Sun (Lian.Sun@informa.com).

Titles in history currently include:

The Indigenization of Christianity in China I
1807–1922
Qi Duan

A Cultural History of the Chinese Character "Ta (她, She)"
Invention and Adoption of a New Feminine Pronoun
Huang Xingtao

A Concise History of China's Population
Jianxiong Ge

Sino-Foreign Cultural Exchange
A Historical Perspective
Cai Hongsheng

A Study of Chinese Characters
Wang Guiyuan

A Study of Excavated Documents in China
Wang Guiyuan

For more information, please visit www.routledge.com/China-Perspectives/book-series/CPH

A Study of Chinese Characters

Wang Guiyuan

LONDON AND NEW YORK

The publication of this title was supported by funds for building world-class universities (disciplines) of Renmin University of China.

First published in English 2024
by Routledge
4 Park Square, Milton Park, Abingdon, Oxon OX14 4RN

and by Routledge
605 Third Avenue, New York, NY 10158

Routledge is an imprint of the Taylor & Francis Group, an informa business

© 2024 Wang Guiyuan

Translated by Zhang Xiaoting, David Golia

The right of Wang Guiyuan to be identified as author of this work has been asserted in accordance with sections 77 and 78 of the Copyright, Designs and Patents Act 1988.

All rights reserved. No part of this book may be reprinted or reproduced or utilised in any form or by any electronic, mechanical, or other means, now known or hereafter invented, including photocopying and recording, or in any information storage or retrieval system, without permission in writing from the publishers.

Trademark notice: Product or corporate names may be trademarks or registered trademarks, and are used only for identification and explanation without intent to infringe.

English Version by permission of China Renmin University Press.

British Library Cataloguing-in-Publication Data
A catalogue record for this book is available from the British Library

Library of Congress Cataloging-in-Publication Data
Names: Wang, Guiyuan, author.
Title: A study of Chinese characters / Wang Guiyuan.
Other titles: Han zi yu chu tu wen xian lun ji. English
Description: Abingdon, Oxon ; New York, NY : Routledge, 2024. | Series: China perspectives | Includes bibliographical references and index. | Contents: v. 1. A study of Chinese characters — v. 2. A study of excavated documents in China. | English with some Chinese.
Identifiers: LCCN 2023034168 (print) | LCCN 2023034169 (ebook) | ISBN 9781032607276 (vol. 1 ; hardback) | ISBN 9781032622972 (vol. 1 ; paperback) | ISBN 9781032612270 (vol. 2 ; hardback) | ISBN 9781032623085 (vol. 2 ; paperback) | ISBN 9781032622965 (vol. 1 ; ebook) | ISBN 9781032623078 (vol. 2 ; ebook)
Subjects: LCSH: Chinese characters—History. | Chinese language—Etymology. | China—Antiquities.
Classification: LCC PL1171 .W334613 2024 (print) | LCC PL1171 (ebook) | DDC 495.11/1—dc23/eng/20231016
LC record available at https://lccn.loc.gov/2023034168
LC ebook record available at https://lccn.loc.gov/2023034169

ISBN: 978-1-032-60727-6 (hbk)
ISBN: 978-1-032-62297-2 (pbk)
ISBN: 978-1-032-62296-5 (ebk)

DOI: 10.4324/9781032622965

Typeset in Times New Roman
by Apex CoVantage, LLC

Contents

List of Figures	*vii*
List of Tables	*viii*

1	Core Issues Regarding the Evolution of Chinese Characters	1
2	The Composition System of Chinese Characters and the Stages of Its Development	27
3	The Evolution of Chinese Characters: An Issue Needs Further Exploration	39
4	The Systematic Transformation of the Chinese Character Composition	50
5	The Motivation and Mechanisms behind the Evolution of the Chinese Characters	69
6	The Process and Mechanism of the Formation of the Stroke System	86
7	The Formation Process and Mechanisms of Radicals	106
8	Symbolisation: The Mechanism of the Transformation from Archaic Characters to New-Style Characters	126
9	On the Official Script Transformation	149
10	Sense Relations Among Same-Origin Chinese Characters (Words)	160

11	Three Issues Regarding the Currently Used Chinese Characters	173
12	Analysis Methods Used in Studies of Characters on Unearthed Texts	182
13	A Study on Characters from Bamboo Slips and Silk Manuscripts	200
14	Discussion on the Original Meaning of *Wu* 物	215
15	The Connotations of *Xie* 偕 in "Fish and Wine" from *Shi Jing*	220
16	An Evaluation of Different Versions of *Shuowen Jiezi*	223
17	Four Misunderstandings about *Shuowen Jiezi*	240
18	New Proofs of *Shuowen Jiezi*	255
19	Mutual Confirmation Between Zhangjiashan Han-Dynasty Bamboo Slips and *Shuowen Jiezi*: Supplement to Proofreading Notes to *Shuowen Jiezi*	260
20	A New Study on the Explanations of *Shuowen Jiezi*	266
21	Mutual Corroboration Between *Shuowen Jiezi* and Chu-State Bamboo Slips	273
22	Chinese Words in *Shuowen Jiezi*: A Probe into the Earliest Word Classification Theory of China	281
23	*Shuowen Jiezi* and an Exploration of Homologous Characters (Same-Origin Characters)	293
	Index	*313*

Figures

1.1	An Unearthed Kneeling Woman Pottery Statue (1)	2
1.2	An Unearthed Kneeling Woman Pottery Statue (2)	2
1.3	An Unearthed Chinese Battle Axe	2
1.4	An Unearthed Figural Lamp Stand	3
2.1	The Composition of 麈	28
2.2	The Composition of 骑	29
2.3	Structures in the Composition System	30
2.4	The Compositional Hierarchy of 骑	31
2.5	Categories of Components and Their Functions	33
3.1	Two Parallel Modifications of 凵	45
3.2	Strokes Modified in Different Ways	47
4.1	Different Forms of 渔 in Oracle-Bone Inscriptions	51
4.2	Different Forms of 执 in Oracle-Bone Inscriptions	51
4.3	Different Small-Seal Forms of 渔	51
4.4	Different Forms of 祀 in Oracle-Bone Inscriptions	52
4.5	Different Forms of 異 in Oracle-Bone and Bronze Inscriptions	52
4.6	Different Forms of 御 in Oracle-Bone Inscriptions	54
4.7	Different Forms of 莫 in Oracle-Bone Inscriptions	54
4.8	Different Small-Seal Forms of 逆	55
4.9	Different Forms of 逆 in Oracle-Bone Inscriptions	55
4.10	Changes in the Form of 企	57
4.11	Forms of 武 in Oracle-Bone and Bronze Inscriptions	61
4.12	Changes in the Composition of 降	63
5.1	Early Relations Among Images, Words, and Chinese Characters	73
5.2	Reasonable Relations Among Images, Words, and Chinese Characters	73
5.3	The Composition of 众	78
5.4	The Composition of 骑	79
8.1	The Relationship Between Chinese Words and Ancient/Current Character Forms	126
8.2	Characters used in *Dongba Sutras*	136
12.1	Classification of Character Samples Based on Functions and Forms	185
12.2	Classification of Character Components	189
17.1	The Original Meaning and Extended and Borrowed Meanings	242
17.2	Development of an Expression Without a Character Form	246

Tables

1.1	The Two Stages of Development of Chinese Characters	2
1.2	Comparison Between Pictographs and Sub-Pictographs	3
1.3	The Character Form Analysis of *Wang* 王 (king)	4
1.4	The Character Form Analysis of *Nv* 女 (woman/girl)	5
1.5	The Character Form Analysis of *Guang* 光 (light)	6
1.6	Characters Used in the Spring and Autumn Period	6
1.7	The Addition of Semantic Components in the Spring and Autumn Period	7
1.8	Comparison Between Western-Zhou-Dynasty and Spring-and-Autumn-Period Characters	8
1.9	Evolutionary Trends From Western Zhou Dynasty to Eastern Han Dynasty	9
1.10	Evolutionary Trends in the Mid- and Late-Warring States Period	10
1.11	Comparison Between the Official Script and the Regular Script	11
1.12	Development Stages of Chinese Characters	12
1.13	Examples of Multitype Modification (1)	13
1.14	Examples of Multitype Modification (2)	14
1.15	Examples of Multitype Modification (3)	14
1.16	Multitype Modifications of Character Component 冃	15
1.17	Modifications of Character Components	16
1.18	Examples of Analogisation	17
1.19	Different Forms of 總	17
1.20	Evolution of 更	18
1.21	Multitype Modifications to the Positions of Character Components	18
1.22	Changes in the Form of 数/數	19
1.23	Changes in the Form of 魏	20
1.24	New Character Forms for New Words	20
1.25	Modifications to Character Forms for Mutual Differentiation	21
1.26	Evolution of 弋	21
1.27	Evolution of 生	21
1.28	Different Forms of Character Component 止	22
1.29	Evolution of 止	23
1.30	Different Forms of Character Component 彳	23

1.31	Different Forms of 學/学	24
1.32	Dunhuang Documents' Influence on Han-Dynasty Character Forms	24
2.1	Development Stages of the Composition System of Chinese Characters	38
3.1	弋 in Western-Zhou-Dynasty Bronze Inscriptions	41
3.2	Evolution of 十	41
3.3	Evolution of 土	41
3.4	Evolution of 廿	42
3.5	Evolution of 卅	42
3.6	Different Forms of Character 弋	42
3.7	Different Forms of Character 弋	43
3.8	Different Forms of Character 弋	43
3.9	Different Forms of Character Component 弋	43
3.10	Different Forms of Character Component 弋 on Chu-State Bamboo Slips	44
3.11	Different Forms of 弋 on Chu-State Bamboo Slips	44
3.12	Different Han-Dynasty Forms of 生	45
3.13	Different Forms of 生 in the Han Dynasty	45
3.14	Different Forms of 牛	45
3.15	Different Forms of Character Component 牛	46
3.16	Different Forms of 步	46
3.17	步 in Ancient Official and Small-Seal Scripts	47
4.1	Requirements for the Orientations and Positions of Character Components in Oracle-Bone Inscriptions	53
4.2	Pictographic Supplements in Oracle-Bone Inscriptions	55
4.3	Examples of Phonetic/Semantic Additions	56
4.4	Changes in the Composition of 塁	57
4.5	Changes in the Form of 析	58
4.6	Changes in the Form of 毓	58
4.7	Changes in the Form of 得	59
4.8	Changes in the Form of 皇	59
4.9	Changes in the Form of 若	59
4.10	Changes in the Form of 牢	60
4.11	Changes in the Form of 鼎	60
4.12	Changes in the Form of 降 and the Form of 陟	63
4.13	Changes in the Form of 監	64
5.1	Shang-Dynasty Oracle-Bone Inscriptions	70
5.2	Shang-Dynasty Oracle-Bone Inscriptions	71
5.3	Shang-Dynasty Oracle-Bone Inscriptions	71
5.4	Shang-Dynasty Oracle-Bone Inscriptions	72
5.5	Shang-Dynasty Character Forms	72
5.6	Symbols on Potteries and Oracle-Bone and Bronze Inscriptions	74
5.7	Changes in the Form of 子	75
5.8	Changes in the Form of 莫	76

x Tables

5.9	Forms of 降 in Oracle-Bone and Bronze Inscriptions	77
5.10	Forms of 洹 in Oracle-Bone and Bronze Inscriptions	77
5.11	Examples of Character Form Changes From the Shang Dynasty to the Late Western Zhou Dynasty	78
5.12	Three Forms of 莫 in Oracle-Bone Inscriptions	80
5.13	Different Forms of the Same Character in Oracle-Bone Inscriptions	81
5.14	Character Form Changes from the Shang Dynasty to the Western Zhou Dynasty	81
5.15	Transition From Shang-Dynasty Oracle-Bone Script to the Small-Seal Script	82
5.16	Transition From Shang-Dynasty Oracle-Bone Script to Western-Zhou-Dynasty Bronze Script	83
5.17	Transition From Shang-Dynasty Bronze Script to the Small-Seal Script	84
5.18	Transition From Pictographic Combinations to Semantic Combinations	85
6.1	The Compositional Structure of Characters in the Archaic and the New-Style Writing Systems	86
6.2	Comparison Between Archaic and New-Style Character Components	87
6.3	The Compositional Structure and Functional Analysis of an Archaic Character	87
6.4	The Compositional Structure and Functional Analysis of a New-Style Character	87
6.5	Comparison Between the Western-Zhou-Dynasty (1046–771 BCE) and the Eastern-Han-Dynasty (25–220) Component Forms	88
6.6	The Characteristics and Durations of the Three Periods in the Evolution of Strokes	89
6.7	Features of the Characters in the Origination Period	90
6.8	Features of the Characters in the Formation Period	91
6.9	The Formation of Rising Strokes	91
6.10	The Evolution of the Vertical-Hook Stroke Embodied in Different Forms of *Xiao* 小 (Small)	92
6.11	The Evolution of the Vertical-Hook Stroke Embodied in Different Forms of *Ding* 丁 (Adult Male)	92
6.12	The Evolution of the Horizontal-Turning-and-Hook Stroke Embodied in Different Forms of *Yue* 月 (Moon)	93
6.13	The Evolution of the Vertical-Curving-and-Hook Stroke Embodied in Different Forms of *Xiong* 兄 (Elder Brother)	93
6.14	The Evolution of the Dot Stroke Embodied in Different Forms of *Yu* 於 (in/at/on)	94
6.15	The Evolution of the Dot Stroke Embodied in Different Forms of *Zhu* 主 (Master)	94
6.16	The Evolution of the Dot Stroke Embodied in Different Forms of *Bing* 病 (Illness)	95

Tables xi

6.17	The Rising Stroke Used in the Manuscripts of the Wei-Jin Period (220–589)	95
6.18	The Vertical-Hook Stroke Used in the Manuscripts of the Wei-Jin Period (220–589)	96
6.19	The Horizontal-Turning-and-Hook Stroke Used in the Manuscripts of the Wei-Jin Period (220–589)	96
6.20	The Vertical-Curving-and-Hook Stroke Used in the Manuscripts of the Wei-Jin Period (220–589)	96
6.21	The Dot Stroke Used in the Manuscripts of the Wei-Jin Period (220–589)	97
6.22	Handwritten Characters with Brush Marks in the Wei-Jin Period (220–589)	98
6.23	Examples of the Principle of Placing Emphasis on Character Forms	99
6.24	Examples of the Principle of Placing Emphasis on Character Forms	99
6.25	Examples of the Principle of Placing Emphasis on Character Forms	100
6.26	Examples of the Modifications Made to Differentiate Characters	100
6.27	Examples of Placing the Emphasis on the Aesthetics of Characters	101
6.28	The Influence of Character Structures on the Formation of Strokes	102
6.29	The Seal-Script Forms of Zhu 朱 (Vermilion), Mo 末 (End), and Wei 未 (Not Yet)	103
6.30	Planned Stroke Combinations	103
6.31	Transformation Through Replacement	104
6.32	Transformation Through Representation and Replacement	104
7.1	Components Using Their Orientation to Indicate Meanings	108
7.2	The Evolution of Si 祀 (Worship) and Fu 福 (Happiness)	113
7.3	The Evolution of Zhi 祇 (to Revere) and Yong 墉 (Fortified Wall)	113
7.4	The Evolution of Ding 鼎 (Tripod Caldron) and Zi 字 (Characters)	114
7.5	The Oracle-Bone-Script Forms of Mu 牡 (Male Animals), Pin 牝 (Female Animals), lao 牢 (fence), and Mu 牧 (Herd)	115
7.6	The Evolution of Feng 凤 (Male Phoenix) and Ji 鸡 (Chicken)	117
7.7	The Evolution of Zhun 屯 (Hardness)	117
7.8	The Oracle-Bone-Script Forms of Chu 出 (Out) and Yu 御 (Manage)	119
7.9	Comparison Between Qin Characters of Different Periods	121
8.1	The Evolution of Wang 王 (King), Nv 女 (Woman/Girl), Guang 光 (Light), and Jian 监 (Supervise)	129
8.2	Comparison Between the Single-Component and Multiple-Component Forms of Feng 凤 (Male Phoenix) and Ji 鸡 (Chicken)	133
8.3	The Evolution of the Character Mai 買 (Buy)	137
8.4	The Evolution of the Character Ni 逆 (Meet Head-On)	137
8.5	The Evolution of the Character Yu 御 (Manage)	139
8.6	The Evolution of the Character Si 祀 (Worship)	139
8.7	The Evolution of the Character She 涉 (to Wade)	140
8.8	The Evolution of the Character Jiang 降 (to Descend)	140
8.9	The Evolution of the Character Zhe 折 (to Break)	141

8.10	The Evolution of the Character *Guan* 祼 (a Worship Ceremony of Pouring Water to Irrigate the Field)	141
8.11	The Evolution of the Character *Xu* 须 (Facial Hair)	142
8.12	The Evolution of *Chi* 齿 (Teeth) and *Ge* 戈 (Dagger-Axe)	143
8.13	The Evolution of the Character *Zhi* 祇 (to Revere)	143
8.14	The Evolution of the Character *Xiu* 羞 (to Offer)	145
8.15	The Evolution of the Character *Zhui* 追 (to Chase After)	145
10.1	Analysis of Sense Relations Among Same-Origin Chinese Characters	162
12.1	Mistaken Copies of Characters from Silk Manuscripts Unearthed in Mawangdui	183
12.2	Examples of Stroke Additions	195
16.1	The Three Versions' Explanations for 釪, 扜, 鐯, and 析	226
17.1	Changes in the Form of 吊	248
17.2	Changes in the Form of 皇	250
17.3	Changes in the Form of 逆	251
23.1	Meaning Analysis	297
23.2	Analysis of Phonetic Components and Core Semes	309

1 Core Issues Regarding the Evolution of Chinese Characters[1]

I. Character Types and the Stages of Their Development

Previous studies generally agree that the evolution of Chinese characters can be split into two stages: the Archaic Stage and the New-Style Stage. On this point, Qi Gong 启功 (1912–2005) made the following statement. "We notice that the character-like symbols on unearthed potteries from the Dawenkou Culture (ca. 4100–2600 BCE), as well as the surviving ancient Chinese fonts and small-seal characters, all feature curved strokes and roundish shapes. Characters on the roughly-inscribed decree slabs of the Qin Dynasty (221–207 BCE), however, begin appearing squarish, characterized by straight strokes and square corners. On the Qin-Dynasty slabs bearing the imperial laws, we can see even more straight strokes and squarish shapes, which indicate the creation of a New-Style writing system that is still in use today. Therefore, we have a reason to name the character fonts created before and after the emergence of the New-Style writing system seal-script fonts and official-script fonts, respectively. The regular-script fonts and Song typeface we use now are all evolved from the official-script fonts."[2] Tang Lan 唐兰 (1901–1979) further pointed out that the great difference between ancient Chinese characters and modern and contemporary Chinese characters was that the former featured seal-script fonts and the latter boasted official-script fonts or cursive script fonts.[3] Chen Mengjia 陈梦家 (1911–1966) described the seal script as a witness to the end of ancient characters and the official script as a pioneer of modern and contemporary characters.[4] Wu Shichang 吴世昌 (1908–1986) called the rise of the official script a major event in the history of Chinese characters and a key link between the big seal script and the regular script.[5] To be more specific, Chinese characters created amid the Archaic Stage are pictograph-like characters, but those created in the New-Style Stage are a mixture of pictographs, ideographs, phonetic-semantic compounds, and others. This transition was caused by a change in the way to create characters: from image-based creation to creation based on pronunciations and meanings.[6]

(I) Pictographs, Sub-pictographs, and the Stages of Their Development

In terms of forms, Chinese characters have experienced a transition from pictographs to sub-pictographs in the Archaic Stage and another transition from the official script to the regular script in the New-Style Stage.

DOI: 10.4324/9781032622965-1

2 Core Issues Regarding the Evolution of Chinese Characters

Table 1.1 The Two Stages of Development of Chinese Characters

Stage of Development	Archaic Stage		New-Style Stage	
Creation Basis	Images		Pronunciations and Meanings	
Character Type	Pictograph	Sub-Pictograph	Official Script	Regular Script

Pictograph-like characters tend to faithfully represent images. Take *nv* 女 (woman/girl) for example. It is  in Shang-Dynasty (ca.1600–1046 BCE) bronze inscriptions and  in early Western-Zhou-Dynasty (ca.1046–771 BCE) bronze inscriptions. Both of the symbols depict a seated woman/girl, similar to unearthed ancient statues of seated women and girls.

Figure 1.1 An Unearthed Kneeling Woman Pottery Statue (1)   *Figure 1.2* An Unearthed Kneeling Woman Pottery Statue (2)

The character *wang* 王 (king) is  in Shang-Dynasty bronze inscriptions and in early Western-Zhou-Dynasty bronze inscriptions. This symbol stands for a battle axe with its edge downwards, which is similar to unearthed ancient battle axes.

Figure 1.3 An Unearthed Chinese Battle Axe

Core Issues Regarding the Evolution of Chinese Characters 3

Another example is *guang* 光 (light). It is 🝁 in Shang-Dynasty bronze inscriptions and 🝂 in early Western-Zhou-Dynasty bronze inscriptions, both evoking a picture of a person holding a lamp. Their creation was probably inspired by the people who attended to lamps at ancient noble banquets.

  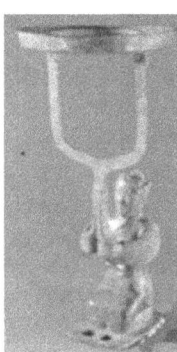

Figure 1.4 An Unearthed Figural Lamp Stand

Sub-pictographs still illustrate images but in a more abstract way in comparison with pictographs. They are still seal-script characters, but they are not all about describing images, which embodies a transition from pictographic characters to semantic-phonetic characters. The following is a comparison of a few characters' pictographic fonts and sub-pictographic fonts.

Table 1.2 Comparison Between Pictographs and Sub-Pictographs

Regular-Script Character	Pictograph	Sub-Pictograph
nv 女 (woman/girl)		
wang 王 (king)		
guang 光 (light)		

These seal-script characters still represent images, but these images are usually not realistic enough. For instance, *nv* 女 (woman/girl) is no longer the image of a sitting woman/girl, *wang* 王 (king), no longer the image of a battle axe, and *guang* 光 (light), no longer the image of a person holding a lamp.

Zhang Taiyan 章太炎 (1869–1936), a philosopher of the last years of the Qing Dynasty (1636–1912), once compared pictographs to Chinese meticulous paintings

4 Core Issues Regarding the Evolution of Chinese Characters

and sketch drawings. He said, "All pictographs are used to represent images, but small-seal-script characters differ from the more old-fashioned pictographs. The former is like sketch drawings, and the latter, to meticulous paintings. For example, *gui* 龟 (turtle), *ji* 鸡 (chicken), and *huan* 环 (ring) are originally written as ▨, ▨, and ▨, vividly picturing relevant objects. In comparison, small-seal-script characters are less image-evoking and less realistic, such as the following examples: ▨ for *ma* 马 (horse), ▨ for *niu* 牛" (ox), ▨ for *quan* 犬 (dog), ▨ for *niao* 鸟 (bird), and ▨ for *yu* 鱼 (fish)."[7] The above-mentioned old-fashioned pictographs or archaic pictographs emerged before small-seal characters, a typical type of sub-pictographs. These archaic pictographs were quoted by Mr. Zhang from the bronze inscriptions that used archaic fonts created before the Western Zhou Dynasty (ca.1046–771 BCE). He was the first person to spot the difference between the archaic pictographs and the sub-pictographs.

Compared to their predecessors, sub-pictographs represent not only images but also pronunciations and meanings, which reflects a change in the basic principles of character creation. Nonetheless, this change must have been very slow and gradual since any sudden change in the written language, an indispensable tool in people's daily lives, would cause unnecessary barriers that hindered effective communication.

When did this change start? The character form analysis of *wang* 王 (king), *nv* 女 (woman/girl), and *guang* 光 (light) can give some insight. Noticeably, the following analysis is based on previous studies on character forms: (1) "A Complete Glyph Table of the Bronze-Inscription Characters of Different Periods of the Western Zhou Dynasty" 西周金文分期字形全表, which is an appendix in a doctoral dissertation titled "*Research on the Composition of the Western-Zhou-Dynasty Bronze-Inscription Characters*" 西周金文构形研究 completed by Tao Quyong 陶曲勇 at the School of Literal Arts of Renmin University of China; (2) "A Complete Glyph Table of the Spring-and-Autumn-Period Bronze-Inscription Characters and a Study on Their Composition" 春秋金文字形全表及构形研究 by Yang Xiuen 杨秀恩; and (3) "A Complete Glyph Table of the Warring-States-Period Bronze-Inscription Characters and Their Composition" 战国金文字形全表及构形研究 by Fan Junli 樊俊利. The above-mentioned studies cover all the ancient Chinese characters in the Western-Zhou-Dynasty, Spring-and-Autumn-Period, and Warring-States-Period bronze inscriptions found before 2010 (including 2010). Due to limited space, the tables below that are quoted from the above studies are abridged. For more details, please refer to the original studies.

Table 1.3 The Character Form Analysis of *Wang* 王 (king)

Early Western Zhou Dynasty	

Core Issues Regarding the Evolution of Chinese Characters 5

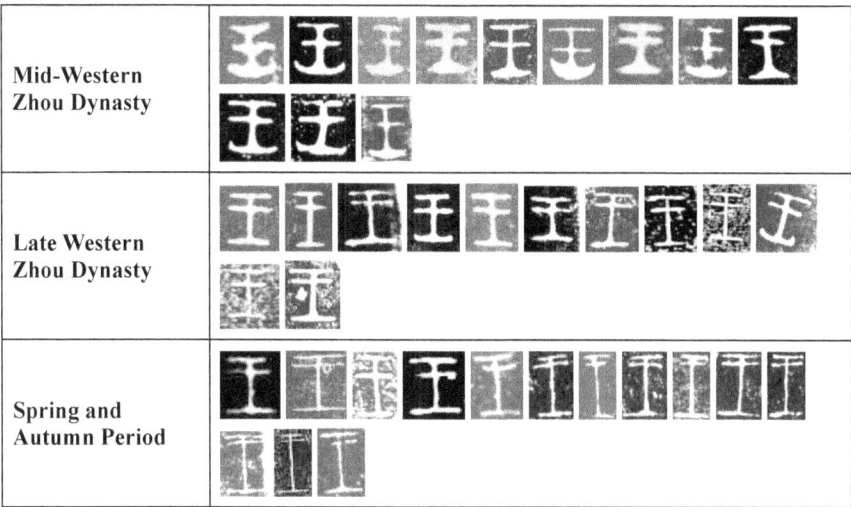

An obvious change occurred to the character *wang* 王 in the late Western Zhou Dynasty: the axe symbol was changed into a horizontal stroke. As a result, the character ceased to represent the image of a battle axe.

Table 1.4 The Character Form Analysis of *Nv* 女 (woman/girl)

Early Western Zhou Dynasty	
Mid-Western Zhou Dynasty	
Late Western Zhou Dynasty	
Spring and Autumn Period	

6 *Core Issues Regarding the Evolution of Chinese Characters*

In late Western Zhou, the part representing the legs of a sitting woman/girl became short and straight, so that the character ceased to represent a woman/girl in a sitting posture.

Table 1.5 The Character Form Analysis of *Guang* 光 (light)

Early Western Zhou Dynasty	
Mid-Western Zhou Dynasty	
Late Western Zhou Dynasty	
Spring and Autumn Period	

Originally, the upper part of *guang* 光 (light) featured an upwards curve that represented a lamp tray, but in the late Western Zhou Dynasty, this curve was replaced by downwards strokes, which did not look like a tray any longer.

The Chinese people developed their writing and reading habits over a long period of time. They changed their character forms only when their understanding of these characters evolved. To look for evidence of this evolution of understanding, it is essential to first study the complex pictographic fonts and then their variants and determine whether these variants have evolved into abstract symbols or sub-pictographs.

Overall, pictographic characters evolved into sub-pictographs in the late Western Zhou Dynasty except that there were still a small number of characters containing pictographic elements, namely big solid dots: *zheng* 正 (just), *tun* 屯 (stock), and *zhong* 终 (end). It was not until the Spring and Autumn Period that such dots were replaced by horizontal strokes. Given this, it is safe to conclude that it was in the Spring and Autumn Period that sub-pictographs were established.

The replacement of such solid dots by lines, which occurred mainly amid the Spring and Autumn Periods, was the most important sign of the transition from pictographs to sub-pictographs. The following is some examples.

Table 1.6 Characters Used in the Spring and Autumn Period

Regular Script	Western Zhou Dynasty	Spring and Autumn Period
Tian 天 (sky)		

Core Issues Regarding the Evolution of Chinese Characters 7

Regular Script	Western Zhou Dynasty	Spring and Autumn Period
Wang 王 (king)		
Hu 祜 (blessing)		
Shi 士 (scholar)		
Tun 屯 (stock)		
Dan 单 (single)		
Zheng 正 (just)		
Zhong 终 (end)		
Rong 戎 (army)		

The adoption of semantic and phonetic components marks the beginning of using pronunciations and meanings as the creation basis for Chinese characters. This adoption process began in the Spring and Autumn Period. In comparison with their Western-Zhou-Dynasty counterparts, characters created during this period contained a lot of semantic components, and sub-pictographs were widely used. Examples are as follows:

Table 1.7 The Addition of Semantic Components in the Spring and Autumn Period

Regular Script	Western Zhou Dynasty	Spring and Autumn Period	Note
Zhang 璋 (flat rectangular jade plate)			The addition of a semantic component 玉 (jade)
Xian 宪 (constitution)			The addition of a semantic component 心 (heart)
Xing 姓 (surname)			The addition of semantic components 女 (woman/girl) and 亻 (person)

(*Continued*)

8 Core Issues Regarding the Evolution of Chinese Characters

Table 1.7 (Continued)

Regular Script	Western Zhou Dynasty	Spring and Autumn Period	Note
Nuo 诺 (promise)			The addition of a semantic component (to speak)
Zheng 郑 (a surname)			The addition of a semantic component (county)
Deng 邓 (a surname)			The addition of a semantic component (county)
Liang 梁 (sorghum)			The addition of a semantic component (grains)
Luan 鑾 (Imperial carriage)			The addition of a semantic component (gold)

The appearance of radicals is the result of the adoption of semantic and phonetic components. Compared with their Western-Zhou-Dynasty counterparts, Spring-and-Autumn characters include radicals that appear in specific positions and forms, as the table shows below.

Table 1.8 Comparison Between Western-Zhou-Dynasty and Spring-and-Autumn-Period Characters

Regular Script	Western Zhou Dynasty	Spring and Autumn Period
Zhong 锺 (bell)		
Si 祀 (ritual)		
Jian 谏 (remonstrate)		
Huang 璜 (semi-annular jade ornament)		
Gui 妫 (a surname)		
Yun 妘 (a surname)		

Core Issues Regarding the Evolution of Chinese Characters 9

Please note that the above-mentioned conclusions are based on available materials. Due to the limitation of these materials, the conclusions may not be completely true.

The evolution of Chinese characters is a natural process that has no naturally defined stages of development. Therefore, the stages of development discussed in this book are also one of the conclusions that may not be completely true and allow for the existence of special cases. Although these conclusions are valid for most of cases, it is not surprising to find several cases that substantially lead over their contemporaries or deliberately imitate ancient writing habits.

(II) The Official Script, the Regular Script, and the Stages of Their Development

The official script emerged from the seal script. It was created together with the New-Style writing system featuring phonetic and semantic symbols. It replaced the seal script's curved strokes and rounded corners with straight lines and square corners, respectively, and standardized the stroke orders. When it reached its mature state, the surviving traits of the seal script that bore by the early official-script characters were eliminated, and the New-Style writing system was established. Chinese characters on the silk manuscripts unearthed from Mawangdui Western-Han-Dynasty (206–8 BCE) Tombs are in the typical early-official-script form, also known academically as the archaic-official-script form. In Eastern-Han-Dynasty (25–220) stele inscriptions, characters bearing traits of the seal script are seldom found.

Table 1.9 Evolutionary Trends From Western Zhou Dynasty to Eastern Han Dynasty

Regular Script	Western-Zhou-Dynasty Bronze Inscriptions	Silk Manuscripts from Mawangdui Han Tombs	Eastern-Han-Dynasty Stele Inscriptions
Shen 神 (deity)			
Fu 福 (happiness)			
Ni 逆 (meet head-on)			
Mo 莫 (denial)			
Fan 番 (rotation)			
Gao 告 (tell)			

(*Continued*)

10 *Core Issues Regarding the Evolution of Chinese Characters*

Table 1.9 (Continued)

Regular Script	Western-Zhou-Dynasty Bronze Inscriptions	Silk Manuscripts from Mawangdui Han Tombs	Eastern-Han-Dynasty Stele Inscriptions
Sang 喪 (lose)			
Shu 述 (relate)			

Academics believe that the emergence of the official script, also known as the official script transformation, probably occurred in the middle or late Warring States Period. In this research, the analysis of all the discovered bronze inscriptions from that period shows that it probably occurred in the late Warring States Period. The following table shows the different Warring-States-Period fonts of three characters.

Table 1.10 Evolutionary Trends in the Mid- and Late-Warring States Period

Jun 君 (power-holder)	Middle Warring States Period	
	Late Warring States Period	
Li 里 (living community)	Middle Warring States Period	
	Late Warring States Period	
Wu 五 (five)	Middle Warring States	
	Late Warring States	

This table shows how late-Warring-States-Period characters differ from their mid-Warring-States-Period counterparts: rounded shapes give way to squarish ones; strokes are restructured; and curved strokes are replaced by straight ones. Such changes support the assertion that the official script was established in the late Warring States Period. There were also historical reasons for such changes. In the middle Warring States Period, there was a large amount of cast inscriptions, such as those on the dagger-axe and halberd of Pingye Lord and the vehicle pass given to the lord of E (today's Hubei Province). In the late Warring States Period, however, all inscriptions on the bronze wares were engravings. This change was an important factor driving the formation of the official script. In the middle Warring States Period, engraved inscriptions still used seal-script characters, such as those on the Zhongshan king's jade ware, but such inscriptions became rare in the late Warring States Period.

The regular script was established as the New-Style writing system, featuring semantic and phonetic components that had evolved and matured. During this process, the strokes, components, and compositional structures of Chinese characters were improved and refined. Among all these improvements, the most important one was the extraction and perfection of strokes. How to write them beautifully and use them to build nice structures also became essential writing techniques; Kaicheng stone scriptures of the Tang Dynasty (618–907) bear typical regular-script characters. The table below compares some characters from the stone scriptures with their counterparts from Eastern-Han-Dynasty stele inscriptions.

Table 1.11 Comparison Between the Official Script and the Regular Script

Regular-Script Character	Official Script (Cao Quan Monument of the Eastern Han Dynasty)	Regular Script (Kaicheng Stone Scriptures of the Tang Dynasty)
Zhu 諸 (all)		
Zi 子 (son)		
Li 離 (leave)		
Feng 風 (wind)		

The official script was created to replace the seal script and build the New-Style writing system, and the regular script was created to perfect the system. In the Eastern Han Dynasty, Chinese characters basically stopped showing any traits of the seal script. Therefore, it is reasonable to deduce that it was during this time that the official script reached its maturity, and the regular script was established towards the end of the Dynasty.[8] Overall, pictograph-like characters prevailed in the Shang and Western Zhou dynasties, sub-pictographs thrived from the Spring and Autumn Period to the middle Warring States Period, and the official script dominated from the late Warring States Period to the Eastern Han Dynasty, followed by the prevailing regular script officially established in the period of the Three Kingdoms (220–280).

Table 1.12 Development Stages of Chinese Characters

Character Type	Pictograph	Sub-Pictograph	Official Script	Regular Script
Period	From the Shang Dynasty to the Western Zhou Dynasty	From the Spring and Autumn Period to the middle of the Warring States Period	From the late Warring States Period to the Eastern Han Dynasty	After the Three Kingdoms Period

II. Multitype Modification and Structural Balance

(I) Multitype Modification

In the process of finding the most suitable new character forms and replacing the seal script with the New-Style writing system, it was likely that many types of modifications were made to character components. The main driving force behind these modifications was probably convenient writing. Such modifications repeatedly occurred during the time from the official script transformation, which happened in the late Warring States Period, to the formation of the present-day Chinese characters, but most of them happened during the official script transformation. This transformation led to the complete disappearance of the traits of the seal script, which shows that the New-Style writing system was formed.

The aforementioned theory about multitype modifications of characters was based on the analyses of many characters from unearthed documents. It is of great importance for the studies on the development of Chinese characters. In previous research, the standard script adopted is usually the seal script defined by *Shuowen Jiezi* 说文解字 (An Explication of Written Characters) or other widely accepted regular script, and the characters do not conform to the adopted script are regarded as popular-form or wrong characters. Such practices often lead to a problem: some reasonable variants of characters were viewed as unacceptable ones. The reason that the researchers chose such practices is that they failed to perceive the official script transformation as a dynamic process: it is both the transformation of the previous seal script and the beginning of the New-Style writing system of Chinese characters. By viewing reasonable and even mainstream variants as popular-form or even wrong characters, such researchers are blind to the mechanism, motivation, and rules behind the overall adjustment of the Chinese character system and changes to individual characters. Due to such directional and dominant errors, previous research fails to offer an accurate and comprehensive analysis of the development of Chinese characters and character fonts.

The aforementioned multitype modifications can be made to strokes, components, and structures of characters.

1. Strokes

After the official script transformation, Chinese characters became phonetic-semantic compounds. The seal-script strokes used to represent images were

Core Issues Regarding the Evolution of Chinese Characters 13

replaced, and abstract symbols were widely used, functioning as single-component characters or character components (used in multicomponent characters). As abstract symbols, the inner composition of a component or a single-component character was no longer important. Therefore, they were simplified for convenience purposes, and there was no certain regularity concerning the style of such simplification. To be more specific, the seal script did not allow any component to change its form and position in a character, but the official or regular script allowed such changes.

The following table shows multitype modifications of the seal-script stroke ∪ by the official script.

Table 1.13 Examples of Multitype Modification (1)

Seal-Script Stroke	Original-Form Characters	Modified Strokes	Modified-Form Characters (from the Silk Manuscripts from Mawangdui Han Tombs)
∪	余	ー	余
	酉	\/	酉
	辛	⊔	辛
	擇	╱	擇
	清	_	清
	竟	‖	竟
	親	∨	親
	屮	⌣	屯
	生	ー ヽ	生
	屮	⸺	半

14 *Core Issues Regarding the Evolution of Chinese Characters*

The following table shows how the seal-script stroke ∩ is modified into official-script strokes.

Table 1.14 Examples of Multitype Modification (2)

Seal-Script Stroke	Original-Form Characters	Modified Stroke	Modified-Form Characters (from the Silk Manuscripts from Mawangdui Han Tombs)
∩	天	—	天
	律		律
	美		美
	帝	⼃	束
	朱		本
	業	⼁⼁	業
	囲		囲
	帝	⼌	帝
	彬		帮

The following table is multiple official-script modifications of the seal-script stroke ⼧.

Table 1.15 Examples of Multitype Modification (3)

Seal-Script Stroke	Original-Form Characters	Modified Strokes	Modified-Form Characters (from the Silk Manuscripts from Mawangdui Han Tombs)
⼧	天	⼈	天
	美		美

Core Issues Regarding the Evolution of Chinese Characters 15

Seal-Script Stroke	Original-Form Characters	Modified Strokes	Modified-Form Characters (from the Silk Manuscripts from Mawangdui Han Tombs)
	甫	十	专
	朱		朱
	耑	十	耑
	㫃		㫃

2. *Components*

The multitype modifications include those made to components, such as rewriting them and replacing them with commonly used simplified components based on their similarity. Such component modifications explain the phenomenon that different components can be used to distinguish the official and regular scripts.

The following table includes multitype modifications of 𦥑, a seal-script component.

Table 1.16 Multitype Modifications of Character Component 𦥑

Seal-Script Component	Modified Components	Modified-Form Characters (from the Silk Manuscripts from Mawangdui Han Tombs)	Small-Seal Components
𦥑	宀	興	興
		長	長
		芜	芦
	艹	芊	芦
		耒	耒
		戒	戒
		具	具

(Continued)

Table 1.16 (Continued)

Seal-Script Component	Modified Components	Modified-Form Characters (from the Silk Manuscripts from Mawangdui Han Tombs)	Small-Seal Components
	大	吳	吳
		昊	昊
	大	矣	矣
		㦵	㦵
	丿丶	水	水

The following table shows component modifications in three characters: *wei* 畏 (fear), *lao* 老 (old), and *yin* 陰 (cloudy).

Table 1.17 Modifications of Character Components

Regular Script	Small Seal Script	Modified Variants (from the Silk Manuscripts from Mawangdui Han Tombs)
wei 畏 (fear),	畏	畏 畏 畏
lao 老 (old)	老	老 老 老
yin 陰 (cloudy)	陰	陰 陰 陰 陰 陰

In silk manuscripts unearthed from Mawangdui Han Tombs, there are three ways to combine components into the character *wei* 畏 (fear). The first way is to combine two components, namely: *gui* 鬼 (ghost) and *zhi* 止 (toe). This composition of *wei* 畏 (fear) also appears in Chu-state slips of the Warring States Period. The second composition of the character differs from the first one in the lower part: the component *zhi* 止 (toe) is replaced by its own cursive form. The lower part in the third composition is no longer the component *zhi* 止 (toe). It looks like the lower part of another character, *liang* 良 (good). Such replacement by simple or similar-looking forms is called analogisation.

Core Issues Regarding the Evolution of Chinese Characters 17

Table 1.18 Examples of Analogisation

Regular Script	Western Zhou Dynasty	Spring and Autumn Period	Warring States Period	Small Seal Script	Western Han Dynasty
Shi 食 (food)					
Liang 良 (good)					
Chang 長 (long)					

As seen from the table above, seal-script *wei* 畏 (fear), *shi* 食 (food), *liang* 良 (good), and *chang* 長 (long), which have different lower parts, share the same lower part after the official script transformation. Among the four, only *liang* 良 (good) gets its new lower part through stroke simplification. The other three characters' original lower parts are replaced with the new one because they share a certain likeness in appearance.

Some characters still have several variants after the official script transformation. For instance, the official-script character *lao* 老 (old) has two variants that have different lower parts: *bi* 匕 (spoon) and *zhi* 止 (toe). The official-script character *yin* 陰 (cloudy) also has two variants discernible by their lower parts namely, *chong* 虫 (worm/insect) and *kou* 口 (mouth).

In Dunhuang documents, *zong* 總 (total) is modified in different ways.

Table 1.19 Different Forms of 總

Small Seal Script	Modified Variants (from Dunhuang Documents)

Apart from changing the component 糸 into 扌, the component 囪 is modified in different ways. The component 囪 is written as ▓ in Western-Zhou-Dynasty bronze inscription. Rong Geng 容庚 (1894–1983) noted, "The component 囪 probably means concerns, worry, or anxiety, because its upper part is a variant of ♦, and its lower part is the symbol representing heart. *Shuowen Jiezi* 说文解字 also agrees that 囪 is a combination of *cong* 囪 (window or cave), which is a variant of ♦, and the heart, and it further points out that 囪 is a phonetic symbol, indicating a transition from pictographs to phonetic-semantic compounds."[9] In silk manuscripts unearthed from Mawangdui Han Tombs, "囪" is ▓, which is like the character's bronze-inscription font. This finding shows that it was quite late that the photographic symbol ♦ above the "heart" component was changed into "囪". *Shuowen Jiezi* says, "When 囪 is on a wall, it is called *you* 牖 (window). When it is inside a room, it is called 囱. It is a pictographic character meaning window or cave." "恖" is changed into "怱" and "怂" in the official script transformation. *Liushu Zhenge* 六书正讹 (Correcting Errors in the Six Categories of Chinese Characters) regards these two variants as the popular forms of 恖. *Zi Hui* 字汇 (Glossary of Characters) only lists 怂 as a variant of 恖. *Ji Yun* 集韵 (Collection of Rhymes) says, "恖 is the archaic form of 怱, and 怂 is the popular form of 怱." *Zheng Zi Tong* 正字通 (Standard Chinese Characters) says, "恖 is written as 怱 in the official script." Some variants of *zong* 總 (total) also include another component *gong* 公 (public), which is evidently a phonetic component in this case. "匆", "勿" and "田" are probably different modifications of "囱", which is complex in structure and not widely used to make characters.

In the vocabulary of contemporary Chinese, there is a word *cong cong* 匆匆 (hurriedly). "匆" is probably a variant of "恖(囱)". In some cases, 恖 and 囱 are regarded as synonymous variants: examples can be found in *Shuowen Jiezi* 说文解字 and *Shuowen Tongxun Dingsheng* 说文通训定声 (Studies on *Shuowen Jiezi*).

3. Structures

Multitype modifications also occurred in character structures, such as adjusting the structures of single-component and multicomponent characters and changing their orientations and positions. The following table shows such modifications made to the Chinese character *geng* 更 (further):

Table 1.20 Evolution of 更

Bronze Inscriptions and Pottery Inscriptions from the Warring States Period	Small Seal Script	Silk Manuscripts from Mawangdui Han Tombs
(images)	(image)	(images)

更 is a two-component character consisting of 丙 and 攴. When it appears in silk manuscripts from Mawangdui Han Tombs, its two components are bonded together in a more cohesive way.

The following table shows modifications to the positions of some character components.

Table 1.21 Multitype Modifications to the Positions of Character Components

Regular Script	Small Seal Script	Silk Manuscripts from Mawangdui Han Tombs
Bao 葆 (keep)	(image)	(images)

Core Issues Regarding the Evolution of Chinese Characters 19

Regular Script	Small Seal Script	Silk Manuscripts from Mawangdui Han Tombs
Ran 然 (right)		
Sheng 聖 (holy)		
Zhi 制 (make)		

(II) Structural Balance

The structural balance, or the spontaneous adjustment and improvement to the character system, occurred under the guidance of the standards proposed by the New-Style writing system. It played an integral role in the establishment of the new system. During the whole process of building the new system, especially after the official script transformation, characters were often modified to achieve structural balance. Such modifications were made to individual characters, words, and the character systems. The modification methods varied, and the method selection was based on actual needs.

1. Structural Balance for Individual Characters

For individual Chinese characters, structural balance means reasonable composition, well-proportioned beauty, and structural stability.

Table 1.22 Changes in the Form of 数/數

Regular Script	Small Seal Script	Silk Manuscripts from Mawangdui Han Tombs	Dunhuang Documents
Shu 數 (number)			

As a component in the Chinese character *shu* 數 (number), *nv* 女 (woman/girl) appears in the lower middle or lower right part of the character in the silk manuscripts from Mawangdui Han Tombs. This shows that the structure of the character was not finalized back then. In *Dictionary for Dunhuang Popular-Form Characters* 敦煌俗字典, there are 17 fonts of the character *shu* 数/數 (number), and the component *nv* 女 (woman/girl) appears in the same position in all these fonts. This is the result of the structural balance.

Table 1.23 Changes in the Form of 魏

Regular Script	Small Seal Script	Silk Manuscripts from Mawangdui Han Tombs	Dunhuang Documents
Wei 魏 (towering)			

In the silk manuscripts from Mawangdui Han Tombs, the character *wei* 魏 (a surname) does not have a uniform, unchanging form either: its component *shan* 山 (hill) can appear in its lower middle or lower right part. In Dunhuang documents and in the small-seal script, however, the character has a definite structure and form.

2. *Structural Balance for Words*

In its early stages, the Chinese vocabulary system mainly relied on the development of Chinese characters to realise its improvement. In the later stages, this improvement mainly depended on the combination of two syllables or two individual characters. There are three ways to expand the vocabulary system through changes in characters. The first is to create new characters by adding phonetic and semantic components to the original characters. The new characters created in this way can be used to replace some of the functions of the original characters and make new words. The second way is to create completely new characters to meet the need for new words. The third way is to use the existing variant forms as new characters and create new words with them to replace some functions of the original characters.

Table 1.24 New Character Forms for New Words

Regular Script	Warring States Period	Small Seal Script	Silk Manuscripts from Mawangdui Han Tombs
Zhen/chen 陳 (formation or statement), zhen 阵 (formation)			
Nai 柰 (a kind of fruit or despite), nai 奈 (despite)			

The component *dong* 東 (east) in the character *zhen/chen* 陳 (formation or statement) originally has a curved stroke in its lower part. Because of the official script transformation, this stroke is replaced by a left-falling stroke and a right-falling one, or by a short horizontal line as seen in the silk manuscripts from Mawangdui Han Tombs. Because of vocabulary development, *zhen* 阵/陣 (formation) gradually becomes an independent character that is used to replace part of 陳's functions and make new words.

Core Issues Regarding the Evolution of Chinese Characters 21

Originally, *nai* 柰 (a kind of fruit or despite) means a kind of fruit and thus has the component *mu* 木 (wood). The component *mu* 木 (wood) is compressed longitudinally and stretched transversely to prevent the character from looking lanky whenever it is placed in the upper part of a character. The same thing happened to the character *li* 李 (plum or a surname).

Table 1.25 Modifications to Character Forms for Mutual Differentiation

Small Seal Script	Silk Manuscripts from Mawangdui Han Tombs
柰	李 李 李 李 李

In the silk manuscripts from Mawangdui Han Tombs, the component *mu* 木 (wood) of *nai* 柰 (a kind of fruit or despite) and *li* 李 (plum or a surname) can also be written as *da* 大 (big). In this case, the component 大 is considered a variant of 木, and the character 奈, a variant of 柰. Nevertheless, due to the development of vocabulary, 奈 gradually becomes an independent character to replace part of 柰's functions.

3. *Structural Balance for the Character Systems*

The multitype modifications made to individual characters could occasionally cause a problem: two different characters were modified into the same form. Such a problem must be solved since it cannot be allowed by any character system.

Table 1.26 Evolution of 弋

Regular Script	Western Zhou Dynasty	Warring States Period
Yi 弋 (hunt with bow and arrow)	弋 弋	弋 弋 弋 弋

Some early forms of *yi* 弋 (hunt with bow and arrow) have a solid dot that is later modified into a short, horizontal line. As a result, its modified form looks exactly like another modified character *ge* 戈 (dagger-axe), which causes problems to the character system. To solve this problem, the short, horizontal line is eliminated.

Table 1.27 Evolution of 生

Regular Script	Small Seal Script	Juyan Bamboo Slips of the Han Dynasty	Eastern-Han-Dynasty Stele Inscriptions
Sheng 生 (life)	生	生 生	生 生

22 *Core Issues Regarding the Evolution of Chinese Characters*

Amid the official script transformation, the curved stroke in the upper part of the seal-script *sheng* 生 (life) was modified in two ways: (1) one left-falling stroke and one horizontal line and (2) one horizontal line. As the second type of modification would produce a character like *zhu* 主 (master), only the first-type modification was widely accepted.

III. Symbiotic Development and Substitutionary Development

The symbiotic development and the substitutionary development are two development modes in the establishment of Chinese character systems. The former refers to a mode that allows different variants of the same original character to develop together with the original character, and the latter refers to a mode that emphasizes the replacement of original characters by their new variants. The process of building the New-Style Chinese character system, which starts from the official script transformation, sees much more symbiotic development than substitutionary development.

The following table includes some character variants containing the component *zhi* 止 (halt). These characters are selected from the silk manuscripts of Mawangdui Han Tombs.

Table 1.28 Different Forms of Character Component 止

Regular Script	Small Seal Script	Silk Manuscripts from Mawangdui Han Tombs
Zao 趮 (fidgety)		
Fa 發 (deliver)		
Qian 前 (front)		
Ni 逆 (meet head-on)		
Zou 走 (go)		
Qi 起 (rise)		
Ti 提 (lift)		
Chi 齒 (teeth)		

Core Issues Regarding the Evolution of Chinese Characters 23

The table above shows the evolution of the component *zhi* 止 (toe) and the variants of the component shown above can be grouped into two categories.

Table 1.29 Evolution of 止

Regular Script	Small Seal Script	Silk Manuscripts from Mawangdui Han Tombs
Zhi (toe)		

Component variants that appear at the same time can be grouped into different categories, and, within each category, the variants evolve through time while maintaining their inherent characteristics. Such a way of evolution allows researchers to explain a difficult character or determine whether it is a popular-form or wrong character by studying its components. Therefore, rules regarding the symbiotic development are of great significance for the aforementioned two types of studies.

Character variants are similar to the component variants. The characters currently regarded as popular or wrong forms of an original character were probably the character's variants for normal use in the past. These character variants, including the one currently deemed as the correct form, coexisted, and went through a symbiotic development process, showing the evolution of the original character. Usually, the characteristics of a character variant can be used to determine the period of its creation. For example, in Dunhuang documents, the radical 彳 is often written as 氵 (得 written as 淂). This practice can be traced back to the Han Dynasty (202 BCE–220 CE). In the Han-Dynasty Bamboo Slips unearthed in Wuwei, all the radicals 彳 are replaced by 氵 in the following characters *fu* 復 (recover), *xu* 徐 (slowly), and *hou* 後 (back). In this case, 氵 is evidently a variant of 彳. The following table gives some insight into this phenomenon: the reason 彳 is written as 氵 is that sometimes the two strokes that form the lower part of 彳 (the written form of 彳) are not combined closely enough.

Table 1.30 Different Forms of Character Component 彳

Regular Script	Han-Dynasty Bamboo Slips Unearthed in Wuwei	Small Seal Script
Fu 復 (recover)		
Xu 徐 (slowly)		
De 得 (obtain)		
Hou 後 (back)		

In Dunhuang documents, the character currently known as *xue* 学/學 (learn) is made up of two components: *wen* 文 (literature) and *zi* 子 (son). The Tang-Dynasty treatise *Zhengming Yaolu* 正名要录 comments that *xue* 學 (learn) is the standard form and regards the one consisting of 文 and 子 (斈) as a wrong character, neglecting the fact that this character variant just changes one component: changing *yao* 爻 (divination diagram) into *wen* 文 (literature).[10] Such a practice dates to the Han Dynasty.

Table 1.31 Different Forms of 學/学

Regular Script	Dunhuang Documents	Han-Dynasty Bamboo Slips, Silk Manuscripts, and Stele Inscriptions	Small Seal Script
Xue 學 (learn)	斈	is the form used in the silk manuscripts from Mawangdui Han Tombs (the form used in the Eastern-Han-Dynasty stele inscriptions)	

Yao 爻 (divination diagram) and *wen* 文 (literature) do share some similarities in appearance, but the replacement of 爻 by 文 is more likely to be a deliberate action. As a character component, 文 can better represent the content of the character *xue* 学/學 (learn) in comparison with 爻. In this sense, the Dunhuang documents just use a variant of the character 学/學, which is not a wrong form of the character.

Table 1.32 Dunhuang Documents' Influence on Han-Dynasty Character Forms

Regular Script	Dunhuang Documents	Han-Dynasty Bamboo Slips and Silk Manuscripts	Small Seal Script
De 德 (morality)		(silk manuscripts from Mawangdui Han Tombs)	
Fu 復 (recover)		(silk manuscripts from Mawangdui Han Tombs)	
Sheng 生 (life)		(Juyan bamboo slips of the Han Dynasty)	

Regular Script	Dunhuang Documents	Han-Dynasty Bamboo Slips and Silk Manuscripts	Small Seal Script
Lao 老 (old)	老	老 (silk manuscripts from Mawangdui Han Tombs)	老
Mei 美 (beautiful)	美	美 (silk manuscripts from Mawangdui Han Tombs)	美

The table above shows some characters selected from Dunhuang documents, which obviously evolve from Han-Dynasty characters. The above-shown forms of *de* 德 (morality), *fu* 復 (recover), *lao* 老 (old) differ from their Han-Dynasty counterparts in components. Those of *sheng* 生 (life) and *mei* 美 (beautiful) differ from their seal-script counterparts in strokes: upward curves are straight, and downward curves are replaced by the combination of a left-falling stroke and a right-falling stroke.

Traditional studies on Chinese characters tend to analyse character forms based on the time of their creation, but the phenomena of symbiotic development show the importance of retrospective analyses in such studies. The comparison of character variants can reveal the motivations and mechanisms behind the evolution of characters.

Notes

1 The original Chinese version was published in the *Studies of the Chinese Language* 中国语文, Issue 1, 2013.
2 启功：《古代字体论稿》，第 27–28 页，北京：文物出版社，1999。
 Qi Gong: *Discussion on Ancient Chinese Character Fonts*, pp. 27–28, Beijing: Cultural Relics Press, 1999.
3 唐兰：《中国文字学》，第 163 页，上海：上海古籍出版社，1979。
 Tang Lan: *Chinese Philology*, p. 163, Shanghai: Shanghai Chinese Classics Publishing House, 1979.
4 陈梦家：《中国文字学》，第 165 页，北京：中华书局，2006。
 Chen Mengjia: *Chinese Paleography*, p. 165, Beijing: Zhonghua Book Company, 2006.
5 吴世昌：《罗音室学术论著》，第 622 页，北京：社会科学文献出版社，1998。
 Wu Shichang: *Luo Yinshi Academic Essays*, p. 622, Beijing: Social Sciences Literature Press, 1998.
6 详王贵元：《汉字形体演化的动因与机制》，《语文研究》，2010（3）。
 Wang Guiyuan: "The Motivation and Mechanisms behind the Evolution of the Chinese Characters", *Linguistic Research*, 2010 (3).
7 章太炎：《论语言文字之学》，《国粹学报》，1906（24）。
 Zhang Taiyan: "On the Studies of Language", *Guocui Xuebao Journal*, 1906 (24).
8 详王贵元：《隶变问题新探》，《暨南学报》，2011（3）。
 Wang Guiyuan: "A New Exploration of the Official Script Transformation", *Jinan Journal*, 2011 (3).

9 容庚：《金文编》，第 692 页，北京：中华书局，1985。
  Rong Geng: *On Bronze Inscriptions*, p. 692, Beijing: Zhonghua Book Company, 1985.
10 《正名要录完整图版》，黄征：《敦煌俗字典》，第587页，上海：上海教育出版社，2005。
  Huang Zheng: "A Complete Copy of '*Zhengming Yaolu*'", *Dictionary for Dunhuang Popular-Form Characters*, p. 587, Shanghai: Shanghai Educational Publishing House, 2005.

2 The Composition System of Chinese Characters and the Stages of Its Development[1]

I. An Analysis of the Composition System of Chinese Characters

(I) Research Methods and Principles for the Analysis of the Composition System

After having a certain number of pictographs, the system of Chinese characters experienced a transition: it stopped being a purely pictographic system and expanded itself by creating new characters with the existing character components. This new method of creating characters adapted to the characteristics of the Chinese language. It was also the most economical, scientific, and convenient way to expand the old character system. Despite that, it must be noted that, without rigorous systematicness, it is impossible to apply this kind of character-forming method based on a limited number of components. The composition system of Chinese characters began to take shape when the oracle-bone script was created, but the system was quite immature back then. Basic components in the oracle-bone script were large in number but simple in structure, and each of them had very limited functions and participated in the composition of a very limited number of characters. Later, when the composition hierarchy matured and allowed basic components that had similar functions to be summarized into one component, the number of components was effectively controlled, and all the components were used efficiently in the hierarchy. Therefore, it is necessary and practical to analyse the composition of Chinese characters by using systematic methods of analysis.

The composition system of Chinese characters consists of character components that has specific forms and functions and are interrelated with one another. The core of this system is the various components and their interconnections. Components used to build characters are basic elements of the composition system, and interconnections between components determine the structure of the composition system. It is hard to discover components and their interconnections through the observation of individual characters. To achieve these goals, it is a must to break down the characters. This breakdown method is of great significance for the studies on the composition system of Chinese characters. The following is a breakdown analysis of the Chinese character *nun* 麕 (aroma). It shows how to break down a character and how to describe the process academically.

28 The Composition System of Chinese Characters

Nun 麕 (aroma) can firstly be broken down into a phonetic component *ma* 麻 (ramie) and a semantic component *xiang* 香 (fragrant). As these two components make up the first level (level 1) of the composition hierarchy, they can be referred to as level-1 components. At the second level (level 2), the level-1 component *ma* 麻 (ramie) is further divided into level-2 components *guang* 广 (wide) and *lin* 林 (woods), and the other level-1 component *xiang* 香 (fragrant), into level-2 components *he* 禾 (standing grain) and *ri* 日 (sun). The level-2 component *lin* 林 (woods) can be regarded as a combination of two level-3 components *mu* 木 (wood). In this hierarchical structure showing the character composition of *nun* 麕 (aroma), components at level 1 are called components of the character, and those at level 2 and level 3 are called subcomponents of the character.

(II) An Analysis of a Character's Compositional Structure

1. Character Morphs

Component morphs are the smallest units of Chinese characters. They have independent structural characteristics and semantic functions and cannot be further broken down. For instance, in the above-shown composition analysis of the character *nun* 麕 (aroma), *guang* 广 (wide), *mu* 木 (wood), *he* 禾 (standing grain), *ri* 日 (sun) are character morphs. Character morphs differ from one another in the following two aspects: (1) form and (2) semantic function. The semantic function describes a morph's contribution to the semantic function of a character. Almost every character can be broken down into a group of character morphs.

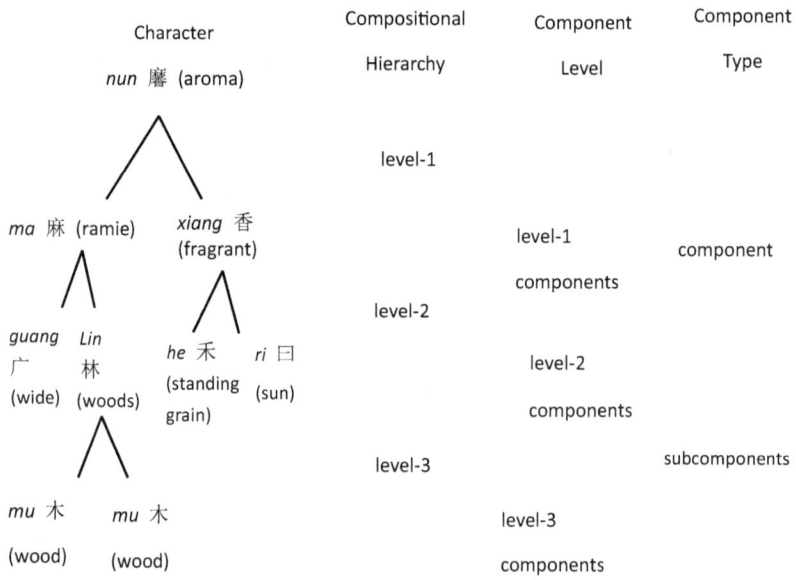

Figure 2.1 The Composition of 麕

The Composition System of Chinese Characters 29

2. *Character Morphemes*

Character morphemes are extracted from different types of character morphs. They are the smallest linguistic unit of a character. A character morpheme is an abstract concept: it is extracted from a group of morphs that have the same semantic function. This concept is a frequently used term in the studies on the composition system of Chinese characters. There are two types of character morphemes: free morphemes and bound morphemes. The former, like single-component characters, has independent meanings and pronunciations. The latter can only serve as character components.

3. *Components*

Components, or level-1, components are extracted from a character on the premise that they can explain the composition and origin of the character. Such components usually can be split further. For instance, as a level-1 component of *nun* 䵅 (aroma), ma 麻 (ramie) can be further split into level-2 components or subcomponents.

A component can contain one or several morphemes, and thus can be divided into mono-morphemic and poly-morphemic components.

(III) Compositional Structures

1. *Compositional Hierarchy—A Vertical Analysis*

The compositional hierarchy refers to the classification of character components. It includes all the components of a character in a vertical hierarchical structure as follows

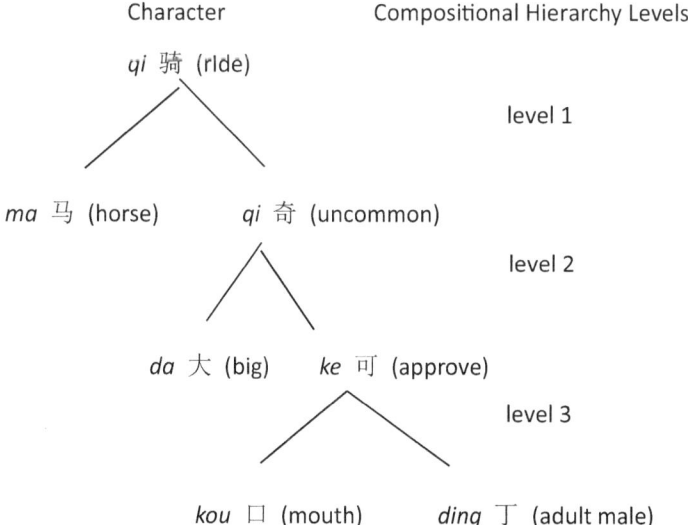

Figure 2.2 The Composition of 骑

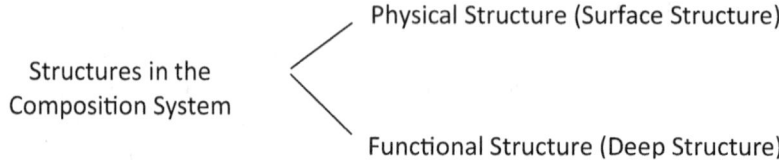

Figure 2.3 Structures in the Composition System

According to the hierarchical structure above, the composition of the character *qi* 骑 (ride) starts from the combination of *kou* 口 (mouth) and *ding* 丁 (adult male) at level 3. At level 2, there are *da* 大 (big) and *ke* 可 (approve), which are form *qi* 奇 (uncommon) at level 1. The two level-1 components *ma* 马 (horse) and *qi* 奇 (uncommon) are combined to make 骑. This three-level structure shows the aforementioned three steps in building the character.

The composition system discusses not only the physical structures of characters but also their functional structures. The former is a surface structure that can be perceived briefly, but the latter is an invisible deep structure.

(1) THE PHYSICAL STRUCTURES AND THE INCLUSIVE RELATIONSHIP
    AMONG THE STRUCTURAL LEVELS

The physical structure analyses are based on individual characters. There is no correspondence between the structural levels and the components. For example, *kou* 口 (mouth) is a level-1 component of *hu* 呼 (exhale), a level-2 component of *shi* 拾 (pick), and a level-3 component of *qi* 骑 (ride). It can also be used as a single-component character. In a word, a component can appear in different places instead of repeatedly appearing at a certain level in the compositional hierarchy.

In the breakdown of *qi* 骑 (ride), there is a clear inclusive relationship among the levels. From the bottom to the top, there is an increase in components. Level-3 components make level-2 components that make level-1 components. Level-1 components build the character. Given such an inclusive relationship, all the morphemes appearing at the upper levels of the hierarchical structure may serve as characters. In other words, the creation of a new character does not require any increase in the number of morphemes, which, to a certain extent, reflects the scientificity and systematicness of the composition of Chinese characters.

(2) THE FUNCTIONAL STRUCTURE AND THE GENERATIVE RELATIONSHIP
    AMONG THE STRUCTURAL LEVELS

The functional structure reflects how the functions of components are combined. It is corresponding to the physical structure.

Different from its counterpart in the physical structure, the inter-level relationship of the functional structure is generative. The generation that implies creation is different from a combination. For instance, the Chinese character *xiu* 休 (rest) is

The Composition System of Chinese Characters 31

just a combination of *mu* 木 (wood) and *ren* 人 (person) in terms of the physical structure. Nevertheless, from a functional point of view, the two components, 木 and 人, seem to have nothing to do with the idea of rest. The generative relationship means that once a new combination of components is created for a new function, the original functions of the components are replaced by the new function. Sometimes, the new function may have something to do with the old functions of the components, but this cannot negate the generative relationship.

2. *Combination Modes—A Horizontal Analysis*

Combination modes describe the different ways that components are combined. This term is used in a horizontal analysis of a hierarchical structure. For example, in the compositional hierarchy of *qi* 骑 (ride), there are three combination modes shown in the following combinations: *ma* 马 (horse) and *qi* 奇 (uncommon), *da* 大 (big) and *ke* 可 (approve), and *kou* 口 (mouth) and *ding* 丁 (adult male). This analysis is different from the vertical analysis in the paragraphs above.

In a horizontal analysis of the compositional hierarchy, there are also discussions on the physical and functional structures of the combination modes.

(1) PHYSICAL COMBINATION MODES

In physical terms, there are four combination structures commonly seen in Chinese characters:

a. Left-right structure: two components arranged side by side;
b. Fully surrounded structure: one component fully surrounded by another (a frequently seen structure in pictograph-like characters);
c. Overlapping structure: overlapping two components; and
d. Overlaid structure: having two adjacent components share some strokes.

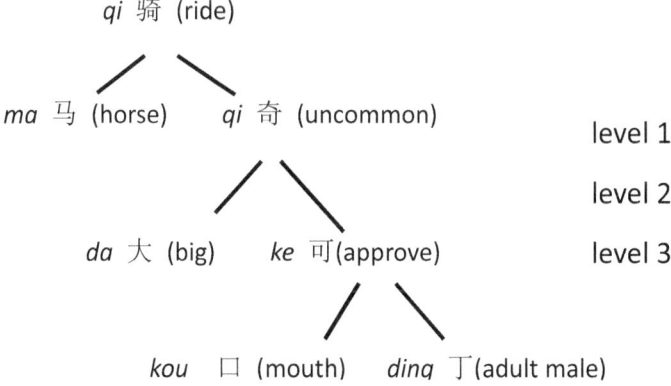

Figure 2.4 The Compositional Hierarchy of 骑

(2) FUNCTIONAL COMBINATION MODES

Functional combination modes are based on the different selections and combinations of components, which are carried out for different functional purposes.

In general, the function-oriented selection of a component seldom corresponds to the selection made for physical composition. This is because a component may have multiple functions and a function can be realised through multiple components. Take the multi-functional component *ren* 人 (person) as an example. It serves as a semantic component in the character *xiu* 休 (rest) and a phonetic component in the character *ren* 认 (recognise). As to the other situation where several multiple-functional components have a common function, these components can replace one another to realise the same phonetic or semantic function in different characters. Apart from this, there is another interesting phenomenon during the evolution of Chinese characters: the increased number of component variants. This phenomenon is caused by the weakening and even the disappearance of some functions, and the need to enhance certain functions. In a word, the realisation of functions is the top priority in the process of creating a Chinese character, and variants can be created for functional purposes.

To understand the functional combination modes, it is essential to first grasp the functional categories of components. Components are classified into different categories according to their different functions: (1) the pictographic category, (2) the semantic category, (3) the phonetic category, and (4) the symbol category. The components belonging to the first category are pictographs, and *tian* 田 (cropland) is one of them. As a pictographic component, 田 depicts a certain shape: it represents the fruit shapes when it appears in the character *guo* 果 (fruit), and it represents the shape of the stomach when it is used to build the character to make the character *wei* 胃 (stomach). Pictographic components evolve from probably the earliest forms of Chinese characters, and the pictographic function is probably the first function of Chinese character components. In later stages of character evolution, many of these pictographic components can hardly evoke images, but they are still regarded as pictographic components if they do not evolve into single-component characters that represent their original meaning. A typical example is 田. As a character, it means the cropland instead of a certain shape. It represents shapes only when it is combined with other components to make characters, such as 果 and 胃. Most pictographic components cannot maintain their original meanings by serving as single-component characters. To achieve this goal, they can only serve as pictographic components in characters. It is noteworthy that pictographic components cannot have semantic or phonetic functions or serve as symbol components.

Semantic and phonetic components that belong to the second and third categories can serve as characters. In such cases, they usually have both semantic and phonetic functions. Components in these two categories are widely used to build new characters when the Chinese characters are no longer pure pictographs. Consequently, they become the most commonly seen character components today. As these components can be used as characters and have both semantic and phonetic functions, their functions in Chinese characters are uncertain. They are sometimes semantic components and sometimes phonetic components.

Components in the fourth category are originally symbols used to describe sequences or numbers. Given the evolution of components after the establishment of the official script, these symbols gradually acquired new a function: serving as bound components. Apart from this new function, they did not gain any pictographic, semantic, or phonetic functions.

Categories of Components and Their Functions:

Given that characters, especially multicomponent characters, are built with a limited number of components in the writing system and that many components can serve as single-component characters with specific functions, the function combination is usually embodied in the combination of level-1 components. Through an analysis of the first levels of the hierarchical structures describing the composition of a character, the following conclusions can be drawn. There are six functional combination modes for the composition of Chinese characters.

a. Pictographic combination: the combination of pictographic functions. In most cases, it is a combination of two or more pictographic components.
b. Phonetic-semantic combination: the combination of semantic and phonetic functions. In most cases, it is a combination of one semantic component and one phonetic component. In rare cases, it may be a combination of one phonetic component and several semantic components or that of two phonetic components and two semantic components.
c. Semantic combination: the combination of semantic functions. In most cases, it is a combination of two or more semantic components.
d. Pictographic-semantic combination: the combination of pictographic and semantic functions. The former is usually realised through bound components (non-character components) and the latter, through free components that can stand alone as characters.

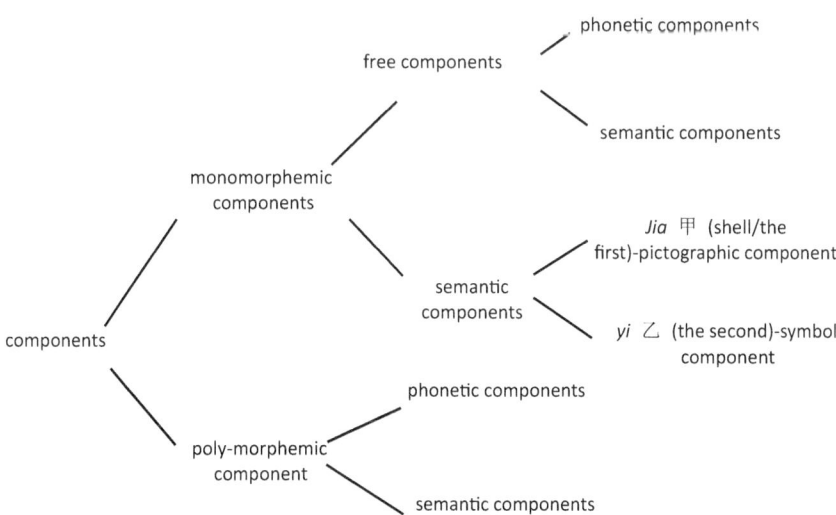

Figure 2.5 Categories of Components and Their Functions

e. Symbolic-semantic combination: the combination of symbolic and semantic functions.
f. Pictographic-phonetic-semantic combination: the combination of pictographic, phonetic, and semantic functions.
g. Symbolic-phonetic combination: the combination of symbolic and phonetic functions.

II. The Development Stages of the Composition System of Chinese Characters

Chinese characters constantly evolved during application, which was embodied in the adjustments and improvements in their compositional structures. Such adjustments and improvements were mainly aimed at the components and structures of Chinese characters. Given the synchronic stability and diachronic evolution in these two aspects, the evolution process of Chinese characters can be divided into three development stages: the early stage, the middle stage, and the late stage. To some extent, the evolution of Chinese characters is the evolution of their compositional structures. In the early stage of evolution, when the oracle-bone script was widely used, most of the characters including both single-component and multiple-component characters were pictographs. They were simple combinations of character components that were still in the process of evolution. Later, as the process of component evolution was completed through assimilation and analogisation, the shapes of the components became stable, as did the quantity of components. This became the prerequisite for the establishment of the composition system of Chinese characters. During its development, the composition system expanded to contain richer contents: hierarchical combination was developed from the simple horizontal combination method for the building of characters; phonetic-semantic and semantic combinations began coexisting with pictographic combinations; and phonetic and semantic components were developed from the original pictographic components. Every evolutionary leap in this composition system of Chinese characters was driven by profound internal reasons, constituting a continuous process of development.

(I) The Stabilisation of the Shapes and Quantity of Components

The oracle-bone script used mainly pictographic characters that consisted of one or more pictographic components, except for a small number of deictic symbols and semantic-phonetic characters. The pictographic expression of this script was the inheritance of the tradition of recording with drawings. It was also the most essential feature of the script. In oracle-bone inscriptions, characters had to faithfully represent images through their strokes and compositional structures, and different forms could be adopted to convey the same meaning or describe the same things. For example, the script allowed many different forms to describe a human body: some forms neglected the depiction of the head; some neglected that of the feet; some depicted a kneeling or standing person; and some depicted the front or side of a human body. Another example is the adoption of various components to describe the action of walking: these components are currently written as *zhi* 止 (toe), 彳, *xing* 行 (walk). In some cases, the script even used the combination of 彳 and 止 to describe the action. These phenomena caused instability in the composition of Chinese characters, which made it hard for people to recognise and use these characters. To solve these problems, assimilation methods were adopted to reduce the number of components. In the meantime, analogisation methods were carried out to turn a multifunction component into a category of components to share the different functions. To be more specific, a multiple-functional component that realised different functions in different characters was developed into several single-function components that were similar in appearance. The stabilization of the component shapes and the quantity of components led to the stabilisation of single-component characters and the character compositional structures, which marked the maturity of the entire composition system of Chinese characters. This evolutionary leap was made from the Western Zhou Dynasty (1046–771 BCE) to the Spring and Autumn Period (770–476 BCE) and embodied in the development of bronze inscriptions used in this period.

(II)   From Horizontal Combination to Hierarchical Combination

As the shapes and quantity of components stabilised, the Chinese people's perception of them shifted in part: these components were no longer just regarded as the representation of images; they began to have phonetic and semantic functions. This change first started among single-component pictographs: as many of them were used as characters, they naturally gained both phonetic and semantic functions while representing images in this process; when they were used to build multiple-component pictographic characters, their phonetic and semantic functions were integrated into those of the new multiple-component characters. In this process, these components consolidated their compositional functions: they gradually acquired fixed shapes and became stable in quantity. Besides, the new multicomponent characters created in this process could be further used as components to make new characters, which led to the appearance of hierarchical structures in character composition. The Chinese vocabulary developed in a very similar method: when the development of one-character words entered a bottleneck, multiple-character words, especially two-character words, were created through the combination of characters. Although the Chinese character composition system matured earlier than the Chinese vocabulary system, there is no denying that their development embodied the same mode of thinking. The maturity of this hierarchical combination method allowed the Chinese to create an infinite number of new Chinese characters with a limited number of components. The establishment of this scientific and systematic composition system marked that the Chinese character composition system crossed the threshold into a new phase of development.

(III) Pictographic Combinations Overtaken by Phonetic-Semantic and Semantic Combinations

When people began creating new characters through hierarchical combination methods, they used components as phonetic-semantic components instead of pure pictographs. In the meantime, pictographic components in the old purely pictographic combinations were influenced by character morpheme assimilation, analogisation and the new hierarchical combination, and began to be perceived as phonetic, semantic, or phonetic-semantic components. Therefore, the old purely pictographic combinations also began to be thought of as phonetic-semantic or semantic combinations. When a pictograph gained phonetic and semantic functions, it would be able to serve as a character. If all the pictographic components had been involved in this transition, all Chinese characters would have become phonetic-semantic or semantic combinations. Nevertheless, things did not go that way. Given that not all pictographic components are transformed, there are still some purely pictographic components in today's Chinese language.

One may question why pictograph-like Chinese characters ceased to be purely pictographic during their evolution. The reason is explained as follows. Originally, Chinese characters were created based on images, hence they were pictographic. When they were created through phonetic-semantic and semantic combinations, their evolution was reflected in the adjustments to the phonetic and semantic combinations, and their pictographic features were diminished.

(IV) Pictographs Overtaken by Phonetic and Semantic Symbols

As the composition system of Chinese characters shifted towards phonetic-semantic and semantic combinations, the significance of pictographic components diminished, leading to some being discarded. This was due to a new emphasis on phonetic and semantic functions over pictographic ones, occurring gradually and synchronously alongside changes to the composition system. Notably, even the remaining pictographic components became less pictographic over time. In fact, many pictographic components used during the Warring States Period (475–221 BCE) could hardly evoke images. This phenomenon became more common among the small-seal-script components. A contradiction arose under such circumstances: the characters did not need to be as pictographic as before, but some pictographic features, such as the many curved lines in the seal script, still survived, which required the people to exert a lot of effort to write them correctly. To solve this contradiction, the curved lines were gradually replaced by strokes. The political environment at that time also accelerated this change: in the Warring States Period, the state sovereigns no longer took orders from the emperor and thus stopped showing respect for the standard forms of Chinese characters recognised by the emperor; when the Qin state thrived and reunited China, the new empire was busy with civil affairs and urgently needed a more convenient writing system. In view of this need, the official script was created.

Since the Han Dynasty (202 BCE–220 CE), the social reasons mentioned above have been regarded as the main reasons for the emergence of the official script, or the official script transformation. Nevertheless, there is still an internal reason for the transformation.

For ease of writing, pictograph-like characters were systematically transformed into phonetic-semantic symbols. When the overall changes happened to the writing system, the symbols or characters needed to respond to the new changes. In other words, changes in the composition system required changes in components and characters. When the pictographs were transformed into phonetic-semantic symbols, the pictographic features were diminished, but this transformation did not affect the already-formed pictographic and phonetic-semantic combinations.

(V) Changes in the Composition Basis

The composition basis for Chinese characters embodies the inherent principles governing the Chinese character composition. In the early development stage of the composition system when all components were pictographs, the composition basis involved shapes and structures. This was especially evident in the composition of single-component characters where each stroke's shape and position had a meaning. In the middle development stage of the composition system, the composition basis became the combination of phonetic and semantic functions. The pictographic function and features were diminished, but they still existed within a certain range. Therefore, shapes still mattered in the character composition during this stage. When Chinese characters evolve into phonetic-semantic symbols, shapes are longer regarded as important, but structures still matter. The structures discussed here refer to the hierarchical combination of components, which include both vertical and horizontal relationships among the components. The phonetic-semantic symbols are no longer subject to pictographic requirements, but they have evolved from pictographic components and have acquired fixed shapes and fixed phonetic and semantic functions. Essentially, Chinese character components must be organically combined according to their functions, and, in a Chinese character, each component plays a unique role in the character composition. (The official script introduced pure symbols into the Chinese character system, and some of these symbols were inherited by the regular script. These symbols are special cases in the current Chinese character system. Their creation is an inevitable consequence of the development of this system.) In a word, when the Chinese characters stopped being pictographic, their composition basis still works.

The above analysis shows that, in the Archaic Stage, the Chinese character composition has already undergone the transition from pictographic combinations to phonetic-semantic and semantic combinations, and the characters have gradually lost their pictographic feature and evolved from pictographs to sub-pictographs. The official script inherits the phonetic-semantic and semantic combinations from the previous scripts and transforms pictographic components into phonetic-semantic symbols. These are the contents of the official script transformation,

Table 2.1 Development Stages of the Composition System of Chinese Characters

Development Stages Classification Basis	Early Stage (the oracle-bone script, and bronze inscriptions of the Western Zhou Dynasty and the Spring and Autumn Period)	Middle Stage (the Warring-States-Period script, and the small-seal script)	Late Stage (after the invention of the official script)
Combination Type	Pictographic combinations	Phonetic-semantic and semantic combinations	Phonetic-semantic and semantic combinations
Character Type	Pictographs	Sub-pictographs	Phonetic and semantic symbols
Composition Basis	Shapes and structures for pictographic purposes	Shapes for pictographic purposes and phonetic and semantic combinations	Phonetic and semantic combinations

which marks the establishment of the new-style system of Chinese characters. Based on the main characteristics of Chinese characters in different periods, the development of Chinese characters is divided into several stages shown in the following table.

Note

1 The original Chinese version was published in the *Journal of Renmin University of China* 中国人民大学学报, 1999, Issue 1.

3 The Evolution of Chinese Characters

An Issue Needs Further Exploration[1]

The evolution of the Chinese character system is essentially split into two different stages (the Archaic Stage and the New-Style Stage) by the establishment of the official script. Before the official script, pictographs dominated the system, and nearly all characters and components were based on images. When the focus of Chinese character expression evolved from images to pronunciations and meanings, the official script was created, starting the long process of building the New-Style Writing System.

The transformation of Chinese characters from pictographs to phonetic-semantic symbols required a holistic and systematic approach, but, in reality, it was impossible to carry out such a transformation after unified planning. Therefore, this transformation was realised through a consensus that was gradually reached through social practice. This reality determined the two characteristics of this transformation: first, the long duration, namely, from the middle Warring States Period to the formation of the modern Chinese characters; second, the widespread usage of variants. This transformation began at a new starting point of the composition system of Chinese characters, and the transformation of the old writing system was embodied in the actual process of using Chinese characters. Our knowledge and theories of Chinese characters are mostly based on the comparison between ancient classics and the standard system of Chinese characters used for printing today. This way of research is unreasonable: contemporary Chinese characters used today are the results of the analogisation of multiple complicated scripts used previously, and they belong to a synchronic system. Ancient Chinese documents (including stele inscriptions and unearthed documents, such as Dunhuang documents) prove that after the Qin Dynasty (221–207 BCE), there was a natural evolution process in the use of Chinese characters. This process features complexity, multitype modification, and systematic self-regulation, and there are still many unsolved mysteries about this process. In recent years, studies of Dunhuang documents and stele inscriptions of different dynasties have become popular. Unfortunately, most of these studies failed to explain the entire evolution process of Chinese characters because they tended to regard some widely recognised character variants that appeared after the invention of the official script as non-standard, illegal, popular-form, or even vulgar-form characters. Nevertheless, the truth is that such character variants appear everywhere in the bamboo slips dating back to the period from the

Qin Dynasty (221–207 BCE) to the Jin Dynasty (265–420). The inscriptions date back to the period of the Northern and Southern dynasties (386–581) to the Ming Dynasty (1368–1644), ancient official documents, including imperial edicts written by emperors themselves and various classical works and calligraphic works.[2] This shows that, in the past, no matter what social class or situation, the use of these variants was not restricted and that these variants were also regarded as formal, mainstream and legitimate forms of Chinese characters back then. The legitimacy of these variants is not something that this research is going to focus on, but they have guiding value for this research. If researchers recognise such a guiding value, their studies on the variants will focus on the rules and mechanisms governing the evolution of the Chinese character system and the motivations behind the evolutionary steps. If they deny the guiding value, just as many researchers do now, they will tend to deem many widely recognised variants as wrong-form characters.

In stele inscriptions and Dunhuang documents, the character component *yi* 弋 (hunt with bow and arrow) is usually written in a form very similar to that of *ge* 戈 (dagger-axe): *dai* 代 (replacement) is written as *fa* 伐 (subjugate), and *shi* 式 (style), as 戓. Most researchers define the two characters containing the 戈 component as wrong characters. For instance, in his book, *Li Bian* 隶辨 (Analysis of the Official Script), the Qing-Dynasty scholar, Gu Aiji 顾蔼吉, pointed out that the character 式 otherwise written as 戓 featured the radical 弋, and those featuring the radical 戈 were wrong.[3] *A Study of Popular-Form Characters in the Stone Inscriptions of the Period from 220 to 979* 六朝唐五代石刻俗字研究 by Ou Changjun 欧昌俊 et al. adopts a similar view from *Shuowen Jiezi* 说文解字 (An Explication of Written Characters): "*Shuowen Jiezi* says that 代 means replacement and consists of the radical *ren* 人 (person) and the phonetic component 弋." Nevertheless, there is also evidence showing that 伐 is an accepted variant of 代: 代 is written as 伐 in the Monument to the Statue of Sun Qiusheng of the Northern Wei Dynasty (386–534) 北魏孙秋生等造像碑 and Epitaph to the Wife of Wei Yi of the Tang Dynasty (618–907) 唐卫义妻高氏墓志.[4] *Shuowen Jiezi* 说文解字 recognises only one standard form of 式, namely a combination of the radical *gong* 工 (work) and the phonetic component 弋. Nonetheless, this did not prevent the variant 戓 from being widely used and recognised. This variant can be seen in the following inscriptions: Northern-Wei-Dynasty inscriptions, including Epitaph to Huangfu Lin of the Northern Wei Dynasty 北魏皇甫驎墓志, Epitaph to Xing Luan's Wife Yuan Chuntuo 北魏邢峦妻元纯陁墓志, Epitaph to Yuan Hui, and Epitaph to Mu Shao 北魏元诲墓志, Epitaph to Yuan Su 北魏元肃墓志, Epitaph to Yuan Su Mu Shao 北魏穆绍墓志; Eastern-Wei-Dynasty (534–550) inscriptions, including Epitaph to Gao Zhan 东魏高湛墓志, Epitaph to Lü Bosheng and His Wife Yuan Zhongying 东魏闾伯升及妻元仲英墓志; Sui-Dynasty (581–618) inscriptions, including Epitaph to Li Ze 隋李则墓志, Epitaph to the Wife of Zhang Tao 隋张涛妻礼氏墓志, Epitaph to Mister Gou's Wife Song Yuyan 隋苟君妻宋玉艳墓志; and Tang-Dynasty (618–907) inscriptions, including Epitaph to Zhang Yao 唐张药墓志, Epitaph to the Wife of Mister Yang 唐杨君妻孙氏墓志, Epitaph to Zhang Luo 唐张洛墓志, and Epitaph to the Wife of Mister Chen 唐陈君妻王氏墓志.[5] Huang Zheng 黄征 noticed this phenomenon and made the following statement in his book, *Dictionary for Dunhuang Popular-Form Characters* 敦煌俗字典. "In Dunhuang manuscripts, 代 and 伐 are used interchangeably in many situations, and there is a tendency for the replacement of 代 by 伐. This is no accident."[6]

Yi 弋 (hunt with bow and arrow) in Western-Zhou-Dynasty (1046–771 BCE) bronze inscriptions.

Table 3.1 弋 in Western-Zhou-Dynasty Bronze Inscriptions

Hu Ding 曶鼎 (*Hu* Tripod Cauldron)	*Fangding* 方鼎 (Rectangular Cauldron)

"In the late Western Zhou Dynasty, the solid dots were gradually replaced by short lines," noted Zhang Zhenlin 张振林. He further pointed out that solid dots were completely replaced by horizontal lines in the Spring and Autumn Period (770–476 BCE) and the Warring States Period (475–221 BCE).[7] Such replacement of dots is a self-regulation principle of the composition system of Chinese characters. It is embodied in the evolution process of many characters, such as *shi* 十 (ten), *tu* 土 (soil), *nian* 廿 (20), and *sa* 卅 (30). *Shi* 十 (10):

Table 3.2 Evolution of 十

	Xiaochenshou Gui Container of the Western Zhou Dynasty
	Xiaochenshou Gui container of the Western Zhou Dynasty
	the ship pass tally given to the lord of the State of E (today's Hubei Province) of the Warring States Period
	Guodian Chu-State Bamboo Slips (No. 38 bamboo slip started with characters "*xing zi ming chu* 性自命出")
	Xinyang Chu-State Bamboo Slips (No. 2–05 bamboo slip)
	Chu-State Bamboo Slips of the Warring States Period: a Collection of Shanghai Museum (Vol. 1-"*Rong cheng shi* 容成氏"-No. 14 bamboo slip)

Tu 土 (soil):

Table 3.3 Evolution of 土

	Yu Ding (*Yu* Tripod Cauldron of the Western Zhou Dynasty)
	Chu-State Bamboo Slips of the Warring States Period: A Collection of Shanghai Museum (Vol. 2 "*Cong zheng* 从政" Part A-No. 2 bamboo slip)

(*Continued*)

42 *The Evolution of Chinese Characters*

Table 3.3 (Continued)

	《上海博物馆藏战国楚竹书二·子羔》简 3 *Chu-State Bamboo Slips of the Warring States Period: A Collection of Shanghai Museum* (Vol. 2 "*Zi gao* 子羔" No. 3 bamboo slip)
	The Chu-State Silk Manuscript (Part B, the 7th line)
	Chu-State Bamboo Slips of the Warring States Period: A Collection of Shanghai Museum (Vol. 1 "*Zi yi* 缁衣" No. 8 bamboo slip)

Nian 廿 (20):

Table 3.4 Evolution of 廿

	Yu Ding (*Yu* Tripod Cauldron of the Western Zhou Dynasty)
	Song Ding (*Song* Tripod Cauldron of the Western Zhou Dynasty)
	Zengji Wuxue Hu (*Zengji* Jugs)
	The vehicle pass tally given to the lord of the State of E (today's Hubei Province) of the Warring States Period
	Guodian Chu-State Bamboo Slips ("*Tang yu zhi dao* 唐虞之道" No. 25 bamboo slip)

Sa 卅 (30):

Table 3.5 Evolution of 卅

	Maogong Ding (Tripod Cauldron of Duke Mao of the Western Zhou Dynasty)
	Baoshan Chu-State Bamboo Slips (No. 107 bamboo slip)
	Chu-State Bamboo Slips of the Warring States Period: A Collection of Shanghai Museum (Vol. 2 "*Rong cheng shi* 容成氏" No. 17 bamboo slip)

Unearthed bamboo slips show that, during the Warring States Period, the dot and the short horizontal line were virtually interchangeable. For instance, in Chu-state bamboo slips, 弋 often has a dot in its lower part and looks very much like 戈.

Table 3.6 Different Forms of Character 弋

	Guodian Chu-State Bamboo Slips ("*Tang yu zhi dao* 唐虞之道" No. 12 bamboo slip)
	Guodian Chu-State Bamboo Slips ("*Tang yu zhi dao* 唐虞之道" No. 18 bamboo slip)

The Evolution of Chinese Characters 43

	Chu-State Bamboo Slips of the Warring States Period: A Collection of Shanghai Museum (Vol. 5 "*Bao Shuya and Xi Peng's Remonstrance* 鲍叔牙与隰朋之谏" No. 1 bamboo slip)
	Chu-State Bamboo Slips of the Warring States Period: A Collection of Shanghai Museum (Vol. 5 "*Bao Shuya and Xi Peng's Remonstrance* 鲍叔牙与隰朋之谏" No. 2 bamboo slip)

Sometimes, the dot in 弋 (戈) is simplified into a short stroke to facilitate fast writing.

Table 3.7 Different Forms of Character 弋

	Guodian Chu-State Bamboo Slips ("*Tang yu zhi dao* 唐虞之道" No. 9 bamboo slip)
	Guodian Chu-State Bamboo Slips ("*Tang yu zhi dao* 唐虞之道" No. 17 bamboo slip)

Sometimes, the dot in the character 弋 (戈) is written as a short horizontal line.

Table 3.8 Different Forms of Character 弋

	Chu-State Bamboo Slips of the Warring States Period: A Collection of Shanghai Museum (Vol. 1 "*Zi yi* 缁衣" No. 2 bamboo slip)
	Chu-State Bamboo Slips of the Warring States Period: A Collection of Shanghai Museum (Vol. 2 "*Rong cheng shi* 容成氏" No. 50 bamboo slip)
	Chu-State Bamboo Slips of the Warring States Period: A Collection of Shanghai Museum (Vol. 5 "*Gu cheng jia fu* 姑成家父" No. 10 bamboo slip)
	Chu-State Bamboo Slips of the Warring States Period: A Collection of Shanghai Museum (Vol. 6 "*Yong ri* 用曰" No. 4 bamboo slip)
	The Chu-State Silk Manuscript (Part B, the 11th line)
	The Chu-State Silk Manuscript (Part A, the 4th line)

The above-mentioned phenomenon also occurs in 弋 (戈) when it serves as a component.

Table 3.9 Different Forms of Character Component 弋

	Baoshan Chu-State Bamboo Slips (No. 150 bamboo slip)		*Baoshan Chu-State Bamboo Slips* (No. 115 bamboo slip)
	Baoshan Chu-State Bamboo Slips (No. 114 bamboo slip)		*Baoshan Chu-State Bamboo Slips* (No. 116 bamboo slip)
	Baoshan Chu-State Bamboo Slips (No. 108 bamboo slip)		*Baoshan Chu-State Bamboo Slips* (No. 117 bamboo slip)

44 *The Evolution of Chinese Characters*

Also, in the Warring-States-Period Chu-State bamboo scroll, 代 is written as 伐, and 式 is written as 弌.

Table 3.10 Different Forms of Character Component 弋 on Chu-State Bamboo Slips

	Baoshan Chu-State Bamboo Slips (No. 61 bamboo slip)
	Chu-State Bamboo Slips of the Warring States Period: A Collection of Shanghai Museum (Vol. 1 "*Zi yi* 缁衣" No. 8 bamboo slip)

The examples above show that whether used as a single-component character or a component, the dot in 弋 (戈) was gradually replaced by a horizontal line during the Warring States. It is worth noting that, in this period, there was still a noticeable difference between the character 戈 and the variant of 弋 which looks like 戈. The following table shows how the former is written in Chu-state bamboo scrolls.

Table 3.11 Different Forms of 弋 on Chu-State Bamboo Slips

	Guodian Chu-State Bamboo Slips ("*Tang yu zhi dao* 唐虞之道" No. 13 bamboo slip)
	Chu-State Bamboo Slips Unearthed at Wulipai (No. 7 bamboo slip)
	Xinyang Chu-State Bamboo Slips (No. 2–028 bamboo slip)
	Bamboo Slips from the Tomb of Marquis Yi of the Zeng State (No. 61 bamboo slip)

In the past, the variant of 弋, which looked like 戈, differed from the character 戈 in only one place: the former had a horizontal line in its lower part, and the latter had a left-falling stroke in its lower part. Gradually, the horizontal line in the variant of 弋 was replaced by a left-falling stroke for the purpose of convenient writing, which made the variant look exactly like the character 戈. Given this, 戈 sometimes was used as a variant of 弋, representing the original meaning of 弋 rather than that of 戈. It was not surprising that 代 and 式 could be written as 伐 and 弌, respectively. Because of the features of the composition system of Chinese characters, the replacement of the dot with a horizontal line led to this systemic conflict. To differentiate 弋 from 戈, the system stopped allowing 戈 to serve as a variant of 弋 any longer at a certain point in time.

Apart from 弋, similar things happened to *sheng* 生 (life). As a component, 生 was often written as 主: the 生 in Dunhuang documents was written as 𡈼 or 𠃓.[8] *A Study of Popular-Form Characters in the Stone Inscriptions of the Period from 220 to 979* 六朝唐五代石刻俗字研究 notices and explains this phenomenon. It

The Evolution of Chinese Characters 45

lists many examples discovered in the stele inscriptions dating back to the period from the Northern Wei Dynasty (386–534) to the Tang Dynasty (618–907), where *xing* 姓 (surname) is written as 妵,[9] and *xing* 性 (nature) as 忄主, and points out that the left-falling stroke in the upper left corner of its phonetic component 生 is omitted.[10] In fact, this phenomenon started as early as the Han Dynasty (202 BCE–220 CE) as shown in the tables below. 生:

Table 3.12 Different Han-Dynasty Forms of 生

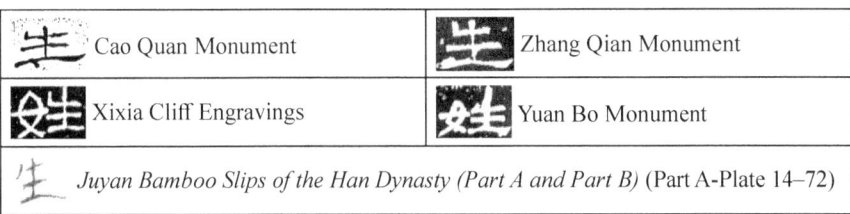

生 Cao Quan Monument	生 Zhang Qian Monument
姓 Xixia Cliff Engravings	姓 Yuan Bo Monument
生 *Juyan Bamboo Slips of the Han Dynasty (Part A and Part B)* (Part A-Plate 14–72)	

主

Table 3.13 Different Forms of 生 in the Han Dynasty

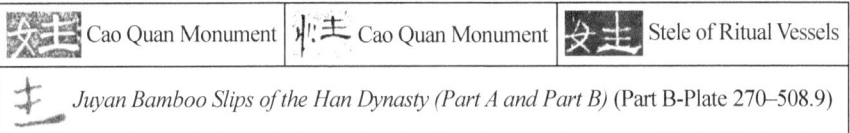

主 Cao Quan Monument	州主 Cao Quan Monument	女主 Stele of Ritual Vessels
主 *Juyan Bamboo Slips of the Han Dynasty (Part A and Part B)* (Part B-Plate 270–508.9)		

This phenomenon was caused by two different measures taken in the transformation of the same curved stroke. After the official script transformation, the composition system of Chinese characters did not allow for the existence of ㇉. Therefore, the following two methods were adopted to transform the stroke.

Figure 3.1 Two Parallel Modifications of ㇉

This change also occurred to other characters that contained a similar stroke or structure. For instance, *niu* 牛 (cattle, originally written as 半) as a character and a component had the following two forms.

Table 3.14 Different Forms of 牛

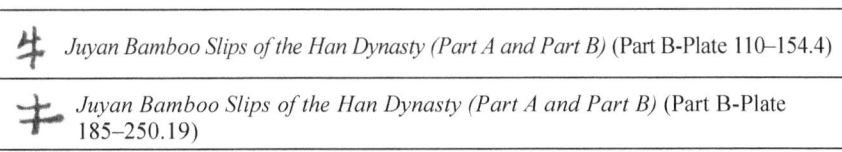

牛	*Juyan Bamboo Slips of the Han Dynasty (Part A and Part B)* (Part B-Plate 110–154.4)
半	*Juyan Bamboo Slips of the Han Dynasty (Part A and Part B)* (Part B-Plate 185–250.19)

Both forms could be used as components to build characters:

Table 3.15 Different Forms of Character Component 牛

Mu 牡 (male)		*Juyan Bamboo Slips of the Han Dynasty (Part A and Part B)* (Part B-Plate 121–169.10)
Pin 牝 (female)		*Juyan Bamboo Slips of the Han Dynasty (Part A and Part B)* (Part A-Plate 160–2218)
Lao 牢 (fence)		*Juyan Bamboo Slips of the Han Dynasty (Part A and Part B)* (Part A-Plate 72–920)
Gao 告 (tell)		*Juyan Bamboo Slips of the Han Dynasty (Part A and Part B)* (Part A-Plate 178–2532B)
Gao 告 (tell)		*Juyan Bamboo Slips of the Han Dynasty (Part A and Part B)* (Part A-Plate 32–255)
Zhu 朱 (vermilion)		*Juyan Bamboo Slips of the Han Dynasty (Part A and Part B)* (Part B-Plate 120–166.10)
Zhu 朱 (vermilion)		*Juyan Bamboo Slips of the Han Dynasty (Part A and Part B)* (Part B-Plate 115–159.2)

In a word, 主, 姓, and 仕 are just the results of a different method used to transform a curved stroke. They are the natural result of their evolution. The reason they are regarded as non-standard characters now is that the system of modern Chinese characters has not chosen them as standard characters. Before the establishment of this system, all of them were widely accepted character variants, and 主 even outshone 生 in terms of popularity. (Similar things have also happened to the following characters and their variants: *dong* 東 (east), *mu* 木 (wood), *wei* 未 (not yet), *tuo* 橐 (a sack), *sheng* 聲 (sound), *he* 禾 (standing grain), *bing* 秉 (grasp), *jian* 兼 (and), *shu* 束 (bind), *ling* 夌 (mount), *gu* 穀 (cereal), *gu* 鼓 (drum), *zhao* 朝 (morning), and *shou* 手 (hand).)

In stele inscriptions and Dunhuang documents. *bu* 步 (step), as a character or a component, is often written as 步:

Table 3.16 Different Forms of 步

Bu 步 (step)		Heng Fang Monument of the Han Dynasty
Zhi 陟 (ascend)		Kong Zhou Monument of the Han Dynasty

A Study of Popular-Form Characters in the Stone Inscriptions of the Period from 220 to 979 六朝唐五代石刻俗字研究 lists a lot of examples of writing 步 as 步 in ancient inscriptions, such as those in Epitaph to Yuan Zhan of the Eastern Wei Dynasty (534–550) 东魏元湛墓志, Records of Magu Immortal Temple of the Tang Dynasty (618–907) 唐麻姑仙坛记, and Epitaph to Sun Zhuo of the Later

Tang Dynasty (923–936) 后唐孙拙墓志. *The Great Chinese Dictionary* 汉语大字典 explains 步 as the wrong form of 步. *Zheng Zi Tong* 正字通 (Proper Forms of Characters) points out that the popular form of 步 features the radical *shao* 少 (inadequate). Kangxi Zidian 康熙字典 (*Kangxi Dictionary*) cites the idea from *Su Shu Zheng E* 俗书正讹 (Non-Standard Popular-Form Characters), saying that that radical of 步 shall be 屮, which is a variant of 止, instead of 少. *A Study of Popular-Form Characters in the Stone Inscriptions of the Period from 220 to 979* 六朝唐五代石刻俗字研究 explains this phenomenon as follows: the phenomenon of writing 步 as 步 is probably caused by the influence of the form of 少 that looks like 屮 (this is a variant of 止)[11]

Table 3.17 步 in Ancient Official and Small-Seal Scripts

![]	*Scattered Bamboo Slips Found in Desert Areas* ("*Tun shu cong can* 屯戍丛残", Plate 5, No. 1 bamboo slip)
![]	*Silk Manuscripts Unearthed from Mawangdui Han Tombs* (Vol. 4, "*Yang Sheng Fang* 养生方", the 195th line)
![]	*Shuowen Jiezi* 说文解字 (the small-seal script)

This research holds that 步 and 步 once coexisted in the writing system and that their difference in form was caused by different modification methods of the vertical stroke with a left turning in 屮.

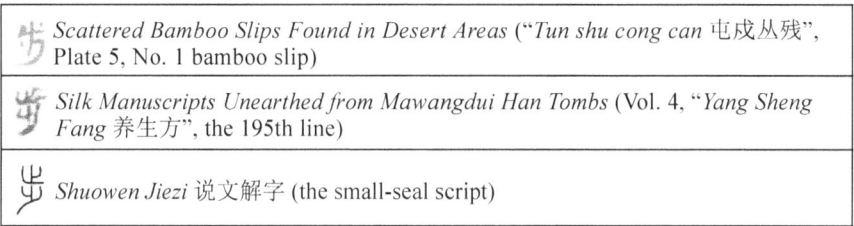

Figure 3.2 Strokes Modified in Different Ways

步 or 步 means *step*, a distinct concept from 少 which means *inadequate*. This distinction may have been the basis for the standardized form of 步 to prevent ambiguity.

Beginning from the appearance of the ancient official script, the modification and adjustment to the composition system of Chinese characters lasted for a very long time. Although there was inevitably some confusion in this process, there were still certain rules to follow. Many changes were carried out for the principle of writing convenience. Most of the time, the modifications were made to curved strokes such as ∪ and ⌐, and the two more commonly used modification methods were straightening and breaking up a curved stroke. The differences caused by these two equally popular methods shall not be considered as features to distinguish between the standard and non-standard-character forms.

Notes

1 The original Chinese version was published in *Academic Research* 学术研究, 2011, Issue 2.
2 黄征：《敦煌俗字无处不在》，见《敦煌俗字典·前言》，上海：上海教育出版社，2005。
 Huang Zheng: *Dunhuang Popular-Form Characters: A Widespread Phenomenon*, the preface of *Dictionary for Dunhuang Popular-Form Characters*, Shanghai: Shanghai Educational Publishing House, 2005.
3 顾蔼吉：《隶辨》，第 235 页，北京：中华书局，1986。
 Gu Aiji: *Analysis of the Official Script*, p. 235, Beijing: Zhonghua Book Company, 1986.
4 欧昌俊、李海霞：《六朝唐五代石刻俗字研究》，第 65 页，成都：巴蜀书社，2004。
 Ou Changjun and Li Haixia: *A Study of Popular-Form Characters in the Stone Inscriptions of the Period from 220 to 979*, p. 65, Chengdu: Bashu Publishing House, 2004.
5 欧昌俊、李海霞：《六朝唐五代石刻俗字研究》，第 67 页，成都：巴蜀书社，2004。
 Ou Changjun and Li Haixia: *A Study of Popular-Form Characters in the Stone Inscriptions of the Period from 220 to 979*, p. 67, Chengdu: Bashu Publishing House, 2004.
6 黄征：《敦煌俗字典》，第 73 页，上海：上海教育出版社，2005。
 Huang Zheng: *Dictionary for Dunhuang Popular-Form Characters*, p. 73, Shanghai: Shanghai Educational Publishing House, 2005.
7 张振林《试论铜器铭文形式上的时代标记》，《古文字研究》第五辑第 67 页，中华书局，1981 年。
 Zhang Zhenlin: *On the Time-Related Features of the Bronze Inscriptions*, Research on Ancient Chinese Characters (Vol. 5), p. 67, Zhonghua Book Company, 1981.
8 详见黄征：《敦煌俗字典》，第 361 页，上海：上海教育出版社，2005。
 Huang Zheng: *Dictionary for Dunhuang Popular-Form Characters*, p. 361, Shanghai: Shanghai Educational Publishing House, 2005.
9 欧昌俊、李海霞：《六朝唐五代石刻俗字研究》，第 96 页，成都：巴蜀书社，2004 。
 Ou Changjun and Li Haixia: *A Study of Popular-Form Characters in the Stone Inscriptions of the Period from 220 to 979*, p. 96, Chengdu: Bashu Publishing House, 2004.
10 欧昌俊、李海霞：《六朝唐五代石刻俗字研究》，第 97 页，成都：巴蜀书社，2004 。
 Ou Changjun and Li Haixia: *A Study of Popular-Form Characters in the Stone Inscriptions of the Period from 220 to 979*, p. 97, Chengdu: Bashu Publishing House, 2004.
11 欧昌俊、李海霞：《六朝唐五代石刻俗字研究》，第 66 页，成都：巴蜀书社，2004。
 Ou Changjun and Li Haixia: *A Study of Popular-Form Characters in the Stone Inscriptions of the Period from 220 to 979*, p. 66, Chengdu: Bashu Publishing House, 2004.

References

[1] Henan Institute of Cultural Relics: *Chu-State Tombs at Xinyang*, Beijing: Cultural Relics Press, 1986.
[2] Hubei Jingsha Railway Archaeological Team: *Baoshan Chu-State Bamboo Slips*, Beijing: Cultural Relics Press, 1991.
[3] Hubei Provincial Museum: *The Tomb of Marquis Yi of the Zeng State*, Beijing: Cultural Relics Press, 1989.
[4] Jingmen Municipal Museum: *Guodian Chu-State Bamboo Slips*, Beijing: Cultural Relics Press, 1998.

[5] Luo Zhenyu and Wang Guowei: *Scattered Bamboo Slips Found in Desert Areas*, Beijing: Zhonghua Book Company, 1993.
[6] Ma Chengyuan, ed.: *Chu-State Bamboo Slips of the Warring States Period: A Collection of Shanghai Museum* (Vol. 1), Shanghai: Shanghai Chinese Classics Publishing House, 2001.
[7] Ma Chengyuan: *Chu-State Bamboo Slips of the Warring States Period: A Collection of Shanghai Museum* (Vol. 2), Shanghai: Shanghai Chinese Classics Publishing House, 2001.
[8] Ma Chengyuan: *Chu-State Bamboo Slips of the Warring States Period: A Collection of Shanghai Museum* (Vol. 5), Shanghai: Shanghai Chinese Classics Publishing House, 2001.
[9] Ma Chengyuan: *Chu-State Bamboo Slips of the Warring States Period: A Collection of Shanghai Museum* (Vol. 6), Shanghai: Shanghai Chinese Classics Publishing House, 2001.
[10] The Collation Team for Silk Manuscripts Unearthed from Mawangdui Han Tombs: *Silk Manuscripts Unearthed from Mawangdui Han Tombs* (Vol. 4), Beijing: Cultural Relics Press, 1985.
[11] Rao Zongyi and Zeng Xiantong: *Three Types of Unearthed Chu-State Documents*, Beijing: Zhonghua Book Company, 1993.
[12] Shang Chengzuo: *Collection of Chu-State Bamboo Slips of the Warring States Period*, Jinan: Shandong Qilu Press, 1995.
[13] The Institute of Archaeology of the Chinese Academy of Social Sciences: *Juyan Bamboo Slips of the Han Dynasty (Part A and Part B)*, Beijing: Zhonghua Book Company, 1980.

4 The Systematic Transformation of the Chinese Character Composition[1]

The Chinese character composition refers to how character components are combined to make characters such as pictographs, single-component ideographs, semantic compounds, and semantic-phonetic characters.[2] A common phenomenon is that the combination, addition, and removal of components often cause changes to character forms in the evolution of Chinese characters, but most of the changes are about the ways to combine components. To be more specific, most of the transformed characters basically keep their original components (in simplified forms) when their original compositional structures are altered. So far, academic circles still have insufficient cognition of this point.

I. Pictographic and Phonetic-Semantic Combinations

The composition of Chinese characters, especially that of early Chinese characters, is an important issue in the studies on Chinese characters. This issue involves the identification of character components, the ways they are combined, and their compositional structures (a hierarchical or flat compositional structure). It is also related to the identification of the historical period of a certain character's emergence and the studies on the evolution of Chinese characters. So far, the research on early Chinese characters, particularly oracle-bone inscriptions, has yielded fruitful results. Although different researchers have come to different conclusions, they share a common habit in research: they tend to infer the compositional structures of early Chinese characters from the compositional structures of their evolved forms. For instance, if the current form of a character is a semantic-phonetic character or semantic-compound character, the researchers tend to think of its early form as a semantic-phonetic or semantic compound but neglect the influence of the systematic transformation of Chinese characters.

The evolution of Chinese characters is a systematic process: at one point in the process, characters went through a transition from pictographs to phonetic-semantic compounds.[3] As was found in this research, all Chinese characters were pictographs representing images before the transition, and their creation was based on drawings, but when they were transformed into phonetic-semantic compounds, their creation was based on the combination of phonetic and semantic components, which led to the emergence of semantic-compound and semantic-phonetic

DOI: 10.4324/9781032622965-4

characters. The tradition of creating characters through phonetic-semantic combinations has been around for many years, but early Chinese characters are often not influenced by this tradition. This is illustrated by the three examples below. The first example is the character *yu* 渔 (fishing). Different forms of 渔 in the oracle-bone inscriptions are shown below.

Figure 4.1 Different Forms of 渔 in Oracle-Bone Inscriptions

The first form depicts a fish with a fishing line in its mouth. The second one looks like the combination of a hand holding a fishing rod and a fish, and the third one, the combination of a hand holding a fishing net and a fish. The fourth depicts two hands pulling a net to catch fish, and the fifth, a fish being fished out of the water. *Shuowen Jiezi* 说文解字 (An Explication of Written Characters) explains that the character 渔 means fishing. This is also reflected in all the above-shown oracle-bone multiple-component pictographs. The only standard for the creation of such pictographic characters is drawing pictures that make sense with a glance. *Shuowen Jiezi* 说文解字 also points out that 渔 is a semantic compound. This is obviously an explanation made after the symbolisation of Chinese characters. Among the five oracle-bone forms of 渔, the fifth one has the same composition as today's 渔, except that its components are still pictographic. The second example is the character *zhi* 执 (capture). In oracle-bone inscriptions, this character has the following forms.

Figure 4.2 Different Forms of 执 in Oracle-Bone Inscriptions

All the three forms are multiple-component pictographs depicting a person in handcuffs, preparing to accept the punishment for his or her sin. *Shuowen Jiezi* 说文解字 explains 执 as both a semantic-compound and a semantic-phonetic character, describing an action to arrest a criminal. According to the book, the character consists of two components *ji* 卂 (catch) and *xing* 幸 (meet), the latter also serving as a phonetic component. This explanation is clearly based on the small-seal character 执, as shown below.

Figure 4.3 Different Small-Seal Forms of 渔

In this small-seal character, the two components are not pictographs, not depicting a person in handcuffs.

52 *The Transformation of the Chinese Character Composition*

Some early pictographic Chinese characters are wrongly regarded as semantic-phonetic characters because of a misunderstanding of the images. A typical example is the character *si* 祀 (worship). In the oracle-bone script, the character is written as follows.

祀

Figure 4.4 Different Forms of 祀 in Oracle-Bone Inscriptions

According to *Shuowen Jiezi* 说文解字, 祀 means worship rituals with a long history, and it is a semantic-phonetic character consisting of *shi* 示 (manifest) and *si* 巳 (child), the latter serving as the phonetic component. This oracle-bone glyph looks almost the same as 祀, which is the contemporary form of the character, but it is not a semantic-phonetic character. In an ancient activity of worshipping an ancestor, a young child who looked like the ancestor would be picked out to evoke the participants' feelings about the ancestor. This child would be held up high to receive the worship on behalf of the ancestor. Today, the character 祀 still contains the component *si* 巳, which means child, and this character component is also written as shi 尸, which means using something or someone to impersonate the dead in some ancient documents, such as *Yi li* 仪礼 (Annotations on the Book of Rites and Rituals) and *Li Ji* 礼记 (The Book of Rites). *Oracle Dictionary* 甲骨文字典, edited by Xu Zhongshu 徐中舒, explains this phenomenon. "The character 祀 originally consisted of *shi* 示 (manifest) and ⼦ (originally written as ⼦, a child chosen to receive worship on behalf of a deceased ancestor), and the latter was wrongly written as 尸 by later generations. The character 祀 was originally written as ⼦, which depicted a person [holding] a child. It was later wrongly written as ⼦ or ⼦ or written in a simplified form ⼂."[4] The character 祀 has a widely accepted variant 禩, and in Shang-Dynasty oracle-bone and bronze inscriptions, its component *yi* 異 (unusual) usually appears in the following forms.

Figure 4.5 Different Forms of 異 in Oracle-Bone and Bronze Inscriptions

All these forms depict an adult holding a child high. The character 祀 is the simplified version of 禩, and the combination of 巳/異 and 示 is simply a pictographic combination instead of a semantic one. Therefore, this character is just an early multiple-component pictographic character. Such a pictographic combination is not rare in the oracle-bone script. For instance, 彳 and *zhi* 止 (toe) are often combined to represent movement.

In studies on the composition of early Chinese characters, researchers often argue about whether a character is a pictograph or semantic compound. This research believes that the early Chinese characters have strong pictographic features as there are strict requirements for the orientation and position of each character component in the writing system.

The Transformation of the Chinese Character Composition 53

Table 4.1 Requirements for the Orientations and Positions of Character Components in Oracle-Bone Inscriptions

Ge 各 (individually)	
Yi 伇 (labour)	
Que 殻 (a musical instrument)	

The three oracle-bone-script characters shown in the table above have various forms, but the forms of a character seldom differ from one another in terms of the position and orientation of character components. For example, in all the forms of *ge* 各 (individually), which originally meant "come", the component representing feet points towards the inside of the upwards-opening component. All the forms of *yi* 伇 (labour) depict a person holding tools behind their back. In all the forms of *que* 殻 (a musical instrument), the component depicting the beater may appear on the right or left side of the one representing the instrument, but the head of the beater always points to the instrument. If these characters were semantic compounds,[5] there would be no such requirements on the components' orientations and positions. Such requirements prove that these characters depict images, boasting strong pictographic characteristics. As to the early forms of some characters, such as *ming* 明 (light) and *ming* 名 (name), whose written forms are not restricted by the above-mentioned requirements, they are also pictograph characters. The reason their components do not follow the restrictions is that they do not rely on positions and orientations to clearly depict the images. This phenomenon is caused by the differences in the images depicted, not the changes in the character composition. All these early characters are pictographs, but this does not prevent the creation of various characters to describe images, actions, and even invisible things.

The fact that early Chinese characters are descriptions of images has already been pointed out by some researchers, but their research results have not been taken seriously. Yao Xiaosui 姚孝遂 is one such researcher. "Characters in oracle-bone and bronze inscriptions depict images. As far as the source of these characters is concerned, they are pictographic characters," said Mr. Yao.[6] "Judging from the structures of oracle-bone-script characters, there is no doubt that they are based on images of objective things. Although many symbols have been linearised and simplified, you can still see that they are developed from images of things."[7]

II. The Pictographic Supplement and the Phonetic/Semantic Addition

The forms of the same early Chinese character often differ from one another in terms of components. The following are the different forms of *yu* 御 (manage) in the oracle-bone script.

54 *The Transformation of the Chinese Character Composition*

Figure 4.6 Different Forms of 御 in Oracle-Bone Inscriptions

Usually, in the analyses of the composition of Chinese characters, the component added to a character that already exists will be regarded as a pictographic component, and the new character created after the addition will be regarded as a semantic-phonetic character. Nevertheless, this kind of thinking pattern is not suitable for the composition of early Chinese characters. An early character may have various forms that consist of different components, and it is hard to determine the order in which these forms appeared. Therefore, it is difficult to determine whether a component is added to or removed from a character form. The fact is that these different forms co-existed at the same time. Even if there was a component added to a character form, the added component was not necessarily a pictographic or phonetic one. Even so, in most cases, added components are pictographic ones. This part discusses these two types of component addition, respectively named the pictographic supplement and the phonetic/semantic addition. The pictographic supplement refers to the addition of a pictographic component for the purpose of perfecting the depiction of an image. This method produces compound-pictograph characters. A typical example is the 10 oracle-bone-script forms of the character *mu* 莫 (sunset) as shown below.

Figure 4.7 Different Forms of 莫 in Oracle-Bone Inscriptions

Shuowen Jiezi 说文解字 says that *mu* 莫 (sunset) consists of components *ri* 日 (sun) and *mang* 茻 (tufted grass), the former enclosed by the latter. The component 日 appears in each of the first eight forms shown above, but the components combine with 日 to make the character differ. As shown above, *cao* 屮 (grass), *mu* 木 (wood), and *he* 禾 (standing grain) can be used to make the characters, and there are no restrictions on their numbers. Given this, it is very unreasonable to call one form that has three 屮 components a semantic-phonetic character for it has an additional 屮 in comparison with another form featuring two 屮 components. For the same reason, it is incorrect to determine that the form featuring four 屮 components or four 木 components is a semantic-phonetic character created by adding two 屮 components or two 木 components to the original form featuring two 屮 components or two 木 components. It is worth noting that in each of the last two forms, there is a pictographic component *zhui* 隹 (short-tailed bird). Birds flying back to their nests are usual sights at sunset. According to *Shuowen Jiezi* 说文解字, a bird resting in a nest is a pictograph describing sunset. Therefore, the component 隹 can be regarded as the pictographic supplement to the two forms. The same phenomenon occurs in the following three oracle-bone-script characters *sang* 丧 (mourning), *wei* 韦 (tanned leather), and *she* 涉 (to wade) as shown below.

The Transformation of the Chinese Character Composition 55

Table 4.2 Pictographic Supplements in Oracle-Bone Inscriptions

Sang 丧 (mourning)	
Wei 韋 (tanned leather)	
She 涉 (to wade)	

The forms of 丧 differ from one another in the number of the component *kou* 口 (mouth). In the different forms of 韋 and those of 涉, the numbers of the component *zhi* 止 (toe) are different. Obviously, this phenomenon is caused by the need for image depiction or the pictographic supplement. None of these components are added for the creation of semantic-phonetic characters.

Some characters in the oracle-bone script are often mistaken for semantic-phonetic characters. A typical example is the character *ni* 逆 (meet head-on), whose small-seal form is shown below.

Figure 4.8 Different Small-Seal Forms of 逆

Shuowen Jiezi 说文解字 describes *ni* 逆 (meet head-on), replaced by *ying* 迎 (meet head-on) in some Chinese dialects, as a semantic-phonetic character consisting of the component *chuo* 辵 (walking) and the phonetic component *ni* 屰 (meet head-on). Given that this small-seal-script character directly inherits its composition from the oracle-bone script, is any of the oracle-bone-script forms of 逆 a semantic-phonetic character?

Figure 4.9 Different Forms of 逆 in Oracle-Bone Inscriptions

In the first form, the upper part seems to be a person standing on his head, representing a person coming from a distance, and the lower part depicts a pair of feet pointing upwards, representing the other person who meets the first person head-on. Compared with the first form, the second form consists of a simplified version of the first form and an extra part: the component 彳 representing a street. The third form, which is the direct source of the small-seal-script form of 逆, depicts a person walking on a street and meeting someone head-on and consists of pure pictographic components. In these forms, 彳 is the pictographic supplement instead of a pictographic component added to expand the original meaning of the character.

The phonetic/semantic addition refers to the addition of a pictographic or phonetic component to create a semantic-phonetic character. Typical examples are *chi* 齿 (teeth), *qiu* 丘 (hill), and *ge* 戈 (dagger-axe) as shown below.

Table 4.3 Examples of Phonetic/Semantic Additions

	Shang Dynasty	Warring States Period
Chi 齿 (teeth)		
Qiu 丘 (hill)		
Ge 戈 (dagger-axe)		

All the forms shown above are pictographs, but some forms include a phonetic component, such as *zhi* 止 (toe) in the Warring-States-Period form of 齿, *qi* 丌 (base) in the Warring-States-Period form of *qiu* 丘 (hill), and some include a semantic component, such as *jin* 金 (metal) in the Warring-States-Period form of *ge* 戈 (dagger-axe).

The functions of components of a character determine the composition type of the character. To judge in what function the components are involved in the composition, it is a must to take into consideration the evolution of the character system instead of analysing individual components. For instance, if a character belongs to the pictographic stage, only a component that has nothing to do with the image that the character describes can be regarded as a phonetic or semantic component. As to the stages of the evolution of the character system, this research draws the following conclusions: the character system was basically pictographic from the Shang Dynasty (ca.1600–1046 BCE) to the Western Zhou Dynasty (1046–771 BCE); it began involving a small amount of phonetic-semantic combinations from the late Warring States Period (475–221 BCE) to the Western Han Dynasty (206 BCE–8 CE); and after the Eastern Han Dynasty (25–220), it began featuring phonetic-semantic combinations.[8]

III. The Symbolisation of Characters and the Transformation of Character Composition

The symbolisation of characters refers to the process where pictographs are transformed into phonetic-semantic symbols. In terms of appearance, this process gradually weakens the pictographic features. When a pictographic component was simplified to the point where it could not represent an image any longer, it completed its own transformation process and became a semantic or phonetic component. Corresponding to the transformed components, the composition of the

The Transformation of the Chinese Character Composition 57

photographic characters was changed into compound-semantic or semantic-phonetic composition. A typical example is the character *wang* 望 (expect).

Table 4.4 Changes in the Composition of 望

Shang Dynasty	Early Western Zhou Dynasty	Middle Western Zhou Dynasty	Late Western Zhou Dynasty	Spring and Autumn Period	Small Seal Script
![]	![]	![]	![]	![]	![]

In the Shang-Dynasty (ca.1600–1046 BCE) bronze inscriptions, the character is a pictograph depicting a person standing on his toes and looking into the distance, and there is an eye drawn vertically in the upper part of the character to emphasize the action of looking. In its early-Western-Zhou-Dynasty (1046–771 BCE) form, the component *yue* 月 (moon) is included to indicate what the person is looking at. In its late-Western-Zhou-Dynasty form, the vertical eye becomes an independent component, making the character no longer a pictograph. The small-seal-script form of this character looks completely different from the original pictograph, and *Shuowen Jiezi* 说文解字 records this character as a semantic compound consisting of *yue* 月 (moon), and *ren* 壬 (carry on a shoulder pole). This is how a pictographic combination is transformed into a semantic compound.

There are two types of composition transformation during the symbolisation process: non-compositional transformation and compositional transformation. The former refers to a transformation process that does change the original composition of a character, and the latter, a transformation process that changes the original composition of a character. They both reduce the pictographic feature of the original components, but the latter includes adjustments and changes to the original components and their combination relationship. The non-compositional transformation occurs in the evolution process of many characters, including *qi* 企 (stand on tiptoe), whose oracle-bone-script and small-seal-script forms are shown below.

Figure 4.10 Changes in the Form of 企

The oracle-bone-script form of the character consists of a component indicating a person and another component depicting the image of a raised heel, but the small-seal-script one has nothing to do with a heel or foot anymore. *Shuowen Jiezi* 说文解字 defines this small-seal-script character as a semantic-phonetic character consisting of the component *ren* 人 (person) and the phonetic component *zhi* 止 (toe). It is worth noting that the transformation from pictographic composition into semantic-phonetic composition is realised through the transformation of the two original components.

58 *The Transformation of the Chinese Character Composition*

Another example of non-compositional transformation is the evolution process of *xi* 析 (to split wood).

Table 4.5 Changes in the Form of 析

Shang Dynasty	Early Western Zhou Dynasty	Middle Western Zhou Dynasty	Small Seal Script

In the oracle-bone script, this character is a pictograph depicting the action of using *jin* 斤 (a tool for cutting trees) to split *mu* 木 (wood), and there is no fixed left-right positional relationship between these two components. The early-Western-Zhou-Dynasty form of the character depicts a hand holding *jin* 斤 (a tool for cutting trees) to split *mu* 木 (wood), but in its middle-Western-Zhou-Dynasty form, the component 斤 is clearly not pictographic enough. The small-seal-script form has even fewer pictographic features because the two pictographic components are further simplified. For this reason, *Shuowen Jiezi* 说文解字 regards this character as a semantic compound consisting of 木 and 斤. The original graphic composition is thus changed into the semantic-compound composition without adding new components or removing any of the original components.

The character *yu* 毓 (give birth to) has also gone through such a non-compositional transformation process.

Table 4.6 Changes in the Form of 毓

Shang Dynasty	Western Zhou Dynasty	Small Seal Script

Shuowen Jiezi 说文解字 describes the character 毓, also written as 育, as a combination of the component *tu* 㐬 (sudden) and the phonetic component *rou* 肉 (flesh), and *Yu Shu* 虞书 (The History of the Yu Dynasty) points out that its radical is *mei* 每 (mother), also written as 母. In the character's Shang-Dynasty and Western-Zhou-Dynasty forms, there are always two components respectively depicting a mother and an upside-down child surrounded by amniotic fluid. In its small-seal-script form, the pictographic components are simplified, turning the pictographic character into a semantic compound. Duan Yucai 段玉裁 (1735–1815), a Qing-Dynasty sinologist, explains this small-seal-script character as a combination of *mei* 每 (mother) and *cao* 艸 (herbage), which means a flourishing life.

The evolution process of *de* 得 (obtain) is also an example of non-compositional transformation.

Table 4.7 Changes in the Form of 得

Shang Dynasty	Western Zhou Dynasty	Spring and Autumn Period	Small Seal Script

In the oracle-bone script, there are a few different forms of the character. All these forms depict a *shou* 手 (hand) opening towards *bei* 贝 (seashell) to convey the meaning "obtain". Some form includes another component 彳, which means to obtain something while walking and emphasizes the meaning of getting something that you did not have before. All these forms are pictographs. The small-seal-script form of the character consists of simplified components inherited from its oracle-bone-script forms, and it is a semantic-phonetic character instead of pictographic one. According to *Shuowen Jiezi* 说文解字, 得 means to obtain something while walking and consists of the component 彳 (walking) and the phonetic component *de* 寻 (obtain).⁹

As to compositional transformation, the evolution process of *huang* 皇 (superior) can serve as a good example.

Table 4.8 Changes in the Form of 皇

Shang Dynasty	Western Zhou Dynasty	Spring and Autumn Period	Warring States Period	Small Seal Script

The original form of the character 皇 is a pictograph depicting a feather crown placed on a throne. In the Spring-and-Autumn-Period (770–476 BCE) forms of this character, there are two types of the "throne" component: one has two horizontal lines, and the other has three. In all these forms, the "throne" component and the "crown" component are connected. These two components are separated in the character's Warring-States-Period (475–221 BCE) form, and the "throne" component is thus changed into *wang* 王 (king). In the character's small-seal-script form, the "crown" component is replaced by *zi* 自 (nose). Under such circumstances, *Shuowen Jiezi* 说文解字 defines this character as a semantic compound.

The evolution of *ruo* 若 (supposing) is another example of compositional transformation.

Table 4.9 Changes in the Form of 若

Shang Dynasty	Western Zhou Dynasty	Spring and Autumn Period	Warring States Period	Small Seal Script

The oracle-bone-script form of the character is usually interpreted as the image of combing hair with both hands. Some forms appearing later include the component *kou* 口 (mouth). In the Warring-States-Period (475–221 BCE) form, the original components are replaced by *cao* 艹 (herbage) and *you* 又 (again). The small-seal-script becomes a semantic compound included in *Shuowen Jiezi* 说文解字, which explains *ruo* 若, which means to pick vegetables and consists of *cao* 艹 (herbage), and *you* 右 (on the right side) refers to the right hand.

The evolution process of *lao* 牢 (fence) also embodies compositional transformation.

Table 4.10 Changes in the Form of 牢

Shang Dynasty	Western Zhou Dynasty	Warring States Period
[image]	[image]	[image]

The Shang-Dynasty (ca.1600–1046 BCE) and Western-Zhou-Dynasty (1046–771 BCE) forms of the character both depict *niu* 牛 (cattle) kept in pens. They are evidently pictographs. In its Warring-States-Period form, the component depicting pens is replaced by the component *mian* 宀 (roofed room), turning the pictographic character into a semantic compound.

The following table shows that the character *ding* 鼎 (tripod caldron) has also undergone a compositional transformation process.

Table 4.11 Changes in the Form of 鼎

Shang Dynasty	Western Zhou Dynasty	Warring States Period
[image]	[image]	[image]

The Shang-Dynasty (ca.1600–1046 BCE) and Western-Zhou-Dynasty (1046–771 BCE) forms are single-component pictographic characters. As the symbolisation process develops, the Warring-States-Period (475–221 BCE) form features the replacement of the pictographic elements that depict the tripod legs with the component *min* 皿 (shallow containers). The appearance of this component is the result of the analogisation of many similar components, and it is a pictographic component. Given this, the other component in the new form becomes a semantic-phonetic component.

The following conclusions can be drawn from the examples given above: in the evolution process of characters, widely used components can be simplified but they are often not replaced, and seldom-used components, especially those appearing in only one character, are often replaced by other components. This phenomenon is not caused by writing errors, but by the overall adjustment of the writing system.

The Transformation of the Chinese Character Composition 61

For the efficiency of the whole system, the practice of creating a new component for the creation of a new word should be prohibited. For the same purpose, analogisation often occurs in the component transformation process: a seldom-used component is often replaced by a commonly used component that looks very similar to itself.

Despite that, in comparison with compositional transformation, non-compositional transformation is still the main transformation type in the symbolisation process of Chinese characters.

The symbolisation process occurred when the composition system of Chinese characters developed from the Archaic Stage to the New-Style stage. It was a systematic transformation of the Archaic writing system, and the starter of the New-Style system. In the symbolisation process, there are four main methods used to transform an old character. The first is to turn a pictographic component into a semantic or phonetic one while maintaining the original composition of the character. Typical examples transformed by this method include *qi* 企 (stand on tiptoe), *xi* 析 (to split wood), and *yu* 毓 (give birth to). The second method is to modify a component through analogisation, turning it into a semantic or phonetic component. Such a method is embodied in the transformation process of *huang* 皇 (superior), *ruo* 若 (supposing), and *lao* 牢 (fence). The third method is to add a semantic or phonetic component. The fourth is to replace the old composition of a pictographic character with a new semantic-compound or semantic-phonetic combination. All these four methods of symbolisation cause changes in the character forms, and the new forms created through such a process need to be defined and explained in a new way.

IV. New Explanations for New Character Forms

The new character forms created through the symbolisation process need new explanations for their composition. The effort to renew the explanations for the characters dates to the Spring and Autumn Period (770–476 BCE). For instance, there is such a statement in *Zuo Zhuan* 左传 (Zuo's Commentary on the Spring and Autumn Annals): *zhi* 止 (toe) and *ge* 戈 (dagger-axe) make the character *wu* 武 (martial), which can be regarded as an explanation for a new character form. This is because the old oracle-bone-script form and the Spring-and-Autumn-Period (770–476 BCE) bronze-inscription forms of 武 are as follows.

Figure 4.11 Forms of 武 in Oracle-Bone and Bronze Inscriptions

The oracle-bone-script form features a lower part that looks like a foot, depicting a person walking. In the bronze-inscription form, the lower part is not pictographic enough, and it is also in this period that the component 止 begins to express the meaning "halt". Given this, *Zuo Zhuan* 左传 interprets the character as stopping warfare. Large-scale efforts to reinterpret the composition of Chinese characters began in the Eastern Han Dynasty (25–220), and the results of the efforts were recorded in Xu Shen's 许慎 (ca.58–147) book, *Shuowen Jiezi* 说文解字.

The changes in the composition of Chinese characters were caused by the symbolisation process, which was a natural phenomenon in the evolution of Chinese characters. When the symbolisation process was completed, people naturally thought of the necessity of defining and interpreting the new character forms. When they started the work, they found that the complexity of this work was beyond their expectation. This was because the symbolisation process caused a series of changes in the composition system of Chinese characters. (1) Some pictographic components lost part of their meanings and functions when their pictographic features were erased. (2) The semantic function of some components evolved when they were used as both single-component characters and character components. The common functions of the former were affected by those of the latter. (3) The semantic-phonetic combinations became mainstream combinations in the composition of Chinese characters. As mentioned above, the symbolisation process aimed to transform pictographs that indirectly suggested pronunciations and meanings into phonetic-semantic symbols that directly indicated pronunciations and meanings. Given this, semantic-phonetic combinations were widely used to transform characters, which underlay the following three important characteristics of this evolutionary stage of the Chinese characters.

① The simplification of character components. In seal scripts, each stroke is a depiction of an object, participating in the composition of characters. The symbolisation process changed this tradition and shifted the focus of composition from individual strokes to components. As this process aimed to create phonetic-semantic symbols, it also helped the various components to develop in fixed directions: becoming phonetic or semantic components. As components became the smallest units in the composition of Chinese characters, the necessity of carefully depicting the components' internal structures with strokes was reduced. Therefore, the strokes within the components were simplified and even blurred.

② The mainstream left-right and up-down structures. As a phonetic-semantic combination usually consisted of two components, many left-right and up-down structured Chinese characters were created during this period.

③ The hierarchical structure. As some old components were integrated to create new phonetic or pictographic components, the hierarchical structure became commonly seen in the analyses of the composition of Chinese characters.

Under such circumstances, traditional-style character composition analyses usually adopt such a default principle: if a Chinese character has certain semantic-phonetic characteristics, it will be preferentially interpreted as a semantic-phonetic character. The following paragraphs illustrate this issue through two examples: *jiang* 降 (to descend) and *zhi* 陟 (to ascend).

The Transformation of the Chinese Character Composition 63

Table 4.12 Changes in the Form of 降 and the Form of 陟

Characters	Shang Dynasty	Western Zhou Dynasty	Spring and Autumn Period	Small Seal Script
Jiang 降 (to descend)				
Zhi 陟 (to ascend)				

The Shang-Dynasty (ca.1600–1046 BCE) form of *jiang* 降 (to descend) depicts two feet pointing downwards walking down the stairs, and that of *zhi* 陟 (ascend), two feet pointing upwards walking up the stairs. Both forms are pictographs. The forms of these two characters used during the Western Zhou Dynasty (1046–771 BCE) and the Spring and Autumn Period (770–476 BCE) are basically unchanged in comparison with their Shang-Dynasty forms. Nonetheless, in their small-seal-script forms, the strokes depicting two feet are integrated into one component. Each newly created component is combined with *fu* 阜 (mound) to make the two characters. In their original forms, there are only two level-1 components. After the transformation, their composition becomes more layered, which needs to be analysed through a hierarchical structure.

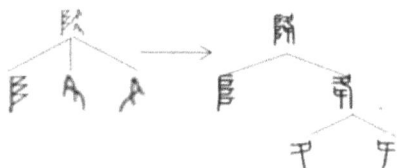

Figure 4.12 Changes in the Composition of 降

These two characters share the same original compositional structure, and their evolution processes are almost the same. When their pictographic features were erased, they should have been regarded as semantic compounds, but this was not the case. The author of *Shuowen Jiezi* 说文解字 somehow regarded the component 夅 as a phonetic component and 降 a semantic-phonetic character, but he explained 陟 as a semantic compound consisting of *fu* 阜 (mound) and *bu* 步 (step).

The phonetic-semantic combination cannot explain every character. When it is hard to determine the phonetic component of a character, the term "simplified phonetic component" is usually adopted to solve the problem, just as in the case of *jian* 監 (supervise).

Table 4.13 Changes in the Form of 监

Shang Dynasty	Early Western Zhou Dynasty	Middle Western Zhou Dynasty	Late Western Zhou Dynasty	Spring and Autumn Period	Small Seal Script

The Shang-Dynasty (ca.1600–1046 BCE) form of the character depicts a person lowering his head to look down at his own reflection in a basin of water. In the upper part of the character, there is a vertical eye that emphasizes the act of observing with the eyes. Influenced by the symbolisation process, the middle-Western-Zhou-Dynasty (1046–771 BCE) form of the character looks quite different from the previous forms: the "eye" part and the part depicting a human body are separated, and these two parts seem to be combined together to make a character component and placed above the component representing the basin of water, building an up-down structured character. *Shuowen Jiezi* 说文解字 forcibly explains this character as a semantic-phonetic character consisting of *jian* 监 (supervise) and a simplified form of the phonetic component *kan* 蚰 (blood), but it is a very far-fetched explanation. The reason for this explanation is that the new form of the character is not pictographic enough to accommodate its original compositional explanation and, in the meantime, it is not a typical semantic compound. *Shuowen Jiezi* 说文解字 offers a solution to this problem, explaining the component that is difficult to explain as a simplified form of a semantic-phonetic component. Such simplified components do exist in Chinese characters, so such an explanation is not unacceptable. This explanation also avoids the existence of meaningless components. The symbolisation process turns most pictographic components into semantic or phonetic ones, except for a few that are turned into pure symbols that have no semantic or phonetic functions. Such a phenomenon is recognised by *Shuowen Jiezi* 说文解字. For instance, the book explains *di* 弟 (sequence) as a symbol that evolved from an archaic symbol, which means the sequence of weaving with tanned leather. This explanation implies the existence of a symbol with the same function in the small-seal script. In the case of 监, its small-seal-script is not such a pure symbol, and both of its two components *wo* 卧 (crouch) and *xue* 血 (blood) can serve as single-component characters.

Another point worth noting is that, in comparison with semantic-phonetic characters created through a strict selection of semantic and phonetic components, those created through the symbolisation process usually feature phonetic components that cannot precisely represent the character pronunciations. Therefore, some characters' phonetic components are not accurate enough.

It must be admitted that not all explanations made by *Shuowen Jiezi* 说文解字 for the new character forms created through the symbolisation process are completely accurate, but most of them are decent enough. Comparative studies of character forms before and after the symbolisation process can improve these explanations. Given the differences caused by the symbolisation, it is unreasonable

The Transformation of the Chinese Character Composition 65

to judge the book's explanations based on character forms created before the symbolisation, namely, in the Shang and Zhou dynasties.

V. The Nature of the Transition from *Wen* 文 to *Zi* 字

There is such a statement in the preface of *Shuowen Jiezi* 说文解字: "Cangjie 仓颉, the legendary cultural hero, invented the Chinese writing system based on images. These earliest pictographic Chinese characters are referred to as *wen* 文, and the characters created through semantic and phonetic combinations later, are referred to as *zi* 字. The latter evolved from the former." The Qing-Dynasty sinologist Duan Yucai 段玉裁 (1735–1815) annotated this statement: "Semantic and phonetic combinations actually refer to two types of combination, namely semantic-phonetic combination and semantic combination. The former features the combination of semantic and phonetic components, and the latter, that of semantic components." Another Qing-Dynasty sinologist, Wang Yun 王筠 (1784–1854), further pointed out the following in his book, *Shuowen Jiezi Judu* 说文解字句读 (Interpretations to *Shuowen Jiezi* 说文解字): "pictographic and single-component ideographs are *wen* 文, and semantic-compound and semantic-phonetic characters are *zi* 字. Xu Shen 许慎 gives examples for each type." It should be noted that character forms created through the above-mentioned semantic and phonetic combinations include only semantic-compound and semantic-phonetic characters and exclude the multicomponent pictographs created through the combination of pure pictographic components. The first two types of characters that are referred to as *zi* 字 (characters) appeared later than the third character type that is also known as *wen* 文. This transition from *wen* 文 to *zi* 字 reflects the transformation process that turns pictographic characters into phonetic-semantic symbols.

The practice of using *zi* 字 to represent Chinese characters is firstly seen in *Shang Jun Shu* 商君书 (The Book of Lord Shang): "有敢定法令，损益一字以上，罪死不赦 (If anyone dares to tamper with any character in a decree, it is a capital crime and will not be pardoned)." Although the time of *Shang Jun Shu* is still controversial, there is other evidence proving that this practice began at least in the Qin Dynasty (221–207 BCE). The character 字 appears in Qin-Dynasty Langyang Stele: "同书文字 (Write with the same characters)". It also appears in a wooden tablet, which is a part of the Qin-Dynasty bamboo slips recently discovered at Liye 里耶秦简. The following words and numbers are written on this tablet 一正.[10]

"[九九]八十一，[八九]七十二，七九六十三，六九五十四，五九卌五，四九卅六，三九廿七，二九十八。八八六十四，七八五十六，六八卌八，五八卌，四八卅二，三八廿四，二八十六。七七卌九，六七卌二，五七卅五，四七廿八，三七廿一，二七十四。六六卅六，五六卅，四六廿四，三六十八，二六十二。五五廿五，四五廿，三五十五，二五而十。四四十六，三四十二，二四而八。三三而九，二三而六，二二而四，一一而二，二半而一。凡千一百一十三字。

$(9 \times 9 = 81, 8 \times 9 = 72, 7 \times 9 = 63, 6 \times 9 = 54, 5 \times 9 = 45, 4 \times 9 = 36, 3 \times 9 = 27, 2 \times 9 = 18.\ 8 \times 8 = 64, 7 \times 8 = 56, 6 \times 8 = 48, 5 \times 8 = 40, 4 \times 8 = 32, 3 \times 8 = 24, 2 \times 8 = 16.\ 7 \times 7 = 49, 6 \times 7 = 42, 5 \times 7 = 35, 4 \times 7 = 28, 3 \times 7 = 21, 2 \times 7 = 14.\ 6 \times$

6 = 36, 5 × 6 = 30, 4 × 6 = 24, 3 × 6 = 18, 2 × 6 = 12. 5 × 5 = 25, 4 × 5 = 20, 3 × 5 = 15, 2 × 5 = 10. 4 × 4 = 16, 3 × 4 = 12, 2 × 4 = 8. 3 × 3 = 9, 2 × 3 = 6, 2 × 2 = 4, One and one are two, and half of two is one. There are 113 characters in total.)

Some researchers think that the appearance of the character 字 in the last sentence "凡千一百一十三字 (There are 113 characters in total)" was caused by some writing error. Some regard it as the name of counting rods. None of these explanations are reasonable enough. The 字 evidently means characters here, and this is probably the origin of the Chinese word *shuzi* 数字 (numbers). This tablet, together with Langyang Stele, provides sufficient evidence that 字 has been used to refer to Chinese characters since the Qin Dynasty. Interestingly, the original meaning 字 is "giving birth to". According to *Shuowen Jiezi* 说文解字, 字 equals to *ru* 乳 (give birth to). Duan Yucai's 段玉裁 (1735–1815) note further points out that the process of humans or birds producing their next generation is called 乳. *Shan Hai Jing* 山海经 (The Classic of Mountains and Seas) also adopts the original meaning of this character: "其上有木焉，名曰黄棘，黄华而员叶，其实如兰，服之不字。(There is a tree on it, which is named huangji. This tree has yellow flowers and round leaves, but you can't have children after eating the fruit of the tree)." The character 字 is originally a combination of two components, describing the process of a fusion of male and female gametes producing an offspring. Similarly, the process of making multicomponent characters through different types of combinations also features fusion and leads to the birth of new things. Given this, it is not surprising that 字 was used to refer to characters after the emergence of many multicomponent characters. It is also reasonable to infer that this practice of using 字 to represent characters must have started after this idea came into being. Coincidentally, many semantic-compound and semantic-phonetic characters appeared right before the Qin Dynasty (221–207 BCE) in the Eastern Zhou Dynasty (770–256 BCE), making it possible for the formation of this idea. This analysis is consistent with the afore-made assertion in this research: it was during the Spring and Autumn Period (770–476 BCE) that the originally photographic Chinese characters were transformed into sub-pictographs.

There is another issue related to the transition from *wen* 文 to *zi* 字: the six means of creating Chinese characters that produce six categories of characters: pictographs, ideographs, semantic compounds, phonetic-semantic compounds, characters created through loan method, and those created through the transfer method. In the Han-Dynasty (202 BCE–220 CE), the specific names of these six means were not finalised: *Han Shu* 汉书 (The History of the Han Dynasty), Zheng Xuan's 郑玄 (127–200) notes to *Zhou Li* 周礼 (Rites of the Zhou Dynasty), and the preface of his book *Shuowen Jiezi* 说文解字 all put forward different names for them and sorted them in different orders. Nevertheless, this term was first mentioned in *Zhou Li* 周礼, a book probably written in the Western Zhou Dynasty (1046–771 BCE), the Spring and Autumn Period (770–476 BCE), the Warring States Period (475–221 BCE), or the Western Han Dynasty (206–8 BCE). In the past, people tended to think that it was created in the Western Zhou Dynasty, but many influential historians, such as Guo Moruo (1892–1978), Gu Jiegang (1893–1980), Fan Wenlan (1893–1969), and

Yang Xiangkui (1910–2000), all believed that it was written in the Warring States Period. As aforementioned, in the Warring States Period, sub-pictographic forms of Chinese characters were fully developed, and the official script transformation was initiated, which led to the creation of semantic-compound and semantic-phonetic characters. The six means of creating Chinese characters came into being in this period, which is also consistent with this assertion.

VI. Summary

Through the above analysis, this chapter puts forward the following viewpoints.

(I) The composition system of Chinese characters has undergone a systematic transition from a stage featuring pure pictographs to a stage featuring semantic-compound and semantic-phonetic combinations. The semantic-compound and semantic-phonetic characters, which are the main part of today's Chinese characters are the results of this transition instead of the inheritance of their original pictographic forms: their current forms are based on the phonetic or semantic components that evolve from pictographs. This transition is systematic, involving nearly all characters in the writing system and enabling the system to develop from the Archaic Stage to the New-Style Stage. The three ways to form semantic-phonetic characters, which are widely recognised by scholars before, are not the main ways to form semantic-phonetic characters. The creation of these characters was mainly realised through the symbolisation of pictographic components in compound pictographs and the explanation efforts exerted to explain these new character forms.

(II) In the early years of Chinese characters, when they were mainly used to express images, their creation was based on drawings; later, when they became phonetic-semantic symbols, their creation was realised through phonetic and semantic combinations. In the Spring and Autumn Period (770–476 BCE), Chinese characters were transformed into sub-pictographs, which started the new tradition of building characters through phonetic and semantic combinations.

(III) The formerly established explanations for the phenomenon that the phonetic component in some semantic-phonetic characters cannot accurately express the pronunciation are as follows: (1) an accurate phonetic component was unavailable at the time of creating the character; (2) the ancient pronunciation of the character is different from its current pronunciation. Through this study, it is found that the transition from the archaic writing system to the New-Style one and the efforts to explain the new character forms created through this transition are also the reasons for this phenomenon.

(IV) The transformation of the character forms caused by the symbolisation process was a natural phenomenon in the evolution of Chinese characters, and the transformed character naturally needed new explanations for their composition. As *Shuowen Jiezi* 说文解字 is intended to explain the transformed character forms, it is unreasonable to find fault with the book through characters formed and created before the transition, namely in the Shang and Zhou dynasties. The composition of characters in each evolution stage has its own characteristics and cannot be mixed up.

(V) The six categories of creating Chinese characters (pictographs, ideographs, semantic compounds, phonetic-semantic compounds, characters created through the loan method, and those created through the transfer method) and *zi* 字 (characters) are terms used to describe characters and their composition after the transition from pictographs to ideograph and semantic-phonetic combinations. The character forms created before this transition are referred to as *wen* 文 (literature), and those created after the transition, referred to as *zi* 字 (characters). These two terms reflect the changes in the composition of Chinese characters.

Notes

1 The original Chinese version was published in *Linguistic Research* 语文研究, 2014, Issue 1.
2 According to Wang Ning, single-component pictographs are "fully-functional non-compositional characters" (《汉字构形学讲座》, 第 58 页, 上海: 上海教育出版社, 2002 *Lectures on Chinese Character Composition*, p. 58, Shanghai: Shanghai Educational Publishing House, 2002)
3 详见王贵元:《汉字形体演化的动因与机制》,《语文研究》, 2010（3）。
Wang Guiyuan: "The Motivation and Mechanisms Behind the Evolution of the Chinese Characters", *Linguistic Research*, 2010 (3).
4 徐中舒:《甲骨文字典》, 第 19 页, 成都: 四川辞书出版社, 2006 年。
Xu Zhongshu: *Oracle Dictionary*, p. 19, Chengdu: Sichuan Lexicographical Publishing House, 2006.
5 Preface in *Shuowen Jiezi*《说文·叙》: "Compound ideographs refer to the characters consisting of two or more components to indicate new meanings." (会意者, 比类合谊, 以见指撝。" 段玉裁注: "先郑《周礼注》曰, 今人用'义', 古人用 '谊'。谊者本字, 义者叚借字。) Duan Yucai noted that *yi* 义 is a loan character based on *yi* 谊.
6 姚孝遂:《古汉字的形体结构及其发展阶段》,《古文字研究》第四辑, 第 15 页, 北京: 中华书局, 1980 年。
Yao Xiaosui: "The Forms and Structures of Ancient Chinese Characters and the Stages of Their Development", *Research on Ancient Chinese Characters* (Vol. 4), p. 15, Beijing: Zhonghua Book Company, 1980.
7 姚孝遂:《古汉字的形体结构及其发展阶段》,《古文字研究》第四辑, 第 11 页, 北京: 中华书局, 1980 年。
Yao Xiaosui: "The Forms and Structures of Ancient Chinese Characters and the Stages of Their Development", *Research on Ancient Chinese Characters* (Vol. 4), p. 11, Beijing: Zhonghua Book Company, 1980.
8 详见王贵元:《汉字发展史的几个核心问题》,《中国语文》, 2013（4）。
Wang Guiyuan: "Core Issues Regarding the Evolution of Chinese Characters", *Studies of the Chinese Language*, 2013 (4).
9 In archaic scripts, the characters *you* 又 (again) and *cun* 寸 (very short) are used interchangeably.
10 湖南省文物考古研究所:《里耶秦简（壹）》, 北京: 文物出版社, 2012 年。
Hunan Provincial Institute of Cultural Relics and Archaeology: *The Qin-Dynasty Bamboo Slips Unearthed at Liye*, Beijing: Cultural Relics Press, 2012.

5 The Motivation and Mechanisms behind the Evolution of the Chinese Characters[1]

I. The Nature of the Transition from the Archaic Writing System to the New-Style One: Pictographs Changed into Phonetic and Semantic Symbols

The establishment of the official script is a major turning point in the evolution of Chinese characters and a dividing point between the Archaic and the New-Style writing systems. This has been established in a basic consensus of academic circles. Nevertheless, problems regarding the nature and internal cause of the evolution of Chinese characters have long remained unsolved. It is generally agreed that the earliest Chinese writing system, which is embodied in the Shang-Dynasty (ca.1600–1046 BCE) oracle-bone and bronze inscriptions, is not mature enough. Despite that it has a relatively mature function of recording language, its character composition system is not mature enough in comparison with its successor: one character or character component often has several different forms. It should also be noted that there is a mistake in such an analysis, which is taking current standards as those of ancient times. This research admits the maturity of the early writing system embodied by the oracle-bone script since it is a practical and effective system in its own time, and such maturity shall not be denied from the perspective of today's researchers. Despite that, this research also admits that the maturity of this early system is different from that of its successor given their difference in the creation basis: the former is created based on images, and the latter is created based on pronunciations and meanings. This transition from pictographs to phonetic and semantic symbols determines the nature of the transition from the Archaic writing system to the New-Style one. When pictographs depicting specific images were changed into phonetic and semantic symbols describing abstract concepts, the Chinese characters were naturally developed from pictographs into sub-pictographs, and their components were simplified. When a character was created to depict an image, just like the characters in the oracle-bone inscriptions, it was hard to unify its forms. This was because different writers might express the image with different strokes and structures if they could evoke vivid images. They were like painters who drew different pictures of the same landscape. When they depicted a person in a character, they had the freedom to choose whether to draw the head or feet, whether to draw his kneeling position or standing position, and whether to draw its front or side. When they expressed movement, they could choose a component from *zhi* 止 (toe),

70 *The Motivation and Mechanisms*

彳, and *xing* 行 (walk) or use both *zhi* 止 and 彳. In a word, it was the focus on the expression of images that unavoidably caused the complexity in the composition of oracle-bone-script characters: characters looked like pictures and had different forms. Given this, such complexity shall be regarded as a natural feature of the oracle-bone script instead of a defect in its character composition system, which harms the early writing system's maturity. When characters were built to express pronunciations and ideas, there was no need for the character components to be as pictographic as before. In return, the simplified components facilitated the following improvements to the composition of characters: characters were simplified; different forms of a character were unified. Under such circumstances, the criteria for judging the maturity of the composition system of Chinese characters changed, and the reasonable phenomena in the previous writing system, such as pictographs and multiple forms for one character, were regarded as a sign of immaturity.

Overall, the evolution of Chinese characters can be divided into two major stages, with the establishment of the official script as the dividing point. In the first stage, the composition basis for Chinese characters was images, and, thus, characters were pictographs and had no uniform forms. To some extent, these characters were drawings. In the middle and late Warring States Period (475–221 BCE), when the composition basis for Chinese characters became pronunciations and meanings, the official script came into being and the old practice of expressing images through characters and the freedom of creating different forms for one character were abolished. The above-mentioned changes were made for writing convenience. They turned "drawings" into "writings".

II. The Shang-Dynasty Characters: The Depiction of Images

The Shang-Dynasty (ca.1600–1046 BCE) characters depict images, which is reflected in the following aspects.

(I) *Single-component Characters and Character Components Usually Have No Fixed Forms*

Table 5.1 Shang-Dynasty Oracle-Bone Inscriptions

Single-Component Character/ Character Component	Oracle-Bone Script of the Shang Dynasty
You 酉 (a wine vessel)	酉 酉 酉 酉 酉 酉 酉 酉 酉
Gui 鬼 (ghost)	鬼 鬼 鬼
Si 祀 (worship)	祀
Fu 福 (happiness)	福

Single-Component Character/ Character Component	Oracle-Bone Script of the Shang Dynasty
Zhu 祝 (pray)	
You 祐 (divine intervention)	

The components in the lower parts of the three oracle-bone-script forms of *gui* 鬼 (ghost) are a depiction of a sitting person, that of a woman or girl, and that of the side of a person. The characters *si* 祀 (worship), *fu* 福 (happiness), *zhu* 祝 (pray), and *you* 祐 (divine intervention) have the same component *shi* 示/礻 (manifest), but in their oracle-bone-script forms, the same component is written in different ways.

(II) Single-component Characters and Character Components Are Basically Pictographs

Table 5.2 Shang-Dynasty Oracle-Bone Inscriptions

Single-Component Character/ Character Component	Oracle-Bone Script of the Shang Dynasty
Che 车 (vehicle)	
Su 宿 (stay overnight)	

The forms of *che* 车 (vehicle) all depict the shape of an ancient Chinese vehicle, and those of *su* 宿 (stay overnight) all include components depicting a person, a mat, and a house. All these forms are pictographs.

(III) Different Forms of a Character May Have Different Numbers of Components

Table 5.3 Shang-Dynasty Oracle-Bone Inscriptions

Characters	Oracle-Bone Script of the Shang Dynasty
Yu 渔 (fishing)	
Yu 御 (manage)	

72 *The Motivation and Mechanisms*

The character *yu* 渔 (fishing) has five forms in the oracle-bone inscriptions: some form consists of the components representing water and fish, some forms are built with a fish component and another component depicting a fishing net, a fishing rope, or a hand, or a pair of hands holding a fishing rod. The hand component is shaped as 又. Different forms of the character *yu* 御 (manage) feature different component combinations: some combinations include components 彳, *zhi* 止 (toe), *pu* 攴 (tap), and another component representing reins; some combinations include 彳, a component representing reins, and another component representing a rider; and some combinations consist of only two components representing reins and a rider, respectively.

(IV) How a Component Is Placed in a Character Is Determined by the Image the Character Describes

Table 5.4 Shang-Dynasty Oracle-Bone Inscriptions

Characters	Oracle-Bone Script of the Shang Dynasty
De 得 (obtain)	
Zhu 祝 (pray)	
Yi 役 (labour)	
Chu 出 (out)	
Ge 各 (individually)	

In all the forms of *de* 得 (obtain), the component representing a hand and that representing a seashell is combined in a similar way: the "hand" reaches out to the "seashell". In all the forms of *zhu* 祝 (pray), the component representing a person always faces the component, meaning a manifestation. In all forms of *chu* 出 (out), the component representing a foot always has its "toes" face the component, representing an exit.

(V) Nearly All Character Forms Are Pictographs

Table 5.5 Shang-Dynasty Character Forms

Characters	Shang-Dynasty Character Compositions
Jian 監 (supervise)	

The Motivation and Mechanisms 73

Characters	Shang-Dynasty Character Compositions
Zhi 執 (hold in hand)	
yin 飲/歆 (drink)	

The forms of the character *jian* 監 (supervise) all depict a person lowering his head to look at his reflection in the water. All the forms of *zhi* 執 (hold in hand) show a person in handcuffs, and those of *yin* 飲 (drink) depict a person lowering his head to drink from a wine jar.

III. Early Relationships among Objects, Words, and Characters Deviated From the Correct Pattern

Studies on the Shang-Dynasty (ca.1600–1046 BCE) characters reveal that early Chinese characters directly expressed objects, but indirectly expressed the pronunciations and meanings of words. The early relationships among objects, words, and characters are shown in the following figure.

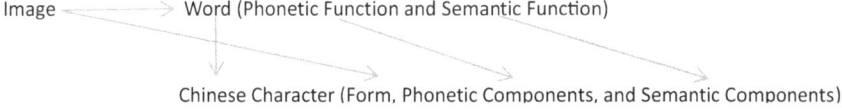

Figure 5.1 Early Relations Among Images, Words, and Chinese Characters

In the ancient Chinese language, one character usually is one word. As symbols used to record the language, the characters should have expressed the meanings and pronunciations of words instead of depicting only objects. That is to say, the correct relationships among objects, words, and characters should be as shown in the following figure.

Figure 5.2 Reasonable Relations Among Images, Words, and Chinese Characters

IV. The Cause of Such Deviation

The main cause of the deviation mentioned in part III is probably the choice of using existing glyphs as writing symbols for the Chinese language. To be more specific, when people started to record their language, they tended to choose existing pictographic glyphs instead of creating new writing symbols. Given this, the primitive

74 *The Motivation and Mechanisms*

glyphs that were created before the early Chinese characters to depict visible objects were used to record an invisible thing: the language. It was also very natural for the people at that time to make such a choice. During the many years before the birth of characters, they got in the habit of expressing their feelings and ideas through pictographic glyphs and getting information by reading such symbols. When they wanted to find some symbols to record their language, the first choice that came to their mind was naturally these pictographs that they had used for years.

Table 5.6 Symbols on Potteries and Oracle-Bone and Bronze Inscriptions

Decorative Symbols on Neolithic-Age Potteries	Oracle-Bone and Bronze Inscriptions of the Shang Dynasty

As they chose to use pictographs as writing symbols and then created new symbols based on the old ones, the early relationships among objects, words, and characters (as shown above) were established. This choice has also established the essential attribute of Chinese characters—expressing meanings through forms—and its influence lasts to this day.

V. The Motivation Behind the Evolution of Early Chinese Characters

As mentioned above, the method of using pictographic glyphs as writing symbols for the Chinese language came into being due to strong historical and customary inertia. Unfortunately, the wide acceptance of this method could not correct the inherent error in this writing system: the pictographic glyphs could not directly express the meanings and pronunciations of characters which were the smallest units of the ancient Chinese language, just like words in English. This defect regarding the relationships among objects, words, and characters required a change in the writing system: pictographs needed to be modified into phonetic and semantic symbols. This need was the internal motivation for the evolution of the early Chinese characters, and it basically determined the direction of this evolution: the pictographic features of the characters needed to be reduced; various forms of a character needed to be unified; and semantic-phonetic characters needed to replace pictographic characters to serve as the mainstream characters.

VI. Mechanisms of the Evolution of the Early Character

(I) The First Stage of the Evolution

1. The Simplification of Shapes and the Reduction in the Number of Components

The evolution of early Chinese characters is mainly concerned with the simplification of components and the reduction in their quantity. The former refers to the process of determining a standard form for a group of pictographs that describe the same object. This process is realised through assimilation, which is the integration of several synonymous pictographs into one. The evolution process of the early forms of *zi* 子 (son) is a typical example.

Table 5.7 Changes in the Form of 子

Oracle-bone Script of the Shang Dynasty	
Bronze Inscriptions of the Western Zhou Dynasty	
Bronze Inscriptions of the Spring and Autumn Period	
Small Seal Script	

76 *The Motivation and Mechanisms*

As to the reduction in the number of components, it is actualized through a process of gradually reaching a consensus about the character composition: each character shall consist of fixed components. The evolution of the early forms of *mu* 莫/暮 (sunset) embodies such a process.

Table 5.8 Changes in the Form of 莫

Oracle-Bone Script of the Shang Dynasty	
Bronze Inscriptions of the Western Zhou Dynasty	
Bronze Inscriptions of the Spring and Autumn Period	
Small-Seal Script	

In the Shang-Dynasty (ca.1600–1046 BCE) oracle-bone script, the character has several forms consisting of different components. The component combinations used to build the character include the following: four *zhi* 之 (grow) components and one *ri* 日 (sun) component; four *cao* 屮 (grass) and two *ri* 日 (sun); four *cao* 屮 (grass), one *ri* 日 (sun), and one *zhui* 隹 (short-tailed bird); four *cao* 屮 (grass) and one *ri* 日 (sun); two *cao* 屮 (grass) and one *ri* 日 (sun); four *mu* 木 (wood), one *ri* 日 (sun), and one *zhui* 隹 (short-tailed bird); three *cao* 屮 (grass) and one *ri* 日 (sun); two *he* 禾 (standing grain) and one *ri* 日 (sun); and two *cao* 屮 (grass) and one *ri* 日 (sun). These forms differ from one another in terms of components and the number of components. In the Western-Zhou-Dynasty (1046–771 BCE) bronze inscriptions, there are only two forms of the character: one consisting of four *cao* 屮 (grass) and one *ri* 日 (sun); the other is built with two *cao* 屮 (grass) and one *ri* 日 (sun).

2. Restrictions on the Position and Orientation of Components

Restrictions on the position and orientation of a component are embodied in the following phenomena: a component usually appears in a fixed position in a character such as the upper or lower part in an up-down structured character or the left or right part in a left-right structured character, and the direction in which a component faces is fixed. The evolution of the early forms of *jiang* 降 (to descend) reflects the formation of such restrictions.

Table 5.9 Forms of 降 in Oracle-Bone and Bronze Inscriptions

Oracle-Bone Script of the Shang Dynasty	
Bronze Inscriptions of the Western Zhou Dynasty	

In the Shang-Dynasty (ca.1600–1046 BCE) oracle-bone script, the *jiang* 降 (to descend) has several forms featuring the following component combinations: a left-placed *fu* 阜 (mound) and two right-placed upside-down *zhi* 止 (toe); two left-placed upside-down *zhi* 止 (toe) and a right-placed *fu* 阜 (mound). In different forms, the two *zhi* 止 (toe) components may face in the same direction or opposite directions. In the Western-Zhou-Dynasty (1046–771 BCE) bronze inscriptions, the character has only one form that consists of a left-placed *fu* 阜 (mound) and two right-placed upside-down *zhi* 止 (toe), and one *zhi* 止 (toe) component faces left and the other faces right. The early forms of *huan* 洹 (the name of a river) undergo a similar evolution process.

Table 5.10 Forms of 洹 in Oracle-Bone and Bronze Inscriptions

Oracle-Bone Script of the Shang Dynasty	
Bronze Inscriptions of the Western Zhou Dynasty	

In the Shang-Dynasty (ca.1600–1046 BCE) oracle-bone script, *huan* 洹 (the name of a river) has several forms that differ from one another in the positions of the components named *shui* 水 (water) and *gen* 亘 (extend cross). The 亘 component can face right or left.

The formation of the restrictions on the shapes, quantity, positions, and orientations of components is a process that gradually turns pictographs into phonetic and semantic symbols. Due to the simplification and abstraction of the shapes, the transformed characters cannot evoke images. Through the assimilation and analogisation of components, a character composition system featuring a limited number of basic components is established.

The above-mentioned process causes a change in the composition of the early characters: the simple combination method used to build characters is replaced by a hierarchical combination approach; pictographic combinations are developed into semantic-compound and phonetic-semantic combinations.

78　*The Motivation and Mechanisms*

Table 5.11 Examples of Character Form Changes From the Shang Dynasty to the Late Western Zhou Dynasty

Characters' Different Historical Periods	*Jian* 監 (supervise)	*Zhi* 執 (hold in hand)	*Yin* 飲/歙 (drink)
Shang-Dynasty Characters			
Late-Western-Zhou-Dynasty Characters			

(II)　The Second Stage of the Evolution

1. *From the Image Depiction to the Phonetic/Semantic Addition*

The depiction of images produces single-component pictographs or compound pictographs featuring non-hierarchical component combinations. It is the fundamental feature of the early Chinese characters. The simple combination method produces non-hierarchical structured characters, whose components cannot be broken up into subcomponents. For instance, *zhong* 众 (crowd) is such a character. It consists of three *ren* 人 (person) components that cannot be further broken up.

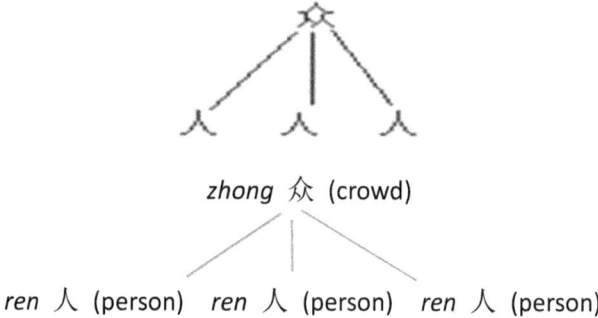

Figure 5.3 The Composition of 众

The phonetic/semantic addition refers to the process of adding a component to express the pronunciation or meaning of a character. Sometimes, such an added component contains subcomponents. In this case, the Chinese character it is added to is a hierarchical-structured character featuring a hierarchical combination of components, such as *qi* 骑 (ride).

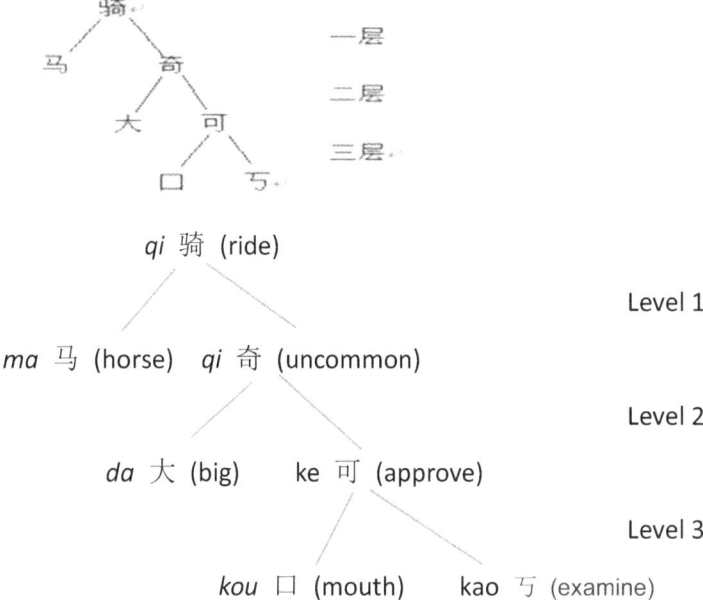

Figure 5.4 The Composition of 骑

It should be noted that the hierarchical combination of components is a conclusion based on the analysis of existing characters and that it does not describe the formation process of the character. In other words, the hierarchical combination of the character is not generated at one time. Instead, it is the result of the method of using a multicomponent character as a component to build a new character.

Early Chinese characters are generally single-component pictographs, as they each represent an image. The seldomly seen multicomponent early characters are just simple combinations of pictographs. When such a multicomponent character is used as a character component, it stops being a representation of an image and begins serving as a semantic-phonetic symbol in the new hierarchical-structured character. The appearance of the hierarchical combinations marks a sharp change in the composition system of Chinese characters: new characters are created through the combination of the existing characters, especially the multicomponent characters, instead of through the invention of new pictographs.

At present, the composition types of some early multicomponent Chinese characters are still controversial: so far, academic circles have not reached a consensus on whether they are pictographic compounds, semantic compounds, or semantic-phonetic characters. This is the main cause of the huge differences in the statistical data of pictographic, semantic-compound characters, and semantic-phonetic characters in oracle-bone and bronze inscriptions. The table below shows the three oracle-bone-script forms of the character *mu* 莫/暮 (sunset).

Table 5.12 Three Forms of 莫 in Oracle-Bone Inscriptions

mu 莫/暮 (sunset) A	mu 莫/暮 (sunset) B	mu 莫/暮 (sunset) C
〔pictograph〕	〔pictograph〕	〔pictograph〕

The form B has two extra *mu* 木 (wood) components in comparison with the form A, and the form C is the form B combined with a component *zhui* 隹 (short-tailed bird). Are form B and form C compound pictographs, semantic compounds, or semantic-phonetic compounds? This research finds that, to answer this question, it is essential to take into consideration the evolutionary stages of the Chinese characters. To be more specific, before determining the compositional structures of these character forms, it is necessary to find out at which evolutionary stage these forms were created. A character form regarded as a compound pictograph in one evolutionary stage might be considered a semantic-compound or semantic-phonetic character in a later stage. Such a change is caused by the transformation of components and the transition in the composition of Chinese characters (Please read the following sections for details). The oracle-bone-script form of *mu* 莫/暮 (sunset) can have two, three, or four *mu* 木 (wood) components, and it is almost impossible to determine the order in which these three forms appear. Nevertheless, this does not affect the judgment on the nature of these forms. The form B is the pictographic form a combined with two 木, which are pictographs, too. Therefore, the form B is a compound pictograph instead of a semantic-compound or semantic-phonetic character. The form C is the form B combined with the pictographic component *zhui* 隹 (short-tailed bird), which describes the sight of a bird flying home at sunset.[5] The form C is also a compound pictograph. Many studies on the oracle-bone-script characters have mistaken such compound pictographs for semantic-phonetic characters. Yao Xiaosui once questioned such a phenomenon. He said, "Some early Chinese characters are regarded as semantic-phonetic characters, but this judgment does not conform to the actual situation. For example, in the oracle-bone script, the character *fu* 俘 (take prisoner) is usually written as semantic compounds such as 〔form〕 or 〔form〕, but it still has another form 〔form〕, which looks like a semantic-phonetic character consisting of a pictographic component 彳 and a phonetic component *fu* 孚 (capture). Nevertheless, this semantic-phonetic character is quite strange: compared with its pictographic component, its phonetic component *fu* 〔孚, capture〕 is more directly related to its meaning, and its pictographic component 彳 actually cannot express the meaning of the character. How does this make sense?"[6] The question that Yao Xiaosui 姚孝遂 put forth is caused by the mistake of inferring the composition of early characters based on the characters' later forms and that of neglecting the influence of the evolutionary stages of the writing system. This serves as a reminder of the importance of differentiating the pictographic supplement and the phonetic/semantic addition for the studies on Chinese characters. The pictographic supplement refers to the addition of a new pictograph to an existing pictographic combination. The addition of two *mu* 木 (wood) components and that of the component *zhui* 隹 (short-tailed bird) to the simplest form of *mu* 莫/暮 (sunset) can be explained as pictographic supplements. Such additions never change the nature of the compound pictographs, turning them into semantic-phonetic characters. Other typical examples of the pictographic supplement include the oracle-bone-script forms of *dian* 奠 (pay respect), *qi* 启 (open), *ni* 逆 (meet head-on), *mu* 牧 (herd), *gou* 遘 (encounter), etc.

Table 5.13 Different Forms of the Same Character in Oracle-Bone Inscriptions

Characters	Oracle-Bone-Script Forms			
Dian 奠 (pay respect)				
Qi 启 (open)				
Ni 逆 (meet head-on)				
Mu 牧 (herd)				
Gou 遘 (encounter)				

The component *fu* 阜 (mound) is added to the simple form of *dian* 奠 (pay respect) to indicate something rising. Its function is like the oracle-bone-script character *zhi* 陟 (ascend). The component *kou* 口 (mouth) is added to the simplest form of *qi* 启 (open) to represent an opening. In a more complex form of 启, the component 彳 is added to represent movement. All these are examples of the pictographic supplement. It should be noted that the term "the pictographic supplement" is applicable only for the studies on early Chinese characters, because in the more evolved forms of characters, the pictographic features are eliminated and some of the previously pictographic components are developed into radicals.

The phonetic/semantic addition refers to the addition of a phonetic or semantic component, just as what occurs to the composition of *xi* 釐 (good luck) and that of *hu* 壺 (bottle) as shown below.

Table 5.14 Character Form Changes from the Shang Dynasty to the Western Zhou Dynasty

Characters Different Historical Periods	*Xi* 釐 *(good luck)*	*Hu* 壺 *(bottle)*
Oracle-Bone Script of the Shang Dynasty		
Bronze Inscriptions of the Western Zhou Dynasty		

According to *Shuowen Jiezi* 说文解字 (An Explication of Written Characters), *xi* 釐 means the happiness of a family. Its oracle-bone-script form consists of *mai* 麦 (wheat) and *pu* 攴 (tap), depicting the image of removing husks from grain. In the bronze inscriptions of the Western Zhou Dynasty (1046–771 BCE), the phonetic component *li* 里 (living community) is added to the original form. Also in the bronze inscriptions, the semantic component *jin* 金 (metal) is added to the original form of *hu* 壶 (bottle), which is created by the oracle-bone script.

The replacement of the image depiction method by the phonetic/semantic 首先 addition marks a change in the composition system of Chinese characters: the old method of creating new characters through new pictographs is replaced by the new method of building new characters with existing characters in the system. The wide adoption of this new method (as well as the character-creating method of weakening the characters' pictographic features but maintaining their compositional structures) leads to the need of adopting a new term, namely 字, to refer to these transformed characters. This is also mentioned in the preface of *Shuowen Jiezi* 说文解字: "The early characters created by Cangjie 仓颉 (the legendary cultural hero who invented the Chinese writing system) are based on images and referred to as *wen* 文, and the characters created through semantic and phonetic combinations later are referred to as zi 字." According to the studies on unearthed documents and stele inscriptions, *zi* 字 was widely used to refer to characters in the Qin Dynasty (221–207 BCE). The relevant evidence includes the Qin-Dynasty stele inscriptions at Mount Tai and the Qin-Dynasty bamboo slips unearthed at Liye. Inferred from this fact, the idea of describing the transformed characters as *zi* 字 probably appeared as early as the Warring States Period (475–221 BCE).

2. *From Pictographic Combinations (Including Single-Component Pictographic Characters) to Semantic-Compound and Phonetic-Semantic Combinations*

There are two ways to develop pictographic combinations into semantic and semantic-phonetic combinations. The first is eliminating the pictographic features of the pictographic components and their combinations. This is how *cheng* 丞 (assist) and *ni* 逆 (meet head-on) are transformed.

Table 5.15 Transition From Shang-Dynasty Oracle-Bone Script to the Small-Seal Script

Characters Different Historical Periods	Cheng 丞 (assist)	Ni 逆 (meet head-on)
Oracle-Bone Script of the Shang Dynasty		
Small-Seal Script		

The oracle-bone-script form of *cheng* 丞 (assist) is a pictograph depicting a pair of hands saving a person who falls into a trap. The small-seal-script of this character is not a pictograph, and *Shuowen Jiezi* 说文解字 defines it as a *combination* of *gong* 廾 (two hands), *jie* 卩 (seal), and *shan* 山 (hill).⁷ In the oracle-bone-script form of *ni* 逆 (meet head-on), 彳 and *zhi* 止 (toe) are two separate components, but in the character's small-seal-script form, the two components are integrated into a semantic radical *chuo* 辵 (walking). *Shuowen Jiezi* explains it as a semantic-phonetic character consisting of *chuo* 辵 (walking) and the phonetic component *ni* 屰 (meet head-on).

The second way to develop pictographic combinations into semantic and phonetic-semantic combinations is the phonetic/semantic addition. The characters *shu* 蜀 (the name of an ancient state), *qiu* 裘 (fur garments), and *qin* 禽 (fowl) are transformed in this way.

Table 5.16 Transition From Shang-Dynasty Oracle-Bone Script to Western-Zhou-Dynasty Bronze Script

Characters Different Historical Periods	Shu 蜀 (the name of an ancient state)	Qiu 裘 (fur garments)	Qin 禽 (fowl)
Oracle-Bone Script of the Shang Dynasty			
Bronze Inscriptions of the Western Zhou Dynasty			

The oracle-bone-script form of *shu* 蜀 (the name of an ancient state) is shaped like a big-headed worm. In the bronze inscriptions of the Western Zhou Dynasty (1046–771 BCE), the semantic component meaning a worm is added to the original character form to further clarify the meaning of the character. Also, in the bronze inscriptions, the phonetic component *you* 又 (again) is added to the oracle-bone-script form of *qiu* 裘 (fur garments), which depicts a fur coat. In comparison with the oracle-bone-script form of *qin* 禽 (fowl), which is a drawing of an animal trapping tool, the bronze-inscription form of the character has one more component: a phonetic component *jin* 今 (now).

(III) The Third Stage of the Evolution

1. From Pictographs and Sub-Pictographs to Phonetic and Semantic Symbols

As this stage features semantic-compound and phonetic-semantic characters, there is no need for the components to be pictographic. They usually express either meanings or pronunciations of characters instead of images. This change is caused by the transition from pictographs to semantic-phonetic symbols and that from "drawing" to "writing". The following table shows how *nv* 女 (woman/girl) and *ri* 日 (sun), two pictographs in the Shang-Dynasty (ca.1600–1046 BCE) bronze inscriptions, gradually develop into sub-pictograph characters in later bronze inscriptions and in the small-seal script. With the establishment of the official script, these two characters become semantic-phonetic symbols.

84 *The Motivation and Mechanisms*

Table 5.17 Transition From Shang-Dynasty Bronze Script to the Small-Seal Script

Characters Different Historical Periods	Nv 女 (woman/girl)	Ri 日 (sun)
Bronze Inscriptions of the Shang Dynasty		
Bronze Inscriptions of the Late Western Zhou Dynasty		
Bronze Inscriptions of the Spring and Autumn Period		
Small-Seal Script		

The preface of *Shuowen Jiezi* 说文解字 describes how the Archaic writing system was abolished. "Back then, the Qin Dynasty (221–207 BCE) burned the works of different schools to ashes, abolished the classics written in archaic-form characters, recruited a large number of people for military service and manual labour, and established a complicated bureaucratic system. For easier writing, the official script came into being, and thus the Archaic writing system was ended."[8] *Han Shu* 汉书 (The History of the Han Dynasty) contains a similar statement. "The official script was established to save time in writing documents and increase the efficiency of the government."[9] This research considers these explanations made in the Han Dynasty (206 BCE–220 CE) as external reasons for the creation of the official script. As to the internal motivation, this research finds that it is the transition from pictographs to semantic-phonetic symbols that essentially determines the birth of the official script.

2. From the Creation Based on Images to That Based on Phonetic and Semantic Functions

The official script, which belongs to the New-Style writing system, is a natural result of the evolutionary process where Chinese characters develop from pictographs to phonetic and semantic symbols. Its establishment marks that the writing system basically gets rid of its old pictographic features. In this natural evolution process, characters change gradually from pictographs to subpictographs and then to phonetic and semantic symbols. When the pictographic features are removed, the transformed characters often keep their original compositional structures. To be more specific, when the pictographic components are transformed, the original component combinations used to build characters are kept.

Table 5.18 Transition From Pictographic Combinations to Semantic Combinations

Composition Basis Characters	Pictographic Combination	Semantic Combination
Xiu 休 (rest)		Xiu 休 (rest)
Lao 牢 (fence)		Lao 牢 (fence)

Notes

1 The original Chinese version was published in *Language Research* 语文研究, 2010, Issue 3.
2 The glyph statistics of the Shang-Dynasty characters are based on "Restudy on the Glyph System of the Dynasty Oracle-Bone Inscriptions" 殷商甲骨文字形系统再研究 (Chen Tingzhu's 陈婷珠 doctoral dissertation at the Research and Application Centre of Chinese Characters of East China Normal University, 2008) and "Study on the Glyphs and Composition of the Shang-Dynasty Bronze-Inscriptions Characters" 商代金文字形表与构形研究 (Gong Xiaohu's 龚小虎 master's dissertation at the School of Literal Arts of Renmin University of China, 2009), similarly hereinafter.
3 The glyph statistics of the Western-Zhou-Dynasty bronze-inscription characters are based on the "A Complete Glyph Table of the Bronze-Inscription Characters of Different Periods of the Western Zhou Dynasty" 西周金文分期字形全表, which is an appendix in "Research on the Composition of the Western-Zhou-Dynasty Bronze-Inscription Characters" 西周金文构形研究 (Tao Quyong's 陶曲勇 doctoral dissertation completed at the School of Literal Arts of Renmin University of China in 2009) and a complete collection of all the Western-Zhou-Dynasty bronze-inscription characters found before 2005 (including 2005), similarly hereinafter.
4 The glyph statistics of the Spring-and-Autumn-Period bronze-inscription characters are based on "A Complete Glyph Table of the Spring-and-Autumn-Period Bronze-Inscription Characters and a Study on Their Composition" 春秋金文字形全表及构形研究 (Yang Xiu'en's 杨秀恩 doctoral dissertation at the School of Arts of Renmin University of China), which includes a complete collection of all the Spring-and-Autumn-Period bronze-inscription characters found before 2005 (including 2005), similarly hereinafter.
5 徐中舒：《甲骨文字典》，第 61 页，成都：四川辞书出版社，1993。
  Xu Zhongshu: *Oracle Dictionary*, p. 61, Chengdu: Sichuan Lexicographical Publishing House, 1993.
6 姚孝遂：《甲骨文形体结构分析》，《古文字研究》第二十辑，第 271 页，北京：中华书局，1999。
  Yao Xiaosui: "Analysis of the Forms and Structures of Oracle-Bone Characters", *Research on Ancient Chinese Characters* (Vol. 20), p. 271, Beijing: Zhonghua Book Company, 1999.
7 王贵元：《说文解字校笺》，第 109、661 页，上海：学林出版社，2002。
  Wang Guiyuan: *Proofreading Notes to Shuowen Jiezi*, pp. 109 and 661, Shanghai: Academia Press, 2002.
8 王贵元：《说文解字校笺》，第 109、661 页 上海：学林出版社，2002。
  Wang Guiyuan: *Proofreading Notes to Shuowen Jiezi*, pp. 109 and 661, Shanghai: Academia Press, 2002.
9 王先谦：《汉书补注》（上册），第 878 页，北京：中华书局，1983 年影印本。
  Wang Xianqian (1842–1917): *Supplement to Han Shu* (Vol. 1), p. 878, Beijing: Zhonghua Book Company, photocopy published in 1983.

6 The Process and Mechanism of the Formation of the Stroke System[1]

The stroke system of Chinese characters is about the types and combinations of strokes, which, taken together, constitute an integral unity. There are several basic strokes in the system, such as the horizontal stroke, the vertical stroke, the left-falling stroke, the right-falling stroke, etc. A stroke combination may have different variations that differ in the length of some strokes, and these different variations create different characters. Typical examples include *li* 力 (capability) and *dao* 刀 (knife); *wei* 未 (not yet) and *mo* 末 (end); *shi* 矢 (arrow) and *shi* 失 (lose); and *wu* 午 (noon) and *niu* 牛 (cattle).

I. The Nature of the Stroke System

(I) The Focus Shift and the Establishment of the Stroke System

In the Archaic writing system, the compositional structures of characters are generally non-hierarchical: components are put together to build characters. In the New-Style writing system, however, hierarchical compositional structures become the mainstream: characters can be broken up into components that can be further broken up into strokes.

Table 6.1 The Compositional Structure of Characters in the Archaic and the New-Style Writing Systems

	The Archaic Writing System	*The New-Style Writing System*
Compositional Structures	Characters	Characters
	Components	Components
		Strokes

It should be noted that the components in the composition structures of the Archaic characters can also be broken up into smaller parts, although they are not listed in the table above. The components of most seal-script characters cannot be written out with one stroke. For example, 𠂇, which is the bronze-inscription form of *yuan* 元 (head) used in the inscriptions on the Yuannian Shidui Gui Container (元年师兑簋) of the Western Zhou Dynasty (1046–771 BCE), is evidently built

DOI: 10.4324/9781032622965-6

The Process of the Formation of the Stroke System 87

with four strokes. The strokes of the Archaic characters are mainly dots (blocks) and lines, as shown in the table below.

Table 6.2 Comparison Between Archaic and New-Style Character Components

	The Archaic Writing System	The New-Style Writing System
Compositional Structures	Characters	Characters
	Components	Components
	Dots and lines	Strokes

The biggest difference between the Archaic and New-Style character composition is as follows: the former is based on images, and the latter is on pronunciations and meanings.[2] In the Archaic writing system, both characters and character components represent images. The only difference is that the former represents overall images and the latter represents parts of the images. The strokes in this system, namely the dots and lines, are used to depict the details of the images. Take 𝌀, the oracle-bone-script form of *zhu* 祝 (pray), as an example. The character, which consists of two components built with lines and dots, depicts a person who opens his mouth to pray in front of a target of worship. The component on the left is an early form of *shi* 示 (manifest), indicating the target of worship. The one on the right depicts a person who is praying. The compositional structure and functional analysis of an Archaic character are shown in the table below.

Table 6.3 The Compositional Structure and Functional Analysis of an Archaic Character

Levels of the Compositional Structure	Functions	
Characters	Overall images	Images
Components		
Dots and Lines	Parts of an image	

The above analysis shows that all three levels of the compositional system of an Archaic character perform the same function: depicting images. Accordingly, a character expresses meanings, and the lines and dots used to build it cannot independently express any meaning. Given this, when analysing the compositional structure of an Archaic character, it is usually unnecessary to consider the lines and dots as a level of the structure.

The compositional structure and functional analysis of a New-Style character are shown in the table below.

Table 6.4 The Compositional Structure and Functional Analysis of a New-Style Character

Levels of the Compositional Structure	Functions
Characters	Semantic and Phonetic Symbols
Components	
Strokes	N/A

Different from the Archaic writing system, the New-Style writing system features characters and character components that represent meanings and pronunciations: characters usually represent the meaning and pronunciation of a word (one-character word), and components serve as semantic or phonetics parts of characters. As they represent abstract ideas, they do not have to be pictographic, and their forms are simplified for convenient writing. These are two reasons for the transformation of the seal script into the official script, and this transformation leads to the creation of the basic strokes of the New-Style characters. These strokes usually cannot serve as semantic or phonetic components or indicate the meanings or pronunciations of words independently. Nevertheless, these abstract strokes are still different from the dots and lines that are used to depict the details of images in the Archaic writing system. In the New-Style stage, the focus once placed on the image depiction where each dot or line conveys some pictographic information is shifted to the combination of components, and the strokes that are not pictographic any longer become pure structural parts of character forms.

(II) Types of Character Components

As mentioned above, the dots and lines in the Archaic characters are part of the image depiction and cannot independently express meanings or pronunciations. Strokes are different. They are not restricted by pictographic characteristics and can be freely combined to make character components. The evolution of the Chinese characters after the official script transformation is closely related to the stroke assimilation: for instance, the formation of the horizontal stroke is the result of assimilating various seal-script structures. The following table shows such a process by comparing some character components forms of Western-Zhou-Dynasty (1046–771 BCE) bronze inscription with their counterparts in the stele inscriptions of the Eastern Han Dynasty (25–220).

Table 6.5 Comparison Between the Western-Zhou-Dynasty (1046–771 BCE) and the Eastern-Han-Dynasty (25–220) Component Forms

Character Components	Bronze Inscriptions of the Western Zhou Dynasty (1046–771 BCE)	Stele Inscriptions of the Eastern Han Dynasty (25–220)
Shi 士 (gentleman)	*Shishang You* Wine Pot	Yang Zhen Monument
Tian 天 (sky)	*Da Yu* Tripod Cauldron	Stele of Ritual Vessels
Zou 走 (go)	Yuannian Shidui *Gui* Container	Huaiyuan Temple Stele at Tongbai
Zheng 正 (proper)	*Yi* Square Wine Pot of the Duke of Xing	Yang Zhen Monument

Character Components	Bronze Inscriptions of the Western Zhou Dynasty (1046–771 BCE)	Stele Inscriptions of the Eastern Han Dynasty (25–220)
Zuo 左 (left)	Plate of Zibai of the State of Guo	Stele of the Cangjie Temple
Si 寺 (temple)	Gui Container of Gugong of the State Si	Yang Zhu Monument
Shi 世 (generation)	Duoyou Tripod Caldron	Shi Chen Monument
Gu 谷 (valley)	Gui Container of the Earl of Ge	Eulogy to Shimen Passage

For further analysis, the components used in both the Archaic and the New-Style writing systems are divided into the following three categories: (1) pictographic components (mainly used in seal scripts); (2) phonetic and semantic components (mainly used in the New-Style writing system); and (3) stroke units (applicable for the strokes used in the New-Style writing system). In this sense, the stroke system is indeed the writing system.

II. The Formation Process of the Stroke System

The study on the formation process of the stroke system should be a segmented study of the forms and quantity of strokes in different evolutionary periods of the Chinese character. It shall list as exhaustively as possible the stroke types used in each period and then compare their differences to reach a comprehensive idea of the formation of strokes. This part, however, uses a backward induction procedure to discuss the origination period, formation period, and perfection period of the strokes based on current strokes. The characteristics and durations of the three periods are shown in the table below.

Table 6.6 The Characteristics and Durations of the Three Periods in the Evolution of Strokes

Evolutionary Period	Characteristic	Duration
Origination Period	The replacement of seal-script structures	From the late Warring States Period (475–221 BCE) to the end of the Western Han Dynasty (206–8 BCE)
Formation Period	The removal of seal-script features and the establishment of the six basic strokes: the horizontal stroke, the vertical stroke, the dot, the left-falling stroke, the right-falling stroke, and the turning stroke.	From the Eastern Han Dynasty (25–220) to the Wei-Jin Period (220–589)

(*Continued*)

Table 6.6 (Continued)

Evolutionary Period	Characteristic	Duration
Perfection Period	The stabilisation of the strokes in terms of forms and quantity, the formation of the rising stroke and the hook, the development of the dot stroke, and the replacement of short vertical strokes and short horizontal strokes by the dot stroke.	Starting from the period of the Northern and Southern dynasties (386–581)

The origination period started in the late Warring States Period (475–221 BCE), when the official script transformation took place. It ended in the last years of the Western Han Dynasty (206–8 BCE). During this period, complicated seal-script forms were replaced by straight lines, squarish shapes, and simple structures. The silk manuscripts from Mawangdui Han Tombs were written in this period. The following table compares some characters from the manuscripts with their counterparts in the small-seal script.

Table 6.7 Features of the Characters in the Origination Period

Characters	Small-Seal Script	Silk Manuscripts from Mawangdui Han Tombs
Si 寺 (temple)		
Tian 天 (sky)		
Lü 律 (regulation)		
Ming 命 (order)		
De 得 (obtain)		
Bing 兵 (troops)		
Feng 奉 (offer)		
Wang 往 (go)		

The Process of the Formation of the Stroke System 91

The formation period lasted from the Eastern Han Dynasty (25–220) to the Wei-Jin Period (220–589). The six types of strokes, namely the horizontal stroke, the vertical stroke, the dot stroke, the left-falling stroke, the right-falling stroke, and the turning stroke, were established in this period. The following table gives some examples of these strokes from Eastern-Han-Dynasty stele inscriptions.

Table 6.8 Features of the Characters in the Formation Period

Characters	Small-Seal Script	Eastern-Han-Dynasty Stele Inscriptions
Tian 天 (sky)		
Shi 示 (manifest)		
Yu 玉 (precious stone)		
Di 帝 (supreme ruler)		
Zhong 中 (central)		

The maturity period started from the period of the Northern and Southern dynasties (386–581), where minor adjustments were made to the existing strokes.

Various types of rising strokes were developed from horizontal strokes in the Wei-Jin Period (220–589), and their standardized form was confirmed in the period of the Northern and Southern dynasties (386–581).[3]

Table 6.9 The Formation of Rising Strokes

Eastern-Han-Dynasty Stele Inscriptions	
Wu-State Bamboo Slip of the Three Kingdoms (220–280)	
Stele Inscriptions of the Wei-Jin Period (220–589)	
Stele Inscriptions of the Period of the Northern and Southern Dynasties (386–581)	

92 *The Process of the Formation of the Stroke System*

A type of the vertical stroke named the vertical hook, which was established in the period of the Northern and Southern dynasties (386–581), was originally a vertical stroke with a left turning. The evolution of this stroke is embodied in the different forms of *xiao* 小 (small) and *ding* 丁 (adult male) as shown in the table below. Before the Wei-Jin Period (220–589), the vertical stroke in the character *xiao* 小 (small) did not have a hook, but in the period of the Northern and Southern dynasties (386–581), the vertical stroke was changed into a vertical-hook stroke.

Table 6.10 The Evolution of the Vertical-Hook Stroke Embodied in Different Forms of *Xiao* 小 (Small)

Eastern-Han-Dynasty Stele Inscriptions	
Wu-State Bamboo Slip of the Three Kingdoms (220–280)	
Stele Inscriptions of the Wei-Jin Period (220–589)	
Stele Inscriptions of the Period of the Northern and Southern Dynasties (386–581)	

Before the Wei-Jin Period (220–589), the character *ding* 丁 (adult male) featured a vertical stroke with a left turning, but in the period of the Northern and Southern dynasties (386–581), this stroke was changed into a vertical-hook stroke.

Table 6.11 The Evolution of the Vertical-Hook Stroke Embodied in Different Forms of *Ding* 丁 (Adult Male)

Eastern-Han-Dynasty Stele Inscriptions	
Wu-State Bamboo Slip of the Three Kingdoms (220–280)	
Stele Inscriptions of the Wei-Jin Period (220–589)	
Stele Inscriptions of the Period of the Northern and Southern Dynasties (386–581)	

The Process of the Formation of the Stroke System 93

The horizontal-turning-and-hook stroke was also established in the period of the Northern and Southern dynasties (386–581). Before the Wei-Jin Period (220–589), the stroke did not have a hook.

Table 6.12 The Evolution of the Horizontal-Turning-and-Hook Stroke Embodied in Different Forms of *Yue* 月 (Moon)

Eastern-Han-Dynasty Stele Inscriptions	
Wu-State Bamboo Slip of the Three Kingdoms (220–280)	
Stele Inscriptions of the Wei-Jin Period (220–589)	
Stele Inscriptions of the Period of the Northern and Southern Dynasties (386–581)	

The vertical-curving-and-hook stroke evolves from a curved stroke that turns right at its end. Take *xiong* 兄 (elder brother) as an example. In the forms appearing before the Wei-Jin Period (220–589), the curved stroke in the lower right part does not have a hook. Nevertheless, in all the forms appearing in the period of the Northern and Southern dynasties (386–581), the curved stroke always has a hook.

Table 6.13 The Evolution of the Vertical-Curving-and-Hook Stroke Embodied in Different Forms of *Xiong* 兄 (Elder Brother)

Eastern-Han-Dynasty Stele Inscriptions	
吴简 Wu-State Bamboo Slip of the Three Kingdoms (220–280)	
Stele Inscriptions of the Wei-Jin Period (220–589)	
Stele Inscriptions of the Period of the Northern and Southern Dynasties (386–581)	

94 *The Process of the Formation of the Stroke System*

The dot stroke originated from the dots in the seal scripts and replaced short horizontal strokes and short vertical strokes in the period of the Northern and Southern dynasties (386–581). Take *yu* 於 (in/at/on) as an example. Prior to the Wei-Jin Period (220–589), the lower right part of the character in its earlier forms featured two short horizontal lines; during the Northern and Southern dynasties period (386–581), these two lines were replaced by two dots.

Table 6.14 The Evolution of the Dot Stroke Embodied in Different Forms of *Yu* 於 (in/at/on)

Eastern-Han-Dynasty Stele Inscriptions	
Wu-State Bamboo Slip of the Three Kingdoms (220–280)	
Stele Inscriptions of the Wei-Jin Period (220–589)	
南北朝碑刻 Stele Inscriptions of the Period of the Northern and Southern Dynasties (386–581)	

The character *zhu* 主 (master) was written with a short horizontal line instead of a dot in its earlier forms prior to the Wei-Jin Period (220–589). However, during the Northern and Southern dynasties Period (386–581), the short horizontal line was replaced by a dot.

Table 6.15 The Evolution of the Dot Stroke Embodied in Different Forms of *Zhu* 主 (Master)

Eastern-Han-Dynasty Stele Inscriptions	
Wu-State Bamboo Slip of the Three Kingdoms (220–280)	
Stele Inscriptions of the Wei-Jin Period (220–589)	
Stele Inscriptions of the Period of the Northern and Southern Dynasties (386–581)	

The Process of the Formation of the Stroke System 95

Prior to the Wei-Jin Period (220–589), the character *bing* 病 (illness) was written with a short vertical line instead of a dot in its earlier forms. This vertical line was replaced by a dot in the period of the Northern and Southern dynasties (386–581).

Table 6.16 The Evolution of the Dot Stroke Embodied in Different Forms of *Bing* 病 (Illness)

Eastern-Han-Dynasty Stele Inscriptions	
Wu-State Bamboo Slip of the Three Kingdoms (220–280)	
Stele Inscriptions of the Wei-Jin Period (220–589)	
Stele Inscriptions of the Period of the Northern and Southern Dynasties (386–581)	

The above analyses are based on character forms appearing in stele inscriptions. Such character forms often feature the inheritance of traditional forms. Therefore, in comparison with commonly used character forms of their times, they usually appear quite old-fashioned. Qiu Xigui once commented that "the character forms used in stele inscriptions are often more old-fashioned than their counterparts used in manuscripts."[4] To avoid analysis errors caused by such a phenomenon, the following analyses include example characters from Loulan bamboo and paper manuscripts from the Wei-Jin Period (220–589).

The rising stroke: this stroke appeared only in the cursive script in the Wei-Jin Period (220–589).

Table 6.17 The Rising Stroke Used in the Manuscripts of the Wei-Jin Period (220–589)

Di 地 (ground)		*Zhu* 珠 (pearls)	
Yu 域 (land within certain boundaries)		*Qin* 勤 (industrious)	
Dong 動 (movement)		*Jin* 覲 (present oneself before a monarch)	

This shows that the rising stroke was not established in the Wei-Jin Period (220–589). This conclusion is the same as that reached in the analyses of stele inscriptions of the same period.

96 The Process of the Formation of the Stroke System

The vertical-hook stroke was not established in the Wei-Jin Period (220–589).

Table 6.18 The Vertical-Hook Stroke Used in the Manuscripts of the Wei-Jin Period (220–589)

Wei 未 (not yet)		Zi 子 (son)	
Xiao 小 (small)		Bie 别 (separate)	
Dao 到 (arrive)		Ze 则 (rules)	
Ke 可 (approve)		Qian 前 (front)	

The horizontal-turning-and-hook stroke was not established in the Wei-Jin Period (220–589), either.

Table 6.19 The Horizontal-Turning-and-Hook Stroke Used in the Manuscripts of the Wei-Jin Period (220–589)

Yue 月 (moon)	
Yong 用 (apply)	

The vertical-curving-hook stroke was not established in the Wei-Jin Period (220–589).

Table 6.20 The Vertical-Curving-and-Hook Stroke Used in the Manuscripts of the Wei-Jin Period (220–589)

Xiong 兄 (elder brother)	
Xian 见 (appear)	

The establishment of the dot stroke was basically realised in the Wei-Jin Period (220–589). This conclusion is based on the analysis of character forms used in Loulan bamboo and paper manuscripts, which differs from the conclusion drawn from analysing the analysis of stele inscriptions of this period.

Table 6.21 The Dot Stroke Used in the Manuscripts of the Wei-Jin Period (220–589)

Yan 言 (to speak)	
Zhu 主 (master)	
Yu 於 (in/at/on)	

To sum up, it is reasonable to conclude that the stroke system of Chinese characters was formed in the period of the Northern and Southern dynasties (386–581).

III.   The Formation Mechanisms of the Stroke System

(I)   Principles Underpinning the Formation of the Stroke System

Wang Fengyang 王凤阳 points out that there are two principles underlying the transformation of seal-script lines into the official-script strokes: "turning curved lines into straight lines" and "avoiding strokes written from right to left and from bottom to top".[5] According to him, these two principles underpin the evolution process of the characters. The first principle led to the transformation of curved lines into straight lines, and the second principle solved the problems caused by old-fashioned strokes that were written from right to left and from bottom to top.[6] Mr. Wang's view is regarded as a summary of the establishment of basic strokes and thus is widely quoted by researchers. Nevertheless, there are two problems with his view. First, these two principles cannot explain all the strokes. Take *dou* 豆 (legumes) as an example, whose seal-script form is 豆. Its lower part ︱ ︱ is transformed into 丶丿, and this transformation has nothing to do with the two principles. The transformation of the following radicals is also not governed by these two principles: 示 transformed into 礻, 衣 transformed into 衤, and 辵 transformed into 辶. The formation of the rising stroke and some hooks cannot be explained by these two principles, either. Second, these two principles describe only phenomena instead of the real motivation, or the real principle. The motivation behind the phenomena of straightening curved lines and avoiding strokes that are written from right to left and from bottom to top is the real principle.

This study holds that the primary principle governing the formation of the stroke system is improving writing convenience, which means making it easier and faster to write characters. Tang Lan 唐兰 (1901–1979) also mentioned this issue by quoting an ancient calligrapher named Wei Heng 卫恒 (?–291): "The official script is a simple and convenient version of the seal script."[7] This judgement is basically appropriate. For the convenience of writing and the improvement in writing speed, the New-Style writing system straightens the lines of the seal scripts and eliminates the strokes that are inconvenient to write. For the same reasons, ︱ ︱, the lower part

98 *The Process of the Formation of the Stroke System*

of the seal-script form of *dou* 豆 (legumes), is transformed into ⟍ ⟋. The two vertical lines are replaced by two slanting lines to shorten the distance that the writing instrument moves. The same adjustment has taken place in other character forms. That's why the two dots in the upper part of some characters such as *shou* 首 (head) and *sui* 㒸 (to follow) are slanting dots. The transformation of the following radicals features the integration of a horizontal stroke and a left-falling stroke, which is carried out to improve writing speed: 示 transformed into 礻 and 衣 transformed into 衤. The rising stroke usually appears in the last stroke of the left part of a left-right structured character. By ending the left part with such a stroke, the distance that the writing instrument moves from the ending point of the left part to the beginning point of the right part is shortened. The left-falling stroke that serves as the first stroke of some characters such as *zi* 自 (nose), *bai* 白 (white) and *xue* 血 (blood) allows the writing instruments to be quickly placed on the starting point of the next stroke. The left-placed radical 氵ends with a rising stroke that allows the writing instrument to be quickly moved to the starting part of the right-placed component. The hook at the end of the curve in the character *xin* 心 (heart) facilitates the writing of the next stroke, which is the dot in the middle. Similarly, the hooks in the characters—such as *nei* 內 (inside), *zhou* 周 (circumference), *yong* 用 (apply), *tong* 同 (together with), *yue* 月 (moon)—all serve the same function. The brush marks in the Loulan bamboo and paper manuscripts offer useful insight into the above-mentioned principle.

Table 6.22 Handwritten Characters with Brush Marks in the Wei-Jin Period (220–589)

Characters	Loulan Bamboo and Paper Manuscripts of the Wei-Jin Period (220–589)	Characters	Loulan Bamboo and Paper Manuscripts of the Wei-Jin Period (220–589)
Shou 首 (head)		Yong 用 (apply)	
Cong 从/從 (follow)		Si 思 (think)	
Di 地 (ground)		Xi 悉 (learn about)	
Yu 域 (land within certain boundaries)		Yin 音 (sound)	

The second principle governing the formation of the stroke system is placing emphasis on character forms. This principle includes the following three aspects. First, when considering written forms, the emphasis is placed on the aesthetics and stability of character forms rather than the forms and positions of components and

The Process of the Formation of the Stroke System 99

strokes. (See Tables 23, 24, and 25 for examples) Second, strokes and their combinations can be modified to reflect the difference among characters. (See Table 26 for examples.) Third, when this principle conflicts with the principle of convenient writing, it is a must to first consider this principle, namely the character forms. (See Table 6.27 for examples.)

See the following tables for examples of the first aspect of the second principle.

Table 6.23 Examples of the Principle of Placing Emphasis on Character Forms

Characters	Small-Seal Script	Stele Inscriptions of the Period of the Northern and Southern Dynasties (386–581)
Zhong 忠 (devotion)		
Yi 怡 (cheerful)		
Gong 恭 (respectful)		

The three small-seal-script characters have the same component *xin* 心 (heart), but the official script presents the component in different forms. The changes made to the component are aimed to ensure that the characters are in perfect square shapes.

Table 6.24 Examples of the Principle of Placing Emphasis on Character Forms

Characters	Small-Seal Script	Stele Inscriptions of the Period of the Northern and Southern Dynasties (386–581)
Quan 券 *(deeds)*		
Zhi 制 (make)		
Bian 辨 (discriminate)		

In the small-seal script, there is only one form for the component *dao* 刀 (knife), but in the official script, this component is written in different forms or simplified to a degree that it can no longer be recognised. These changes are also made for the perfect square shapes of the characters.

Table 6.25 Examples of the Principle of Placing Emphasis on Character Forms

Characters	Small-Seal Script	Stele Inscriptions of the Period of the Northern and Southern Dynasties (386–581)
Shi 食 (food)		
Yang 養 (provide for)		
Yu 餘 (surplus)		
Yin 飲 (drink)		

As a single-component character or a component, *shi* 食 (food) appears in only one form in the small-seal script. Nevertheless, it appears in different forms in the stele inscriptions: one form looks even more complicated than its small-seal-script form, which takes up more space to prevent the character from appearing unbalanced and top-heavy; the other form is a simplified form, which saves space for the component placed on its right side.

In the Archaic writing system, a component tends to keep its form no matter where it appears, including the situation when it serves as a single-component character. Nevertheless, in the New-Style writing system, a component often has different forms when it appears in different positions. This phenomenon is caused by the principle of placing emphasis on character forms. It also shows that the New-Style writing system is a highly abstract and symbolic writing system.

See the following table for examples of the second aspect of the second principle.

Table 6.26 Examples of the Modifications Made to Differentiate Characters

Small Seal Script			
Eastern-Han-Dynasty Stele Inscriptions			
Regular Script	*Wu* 午 (noon)	*Niu* 牛 (cattle)	*Cai* 才 (gift)

In the small-seal script, the vertical stroke in *wu* 午 (noon) and *niu* 牛 (cattle) is started above the first horizontal stroke. In the regular script, the vertical stroke in 午 is started from the first horizontal line to differentiate the character from 牛. Another possible choice to transform the small-seal-script form of 午 is to straighten its first horizontal stroke ⌒. This choice was not adopted probably because it would turn 午 into *cai* 才 (gift).

See the following table for examples of the third aspect of the second principle.

Table 6.27 Examples of Placing the Emphasis on the Aesthetics of Characters

Characters	Loulan Bamboo and Paper Manuscripts	
Lai 来 (come)	来	来
Dong 东 (east)	東	東

In Loulan bamboo and paper manuscripts, *lai* 来 (come) and *dong* 东 (east) each has two written forms. The forms listed in the second column of the table are easier and faster to write, and, thus, they save time, but they are not accepted as standard forms as listed in the third column for aesthetic needs.

(II) Two Aspects of the Generation of the Stroke System

The transformation of the seal script into the official script is, to some extent, a transcription process. There are certain rules for the transformation of the seal-script lines and dots into strokes. Given this, the New-Style writing system basically inherits the character components and component combinations of the Archaic writing system. Governed by the rules, an official-script line or dot may be transformed into one stroke. It may also be replaced by several strokes or stroke combinations. For example, ∪ in the seal script is transformed in the following three ways: 一, ノ ㇏, and *ba* ⋎ (number eight). The first form is created by straightening the curved line of ∪. The second one is produced by a process that divides the curved line into two parts, the left part and right part; the left part is straightened into a left drop line and the right part into a horizontal line. The third form featuring two slanting dots is a commonly used simplified form of the curved lines like ∪. For instance, there are also three transformed forms of ⌒: the straightened form 一, ハ, and 冂. Its second form is created by breaking the curved line into a left part and a right part, while its third form is created by turning the curve into a squarish structure.

The main reason why a seal-script line or dot can be changed into multiple forms is the multitype modification made to the seal script during the official script transformation. One typical example is that a character may have a few forms consisting of the same components that are written in different ways. There is also a secondary cause for this phenomenon: the influence of the character structures. For instance, *ba* ⋎ (number eight), one of the transformed forms of ∪, often appears in the middle part of characters, such as *yin* 音 (sound) and *di* 帝 (supreme ruler), and ノ 丶, another transformed form of ∪, usually appears in the top part of characters, such as *sheng* 生 (life) and *niu* 牛 (cattle).

Table 6.28 The Influence of Character Structures on the Formation of Strokes

Characters	Small-Seal Script	Stele Inscriptions of the Eastern Han Dynasty (25–220)
Yin 音 (sound)		
Di 帝 (supreme ruler)		
Tong 童 (child)		
Jing 競 (contend)		
Zhang 章 (composition)		
Jing 竟 (finish)		
Sheng 生 (life)		
Niu 牛 (cattle)		
Zhu 朱 (vermilion)		

The appearance of multiple transformed forms is a natural phenomenon that occurs in the evolutionary process of characters, arising spontaneously rather than through deliberate planning. The multiple forms likely provided people in the past with a broader range of options for distinguishing between different characters in written form. Additionally, they established a sensible guideline while providing ample leeway and room for experimentation in the development of the stroke system.

Although it is a spontaneous process, there must also be some planning in it. This is because the Archaic and the New-Style writing systems use different ways to distinguish characters. The analysis of the examples below offers some useful insight into this issue.

Table 6.29 The Seal-Script Forms of *Zhu* 朱 (Vermilion), *Mo* 末 (End), and *Wei* 未 (Not Yet)

The above-listed seal-script characters are obviously different from one another. Nevertheless, when their ∪ is replaced by 一 and their ∩ is replaced by 八, these three characters will be transformed into the same form. Only by planning ahead can you avoid such a problem. Thanks to such planning, ∪ in the first character is replaced by ノ ヽ, turning the character into 朱. Similar adjustments were made for the second and third characters to differentiate between 末 and 未. In the second character, the short horizontal line was placed below the long one, while in the third character, it was positioned above the long line.

The above analysis shows that only reasonable planning can make the New-Style writing system more scientific and that there is evidence supporting the existence of such planning. Given this, it is reasonable to conclude that the formation of the stroke system is not only a completely spontaneous process governed by the principles and that it must involve some systematic and proactive planning efforts. The planning is carried out in the following two aspects: (1) the transformation of strokes, turning the irregular lines and dots of the seal script into a limited number of stroke types; (2) the replacement of the seal-script structures by stroke combinations. This research refers to them as the two aspects for the stroke system generation.

As the first aspect has been discussed in the previous paragraphs, the following analysis is focused on the second aspect. There are two methods used to replace the seal-script structures by stroke combinations. The first method is representing the original seal-script structure with stroke combinations, but the application of this method is heavily influenced by the trend of replacing a group of similar seal-script structures with a commonly used stroke combination.

Table 6.30 Planned Stroke Combinations

Characters	Small Seal Script	Eastern-Han-Dynasty Stele Inscriptions	Seal-Script Structure	Stroke Combination
Mei 每 (mother)			ᴗ	
Fang 方 (a square or rectangle)				*Tou* 亠 (a radical)
Yi 亦 (also)				
Zhu 主 (master)			ᴗ	

(Continued)

104 *The Process of the Formation of the Stroke System*

Table 6.30 (Continued)

Characters	Small Seal Script	Eastern-Han-Dynasty Stele Inscriptions	Seal-Script Structure	Stroke Combination
Di 帝 (supreme ruler)				
Gao 高 (high or tall)				
Liu 六 (number six)				
Chong 充 (be full)				

The second method is replacing seal-script structures with simplified stroke combinations that may share some similarities with the original structures.

Table 6.31 Transformation Through Replacement

Characters	Small-Seal Script	Stele Inscriptions of the Period of the Northern and Southern Dynasties (386–581)	Seal-Script Structure	Stroke Combination
Sai 塞 (block up)				
Han 寒 (cold)				
Xiang 襄 (aid)				

Sometimes, these two methods are combined in the transformation of a seal-script structure.

Table 6.32 Transformation Through Representation and Replacement

Characters	Western Zhou Dynasty (1046–771 BCE)	Small-Seal Script	Western Han Dynasty (206–8 BCE)	Eastern Han Dynasty (25–220)	Period of the Northern and Southern Dynasties (386–581)
Shi 食 (food)					

Characters	Western Zhou Dynasty (1046–771 BCE)	Small-Seal Script	Western Han Dynasty (206–8 BCE)	Eastern Han Dynasty (25–220)	Period of the Northern and Southern Dynasties (386–581)
Liang 良 (kindhearted)					
Chang 長 (long)					

The application of the representation method is more evident in the transformation of *liang* 良 (kind-hearted), and the replacement method is more evident in the transformation of the other two above-listed characters.

The replacement method is mainly aimed at complicated-looking and seldomly used seal-script components. Essentially, it is also a way to optimize the composition system.

Notes

1 The original Chinese version was published in *Linguistic Sciences* 语言科学, 2014, issue 5.
2 详见王贵元：《汉字形体演化的动因与机制》，《语文研究》，2010（3）。
  Wang Guiyuan: "The Motivation and Mechanisms Behind the Evolution of the Chinese Characters", *Linguistic Research*, 2010 (3).
3 The following character forms are quoted from Shi Xiaoxi 史晓曦's master dissertation "Study on Characters in the Eastern-Han-Dynasty Inscriptions and Related Issues" 东汉碑刻文字编及相关问题研究, Zhang Xiang 张翔's "Study on the Character Composition of Wu-State Bamboo Slips Unearthed in Zoumalou" 走马楼三国吴简文字编及构形研究 and Zhang Yinghui 张颖慧's "Study on the Stele Inscriptions of the Wei-Jin Period and the Period of the Northern and Southern Dynasties" 魏晋南北朝石刻文字研究. Please refer to the character form tables in the above-mentioned paper for the source of these forms.
4 裘锡圭：《文字学概要》，第 93 页，北京：商务印书馆，1990。
  Qiu Xigui: *A Summary of Chinese Philology*, p. 93, Beijing: The Commercial Press, 1990.
5 王凤阳：《汉字学》，第 222–223 页，长春：吉林文史出版社，1989。
  Wang Fengyang: *Chinese Philology*, pp. 222–223, Changchun: Jilin Literature and History Press, 1989.
6 王凤阳：《汉字学》，第 763 页，长春：吉林文史出版社，1989。
  Wang Fengyang: *Chinese Philology*, p. 763, Changchun: Jilin Literature and History Press, 1989.
7 唐兰：《中国文字学》，第 165 页，上海：上海古籍出版社，1979。
  Tang Lan: *Chinese Philology*, p. 165, Shanghai: Shanghai Chinese Classics Publishing House, 1979.

7 The Formation Process and Mechanisms of Radicals

The radical system of Chinese characters has been deliberately and gradually established during the evolution of the composition system of Chinese characters. Its establishment is a symbol of maturity for the composition system. The author of *Shuowen Jiezi* 说文解字 (An Explication of Written Characters) discovered the significance of radicals in the composition system of Chinese characters and thus arranged 9,353 characters under 540 radicals to reflect it. In comparison with today's radicals, which are used to search for characters in dictionaries, *Shuowen Jiezi* contains many more radicals. This is because radicals have been modified over the years for the improvement of the character-searching method based on radicals. Although current radicals are also derived from characters, they cannot reflect the original radical system any longer. Up to now, academic research on Chinese radicals basically focused on the arrangement and consultation of characters under radicals and neglects an important subject in the studies of Chinese characters and their history: the formation process and mechanisms of the radical system.

I. The Nature and Characteristics of Radicals

(I) The Nature of Radicals

Classical Chinese 古代汉语, edited by Wang Li 王力, points out that "the 540 radicals of *Shuowen Jiezi* 说文解字 are of high research value because they reflect the six means of creating Chinese characters, and they are determined according to the principles of philology, not for a character-research method."[1] This assertion is correct. These radicals, chosen based on philological principles, are the assimilation results of character components. They reflect the original radical system in the composition system of Chinese characters, just as Chinese Pinyin reflects the phonetic system of Chinese characters. In fact, *Shuowen Jiezi* is not a usual dictionary. It focuses on explaining individual characters. Xu Shen 许慎 (ca. 58–147)'s purpose in writing the book was to explain the compositional and semantic systems of Chinese characters and to correct the haphazard interpretations of Chinese characters at that time. Therefore, the book was not intended to provide a dictionary for general checking of the form, pronunciations, and meaning of Chinese characters; it was intended to demonstrate the original form and meaning of Chinese characters in a philological method. In comparison with *Shuowen Jiezi*, the Ming-Dynasty (1368–1644) scholar Mei Yingzuo's 梅膺祚 (?–?) book, *Zi Hui* 字汇 (A Collection of Words), which was designed as an easy-to-use dictionary, contains only 200-plus radicals. This author further assimilated the radicals in accordance with their appearance and neglected their compositional and semantic functions and philological principles for a convenient method of searching characters. The preface to *Shuowen Jiezi* also explains this issue and states that this book arranges characters under radicals based on their forms and functions. In other words, radicals' forms and functions can be used to distinguish different groups of Chinese characters, and they provide useful insight into the composition system of Chinese characters. This is the nature of radicals.

(II) The Characteristics of Radicals

As the first book to systematically record the radical system, *Shuowen Jiezi* 说文解字 arranges 9,353 characters under 540 radicals. Given that it analyses mainly the small-seal-script characters, it is reasonable to infer that the radical system of Chinese characters was basically established when the small seal-script was formed. What are the characteristics of this radical system from the point of view of the composition system of Chinese characters? This question will be discussed in the following paragraphs.

1. Radicals Usually Appear in Similar Positions in Characters

Radicals usually appear in similar positions in characters. This is one of the most important characteristics of radicals. For instance, 54 of the 62 characters arranged under the radical *shi* 示 (manifest) have the radical placed on the left side, and 87 of the 91 characters arranged under the radical *ye* 页 (page) have the radical placed on the right side. All the 24 characters under the radical *min* 皿 (shallow containers) have the radical placed at the bottom.

There are three questions to be asked about this phenomenon.

(1) Why do radicals tend to appear in similar positions in characters? This study finds that the reason lies in the radicals. As a symbol of maturity for the composition system of Chinese characters, the establishment of radicals is the result of the assimilation of components. To distinguish different types of Chinese characters, they had better appear in similar positions in characters to indicate the types to which they belong.

(2) Why are there usually a few special cases where a radical does not appear where it should? There are two reasons. Firstly, although the formation of radicals is influenced by human choices, it is a natural phenomenon that occurs during the evolution of character composition rather than a planned action. It is normal for the radical system to be imprecise in some respects. Second,

in terms of character composition, the New-Style writing system places the emphasis on character forms.² To ensure that characters meet the aesthetic standards, it allows adjustments made to the radical positions. Take *ji* 祭 (worship) as an example. Its radical *shi* 示 (manifest) is usually a left-placed radical, but the composition system allows it to serve as the lower part of the character to prevent the character from becoming rectangular instead of squarish. Similar adjustments have been made to other characters, such as *ying* 祡 (a type of worship ritual) and *ying* 禜 (a type of worship ritual) to ensure the square shapes of the characters.

(3) How can the radicals have different default positions? Why are some of them usually placed on the left or right? Why do some usually appear in the upper or lower parts of characters? There are many reasons for these phenomena. Some reasons are related to the shape characteristics and combination of components. Radicals such as *mian* 宀 (roofed room) and *xue* 穴 (cave) naturally leave space for components placed under them. Some reasons are related to the functions of radicals: *shou* 収 (collect), which means holding with both hands, usually serves as a lower part of a character. Some reasons have to do with the convenience and comfort of writing; radicals, such as *ye* 页 (page) and *qian* 欠 (yawn) are usually left-placed to ensure the convenience of writing. In addition to this, the left-right structured characters usually feature left-placed radicals since characters are written from left to right and the left part is usually reserved for components indicating the type of the characters. In a pictographic writing system, a component's orientation can be utilized to denote its relationship to other components within a character.

Table 7.1 Components Using Their Orientation to Indicate Meanings

Xing 姓 (surname)		Mei 妹 (younger sister)	
Xie 媟 (act indecently)		Mu 牧 (herd)	
Yi 劓 (cut off the nose as a punishment)		Tian 畋 (hunt)	
Yi 役 (labour)		Que 殼 (a musical instrument)	

In the characters listed above, *nv* 女 (woman/girl), *pu* 攴 (tap), *li* 力 (capability), and *shu* 殳 (long pole) are all components that utilize their orientation to express meanings. More specifically, whether such a component is placed on the left or right side of a character, it must face the other component. Most of such components are right-placed components. This is probably related to the convenience of writing: to write the components on the left, it is a must to write out their mirror

The Formation Process and Mechanisms of Radicals 109

images, which is a difficult thing to do. When such components are transformed into new forms during the evolution of characters, they naturally become right-placed components.

2. Radicals Are Defined Their Forms and by Their Functions

The function of radicals refers to their contribution to the expression of meanings. From a philological viewpoint, radicals are defined not only by their forms but also by their functions. As such, they facilitate the analogisation of character forms and meanings. Some radicals listed in *Shuowen Jiezi* have obviously pictographic features, but they also have semantic functions. For instance, *xun* 熏 (smoke), a character arranged under the radical *cao* 艸 (grass) in the book, uses the radical to indicate the upward movement. Grass grows upwards, and so does smoke. These two images do share similarities.

3. Radicals Possess Two Major Functions

Radicals possess two major functions. They can participate in the character composition either with their original meanings or with abstract meanings. The former usually refers to a concrete thing, and the latter to an abstract concept or category. Take the characters arranged under the radical *niu* 牛 (cattle) in *Shuowen Jiezi* as an example. It retains its original meaning in the following characters.

(1) *Du* 犊 (calf), consisting of the radical *niu* 牛 (cattle) and the simplified form of the phonetic component *du* 渎 (ditch);
(2) *San* 犙 (three-year-old cattle), consisting of the radical *niu* 牛 (cattle) and the phonetic component *can* 参 (intervene);
(3) *Si* 牭 (four-year-old cattle), consisting of the radical *niu* 牛 (cattle) and the radical and phonetic component *si* 四 (number four); and
(4) *Mou* 牟 (the sound that cattle make), featuring the radical *niu* 牛 (cattle) and depicting the image of the animal opening its mouth and going "moo".

The radical is used to refer to domesticated animals.

(5) *Mu* 牡 (male animals), consisting of the radical *niu* 牛 (cattle) and the phonetic component *tu* 土 (soil);
(6) *Pin* 牝 (female animals), consisting of the radical *niu* 牛 (cattle) and the phonetic component *bi* 匕 (spoon);
(7) *Xi* 犠 (cattle offered as a sacrifice), consisting of the radical *niu* 牛 (cattle) and the phonetic component *xi* 羲 (gas); and
(8) *Chan* 犣 (domestic animals), consisting of the radical *niu* 牛 (cattle) and the phonetic component *chan* 產 (give birth).

The above analysis shows that the radical *niu* 牛 (cattle) can mean cattle or domesticated animals: the former is its original meaning, and the latter is its abstract meaning. Another example is the radical *zu* 足 (foot). It retains its original meaning in the following characters.

(9) *Gen* 跟 (heel), consisting of the radical *zu* 足 (foot) and the phonetic component *gen* 艮 (mountain);
(10) *Huai* 踝 (ankle), consisting of the radical *zu* 足 (foot) and the phonetic component *guo* 果 (fruit);
(11) *Zhi* 跖 (sole of the foot), consisting of the radical *zu* 足 (foot) and the phonetic component *shi* 石 (stone); and
(12) *Qi* 踦 (a foot), consisting of the radical *zu* 足 (foot) and the phonetic component *qi* 奇 (uncommon).

The radical is used to refer to the action of walking.

(13) *Cu* 踧 (travel fast on the flat road), consisting of the radical *zu* 足 (foot) and the phonetic component *shu* 叔 (father's younger brother);
(14) *Qu* 躣 (walking), consisting of the radical *zu* 足 (foot) and the phonetic component *qu* 瞿 (frightened);
(15) *Ji* 踖 (run fast), consisting of the radical *zu* 足 (foot) and the phonetic component *xi* 昔 (dried meat); and
(16) *Ju* 踽 (walk slowly), consisting of the radical *zu* 足 (foot) and the phonetic component *yu* 禹 (the reputed founder of the Xia Dynasty).

The above analysis shows that the radical *zu* 足 (foot) can mean either "foot" or "walking": the former is its original meaning, and the latter, its abstract meaning.

II. Formation Pathways of Radicals

This study holds that the analogisation phenomenon is not something that occurs at the very beginning of the composition system of Chinese characters. Regarding the compensation system of Chinese characters, there are two stages of development: in the primary stage, the focus is placed on building characters for accurate expression; in the advanced stage, the emphasis is shifted to classifying the characters in accordance with their meanings, and radicals are established for this purpose. As early Chinese characters are created based on images, most of them are naturally pictographs that do not share many similarities in appearance. These pictographs independently express meanings instead of being subordinate to a character system. In the advanced stage, characters are created as phonetic-semantic symbols. Therefore, they become more abstract and stop being pictographic. It is also at this stage that they are divided into different categories in accordance with their forms and meanings.[3]

Some components that are frequently used to build early Chinese characters can be considered early radicals, such as *kou* 口 (mouth), *er* 耳 (ear), *zhi* 止 (toe), *ren* 人 (person), *nv* 女 (woman/girl), *shi* 示 (manifest), *shou* 手 (hand), *mu* 木 (wood), *pu* 攴 (tap), *huo* 火 (fire), *shui* 水 (water), *mian* 宀 (roofed room), *niu* 牛

(cattle), *ma* 马 (horse), and *niao* 鸟 (birds). Although they do not form a system, they do serve as radicals in the early days. Does this mean that the analogisation process starts together with the establishment of the composition system of Chinese characters? This is not the case. The creation of these often-used components is not a result of the analogisation process. It is caused by natural selection during the process of creating pictographs. Components highly related to human bodies were often used to express meanings since people needed to rely on their senses to understand things, such as *ren* 人 (person), *nv* 女 (woman/girl), *kou* 口 (mouth), *er* 耳 (ear), *rou* 肉 (flesh), *zu* 足 (foot), *shou* 手 (hand), and *shou* 首 (head). Components representing commonly seen things in daily life also frequently appeared in early characters, such as *shui* 水 (water), *huo* 火 (fire), *mu* 木 (wood), *he* 禾 (standing grain), *niu* 牛 (cattle), *ma* 马 (horse), and *mian* 宀 (roofed room). Not all these components have become radicals, but they are the foundation for the formation of radicals. This is because most radicals are developed from often-used components. In the development of Chinese characters, many frequently used early components were deliberately used to build more characters, which further broadened the scope of their application. From another point of view, this facilitated the analogisation of characters, making it possible to divide them into different groups featuring different often-used components. With the continuous extension of their scope of use, these oft-used components gradually formed a system: the radical system. There are four pathways for such extension: addition, selection, modification, and creation.

(I) Addition

The first pathway for the extension of component usage is the addition of a component. As shown below, many early Chinese characters have been added with an often-used component.

1. The addition of *shi* 示 (manifest). In the oracle-bone inscriptions and the Western-Zhou-Dynasty (1046–771 BCE) and Spring-and-Autumn-Period (770–476 BCE) bronze inscriptions, 彔 is used to express happiness. Later, the component *shi* 示 (manifest) is added to the character, making it *lu* 禄 (happiness). Given its appearance in the Warring-States-Period (475–221) seals and the Qin bamboo slips unearthed at Shuihudi, the form 禄 probably appeared in the late Warring States Period. In the oracle-bone inscriptions and the Western-Zhou-Dynasty (1046–771 BCE) and Spring-and-Autumn-Period (770–476 BCE) bronze inscriptions, 且 is used to indicate ancestors. This character is later changed in *zu* 祖 (ancestors) by adding the component *shi* 示 (manifest). According to the archaeological evidence found so far, 祖 appeared in the middle Spring and Autumn Period (770–476 BCE), but in the late Spring and Autumn Period 且 was still more commonly used than 祖. The Shang-Dynasty (ca. 1600–1046 BCE) character of *ji* 祭 (worship) was modified in the Western Zhou Dynasty (1046–771 BCE) through the addition of the component *shi* 示 (manifest).

112 *The Formation Process and Mechanisms of Radicals*

2. The addition of *shui* 水 (water). The character *jiu* 酒 (alcoholic beverages) is created by adding the component *shui* 水 (water) to 酉, which is used in the Western-Zhou-Dynasty (1046–771 BCE) and Spring-and-Autumn-Period (770–476 BCE) bronze inscriptions to indicate wine. Given its appearance in the Qin bamboo slips unearthed at Shuihudi, the creation of 酒 probably occurred in the late Warring States Period (475–221 BCE).
3. The addition of *yu* 玉 (precious stone). The character *zhang* 璋 (a jade tablet) was created in the late Spring and Autumn Period (770–476 BCE) by adding the component *yu* 玉 (precious stone) to its early character form 章 appearing in Man Gui Container (鄸簋) of the Western Zhou Dynasty (1046–771 BCE).
4. The addition of *yan* 言 (to speak). The character *nuo* 诺 (promise) was created in the early Spring and Autumn Period (770–476 BCE) by adding the component *yan* 言 (to speak) to its early form 若 appearing on Hu tripod cauldron of the Western Zhou Dynasty (1046–771 BCE).
5. The addition of *mi* 糸 (silk). The character *zhong* 终 (end) was created in the early Warring States Period (475–221 BCE) by adding the component *mi* 糸 (silk) to its early character form 夂. The bamboo slips unearthed from the Tomb of Marquis Yi of the Zeng State offer relevant evidence. As evidenced by the bamboo slips unearthed at Guodian, the character *ji* 纪 (threads) was created in the middle Warring States Period (475–221 BCE) by adding the component *mi* 糸 (silk) to its early character form 己. The character *zhi* 織 (weave) first appears in the Qin bamboo slips unearthed at Shuihudi, which dates to the late Warring States Period. Before this period, the character is written as 戠.
6. The addition of *jin* 金 (metal). Characters *cheng* 鎗 (a wine vessel) and *cong* 鏓 (chime) were created in the late Western Zhou Dynasty (1046–771 BCE) by adding the component *jin* 金 (metal) to 倉 and 恖. Characters *dun* 錞 (a copper utensil) and *liu* 鏐 (pure gold) were created in the late Spring and Autumn Period (770–476 BCE) by adding the component jin 金 (metal) to 辜 and 翏.
7. The addition of *ren* 人 (person). The character *chang* 償 (return) first appeared in the bamboo slips unearthed at Longgang. It is written as 賞 in earlier literature. The character *yi* 儀 (ceremony) first appeared in Eastern-Han-Dynasty stele inscriptions.

This character was previously written as 義.

Some of the above-mentioned component additions are intended to enhance the semantic function of characters. Some are for the analogisation of characters and new derivative characters. All of them extend the use of certain components.

(II) Selection

The establishment of radicals corresponds to that of the composition system of Chinese characters. That is to say, the maturity of the radical system to some extent equals the maturity of the composition system. During the Shang Dynasty (ca.1600–1046 BCE) and the Western Zhou Dynasty (1046–771 BCE), a character might have several forms that differed from one another in terms of the number and

The Formation Process and Mechanisms of Radicals 113

position of components. This is a natural phenomenon for pictographs used during that period, and it naturally disappears in the process of developing pictographs into phonetic-semantic symbols. There are some forms destined to be eliminated or selected as standard forms in this process, and such selection is closed related to the development of radicals. In the process of developing often-used components into radicals, requirements on their forms and positions gradually appeared, which leads to the standardization of the radicals.

Table 7.2 The Evolution of *Si* 祀 (Worship) and *Fu* 福 (Happiness)

	Western Zhou Dynasty (1046–771 BCE)	Spring and Autumn Period (770–476 BCE)
Si 祀 (worship)		
Fu 福 (happiness)		

(III) Modification

The modification method mainly targets single-component characters that cannot or seldomly serve as character components. Sometimes, it also influences derivative characters. These characters are transformed to simplify the components in the composition system and clarify the character category they belong to. Such modifications can be divided into two types: overall modifications and partial modifications.

1. Overall Modifications

Table 7.3 The Evolution of *Zhi* 祇 (to Revere) and *Yong* 墉 (Fortified Wall)

	Shang Dynasty (ca. 1600–1046 BCE)	Western Zhou Dynasty (1046–771 BCE)	Spring and Autumn Period (770–476 BCE)	Small-Seal Script
Zhi 祇 (to revere)				
Yong 墉 (fortified wall)				

The early forms of *zhi* 祇 (to revere) and *yong* 墉 (fortified wall), used before the Warring States Period (475–221 BCE), are single-component pictographs. In the small-seal script, they are modified into two characters featuring the radical *shi* 示 (manifest) and the radical *tu* 土 (soil), respectively.

114 The Formation Process and Mechanisms of Radicals

2. Partial Modifications

Table 7.4 The Evolution of *Ding* 鼎 (Tripod Caldron) and *Zi* 字 (Characters)

	Shang Dynasty (ca.1600–1046 bce)	Western Zhou Dynasty (1046–771 BCE)	Warring States Period (475–221 BCE)
Ding 鼎 (tripod caldron)			

The pictographic form of *ding* 鼎 (tripod caldron) used in the Shang Dynasty (ca.1600–1046 BCE) and the Western Zhou Dynasty (1046–771 BCE) is a single-component character, but there are two modified forms of this character created in the Warring States Period (475–221 BCE). In the first modified form, its original pictographic lower part representing tripod legs is replaced by the component *min* 皿 (shallow containers), which indicates a certain type of utensil. This composition is explained as a combination of 皿 and the simplified form of the phonetic component *ding* 鼎 (tripod caldron). In the second form, the pictographic lower part is replaced by the component *huo* 火 (fire), which means utensils you use for cooking with fire. In this case, the component 火 can be considered a semantic component.

The character *chang* 嘗 (taste) is arranged under the radical *zhi* 旨 (delicious) in *Shuowen Jiezi* 说文解字, but its meaning is extended in its application: it is often used to refer to the worship ceremony dedicated to the autumn season, whose core worship procedure is to taste the newly harvested grains. Many documents can prove this meaning extension. *Erya* 尔雅 (Erya Dictionary), which is widely regarded as the first Chinese dictionary, explains this character as the worship ceremony dedicated to the autumn season. Guo Pu (276–324) made comments on this explanation: "嘗 (taste) means to taste new grains." *Baihu Tongyi* 白虎通义 (Standard Explanations to Classics Made at Baihu Taoist Temple) also gives a similar explanation to this character: "the worship ceremony named 嘗 is performed in the autumn to taste the newly harvested grains." Gradually, *zhi* 旨 (delicious), the original semantic component of the character is replaced by *shi* 示 (manifest), and a derivative character 嘗 (appearing in the Spring and Autumn Period (770–476 BCE)) is created for the worship ceremony dedicated to the autumn season.

(IV) Creation

This way of extending the use of components is to create new characters with frequently used components.

III. The Development of Their Compositional Function

In early Chinese characters, components are usually non-polysemous, and they often represent concrete things. With the evolution of the writing system, components representing abstract ideas were used for the composition of characters, and those inherited from the early characters were modified by transformation or replacement.

(I) Non-Polysemous Components Transformed into Abstract Components

With the evolution of Chinese characters, non-polysemous character components were gradually transformed into abstract components that are used to express a kind of thing or phenomenon. The completion of such a transformation marks the establishment of radicals. The evolution of the characters *mu* 牡 (male animals), *pin* 牝 (female animals), *lao* 牢 (fence), and *mu* 牧 (herd) can give some useful insight into such a transformation process.

Table 7.5 The Oracle-Bone-Script Forms of *Mu* 牡 (Male Animals), *Pin* 牝 (Female Animals), *lao* 牢 (fence), and *Mu* 牧 (Herd)

Oracle-Bone Script	Character forms featuring the radical *niu* 牛 (cattle)				
	Character forms featuring the radical *yang* 羊 (sheep and goats)				
	Character forms featuring the radical *shi* 豕 (pigs and boars)				
	Character forms featuring the radical *ma* 马 (horse)				
Small-Seal Script	Character forms featuring the radical *niu* 牛 (cattle)				
Regular Script	Character forms featuring the radical *niu* 牛 (cattle)	牡	牝	牢	牧

Among the combinations shown above, the combination of *niu* 牛 (cattle) and *tu* 土 (soil) means bull, that of *yang* 羊 (sheep and goats) and *tu* 土 (soil) means ram, and that of *shi* 豕 (pigs and boars) and *tu* 土 (soil) means boar. The component *tu* 土 (soil) seems to represent an abstract concept of "a male animal" in these characters, instead of retaining its original meaning. Previous researchers have already pointed out this phenomenon. Yang Shuda 杨树达 (1885–1956), a famous scholar, noted, "Analyses of the composition of the characters that are included in the parts about animals and livestock in the dictionary *Erya* 尔雅 and arranged under the radicals *niu* 牛 (cattle) and *ma* 马 (horse) in *Shuowen Jiezi* show that there are lots of character components created to refer to different kinds of animals, which is probably a legacy of the animal husbandry era when people created a character for each different wild or domestic animal. It seems that these components can be combined with a part of *pin* 牝 (female animals) or *mu* 牡 (male animals) to build characters that indicate animals of different genders. For example, 牝 means female cattle, and *you* 麀 means female deer. If you do not think that the latter contains a gender component derived from the former, do you think that the component *tu* 土 (soil) in *mu* 牡 (male animals) means the same thing as it does in *chen* 尘 (dust)?"[4] Other scholars also pointed out that some components that seemed to represent a concrete thing actually had a broader meaning. Qu Runmin 瞿润缗 said, "Before, we did not distinguish the differences between the two characters *lao* 牢 (fence) and '牢'. In fact, '牢' is a small fence, which is never described with the character *lao* 牢 (fence). These two characters are different."[5] Xu Zhongshu's 徐中舒 *Oracle Dictionary* 甲骨文字典 further extends Qu Runmin's view: "*Lao* 牢 (fence) and '牢' refer to two different things. The former is used to hold cattle for sacrifice ceremonies, the latter holds sheep or goats for sacrifice ceremonies. In the past, these two characters were thought to represent fences of different sizes. It does conform to the reality of the Shang Dynasty."[6]

Xu Zhongshu's judgment is supported by the discovery that 牡 and 牝 can appear in the same piece of oracle inscription.

(1) Consult with Oracle Yisi 乙巳 on the *bing*-10 丙十 day about whether Bibing 妣丙 will deliver a child, offering the following sacrifices: three *mu* 牡, one 牝, and white . . . (Oracle-Bone Inscriptions Unearthed at the Ruins of Yin 殷墟甲骨刻辞类纂)

(2) Consult with Oracle Xinsi 辛巳 about whether Bigeng 妣庚 and Bibing 妣丙 will deliver children, offering the following sacrifices: *mu* 牡, 牝, and *baishi* 白豕 (white pig). (Oracle-Bone Inscriptions Unearthed at the Ruins of Yin)

(3) Consult with Oracle Xinsi 辛巳 about whether Bigeng 妣庚 and Bibing 妣丙 will deliver children, offering the following sacrifices: mu 牡, 牝, and *baiquan* 白犬 (white dog). (Oracle-Bone Inscriptions Unearthed at the Ruins of Yin)

(4) Consult with Oracle Xinwei 辛未 after offering 牝 and 豺 to the ancestors. (Oracle-Bone Inscriptions Unearthed at the Ruins of Yin)

(5) Consult with Oracle . . . about whether Geng 庚 and Bibing 妣丙 . . . will deliver children. 牝 犰 (Oracle-Bone Inscriptions Unearthed at the Ruins of Yin)

With the evolution of Chinese characters, *mu* 牡 (male animals) and *pin* 牝 (female animals) gradually became abstract symbols referring to different genders of animals, resulting in the elimination of many relevant character forms. The component *niu* 牛 (cattle) in these two characters also gradually becomes an abstract symbol representing domesticated animals.

(II) Non-Polysemous Components Replaced by Abstract Components

Pictographic characters are intended to depict images, so their compositional system is closely related to the physical features of the things that they describe. Systematisation of character forms was never the goal of such a system. With the development of the composition system of Chinese characters, the importance of systematising character forms became increasingly prominent. This is because to ensure the convenience and effectiveness of writing and reading, the composition of characters must be simplified to reduce the barriers to reading and writing characters. One of the important ways to realise the systematisation

The Formation Process and Mechanisms of Radicals 117

of character forms is the analogization of character components, which is indeed a way to classify Chinese characters according to their forms and meanings and improve the effectiveness of the character system by reducing the number of rarely used components. The following examples may help to illustrate this point.

Table 7.6 The Evolution of *Feng* 凤 (Male Phoenix) and *Ji* 鸡 (Chicken)

	Oracle-Bone Script	*Small-Seal Script*
Feng 凤 (male phoenix)		
Ji 鸡 (chicken)		

The oracle-bone-script form of *feng* 凤 (male phoenix) features a non-polysemous, pictographic component that depicts the bird, but, in its small-seal-script, the component is replaced by the component *niao* 鸟 (bird), which is more an abstract symbol representing a concept instead of a pictograph. The non-polysemous and pictographic component in the oracle-bone-script form of *ji* 鸡 (chicken), which depicts the image of the bird, is replaced by the abstract component *zhui* 隹 (short-tailed bird) in the small-seal script.

The character *zhun* 屯 (hardness), which is arranged under the radical *cao* 屮 (grass), in the book *Shuowen Jiezi*, it is originally a pictograph depicting a bud exerting all its effort to break out of the ground. Given this, its original form consists of a pictograph representing a bud and a horizontal line representing the ground. According to *Yi* 易 (The Book of Changes), this form describes the hardness experienced by the tender bud as it breaks through the hard ground.

Table 7.7 The Evolution of *Zhun* 屯 (Hardness)

Zhun 屯 (hardness)	*Shang Dynasty (ca. 1600–1046 BCE)*	*Western Zhou Dynasty (1046–771 BCE)*	*Spring and Autumn Period (770–476 BCE)*	*Small-Seal Script*

Gao Hongjin said, "The original form of the character 屯 depicts the growth of a seed that has sprouted but has not yet shelled, so it is used to describe hardness." Seeds with shells must first take root in the soil and then break out of the ground with their shells. The horizontal line that represents the ground in the oracle-bone-script form of the character is derived from a single-component pictographic character, and the other component in this form is replaced by the abstract component *cao* 屮 (grass). Therefore, *Shuowen Jiezi* describes this character as a combination of *cao* 屮 (grass) and *yi* 一 (one).[7]

118 *The Formation Process and Mechanisms of Radicals*

IV. The Development Stages of Radicals

(I) Pre-Radical Period

Was the concept of radicals in existence during the emergence of Chinese characters, or did it evolve gradually during their development? There is no definitive research on this topic. Although attempts have been made to summarize the radicals of the oracle-bone-script characters, they have been unsuccessful, likely due to the following reasons.

1. In the oracle-bone inscriptions, there are many single-component pictographs that never serve as character components, such as the oracle-bone-script forms of *di* 帝 (supreme ruler), *zhi* 祇 (to revere), *cong* 琮 (octagonal piece of jade with hole in middle), *mang* 笀 (tiny thorns), *cai* 蔡 (wild grass), *ruo* 若 (supposing), *zeng* 曾 (increase), *zhou* 周 (circumference), *sui* 岁 (planet Jupiter), *dun* 盾 (shield), *ji* 箕 (winnowing basket), *lu* 盧 (a vessel for holding cooked rice), *she* 射 (to shoot), *ji* 檵 (a kind of tree), *tuo* 橐 (a sack), *mu* 穆 (a king of grain), *qiu* 裘 (fur garments), *mao* 髦 (long hair), *bao* 豹 (leopard), *liao* 尞 (fuel used for worship ceremonies), *lei* 雷 (thunder), *guo* 馘 (to cut the left ears of the slain), *min* 捪 (touch), *huo* 或 (or), *qi* 戚 (a kind of axe), *se* 瑟 (large stringed musical instrument), *fa* 發 (deliver), *pei* 轡 (reins), *hong* 虹 (rainbow), *shan* 蟺 (earthworm), *fu* 蝠 (bats), *qiu* 蛷 (multi-legged insects), *zhu* 鼄 (spider), *yong* 墉 (fortified wall), *zhu* 助 (help), *qin* 禽 (fowl), *wan* 萬 (scorpion), *mi* 麋 (elk), *jia* 豭 (male pig), *xu* 须 (facial hair), *er* 爾 (decorative pattern), *qiu* 秋 (autumn), *tai* 臺 (platform), and *zi* 髭 (moustache). These character forms cannot be broken down into components and thus can only be regarded as "radicals". Such "radicals" without the function of classifying characters are not real radicals.
2. The radical system of the oracle-bone characters is immature, as many characters have not yet been added with radicals, such as 豊-*li* 禮 (social rites), 录-*lu* 禄 (happiness), 羊-*xiang* 祥 (good omen), 且-*zu* 祖 (ancestors), 癶-*ji* 祭 (worship), 帝-*di* 禘 (imperial ancestor worship), 复-*fu* 復 (recover), 忌-*ji* 跽 (kneel for a long time), 雚-*guan* 觀 (observe), 酉-*jiu* 酒 (alcoholic beverages), 冬-*zhong* 终 (end), 宾-*pin* 嬪 (court lady), 匕-*bi* 妣 (one's deceased mother), 尃-*bo* 搏 (combat), 乍-*zuo* 作 (get up), 畐-*bi* 鄙 (500 families), 鄉-*xiang* 饗 (banquet), 易-*ci* 赐 (bestow favours), 易-*yang* 昜 (rising sun), 每-*hui* 晦 (last day of the lunar month), 晦-*hui* 誨 (teach), 散-*wei* 微 (walk clandestinely), 吏-*shi* 使 (order), 卜-*wai* 外 (outside), and 白-*bo* 伯 (eldest of brothers).
3. Components do not appear in fixed positions in the oracle-bone script and do not have the functions of indicating the compositional structures and meanings of characters.
4. Many oracle-bone characters have variants that differ from one another in the number and type of components. Under such circumstances, it is hard to determine their radicals.

Table 7.8 The Oracle-Bone-Script Forms of *Chu* 出 (Out) and *Yu* 御 (Manage)

Chu 出 (out)	
Yu 御 (manage)	

5. The oracle-bone components are basically non-polysemous components. Only a few of them are abstract components, which is the primary characteristic of radicals.

Why is it hard to summarize the radicals of the oracle-bone-script characters? The underlying reason is that the Shang-Dynasty (ca. 1600–1046 BCE) oracle-bone characters are pictographs and their character forms, components, and component combinations are based on image depiction instead of being governed by a composition system. Characters created during this period feature various components and component combinations: one component often has several forms, and various components can be combined in different ways to make characters. These early characters focus on depicting images. They have not yet evolved into the stage where often-used components or radicals are used to indicate compositional structures and meanings of characters and where the composition of individual characters is subject to the character system.

(II)   The Establishment of the Radical System

The composition system of the Chinese characters has been established and improved over a long period, and so has the radical system. The emergence of abstract components in batches is an important symbol of the establishment of the radical system. Through a general survey of the Shang-Dynasty (ca. 1600–1046 BCE) and Zhou-Dynasty (1046–256 BCE) character forms, this study discovers that many abstract components appeared in the middle Western Zhou Dynasty (1046–771 BCE). For instance, there are no characters featuring the radical *jin* 金 (metal) in the Shang-Dynasty and Zhou-Dynasty character forms, but among the middle-Western-Zhou-Dynasty characters, there are 13 such characters, including *xi* 錫 (tin), *zhu* 鑄 (cast), *zhong* 錘 (a type of wine utensil), *zhong* 鐘 (bell), *ling* 鈴 (bell), *jun* 鈞 (unit of measure equivalent to 30 catties), *xing* 鋞 (a kind of wine utensil), *tuo* 鉈 (a short spear), *ying* 鎣 (polish), *tiao* 銚 (iron), *jin* 䘳 (collar of a robe formerly worn by the literati), *shi* 鈇 (arrowhead), and 鐳. The new characters created in the late Western Zhou Dynasty, those created in the Spring and Autumn Period (770–476 BCE), and those created in the Warring States Period (475–221 BCE), respectively, contributed 13, 31, and 25 new characters with the radical *jin* 金 (metal). As a character component, this radical represents an abstract concept of "metal". All the characters featuring this radical refer to a certain kind of metal. The character *shu* 蜀 (name of an ancient state) also first got its radical *chong* 虫 (worm/insect) in the mid-Western Zhou Dynasty.

Ban Gui Container (班簋)

As the original form of 蜀 is a pictograph depicting a big-headed worm, the Western-Zhou-Dynasty form uses the component *chong* 虫 (worm/insect) as its radical. The above analysis suggests that the radical system of Chinese characters started in the mid-Western Zhou Dynasty. Previous studies have argued that, in the late Western Zhou Dynasty, Chinese characters were transformed from pictographs to phonetic-semantic symbols named sub-pictographs. The establishment of the radical system (starting in the mid-Western Zhou Dynasty), discussed in this study does not perfectly coincide with the removal of pictographic features (beginning in the late Western Zhou Dynasty). Nevertheless, the time difference is not great.

During the Spring and Autumn Period (770–476 BCE) and the Warring States Period (475–221 BCE), different states used different types of characters. Surprisingly, in the late Warring States Period, the Qin State's characters developed to an advanced level.

1. In the character system of the Qin state, characters seldom have variants. For comparison, the Chu-state characters used in the same period often have variants.
2. In the character system, there are many multicomponent characters. In comparison with the literature of previous periods, Qin bamboo slips unearthed at Shuihudi have 524 new multicomponent characters (including new variants of the existing characters).[8]

Such new characters and variants include *lu* 祿 (happiness), *mei* 禖 (praying for a child), *sui* 祟 (evil spirit), *mei* 袜 (demon), *zhu* 珠 (pearls), *da* 荅 (red bean), *you* 莠 (green foxtail), *chen* 苣 (fragrant plant), *lin* 蘭 (Chinese iris), *pu* 蒲 (cattail), *bao* 苞 (bulrush), *yuan* 苑 (garden), *fu* 苖 (a kind of grass), *ruo* 若 (supposing), *bao* 葆 (luxuriant), *jian* 薦 (grass), *li* 犁 (plough), *wen* 吻 (lips), *qian* 前 (front), *gui* 歸 (return), *sui* 隨 (follow), *ta* 遝 (crowded and repeated), *lie* 邋 (the waving of the flag), *zhi* 迣 (to leap over), *bi* 彼 (to impose), *jiao* 徼 (to go on a tour of inspection), *xun* 循 (to follow), *xu* 徐 (slowly), *shu* 術 (road), *chong* 衝 圖 (to rush at), *jian* 踐 (to trample), *bian* 扁 (to inscribe on the door), *ye* 謁 (to report), *zhu* 諸 (various), *mou* 謀 (plan), *lun* 論 (to discuss), *shi* 識 (to recognise), *cheng* 誠 (honest), *ke* 課 (to examine), *shi* 試 (to try out), *shuo* 說 (to speak), *zhui* 諈 (to entrust), *tong* 詷 (common), *bu* 誧 (to admonish), *hu* 謼 (to shout), *ya* 訝 (to express surprise), *tuo* 詑 (to cheat), *zha* 詐 (to express shame), *wu* 誣 (to make false accusation), *bang* 謗 (to slander), *wu* 誤 (to make mistakes), *zi* 訾 (to slander), *xu* 訏 (to exaggerate), *qian* 譴 (to reprimand), *rang* 讓 (to concede), *sui* 誶 (to speak ill of), *jie* 詰 (to question), *xun* 詢 (to consult), *you* 誘 (to entice), *xun* 訊 (to inquire), *dian* 殿 (hall), *xiao* 殽 (confused), *shou* 收 (accept), *min* 敃 (to defy), *chen* 瞋 (to glare with anger), *mi* 眯 (to narrow one's eyes), *ya* 雅 (graceful), *meng* 瞢 (eyesight obscured), *chun* 脣 (lips), *shen* 腎 (kidney), *nao* 臑 (upper limbs), *gu* 股 (thighs), *jiao* 脚 (foot), *heng* 胻 (the upper part of shin bone), *dui* 脫 (to peel off), *die* 胅 (hips), *sui* 隋 (residual meat), *fu* 脯 (dried meet), *jiao* 膠 (glue), *qiang* 腔 (cavity), and *jin* 筋 (tendon). Most of these characters are created through the addition of a

The Formation Process and Mechanisms of Radicals 121

semantic component, which further clarifies the meaning of these characters and strengthens the relationship between the character system and the vocabulary system of the Chinese language.

3. There are obvious differences between the single-component characters used in Qin bamboo slips unearthed at Shuihudi and those used in Qin literature of earlier periods. They are simplified and analogised.

Table 7.9 Comparison Between Qin Characters of Different Periods

Shang 商 (estimate)	Bell of the Duke of Qin (Piece B) 秦公鎛乙	Qin bamboo slips unearthed at Shuihudi 睡虎地秦简
Xun 讯 (to interrogate)	Lid of the Qin-Dynasty Buqi Gui Container 秦不其簋盖	Qin bamboo slips unearthed at Shuihudi 睡虎地秦简
Xia 夏 (Chinese/China)	Lid of the Gui Container of Duke Qin 秦公簋盖	Qin bamboo slips unearthed at Shuihudi 睡虎地秦简
Shuai 帅 (shawl)	Lid of the Gui Container of Duke Qin 秦公簋盖	Qin bamboo slips unearthed at Shuihudi 睡虎地秦简
Yi 宜 (suitable)	The Gui Container of Duke Qin 秦公簋器	Qin bamboo slips unearthed at Shuihudi 睡虎地秦简
Gui 归 (return)	Lid of Qin-Dynasty Buqi Gui Container 秦不其簋盖	Qin bamboo slips unearthed at Shuihudi 睡虎地秦简
Shi 是 (right)	Lid of the Gui Container of Duke Qin 秦公簋盖	Qin bamboo slips unearthed at Shuihudi 睡虎地秦简
Ruo 若 (supposing)	Curse on the King of Chu (Stele Inscription) 诅楚文	Qin bamboo slips unearthed at Shulhudi 睡虎地秦简

As shown in the table above, apart from the characters, such as *shang* 商 (estimate), *yi* 宜 (suitable), and *xia* 夏 (Chinese/China), which are clearly simplified, the transformed characters shown above feature components being analogised: seldom-used, pictographic components are removed. For instance, *ruo* 若 (supposing) gives up its pictographic form that depicts a person tidying his hair with both hands. The seldom-used components in the original forms of *shi* 是 (right) and *xun* 讯 (to interrogate) are, respectively, replaced by two combinations of commonly used components: the combination of *ri* 日 (sun) and *zheng* 正 (proper), and that of *yan* 言 (to speak) and *xun* 卂 (to fly rapidly). The seldom-used components in the original forms of *shuai* 帅 (shawl) and *gui* 归 (return) are replaced by the similar-looking component *dui* 自 (to pile up).

The Buqi Gui Container (不其簋) and the Bell of Duke Qin (秦公鎛) both have ancient origins, with the former dating back to several years prior to Qin Lord Zhuanggong's (856–778 BCE) reign in 822 BCE, and the latter is believed to have originated around 697 BCE when Qin Lord Wugong (?–678 BCE) assumed power. The Gui Container of Duke Qin (秦公簋) was built around 576 BCE when Qin Lord Jinggong (?–537 BCE) came to the throne, and the Stele Inscription "Curse on the King of Chu" was created in 312 BCE during the reign of King Huiwen of Qin (356–311 BCE). As to the creation of Qin bamboo slips unearthed at Shuihudi, Chen Wei believes that they were made in the late Warring States Period (475–221 BCE) when Ying Zheng 嬴政 (259–210 BCE), who later become the first Qin Emperor, reigned the State of Qin.[9] His claim is supported by the use of the following characters in the bamboo slips: *li* 吏 (official), *shi* 事 (government post), *qing* 卿 (high official), *xiang* 郷 (village), *you* 酉 (a wine vessel), *jiu* 酒 (alcoholic beverages), *shang* 賞 (reward), and *chang* 償 (return).[10]

As shown in the above analysis, the characters of the Qin State in the late Warring States Period seem quite standardised and systematised. This point has also been made by Zhao Ping'an. In his research "On the Three Qin Campaigns to Standardize Character Form" 试论秦国历史上的三次 "书同文", he divides the development history of Qin characters into the following three stages: (1) the first stage began with the publication of *Shiliu Pian* 史籀篇 (Shiliu Literacy Book); (2) the second stage began from the mid-Warring States Period when the State of Qin spread its characters in the places it conquered; (3) the third stage started when the Qin State unified China and standardised the country's writing system with the small-seal script.[11] Nevertheless, it should be noted that the "standardisation" discussed in Zhao Ping'an's article is different from the "standardisation" discussed in this study. The former is about how the Qin State standardised the writing system by disseminating its characters, and the latter is about the state's efforts to sort and standardise its character forms.

The Qin State's endeavour to unify China started with its annexation of the State of Han in 230 BCE. Ten years after that, it successfully completed this feat. As different states used different writing systems before the unification when China was split into several states in the Warring States Period (475–221 BCE), the Qin State had to unify these systems by spreading its own system to enhance the unification. To smoothly popularize its own writing system, it had to first systematise and standardise this system. Under this assumption, the endeavour to systematise and standardise the writing system of the Qin State should begin from the annexation of the State of Han and during the reign of Ying Zheng 嬴政.[12] In the written history of Qin characters, there are not many records regarding these systematisation and standardisation efforts. This is understandable because there is no need to elaborate too much on the unification of the writing system, which is an inherent part of the unification of the country. Although there are few records in official history, there are some other written records that have long been treated as legends. Zhang Huaiguan 张怀瓘, a Tang-Dynasty calligrapher and calligraphy theorist, said in his book, *Shuduan* 书断 (Calligraphy Appreciation): "Cai Yong 蔡邕 [133–192, an Eastern-Han-Dynasty calligrapher and writer] mentioned in 'Shenghuang Pian' 圣皇篇 (Holy Emperor) that it was Cheng Miao 程邈 [a Qin-Dynasty calligrapher] who established the official script to replace the ancient writing system." Wei Heng 卫恒 (?-291) recorded one such legend in his *Siti*

Shushi 四体书势 (The Four Scripts and Their Calligraphic Styles): "Cheng Miao 程邈, a native of Xiagui once served as a low-ranking government official. As he offended Emperor Qin Shi Huang (the first Emperor of the Qin Dynasty), he was imprisoned in Yunyang for 10 years. In the prison, he modified the big seal script by simplifying the complicated parts, strengthening the weak points, and standardising the strokes. When his work was reported to Emperor Qin Shi Huang, the emperor was impressed and made him a high-ranking official and his script became the standard script. Some people say that the script Cheng Miao created is the official script. The preface of *Shuowen Jiezi*, however, provides a conflicting statement about Cheng Miao: "The third script is the small-seal script. It is said to be created by Cheng Miao, a native of Xiagui, under the command of Emperor Qin Shi Huang. The fourth script is called the official script of Qin." Duan Yucai 段玉裁 (1735–1815), a Qing-Dynasty sinologist, made a note of this statement and pointed out that it might be wrong. "As it is clearly stated in previous paragraphs that *Li Si* 李斯 (?–208 BCE), Zhao Gao 赵高 (?–207 BCE) and Hu Wu 胡毋 (269–318) were the ones who created the small-seal script by modifying the big seal script. This statement clearly contradicts the pre-said conclusion. Cai Yong 蔡邕 pointed out in 'Shenghuang Pian' 圣皇篇 (Holy Emperor) that Cheng Miao 程邈 was the creator of the official script, and this statement is widely agreed by such scholars as Cai Yan 蔡琰, Wei Heng 卫恒 (?–291), Yang Xin 羊欣 (370–442), Jiang Shi 江式 (?–523), Yu Jianwu 庾肩吾 (487–551), Wang Sengqian 王僧虔 (426–485), Li Daoyuan 郦道元 (ca. 470–527), and Yan Shigu 颜师古 (581–645). Only folk stories offer some different explanations," noted Duan Yucai. Both Xu Shen 许慎 (ca. 58–147, the author of *Shuowen Jiezi*) and Cai Yong 蔡邕 (133–192) are well-respected scholars. Given their views on the creation of the official script and the development history of the Qin character system, it is reasonable to infer that the Qin State did exert effort to create this script before it unified China. The reason why some records regarding its creation mention Emperor Qin Shi Huang is that people tended to use this title to refer to Ying Zheng 嬴政, sometimes neglecting the fact that he was not known as an emperor before he unified the country. Given this, it is not surprising that the official historical records only show the emperor's efforts to standardise the small-seal script after the unification of China, not those to standardise the official script.

Researchers have long been baffled by the question: why did the Qin Dynasty (221–207 BCE) not take any measures to standardize the widely used official script following the unification of China? If the above inference is consistent with historical facts, the answer to a long-standing problem in Chinese philology has been found. It was unnecessary for the Qin Dynasty to do so, as the standardisation of its official script was completed before the unification of China. This view is supported by a lot of archaeological evidence: many unearthed Qin-Dynasty bamboo slips featuring the official-script characters created before the unification instead of the small-seal script. It can be reasonably inferred that the standardisation of the small-seal script was just an action to highlight the newly established Dynasty's prominent status and power. There were many similar actions taken during this period: the supreme ruler's title was changed from *wang* 王 (king) to *huangdi* 皇

帝 (emperor), the first-person pronoun he used was changed to *zhen* 朕 (pronoun "I"), and the names of his orders were changed from *ming* 命 (order) and *ling* 令 (command) to *zhi* 制 (system) and *zhao* 诏 (decree), respectively.

When Ying Zheng 嬴政 (259–210 BCE) reigned the State of Qin, the characters used by the state were standardised and systematised. First, many variant characters were eliminated, which facilitated the determination of radicals. Second, many new multicomponent characters were created through the addition of semantic components, which further improved the radical system. Third, through modifying existing components and creating new components, some single-component characters that did not conform to the new system, featuring multiple-component characters, were eliminated. Besides, the assimilation and analogisation of components also contributed to the establishment of the radical system. Therefore, it is reasonable to conclude that the radical system of Chinese characters was established in the late Warring States Period.

Notes

1 王力主编：《古代汉语》（修订本）第二册，第166页，北京：中华书局，1981。
   Wang Li, ed.: *Classical Chinese (Revised Edition,* Vol. 2), p. 166, Beijing: Zhonghua Book Company, 1981.
2 王贵元：《汉字笔画系统的形成过程与机制》，《语言科学》，2014 (5).
   Wang Guiyuan: "The Process and Mechanism of the Formation of the Stroke System", *Linguistic Sciences,* 2014 (5).
3 The Archaic writing system to the New-Style system is the transformation of the pictographs to phonetic-semantic symbols, see Wang Guiyuan: "The Motivation and Mechanisms Behind the Evolution of the Chinese Characters", *Linguistic Research,* 2010 (3)
   王贵元：《汉字形体演化的动因与机制》，《语文研究》，2010（3）.
4 杨树达：《积微居甲文说·卜辞锁记》，第 3 页，北京：中国科学院出版，1954.
   Yang Shuda: *Jiweiju Studies on the Oracle-Bone Script and Records About the Oracle-Bone Inscriptions,* p. 3, Beijing: Chinese Academy of Sciences Press, 1954.
5 容庚、瞿润缗：《容庚学术著作全集·殷契卜辞》，第 125 页，北京：中华书局，2011.
   Rong Geng and Qu Runmin: *The Complete Works of Rong Geng · Oracle-Bone Inscriptions of the Shang Dynasty,* p. 125, Beijing: Zhonghua Book Company, 2011.
6 徐中舒主编：《甲骨文字典》，第 82–83 页，成都：四川辞书出版社，1989.
   Xu Zhongshu, ed.: *Oracle Dictionary,* pp. 82–83, Chengdu: Sichuan Lexicographical Publishing House, 1989.
7 高鸿缙：《中国字例》，第 223 页，台湾：三民书局，2008.
   Gao Hongjin: *Chinese Characters,* p. 223, Taiwan: San Min Book Co. Ltd., 2008.
8 This statistic is based on the following materials. (1) *A New Collection of Oracle-Bone Characters* 新甲骨文编 edited by Liu Zhao 刘钊; (2) *A New Collection of Bronze-Inscription Characters* 新编金文编 edited by Wang Guiyuan 王贵元. This is a key social science project funded by the Ministry of Education of the PRC and a complete collection of the bronze-inscription characters from the Shang Dynasty (ca.1600–1046 BCE) to the Warring States Period (475–221 BCE), discovered before February 2012; (3) *A Collection of Chu-State Characters* by Li Shoukui 李守奎《楚文字编》; (4) *A Collection of Qin Characters* by Wang Hui 王辉主编《秦文字编》; (5) *A Collection of Characters on Qin Bamboo Slips Unearthed at Shuihudi* by Zhang Shouzhong 张守中《睡虎地秦简文字编》. Possible statistical errors are caused by the following two aspects: (1) the unearthed documents did not include all the Chinese character forms used back then; (2) the above-mentioned materials may inadvertently ignore some character forms. These errors have a very limited effect on the analysis in this research.

9 陈伟主编：《秦简牍合集·序言》（壹）上，第3页，武汉：武汉大学出版社，2014.
　Chen Wei, ed.: *A Collection of Qin Bamboo Slips* (Vol. 1–1), p. 3, Wuhan: Wuhan University Press, 2014.
10 陈侃理：《里耶秦方与"书同文字"》，《文物》，2014（9）.
　Chen Kanli: "Qin Bamboo Slips Unearthed at Liye and the Standardization of Character Forms", *Cultural Relics*, 2014 (9).
11 赵平安：《试论秦国历史上的三次"书同文"》，《河北大学学报》，1994（3）.
　Zhao Ping'an: "On the Three Qin Campaigns to Standardize Character Form", *Journal of Hebei University*, 1994 (3).
12 From 236 BCE, the Qin State began to invade and occupy part of the land of the Zhao State, the Han State, and the Wei State.

8 Symbolisation

The Mechanism of the Transformation from Archaic Characters to New-Style Characters

I. Introduction

As the oldest known writing system that is still in use today, Chinese characters boast super vitality. How did they keep developing in the past thousands of years? What are the mechanisms that enable ancient Chinese characters to evolve into their current forms? Why do semantic-phonetic characters become mainstream characters? Why are today's Chinese characters often left-right and up-down structured? What is the significance of the transformation of pictographic lines into strokes? Academic circles seldom discuss these problems in depth.

II. Symbolisation

According to their nature, characters can be divided into two categories: *wufu* 物符 (object glyphs) and *cifu* 词符 (word symbols). The former directly depicts images of objects and indirectly represents the pronunciations and meanings of words. The latter, however, often directly represents the pronunciations and meanings of words. The development process where ancient Chinese character forms evolve into their current forms is essentially the transformation of *wufu* into *cifu*. The relationship between Chinese words and ancient/current forms of Chinese characters is shown below.

Figure 8.1 The Relationship Between Chinese Words and Ancient/Current Character Forms

The symbolisation discussed in this study refers to the transformation of image-depicting Archaic characters into New-Style phonetic-semantic characters.

The symbolisation process is crucial for the development of Chinese characters. It is one of the core issues regarding the history of Chinese characters. Its

DOI: 10.4324/9781032622965-8

importance is reflected in two aspects: first, it is the key link in the transformation between the Archaic and the New-Style composition systems; second, it determines the composition system and features of the New-Style composition system.

Early Chinese characters are pictographs depicting images of concrete things, which has been pointed out by many previous studies. Tang Lan 唐兰 (1901–1979) said, "The process where primitive characters evolved into modern characters can be divided into three phases. The first one is the primitive phase where drawings were developed into *xiangxing* 象形 -pictographic characters. The second one is the ancient phase where *xiangyi* 象意 -pictographic characters were invented and perfect. The third one is the near-ancient phase where semantic-phonetic characters were established."[1] He also pointed out that "*xiangxing* and *xiangyi* pictographs that were based on images were used in the ancient phase" and that "semantic-phonetic characters featuring the addition of phonetic components emerged in the near ancient phase."[2] It is worth noting that Tang Lan defines most pictographs as *xiangyi* pictographs. He noted, "*Xiangyi* pictographs are mainstream pictorial characters used in the ancient phase. Before the invention of semantic-phonetic characters, there were mainly *xiangyi* pictographs and a small number of *xiangxing* pictographs in use."[3] The "*xiangyi* pictographs" he discusses are compound pictographs and single-component pictographs that depict images in a more abstract and concise way. Given this, it can be included that Tang Lan 唐兰 (1901–1979) regards all early Chinese characters as pictographs. His view is supported by Yao Xiaosui's statement: "All oracle-bone characters are based on images of objective things."[4]

Xu Shen (ca. 58–147), the Han-Dynasty (202 BCE–220 CE) scholar who wrote the book *Shuowen Jiezi* 说文解字 (An Explication of Written Characters), also held that Chinese characters evolved from pictographs to phonetic-semantic symbols. His attitude is illustrated through the title of his book, which consists of two Chinese words: *shuowen* 说文 and *jiezi* 说文解字. According to the book, the verb *shuo* 说 equals to the verb *jie* 解, both meaning "to explain". Xu Shen named his book this way because he believed that *wen* 文 and *zi* 字 are different. In the preface of his book, he stated his views directly, "What Cangjie 仓颉 (the legendary inventor of Chinese characters) created to express images is named *wen* 文, and characters built through semantic and phonetic combinations are named *zi* 字. The development of *wen* 文 is limited by concrete images, but that of *zi* 字 is infinite." This statement conveys the following three points. First, the development of Chinese characters can be divided into two stages: the first stage featuring the development of *wen* 文 and the second stage boasting the creation of *zi* 字. Second, *wen* 文 tends to be single-component pictographs, but *zi* 字 is usually component combinations. Third, the creation of *wen* 文 is realised through the depiction of images, but that of *zi* 字 is carried out through combinations of character components.

Shuowen Jiezi 说文解字 explains *wen* 文 as pictures and descriptive lines, indicating that its creation is based on images. Such a creation needs to classify objective things first: *niao* 鸟 (long-tailed bird) and *zhui* 隹 (short-tailed bird) are typical examples. The creation of *wen* 文 embodies two of the six means of creating Chinese characters: depiction and representation. In his book, *Notes to Shuowen Jiezi* 说文解字注, the Qing-Dynasty sinologist Duan Yucai 段玉裁 (1735–1815) explains that "pictographs are created through depiction and representation of images." The representation method is to use some lines or dots to represent images. For instance, *ren* 刃 (knife edge) and *yi* 亦 (armpits), both explained as pictographs by *Shuowen Jiezi*, use dots to point out the things they describe.

As to the semantic and phonetic combinations mentioned by *Shuowen Jiezi*, Duan Yucai 段玉裁 gave the following explanation in *Notes to Shuowen Jiezi* 说文解字注: "The semantic and phonetic combinations actually refer to two types of combination, namely the semantic-phonetic compounds and semantic compounds." Wang Yun 王筠 (1784–1854) noted in his book, *Shuowen Jiezi Judu* 说文解字句读 (Interpretations to *Shuowen Jiezi*), that "Xu Shen gives examples for both pictographs known as *wen* 文 and semantic-phonetic characters known as *zi* 字." Interestingly, the character *zi* 字, which consists of the phonetic component *zi* 子 (son) and the component *mian* 宀 (roofed room), originally means "to give birth to". This can be proved by ancient classics such as *Shuowen Jiezi* and *Shan Hai Jing* 山海经 (The Classic of Mountains and Seas). The character *zi* 字 is arranged under the radical *zi* 子 (son) in *Shuowen Jiezi* and explained to be equal to the character *ru* 乳 (give birth to), which is arranged under the radical *yi* 乙 (the second) in the book. It is worth noting that these two characters refer to only human reproduction and that the reproduction of animals is described with the character *chan* 产 (to give birth to). *Shan Hai Jing* records a strange tree named *huangji* 黄棘, which has yellow flowers, round leaves, and orchid-like fruit that caused *bu zi* 不字 (infertility). Guo Pu (276–324) noted, "The *zi* 字 here means 'to give birth to'." Why could the character *zi* 字 be used to describe characters when semantic-compound and semantic-phonetic characters became mainstream characters? This was because the combination methods used to create semantic-compound and semantic-phonetic characters were, to some extent, like the reproduction mode of human beings, which requires the combination of male and female reproductive cells. There are different methods used to realise semantic and phonetic combinations in the development of Chinese characters: the combination of two or more single-component characters or the creation of semantic-compound/semantic-phonetic characters through the addition of semantic/phonetic components. Generally, the latter method is more commonly used. According to the above analysis, the following conclusions can be drawn. First, *zi* 字 refers to semantic-compound and semantic-phonetic characters, excluding compound pictographs. Second, *wen* 文 refers to early pictographic characters, and *zi* 字 refers to characters created through semantic and phonetic combinations after *wen* 文. Third, the development from *wen* 文 to *zi* 字 is essentially the transition from pictographs to phonetic-semantic symbols, which is the symbolisation process.

III. The Beginning and Completion of the Symbolisation Process

The symbolisation is a slow, gradual process beginning within the seal script. The early symbolisation phenomena are mainly manifested in the following two aspects.

(I) The first aspect is the reduction of the pictographic characteristics regarding character components and the compositional structures of characters.

Table 8.1 The Evolution of *Wang* 王 (King), *Nv* 女 (Woman/Girl), *Guang* 光 (Light), and *Jian* 監 (Supervise)

	Shang Dynasty	Early Western Zhou Dynasty	Middle Western Zhou Dynasty	Late Western Zhou Dynasty	Spring and Autumn Period
Wang 王 (king)					
Nv 女 (woman/girl)					
Guang 光 (light)					
Jian 監 (supervise)					

The Shang-Dynasty (ca. 1600–1046 BCE) form of *wang* 王 (king) is a pictographic character depicting a hanging battle-axe with its cutting edge facing downward. In comparison with that, the form of this character created in the late Western Zhou Dynasty (1046–771 BCE) is quite different: the part representing the cutting edge is turned into a horizontal line, making the character not a depiction of a battle-axe any longer. The original form of *nv* 女 (woman/girl) depicts a woman or girl sitting gracefully with her hands crossed on her chest, but its form used in the late Western Zhou Dynasty does not look like a sitting woman or girl: the part depicting the legs is shortened and straightened. In the original form of *guang* 光 (light), which depicts a person holding a lamp with plates containing combustibles, there are up-curved lines depicting the lamp plates. In its late-Western-Zhou-Dynasty form, however, the up-curved lines are replaced by slashes that slope downward. The character *jian* 監 (supervise) originally depicts a person looking down at his or her reflection in a basin of water, but in its late-Western-Zhou-Dynasty form, the structure of the components that originally represent the eye, the body, and the water storage container is changed. Such changes remove nearly all the pictographic characteristics of the original character.

(II) The second aspect is the formalisation of seal script. Such formalisation reaches its acme with the establishment of the small-seal script, which is also considered to be the end of the development of the seal script. Small-seal-script characters have two features. First, they are non-pictographic characters that appear like pictographs. For instance, ⊖ (the small-seal-script character of the sun) and 犬 (the small-seal-script character of the dog). Second, character components have fixed positions and orientations, which facilitates the complete symbolisation of Chinese characters. The removal of pictographic characteristics reflects that the creation of characters does not rely on images anymore.

This study finds that the overall removal of pictographic characteristics seems to begin in the late Western Zhou Dynasty (1046–771 BCE) and that characters used in the Spring and Autumn Period (770–476 BCE) are sub-pictographs. Given this, it concludes that the symbolisation of Chinese characters began in the late Western Zhou Dynasty.[5]

The completion of the symbolisation process is marked by the establishment of *cifu* 词符 (word symbols). The establishment of *cifu* is realised through the removal of pictographic characteristics of *wufu* 物符 (object glyphs). When the removal is completed, the symbolisation is concluded. It is worth noting that the completion of the symbolisation process does not mean that the *cifu* system does not need to be further improved. Nevertheless, there is no direct correlation between the improvements made to the *cifu* system and the symbolisation process. Characters used in the Eastern-Han-Dynasty (25–220) stele inscriptions clearly belong to a *cifu* system since they do not have any seal-script characteristics that are evident in the Western-Han-Dynasty (206–8 BCE) characters. Characters appearing in the unearthed early-Western-Han-Dynasty burial item lists still have obvious seal-script characteristics, such as those unearthed at No.1 Luobowan Tomb in Gui County of Guangxi Province, No.1 and No.3 Mawangdui Tombs in Changsha of Hunan Province, No. 8 and No.9 Fenghuangshan Tombs in Jiangling of Hubei Province, No.26 Xiaojia Caochang Tomb in Sha City of Hubei Province, and No.18 Gaotai Tomb in Jiangling of Hubei Province. There are only a small number of unearthed bamboo and silk manuscripts dating back to the middle Western Han Dynasty, and thus those unearthed at No.5 Huchang Tomb in Hanjiang of Jiangsu Province, which date back to this period, provide a valuable reference. Most of the characters used in the unearthed document do not have any seal-script features, except for *gong* 公 (just), *nv* 女 (woman/girl), *zhi* 致 (deliver), *wu* 吴 (to peal), and *yin* 尹 (administer). Characters used in the late Western Han Dynasty have few seal-script features, which is proved by the following unearthed bamboo and wooden slips: the bamboo slips from No.6 Han Tomb at Yinwan Village, Donghai Country, Jiangsu Province and No.101 Han Tomb in Xupu County, Yizheng City, Jiangsu Province; unearthed wooden slips from the Han Tombs at Mount Huaguo, Lianyungang City, Jiangsu Province; bamboo scrolls from No.6 Han Tomb at Mojuzi Village, Wuwei City, Gansu Province (this tomb dates back to the reign of Wang Mang 王莽, namely from 9 to 25). Among those bamboo scrolls unearthed from No.6 Mojuzi Tomb, there is a bamboo-scroll copy of *Yi li* 仪礼 (Annotations on the Book of Rites and Rituals), which is probably even older than the age of this tomb. Characters used in those bamboo scrolls have very few seal-script features. As to the bamboo scrolls about medicine unearthed at Wuwei 武威医简 and the Wangzhangshi bamboo scrolls 王杖十简 excavated from the No.18 Mojuzi Tomb, they were buried in the early Eastern Han Dynasty, but they were probably created in the late Western Han Dynasty. They also bear characters that have very few seal-script features.

IV. The "Semantic-Phonetic" and "Semantic-Compound" Characters in the Oracle-Bone Script

Theoretically speaking, *cifu* 词符 (word symbols) such as semantic-compound and phonetic-semantic characters could never appear in the period of *wufu* 物符 (object glyphs) when glyphs represented images of objects. Regarding some of such glyphs as semantic-phonetic and semantic-compound characters is as ridiculous as discovering bronze wares in Stone-Age ruins or iron wares in Bronze-Age ruins. Nevertheless, many researchers still hold that there are a certain number of semantic-phonetic and semantic-compound characters among the oracle-bone glyphs. Some researchers even gave specific statistics: for instance, Chen Tingzhu 陈婷珠 once stated that there are 875 semantic compounds and 330 semantic-phonetic compounds among the oracle-bone glyphs found so far.[6] The main reason for this mistake is the influence of inertial thinking. They tend to regard the character composition structures defined by *Shuowen Jiezi*, which is a Han-Dynasty (202 BCE–220 CE) book created to explain the Qin-Dynasty (221–207 BCE) small-seal script, as the universal compositional structures that govern all Chinese characters created in various periods. Therefore, they fail to see the differences between the compositions of Chinese characters of different periods and wrongly apply the rules governing the creation of semantic-phonetic and semantic-compound characters to that of early pictographic characters.

Some researchers have pointed out this problem before, but their views have not been paid attention to or attached importance to. For example, Tang Lan 唐兰 once directly pointed out that there were no semantic compounds among the Chinese characters created before the Qin Dynasty (221–207 BCE). "Xu Shen regards the form of *wu* 武 (martial) used in *Zuo Zhuan* 左传 (Zuo's Commentary on The Spring and Autumn Annals) and that of *xin* 信 (honest) used in *Guliang* 谷梁 (The Guliang School's Records about the Spring and Autumn Period) as semantic compounds. His analysis seems reasonable, but from an academic perspective, it is wrong. He mistook *xiangyi* pictographs as ideographs. The former expresses meaning through drawings, but the latter express meanings that may not be related to the images. For example, there are two components *ge* 戈 (dagger-axe) and *zhi* 止 (toe) used to build the character *wu* 武 (martial). When being used as a semantic component, *zhi* 止 means 'to halt'. Obviously, this component is not used this way in this character. What these two components form is a *xiangyi* pictograph instead of an ideograph," noted Tang Lan.[7] He also argued that "among the Archaic characters created before the Qin Dynasty (221–207 BCE), no one is built with multiple existing characters (a common way to build compound ideographs)."[8] Tang Lan's 唐兰 view is not completely unappreciated by other researchers. Wang Fengyang highly praised his viewpoint by saying, "Tang Lan 唐兰 holds that there are no compound-ideograph Archaic characters, which is an accurate argument that hits the nail on the head."[9]

The difference between *xiangyi* pictographs and semantic compounds is caused by the different functions of their character components: the former boasts pictographic components, and the latter features semantic components. Take the character *wu* 武 (martial) as an example again. Its oracle-bone form consists of two pictographic components *ge* 戈 (dagger-axe) and *zhi* 止 (toe), sketching a basic outline of a walking soldier with a dagger-axe in hand. In the latter forms of the character, the pictographic features of the components are reduced, and they gradually become semantic components: *ge* 戈 means "weapon", and *zhi* 止 means "to halt". Under such circumstances, the character is gradually regarded as a compound ideograph. Qiu Xigui 裘锡圭 also discussed this issue. He said, "There are some multi-compound Archaic characters, often consisting of two or more pictographic components. They express meaning through their pictorial forms. As mentioned above, many researchers regard *li* 立 (stand) and *bu* 步 (step) as compound ideographs when discussing the six means of creating Chinese characters, but these two characters are different from real compound ideographs, such as *wai* 歪 (wry)." In his book, *Liushu Lue* 六书略 (On the Six Means of Creating Characters), the Song-Dynasty scholar Zheng Qiao 郑樵 (1104–1162) lists these two characters as pictographic characters and states the following explanation: *li* 立 (stand) depicts a standing person, and *bu* 步 (step) consists of two "toe" components arranged one after another. His explanation for these two characters is better than that made by *Shuowen Jiezi*. In *Wen Yuan* 文源 (The Origin of Characters), a philological book by Lin Yiguang 林义光 (?-1932), there is such a statement: "*Wu* 武 (martial) and *xin* 信 (honest) are ideographic characters respectively featuring the combination of *zhi* 止 (toe) and *ge* 戈 (dagger-axe) and that of *ren* 人 (person), and ▨ (*she* 射, to shoot), ▨ (*she* 涉, to wade), ▨ (*chong* 舂, to grind grains in mortar), and ▨ (*zheng* 争, to contend) are pictographic characters depicting images. This viewpoint is reasonable."[10] Wang Ning 王宁 discussed this issue through the example of *shi* 示 (manifest). "The oracle-bone form of the character *zhu* 祝 (pray) depicts a person speaking to or reaching out to an idol, and the component representing the idol is the early form of *shi* 示 (manifest). The component *shi* 示 (manifest) is originally pictographic, but it gradually becomes ideographic as it is usually used as a left-placed component to build characters, such as *fu* 福 (happiness), *si* 祀 (worship), *si* 祠 (worship events in spring), *dao* 祷 (to pray) and influenced by the meanings of these multiple-component characters."[11] Wang Ning obviously disagrees with the explanation that *Shuowen Jiezi* makes for *zhu* 祝 (pray). *Shuowen Jiezi* regards this character as a compound ideograph, but Wang Ning 王宁 holds that the component *shi* 示 (manifest) in the character is an ideograph that evolves from a pictograph and that the oracle-bone form of the character must be a pictographic character.

As mentioned above, Tang Lan 唐兰 holds that there are no compound ideographs among the ancient characters created before the Qin Dynasty (221–207 BCE). Wang Fengyang agrees with him but points out a loophole in his point of view. Wang Fengyang said, "Mr. Tang's viewpoint needs to be revised a little: the periods he discusses need to be more clearly divided. For instance, it is correct to say that people did not create any compound ideograph for oracle-bone inscriptions and early bronze inscriptions, but it is incorrect to claim that people in the Spring and Autumn Period (770–476 BCE) and the Warring States Period (475–221 BCE) did not create any compound ideograph. This is because in these two periods, people begin to interpret some multi-component characters as combinations of characters, such as explaining *wu* 武 (martial) and *gong* 公 (just), respectively, as the combination of *zhi* 止 (toe) and *ge* 戈 (dagger-axe) and the antonym of *si* 厶 (private). This way of interpreting characters will inevitably affect the way they create characters."[12] Wang Fengyang's point of view is correct and can be supported by the interpretation of character composition in *Zuo Zhuan*.

The above analysis clarifies that the statement that there are some compound ideographs in the oracle-bone script is wrong. This mistake is caused by neglecting the difference between character components' pictographic and ideographic functions and the tendency of applying the compositional structures of the transformed forms of characters to their original forms.

Different from his views on oracle-bone-script compound ideographs, Tang Lan 唐兰 admitted that there were semantic-phonetic characters in the oracle-bone script. He said, "The formation of semantic-phonetic characters is closely related to the development of society and that of culture. In the oracle inscriptions, there are many characters describing locations or referring to certain women or girls. Based on this, it can be reasonably inferred that the formation of semantic-phonetic characters probably occurred in a matriarchal society."[13] In his statement that "the third one (development phase of Chinese characters) is the near ancient phase where semantic-phonetic characters were established,"[14] the term "near ancient phase" includes Shang (ca. 1600–1046 BCE) and Zhou (1046–256 BCE) dynasties. "The writing systems used by the Shang, Western Zhou, and Eastern Zhou dynasties are early systems of the near ancient phase, which is closely related to those used in the ancient phase," noted Tang Lan 唐兰.[15] As analysed above, there are no oracle-bone-script compound ideographs, which is in line with theoretical inference. Do these oracle-bone-script "semantic-phonetic" characters, which are not in line with theoretical inference, really exist?

In most cases, "semantic-phonetic" characters discovered in oracle-bone inscriptions are pictographic characters mistaken by researchers. For example, the oracle-bone-script forms of *gao* 高 (high or tall), *deng* 登 (get on a vehicle), *diao* 弔 (mourn), *zhu* 祝 (pray), *zhi* 之 (grow), *you* 友 (friend), and *fu* 孚 (capture) are all wrongly defined as semantic-phonetic characters in Chen Tingzhu's *Restudy on the Glyph System of the Shang-Dynasty Oracle-Bone Characters*. Even *Shuowen Jiezi* does not explain them as semantic-phonetic characters. In a few cases, some oracle-bone characters do contain phonetic components. Nevertheless, in these seemingly semantic-phonetic characters, the "semantic" and "phonetic" components cannot be equated with the semantic and phonetic components in real semantic-phonetic characters.

Table 8.2 Comparison Between the Single-Component and Multiple-Component Forms of *Feng* 凤 (Male Phoenix) and *Ji* 鸡 (Chicken)

Feng 凤 (male phoenix)	
Ji 鸡 (chicken)	

134 *Symbolisation*

The original pictographic forms of the characters *feng* 凤 (male phoenix) and *ji* 鸡 (chicken), listed in the second column, look very similar. Their forms in the third column feature the addition of phonetic components, but they are still pictographs that are essentially different from real semantic-phonetic characters whose semantic component is more ideographic than pictographic. In her science of Chinese character composition, Wang Ning 王宁 defined such characters as pictographic-phonetic combinations and real semantic-phonetic characters as ideographic-phonetic characters. She said, "Adding a phonetic component to a pictograph is an important character-constructing method for the oracle-bone script. This method is used to distinguish some pictographs that look very similar or further clarify their meanings. Characters built through this method are pictographic characters with phonetic components."[16] Wang Ning 王宁 also emphasised that "semantic-phonetic characters are combinations of semantic and phonetic components."[17] These judgments made by Wang Ning are correct.

The phonetic components used to build real semantic-phonetic characters are referred to as phonetic radicals. In general, phonetic radicals have two major functions: (1) distinguishing character forms and (2) transcribing the pronunciation of Chinese characters. Some researchers also believe that phonetic radicals have the function of signifying the origins of characters, but this function is not a planned thing: it is actually a phenomenon formed over the process where character derivatives were created through the addition of components. This so-called function is essentially different from the distinguishing and transcribing functions mentioned above. The main function of early phonetic radicals is distinguishing character forms, which has been discussed by many researchers. Xu Zhongshu 徐中舒 said, "Semantic-phonetic characters appeared in the oracle-bone script. Some simple line drawings, or simple pictographs, often confused the character users, so they added phonetic components to distinguish them. For example, the original pictographic forms of *ji* 鸡 (chicken) and *feng* 凤 (male phoenix) both look like birds. To distinguish them, the phonetic components *xi* 奚 (slave) and *fan* 凡 (all) were added to make 奚 and 凡. The original forms of *xing* 星 (star), 晶 and 星, are similar to that of *kou* 口 (mouth) or *ri* 日 (sun), so a phonetic component is added to the original form to make 星 and 星."[18] Chang Zonghao also mentioned, "The original right-placed component of the character *ji* 鷄 (chicken) is a pictographic character that is easily confused with the original pictographic form of the character *feng* 凤/鳳 (male phoenix). Given this, a phonetic component *xi* 奚 (slave) is added to indicate the pronunciation of the character while distinguishing it from similar-looking characters."[19]

When early single-component pictographic characters were developed into compound-pictograph characters, some phonetic components participated in the composition of some characters that could only be regarded as quasi-semantic-phonetic characters. The term "semantic-phonetic characters" refers to characters created after pictographic components were transformed into ideographs. After the same transformation process, compound-pictograph characters were developed into compound-ideograph and semantic-phonetic characters.

It is worth noting that the earliest semantic-phonetic characters that are combinations of pictographs and characters created through the loan method are not real semantic-phonetic characters either. In such characters, the pictographic components are not transformed into semantic components. Only when such a transformation is completed, can these characters become real semantic-phonetic characters.

Previous studies on Chinese characters usually regard the six means of creating Chinese characters as universal rules governing the composition of Chinese characters in different periods. Nonetheless, just as Wang Ning 王宁 observed, "The term 'the six means of creating Chinese characters' actually refers to the rules embodied in the composition of the Qin-Dynasty (221–207 BCE) small-seal-script characters".[20] It is appropriate to use this term to describe the character-making rules of the Qin-Dynasty small-seal script, but it is not applicable to the composition of Chinese characters in all periods.[21] For example, the semantic combination and the semantic-phonetic combination—two of the six means of creating Chinese characters—appeared long after the creation of early Chinese characters. They came into being after the Chinese characters developed to a certain stage.

V. The Motivation Behind the Symbolisation Process

An important symbol of the symbolisation process is the emergence and establishment of the official script. Traditionally, the establishment of this script is attributed to the need to improve office efficiency. *Han Shu* 汉书 (The History of the Han Dynasty) says that "the official script was created to reduce the workload of government workers and officials". In the preface of *Shuowen Jiezi*, there is such a statement. "Back then, the Qin Dynasty burned the works of different schools to ashes, abolished the classics written in archaic-form characters, recruited a large number of people for military service and manual labor, and established a complicated bureaucratic system. For easier writing, the official script came into being, and thus the Archaic writing system was ended." There is no doubt that, with the quickening pace of life, people would naturally ask for a faster writing speed. Nevertheless, the increase in the writing speed could hardly be realised without making any changes to the pictographic characters. This is because the small-seal-script characters just cannot be written as fast as the regular-script characters. If the need for a faster writing speed is the external cause of the establishment of the official script, what is its internal cause? This study finds that the internal cause is the restoration of the Chinese characters' function of recording the Chinese language.

Early Chinese characters depict images instead of recording the Chinese language. What causes such a situation? Given the primitive conditions for early character inventors, it was difficult to create an utterly new set of written symbols for the Chinese language. Regarding the composition of the brand-new written symbols, they needed to first sort out the basic units of the symbols, which was a highly challenging job. Besides, it was not easy for a brand-new symbol system to be accepted and widely spread. Therefore, pictorial symbols that the people usually used to communicate their feelings towards nature and society were adopted in the creation of early Chinese characters. As these pictorial symbols were not enough for recording the Chinese language, more symbols in a similar style were created. Some ethnic minorities in China still use such pictographs, and the Naxi ethnic group is a typical example. The Naxi people use Dongba characters that have two main characteristics. First, these characters cannot fully record the Naxi language. Sentences written in Dongba characters are indeed a series of keywords and needed to be explained by the local clergy named Dongba. Second, Dongba characters and their combinations usually depict images.

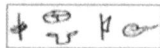

Figure 8.2 Characters Used in *Dongba Sutras*

What is shown above is a sentence from the *Dongba Sutras* 东巴经, consisting of four Dongba characters: ♦ (tree), ♀ (the east), ♯ (gate), and ☞ (*duangui* ghost). The meaning of this sentence is "using wood to shut the eastern *duangui* gate." Interestingly, in terms of word order, the character meaning "gate" shall be placed after the character representing "*duangui* ghost". Nevertheless, the actual situation is just the opposite: "shutting the *duangui* gate" is written as "shutting the gate on *duangui*" to emphasize the function of the gate, which is to keep *duangui* ghost out.[22][23]

The pictographic early Chinese characters were created under certain historical conditions, utilizing primitive pictorial symbols to record the meaning of words. Nonetheless, as written symbols for the Chinese language, they should be more directly related to the language than images. The need to correct this deviation constitutes the internal and essential cause of the transformation of *wufu* 物符 (object glyphs) into *cifu* 词符 (word symbols).

Generally, one system develops into another system only after it is fully developed, and the former system's maturity often provides prerequisites for the development of the latter system. The maturity of the Shang-Dynasty (ca. 1600–1046 BCE) oracle-bone script made it possible for the establishment of a more symbolised written system, and an external cause, namely the gradual decline of the imperial power of the Western Zhou Dynasty (1046–771 BCE), also played a significant role in the transformation of the writing system. The weakening power of the Western Zhou Dynasty led to many ideological changes, including changes in people's attitudes towards the Chinese characters used by the Dynasty.

The symbolisation process is caused by internal and external reasons. The internal reason is the need to make Chinese characters more directly related to the Chinese language than images, and the external reason is the ideological changes including the call for a faster writing speed.

VI. The Pathways to Realise Symbolisation

The symbolisation of Chinese characters is an all-around transformation of the composition system of Chinese characters: it ends the old pictographic system and establishes a new system featuring multicomponent characters and standardised components and characters. The replacement of the old system with the new system is carried out for the following two purposes: recording the pronunciations and meanings of words; making characters conform to certain combination standards. The combination standards refer to the requirements for character component combinations to be phonetic-semantic,

Symbolisation 137

which express abstract things, such as meanings and pronunciations, instead of images. These two purposes are also embodied in the six pathways mentioned below.

(I)   Turning Pictographic Components into Semantic and Phonetic Ones

1.   Turning Pictographic Components into Semantic Ones

The transformation of pictographic components into semantic symbols leads to the removal of their pictographic features, which develops the pictographic characters into official-script characters. Take the evolution of *mai* 買 (buy) as an example.

Table 8.3 The Evolution of the Character *Mai* 買 (Buy)

	Shang Dynasty (ca. 1600–1046 BCE)	*Western Zhou Dynasty (1046–771 BCE)*	*Spring and Autumn Period (770–476 BCE)*	*Eastern Han Dynasty (25–220)*
Mai 買 (buy)				

Shuowen Jiezi explains *mai* 買 (buy) as a combination of *wang* 网 (net) and *bei* 貝 (seashell), and *Mengzi* 孟子 (Mencius) interprets this character as an act of gaining a market advantage by gaining a monopoly. The original meaning of this character is to make money in business, and the original forms of its two components are pictographs depicting a net and a shell, respectively. In the Shang-Dynasty (ca. 1600–1046 BCE) and Western-Zhou-Dynasty (1046–771 BCE) forms of the character, both components are pictographs, but in its Spring-and-Autumn-Period (770–476 BCE) form, the two components are not pictographic enough. In the Eastern-Han-Dynasty (25–220) form of the character, the symbolised components, which are semantic symbols, can hardly evoke the image of a net and that of a shell.

2.   Turning Pictographic Components into Phonetic Ones

In the symbolisation process, some pictographic components are influenced by the trend of phonetic-semantic component combinations. They are re-interpreted as phonetic components. The evolution of the character *ni* 逆 (meet head-on) is a typical example.

Table 8.4 The Evolution of the Character *Ni* 逆 (Meet Head-On)

	Shang Dynasty (ca. 1600–1046 BCE)	*Western Zhou Dynasty (1046–771 BCE)*	*Warring States Period (475–221 BCE)*	*Small Seal Script*	*Eastern Han Dynasty (25–220)*
Ni 逆 (Meet Head-on)					

Shuowen Jiezi describes *ni* 逆 (meet head-on), replaced by *ying* 迎 (meet head-on) in some Chinese dialects, as a combination of the component *chuo* 辵 (walking) and the phonetic component *ni* 屰 (meet head-on). In the first Shang-Dynasty form of this character, the upper part seems to be a person standing on his head, representing a person coming from a distance, and the lower part depicts a pair of feet pointing upwards, representing the other person who meets the first person head-on. The second Shang-Dynasty form of the character consists of two parts: a simplified version of the first form and the component 彳 representing a street. The third form, which is the direct source of the small-seal-script form of 逆, depicts a person walking on a street and meeting someone head-on, but it still consists of pure pictographic components. In the small-seal-script form of the character, there is one semantic component *chuo* 辵 (walking), which consists of 彳 and *zhi* 止 (toe), and one phonetic component 屰. The component 屰 is a symbolised version of the pictographic component representing a person in the character's pictographic forms. It is explained as a phonetic component in *Shuowen Jiezi*.

(II) The Shaping, Quantifying, Positioning, and Orientating of Character Components

The Archaic writing system allows a character to have several forms or variants. In a few cases, a character can have up to 10 different variants. This is a natural phenomenon for a pictographic writing system, as it highlights vivid depictions of images instead of standardised written symbols. The various images and different ways to perceive and depict them then determine that the pictographic characters can be written in different ways. This is like different artists drawing different pictures of the same landscape.

The variants of Archaic characters can be divided into the following four types:

(1) There are character variants caused by different depictions of the same thing. For example, when depicting a person with a character, the writer had the freedom to choose whether to draw the head or feet, whether to draw his kneeling position or standing position, and whether to draw its front or side. The writer could also choose to portray a man or a woman. Under such circumstances, the character depicting a person had multiple forms.
(2) There are character variants caused by differences in the number of components: an Archaic character may consist of one, two, three, or four components.
(3) There are character variants caused by differences in the positions of components: a left-placed component may be placed on the right to make a character variant.
(4) There are character variants caused by differences in the orientations of components: the same component may face the left or the right to make different character variants. The symbolisation process requires the removal of the excessive variants, and this is realised through the shaping, quantifying, positioning, and orientating of character components. To be more specific, "shaping" means to unify the multiple forms of a character into one standard form, and "quantifying", "positioning", and "orientating" mean to determine the quantity, positions, and orientations of components in a character.

The evolution of the character *yu* 御 (manage) can provide some useful insight into the shaping of characters and the quantifying of character components.

Table 8.5 The Evolution of the Character *Yu* 御 (Manage)

Yu 御 (manage)	Western Zhou Dynasty (1046–771 BCE)	Small-Seal Script	Eastern Han Dynasty (25–220)

There are three Western-Zhou-Dynasty (1046–771 BCE) forms of the character *yu* 御 (manage), which have different numbers of components. The first form consists of 彳, *zhi* 止 (toe), *wu* 午 (noon), and *jie* 卩 (seal). The second consists of 彳, *wu* 午 (noon), and *jie* 卩 (seal). The third one contains only two components *wu* 午 (noon) and *jie* 卩 (seal). It is worth noting that *wu* 午 (noon) and *jie* 卩 (seal), which appear in all three forms, are written in different ways in these different forms. In the small-seal script and the writing system used in the Eastern Han Dynasty (25–220), the character has only one form.

The evolution of the character *si* 祀 (worship) embodies the positioning and orientating of character components.

Table 8.6 The Evolution of the Character *Si* 祀 (Worship)

Si 祀 (worship)	Western Zhou Dynasty (1046–771 BCE)	Small-Seal Script	Eastern Han Dynasty (25–220)

In the Western-Zhou-Dynasty (1046–771 BCE), forms of the character *si* 祀 (worship), *shi* 示 (manifest) can be a left- or right-placed component, and *si* 巳 (child) can face right or left. In the character's small-seal-script and Eastern-Han-Dynasty (25–220) forms, these two components appear in fixed positions and face fixed directions.

(III) Rearranging Components and Reinterpreting Component Combinations

The Archaic writing system allows not only single-component characters but also compound pictographs that depict images through its component combinations. In the process of symbolising such characters, their components are rearranged while being turned into semantic or phonetic components. After undergoing this process, the transformed characters are reinterpreted as compound-ideograph or semantic-phonetic characters. The evolution processes of the characters listed below are typical examples.

140 *Symbolisation*

Table 8.7 The Evolution of the Character *She* 涉 (to Wade)

She 涉 (to wade)	Shang Dynasty (ca. 1600–1046 BCE)	Western Zhou Dynasty (1046–771 BCE)	Warring States Period (475–221 BCE)	Small-Seal Script	Eastern Han Dynasty (25–220)

She 涉 (to wade), a character included in *Shuowen Jiezi*, is originally a compound-pictograph character. Its Shang-Dynasty (ca. 1600–1046 BCE) and Western-Zhou-Dynasty (1046–771 BCE) forms depict a river and one foot on each side of it. The component representing the river is later developed into the left-placed component *shui* 水 (water), and the two "foot" components, into *bu* 步 (step). As a result, the compound pictograph is turned into a compound ideograph. The reason the character has two Warring-States-Period (475–221 BCE) forms is that this period is the transition period in the symbolisation process of this character.

The evolution of *jiang* 降 (to descend) is another example of re-combination and re-interpretation.

Table 8.8 The Evolution of the Character *Jiang* 降 (to Descend)

Jiang 降 (to descend)	Shang Dynasty (ca. 1600–1046 BCE)	Western Zhou Dynasty (1046–771 BCE)	Spring and Autumn Period (770–476 BCE)	Small-Seal Script	Eastern Han Dynasty (25–220)

The Shang-Dynasty (ca. 1600–1046 BCE) form of *jiang* 降 (to descend) depicts two feet pointing downwards and walking down the stairs. The forms of this character used during the Western Zhou Dynasty (1046–771 BCE) and the Spring and Autumn Period (770–476 BCE) remain basically the same, except for the merging of the two "foot" components into one component. Therefore, in *Shuowen Jiezi*, the character is explained as a semantic-phonetic character consisting of the merged component and *fu* 阜 (mound) and a phonetic component *jiang* 夅 (to descend).

Tang Lan 唐兰 once discussed such phenomena. "Multicomponent *xiangyi* pictographs seem to be semantic-phonetic characters, but they are not. They are still pictorial characters depicting images. As long as you can infer the meaning of a character from its form, it is a *xiangyi* pictograph. Even if they may be developed into semantic-phonetic characters later, but this does not change the fact that they are originally *xiangyi* pictographs,"[24] noted Tang Lan 唐兰. "Once created, semantic-phonetic characters gained an absolute advantage over pictorial characters.

Under their influence, the *xiangyi* pictographs with phonetic components and a small number of multicomponent pictographs were developed into or reinterpreted as semantic-phonetic characters."[25]

(IV) Modifying Pictographic Characters

There are two main types of modifications that turn pictographs into compound ideographs and semantic-phonetic characters.

1. Component Analogisation

Many components that are not used frequently enough are regarded as analogous to and replaced by commonly used components. The two parties involved in such a replacement shall first share similarity in semantic or phonetic function, and they had better look similar. Take the evolution of *zhe* 折 (to break) as an example.

Table 8.9 The Evolution of the Character *Zhe* 折 (to Break)

Zhe 折 (to break)	Shang Dynasty (ca. 1600–1046 BCE)	Western Zhou Dynasty (1046–771 BCE)	Spring and Autumn Period (770–476 BCE)	Small-Seal Script	Eastern Han Dynasty (25–220)

The original form of *zhe* 折 (to break) depicts the image of *jin* 斤 (a tool for cutting trees) cutting weeds. In its small-seal-script, the "weed" component is replaced by a similar-looking component *shou* 手 (hand) that is also used to indicate an operation done by hand. A similar replacement happens to the original forms of *feng* 鳳/凤 (male phoenix) and *ji* 雞 (chicken). Their pictographic components are replaced by *niao* 鸟 (long-tailed bird) and *zhui* 隹 (short-tailed bird), respectively.

The evolution of *guan* 祼 (a worship ceremony of pouring water to irrigate the field) is also a typical example.

Table 8.10 The Evolution of the Character *Guan* 祼 (a Worship Ceremony of Pouring Water to Irrigate the Field)

Guan 祼 (a worship ceremony of pouring water to irrigate the field)	Shang Dynasty (ca. 1600–1046 BCE)	Western Zhou Dynasty (1046–771 BCE)	Small-Seal Script

The Shang-Dynasty (ca. 1600–1046 BCE) and Western-Zhou-Dynasty (1046–771 BCE) forms of *guan* 祼 (a worship ceremony of pouring water to irrigate

142 *Symbolisation*

the field) depict a person holding a wine vessel for a worship ceremony. With the development of the small-seal script, this pictograph is regarded as a phonetic component and replaced by a similar-looking component *guo* 果 (fruit). *Shuowen Jiezi* explains the small-seal-script form of this character as a combination of the semantic component *shi* 示 (manifest) and the phonetic component *guo* 果 (fruit).

Component analogisation is aimed to replace the complicated, pictographic, and seldomly used character components with frequently used components. In most cases, such a pictographic component is designed for only one character. This type of replacement can be regarded as an improvement made to the character composition system.

2. *Splitting Single-Component Characters*

Most pictographic characters are single-component characters, but most characters expressing the meaning of Chinese words are multiple-component characters. Given this, turning single-component characters into multiple-component characters is also a part of the symbolisation process.

Table 8.11 The Evolution of the Character *Xu* 须 (Facial Hair)

	Shang Dynasty (ca. 1600–1046 BCE)	Western Zhou Dynasty (1046–771 BCE)	Spring and Autumn Period (770–476 BCE)	Warring States Period (475–221 BCE)	Small-Seal Script
Xu 须 (facial hair)					

The original form of *xu* 须 (facial hair) is a single-component pictograph highlighting a man's facial hair. Its small-seal-script form is a multiple-component character that is explained by *Shuowen Jiezi* as a combination of *ye* 頁 (head) and *shan* 彡 (hair).

(V) Adding a Semantic or Phonetic Component

The Shang-Dynasty (ca. 1600–1046 BCE) form of the character *chi* 齿 (teeth) is a single-component pictograph. Its Warring-States-Period (475–221 BCE) form includes a phonetic component *zhi* 止 (toe). A semantic component *jin* 金 (metal) is added to another Shang-Dynasty single-component pictograph *ge* 戈 (dagger-axe) to make the character's Warring-States-Period form. Generally, in the former case, the original pictographic form of the character is turned into a semantic component in the transformed form of the character, and in the latter case, the original pictograph is turned into a phonetic component. Having been transformed in these two ways, pictographs become semantic-phonetic characters.

Table 8.12 The Evolution of *Chi* 齿 (Teeth) and *Ge* 戈 (Dagger-Axe)

	Shang Dynasty (ca. 1600–1046 BCE)	Warring States Period (475–221 BCE)
Chi 齿 (teeth)		
Ge 戈 (dagger-axe)		

Previous studies generally believe that the addition of semantic and phonetic components is intended to better express the pronunciations and meanings of words. In fact, there is another important reason for such an addition: the trend of building multicomponent characters through phonetic-semantic combinations.

(VI) Creating New Characters

In some cases, old pictographs are replaced by newly created compound-ideograph or semantic-phonetic characters.

Table 8.13 The Evolution of the Character *Zhi* 祇 (to Revere)

	Shang Dynasty (ca. 1600–1046 bce)	Western Zhou Dynasty (1046–771 BCE)	Spring and Autumn Period (770–476 BCE)	Warring States Period (475–221 BCE)	Small-Seal Script	Eastern Han Dynasty (25–220)
Zhi 祇 (to revere)						

The forms of the character *zhi* 祇 (to revere) used in and before the Warring States Period (475–221 BCE) are compound-pictograph characters. Its small-seal-script form is a semantic-phonetic character that has no connection to the previous forms of the character. *Shuowen Jiezi* 说文解字 explains this newly created form as a combination of *shi* 示 (manifest) and the phonetic component *di* 氐 (low).

Among the six above-mentioned pathways to realise the symbolisation of characters are modifying pictographic characters, adding a phonetic or semantic component, and creating new characters remain mainstream through the whole symbolisation process. They are used to symbolise existing pictographs as well as to create new characters. Different from them, the other three pathways are used only to realise the symbolisation process and cannot be used to create new characters: turning pictographic components into ideographs and phonetic ones; the shaping, quantifying, positioning, and orientating of character components; and rearranging components and reinterpreting component combinations. The symbolisation process is realised by creating new characters and adding a phonetic or semantic component is completed in an instant, but that is also realised through modifying pictographic characters that may be completed gradually or instantaneously.

144 *Symbolisation*

Symbolisation actualized through the other three pathways is usually completed in a gradual way over time.

VII. Changes Caused by Symbolisation to the Composition System of Chinese Characters

The symbolisation process is essentially a change in the creation basis for the composition of Chinese characters: the depiction of images is replaced by the expression of pronunciations and meanings. This process leads to the following series of changes in the composition system of Chinese characters.

(I) The Formation of the Strokes

Strictly speaking, the lines and dots used to write Archaic characters cannot be referred to as Chinese character strokes because they are basically equivalent to lines and points in painting. The character strokes are created to increase the writing speed, and the premise of fast writing is that Chinese characters do not rely on complicated pictographic forms to express meanings. Therefore, the replacement of pictographs with phonetic-semantic symbols constitutes an important precondition for the formation of strokes. In other words, the fundamental reason for the emergence of Chinese character strokes is the symbolisation of Chinese characters, which turns pictographs into phonetic-semantic symbols.

(II) Inaccurate Phonetic Components

The phonetic components of often-used semantic-phonetic characters are frequently unable to express pronunciation accurately. According to Li Yan and Kang Jiashen, only 55.68% of the currently used semantic-phonetic characters have basically accurate phonetic components: 37.51% of the currently used semantic-phonetic characters have phonetic components that accurately express the pronunciation and tone of the characters, and 18.17% of them have phonetic components that only accurately indicate the pronunciations.[26] Previous studies usually give two reasons for this phenomenon: the difference between ancient and current pronunciations, and the careless choice of phonetic components. This study attributes this phenomenon mainly to the symbolisation of Chinese characters. Compared with the newly created semantic-phonetic characters, the semantic-phonetic characters created through other pathways of the symbolisation usually have inaccurate phonetic components. Take the evolution of *xiu* 羞 (to offer) as an example. The forms of this character used in and before the Warring States Period (475–221 BCE) consist of two components: *yang* 羊 (sheep and goats) and *you* 又 (again). In these forms, *you* 又 (again) is equivalent to *shou* 手 (hand), so this character means "to offer". During the symbolisation process, this character is turned into a semantic-phonetic character, and its component *you* 又 (again) is replaced by *niu* 丑 (a knot that can be undone by a pull), because it has a pronunciation similar to that of the character.

Table 8.14 The Evolution of the Character *Xiu* 羞 (to Offer)

Xiu 羞 (to offer)	Shang Dynasty (ca. 1600–1046 BCE)	Western Zhou Dynasty (1046–771 BCE)	Spring and Autumn Period (770–476 BCE)	Warring States Period (475–221 BCE)	Small-Seal Script

In terms of pronunciation, *niu* 丑 (a knot that can be undone by a pull) and *xiu* 羞 (to offer) are two syllables sharing the same *yunmu* 韵母 (the final part of a Chinese syllable).[27] As their *shengmu* 声母 (the initial part of a Chinese syllable) are quite different, the view that *niu* 丑 is the original phonetic component of *xiu* 羞, which is shared by Yan Xuejiong and Yahontov, is wrong.[28] These two researchers did not take into consideration the transformation of characters cause by the symbolisation process.

(III) Mainstream Semantic-Phonetic Combinations

Semantic-phonetic characters account for more than 80% of currently used Chinese characters. This is because they could best achieve the purpose of the New-Style writing system: recording the pronunciations and meanings of words with simplified written symbols. The creation of semantic-phonetic characters is also a result of the symbolisation of Chinese characters.

(IV) The Further Development of the Binary Structure

The Binary Structure of Chinese characters refers to the most often-seen two-component combinations: a character often consists of two components. It has been the mainstream structure of character composition since the early development stage of Chinese characters because it allows characters to contain more information in a concise form. The symbolisation process leads to the transformation of many pictographic characters into two-component characters, and many new two-component characters are created during this process. Because of the symbolisation process, the Binary Structure has basically dominated the composition of Chinese characters. Most Chinese characters are left-right or up-down structured, embodying the Binary Structure. Take *zhui* 追 (to chase after) as an example.

Table 8.15 The Evolution of the Character *Zhui* 追 (to Chase After)

Zhui 追 (to chase after)	Western Zhou Dynasty (1046–771 BCE)	Spring and Autumn Period (770–476 BCE)	Warring States Period (475–221 BCE)	Small-Seal Script	Eastern Han Dynasty (25–220)

146 *Symbolisation*

The forms of the character *zhui* 追 (to chase after) used in and before the Warring States Period (475–221 BCE) contain three components: 彳, *zhi* 止 (toe), and *dui* 𠂤 (to pile up). In its small-seal-script form, the components 彳 and *zhi* 止 (toe) are merged into one component *chuo* 辵 (walking). *Shuowen Jiezi* explains this form as a combination of *chuo* 辵 (walking) and the phonetic component *dui* 𠂤 (to pile up)

It should be noted that the further development of the Binary Structure also leads to the development of the compositional structure of characters: the one-level compositional structure is developed into a multilevel hierarchical structure. For instance, the early forms of *zhui* 追 (to chase after) are a simple combination of three components 彳, *zhi* 止 (toe), and *dui* 𠂤 (to pile up), and they have no subcomponents. Its later forms, however, feature a multilevel hierarchical structure: among the two components of the character *chuo* 辵 (walking) and *dui* 𠂤 (to pile up), *chuo* 辵 (walking) can be further broken up into subcomponents 彳 and *zhi* 止 (toe).

VIII. Conclusion

Most of the ancient pictographic writing systems in the world have been replaced by alphabetic writing systems, but Chinese characters have survived. The above analysis shows that the most important reason for the survival is the timely innovation and transformation of the Chinese writing system. Different from alphabetic writing systems that record only pronunciations, transformed Chinese characters, mainly semantic-phonetic and compound-ideograph characters, record both pronunciations and meanings. As compound-ideograph characters record only meanings, so semantic-phonetic characters become the mainstream of the transformed characters. While maintaining the tradition of expressing meaning through character forms, the current Chinese writing system allows the subcomponents of characters to be further simplified in writing. The currently used Chinese characters can be written quickly, meeting the needs of a fast-paced world. When the seal script featuring pictographic and complicated-looking characters is replaced by the official script, the curvy line and various dots used for writing are straightened and transformed into abstract and easy-to-write strokes, and the stroke order is created to solve the problems that some seal-script lines are written from right to left or from bottom to top.[29] Thanks to these changes, it is hard to fault the current Chinese writing system for being not ergonomic or efficient enough, which helps the system to survive instead of being replaced by an alphabetic writing system.

Notes

1 唐兰：《古文字学导论》（增订本），第 83 页，济南：齐鲁书社，1981。
 Tang Lan: *Introduction to Chinese Paleography (Revised Edition)*, p. 83, Jinan: Shandong Qilu Press, 1981.
2 唐兰：《中国文字学》，第 61 页，上海：上海古籍出版社，2005。
 Tang Lan: *Chinese Philology*, p. 61, Shanghai: Shanghai Classics Publishing House, 2005.
3 唐兰：《中国文字学》，第 62 页，上海：上海古籍出版社，2005。
 Tang Lan: *Chinese Philology*, p. 62, Shanghai: Shanghai Classics Publishing House, 2005.

4 姚孝遂：《姚孝遂古文字论集》，第 58 页，北京：中华书局，2010。
Yao Xiaosui: *Collection of Studies on Ancient Chinese Characters by Yao Xiaosui*, p. 58, Beijing: Zhonghua Book Company, 2010.
5 王贵元：《汉字发展史的几个核心问题》，《中国语文》，2013（1）．
Wang Guiyuan: "Core Issues Regarding the Evolution of Chinese Characters", *Studies of the Chinese Language*, 2013 (1).
6 陈婷珠：《殷商甲骨文字形系统再研究》，第 251 页，上海：上海人民出版社，2010．
Chen Tingzhu: *Restudy on the Glyph System of the Shang-Dynasty Oracle-Bone Characters*, p. 251. Shanghai: Shanghai People's Publishing House, 2010.
7 唐兰：《中国文字学》，第 57 页，上海：上海古籍出版社，2005．
Tang Lan: *Chinese Philology*, p. 57, Shanghai: Shanghai Classics Publishing House, 2005.
8 唐兰：《中国文字学》，第 58 页，上海：上海古籍出版社，2005．
Tang Lan: *Chinese Philology*, p. 58, Shanghai: Shanghai Classics Publishing House, 2005.
9 王凤阳：《汉字学》，第 514 页，长春：吉林文史出版社，1989．
Wang Fengyang: *Chinese Philology*, p. 514, Changchun: Jilin Literature and History Press, 1989.
10 裘锡圭：《文字学概要》，第 99 页，北京：商务印书馆，1988．
Qiu Xigui: *A Summary of Chinese Philology*, p. 99, Beijing: The Commercial Press, 1988.
11 王宁：《汉字构形学讲座》，第 51 页，上海：上海教育出版社，2002．
Wang Ning: *Lectures on the Composition of Chinese Characters*, p. 51, Shanghai: Shanghai Educational Publishing House, 2002.
12 王凤阳：《汉字学》，第 514 页，长春：吉林文史出版社，1989．
Wang Fengyang: *Chinese Philology*, p. 514, Changchun: Jilin Literature and History Press, 1989.
13 唐兰：《中国文字学》，第 78 页，上海：上海古籍出版社，2005．
Tang Lan: *Chinese Philology*, p. 78, Shanghai: Shanghai Classics Publishing House, 2005.
14 唐兰：《古文字学导论》（增订本），第 83 页，济南：齐鲁书社，1981．
Tang Lan: *Introduction to Chinese Paleography (Revised Edition)*, p. 83, Jinan: Shandong Qilu Press, 1981.
15 唐兰：《古文字学导论》（增订本），第 84 页，济南：齐鲁书社，1981．
Tang Lan: *Introduction to Chinese Paleography (Revised Edition)*, p. 84, Jinan: Shandong Qilu Press, 1981.
16 王宁：《汉字构形学讲座》，第 63 页，上海：上海教育出版社，2002．
Wang Ning: *Lectures on the Composition of Chinese Characters*, p. 63, Shanghai: Shanghai Educational Publishing House, 2002.
17 王宁：《汉字构形学讲座》，第 64 页，上海：上海教育出版社，2002．
Wang Ning: *Lectures on the Composition of Chinese Characters*, p. 64, Shanghai: Shanghai Educational Publishing House, 2002.
18 徐中舒：《徐中舒历史论文选辑》，第 1406 页，北京：中华书局，1998．
Xu Zhongshu: *Selected Historical Papers by Xu Zhongshu*, p. 1406, Beijing: Zhonghua Book Company, 1998.
19 常宗豪：《当前的汉字规范化问题》，《中国语文研究》，1980（1）．
Chang Zonghao: "Problems Existing in the Current Effort to Standardize Chinese Characters", *Studies in Chinese Linguistics*, 1980 (1).
20 王宁：《汉字构形学讲座》，第 17 页，上海：上海教育出版社，2002．
Wang Ning: *Lectures on the Composition of Chinese Characters*, p. 17, Shanghai: Shanghai Educational Publishing House, 2002.
21 王宁：《汉字构形学讲座》，第 16 页，上海：上海教育出版社，2002．
Wang Ning: *Lectures on the Composition of Chinese Characters*, p. 16, Shanghai: Shanghai Educational Publishing House, 2002.
22 Translator's note: *duangui* is a word transliterated according to its Mandarin Chinese pronunciation.

23 邓应章、常丽丽：《纳西东巴经特殊字序研究》，《中央民族大学学报》，2014（4）.
Deng Yingzhang and Chang Lili: "A Study on the Special Character Order of the Naxi Dongba Sutras", *Journal of the Minzu University of China*, 2014 (4).
24 唐兰：《中国文字学》，第62页，上海：上海古籍出版社，2005.
Tang Lan: *Chinese Philology*, p. 62, Shanghai: Shanghai Classics Publishing House, 2005.
25 唐兰：《中国文字学》，第78页，上海：上海古籍出版社，2005.
Tang Lan: *Chinese Philology*, p. 78, Shanghai: Shanghai Classics Publishing House, 2005.
26 李燕、康加深：《现代汉语形声字声符研究》，《现代汉字学参考资料》，第152页，北京：北京大学出版社，2001.
Li Yan and Kang Jiashen: "A Study of the Phonetic Components of Modern Chinese Semantic-Phonetic Characters", *References for Studies on Modern Chinese Characters*, p. 152, Beijing: Peking University Press, 2001.
27 严学宭：《原始汉语复声母类型的痕迹》，《古汉语复声母论文集》，第136页，北京：北京语言文化大学出版社，1998.
Yan Xuejiong: "Traces Left by the Polyconsonant Initial Sounds of Early Chinese Characters", *A Collection of Papers on Polyconsonant Initial Sounds of Ancient Chinese Characters*, p. 136, Beijing: Beijing Language and Culture University Press, 1998.
28 雅洪托夫：《上古汉语的复辅音声母》，《古汉语复声母论文集》，第304页，北京：北京语言文化大学出版社，1998.
Yahontov: "The Polyconsonant Initial Sounds of Early Chinese Characters", *A Collection of Papers on Polyconsonant Initial Sounds of Ancient Chinese Characters*, p. 304, Beijing: Beijing Language and Culture University Press, 1998.
29 王凤阳：《汉字学》，第222–223页，长春：吉林文史出版社，1989.
Wang Fengyang: *Chinese Philology*, pp. 222–223, Changchun: Jilin Literature and History Press, 1989.

9 On the Official Script Transformation[1]

I. Geographical and Factional Issues about the Official Script Transformation

During the Warring States Period (475–221 BCE), people of different states or regions used different characters. Given the geographical and factional differences, the Warring-States-Period characters can be classified into several types, and there are several different classification methods: (1) Qin characters, Chu characters, Jin characters, Qi characters, and Yan characters; (2) western-region characters and eastern-region characters; (3) Qin characters and six-state characters. Was the official script transformation a common phenomenon occurring in all these types or a phenomenon unique to Qin characters? This has always been a highly controversial issue. Some researchers argue that this phenomenon happened only to Qin characters. For instance, in *A Course in Philology* 文字学教程, Jiang Baochang 姜宝昌 defines the official script transformation as a process of transforming the original Qin seal script into the official script,[2] and in *On the Official Script Transformation* 隶变纵横谈, Zhao Ping'an 赵平安 defined it as a process of transforming characters that have seal-script elements into archaic official-script characters and then into the bafen-official-script characters.[3] Some researchers hold that the official script transformation occurred to all the character types used in the Warring States Period. Tang Lan 唐兰 (1901–1979) said in *Chinese Philology* 中国文字学, "The simplified or cursive character forms appearing in all the six states' writing systems are early experimental official-script forms."[4] He also noted, "As the characters of the six states gained increasingly distinct local characteristics, people at that time even felt the need to unify all types of characters. Except for the pictorial characters, there was a common evolutionary trend in the development of characters in all states: simplification. People began using cursive forms when carving or writing characters, which initiated the official script transformation."[5] In *The Calligraphic Art of Chu-State Silk Manuscripts* 楚帛书之书法艺术, Rao Zongyi 饶宗颐 said, "*Liuti Shulun* 六体书论 (The Six Script Types and Their Calligraphic Styles), a book written by a Tang-Dynasty calligrapher and calligraphy theorist named Zhang Huaiguan 张怀瓘, names Cheng Miao 程邈 as the inventor of the official script, which is also known as *zhenshu* 真书. The so-called Qin and Han official script do not all originate from the Qin state, so this statement probably describes only the origin of the Qin seal script. The characters on the Chu-State Silk Manuscript that date back to this period also have strong seal-script characteristics: they are in roughly square shapes and structured with abstract strokes, looking like early forms of the Han official script. Given this, it may be incorrect to give Cheng Miao 程邈 all the credits for the establishment of the official script."[6] Apart from clarifying that characters of the six states also underwent the official script transformation, Tang Lan and Rao Zongyi also pointed out that the characters of the six states were also the source of the standard official-script characters. This view is unacceptable to the advocates for the official script transformation unique to the Qin characters. Apart from the researchers who hold the above-mentioned two seriously opposing views, there are some other researchers who have also noticed the official-seal transformation phenomena in the six states but have not asserted that the transformed characters of the six states are early forms of the standard official-script characters. "The Dialectical Development of Ancient Chinese Characters", an academic paper by Guo Moruo 郭沫若 (1892–1978), notices the difference between the seal-script characters written on the Chu-State Silk Manuscript and those carved on bronze wares in the Warring States Period and concludes that the former shares more similarities with the standard official script as it is more simplified and squarish in shape.[7] *Ancient Chinese Philology*, a book by Jiang Liangfu 姜亮夫, contains this statement: "There are many simplified- or cursive-form characters among the characters used by the six states of the late Warring States Period, which shares a lot of similarities with the standard official-script characters."[8]

There is a reason for the emergence of the above-mentioned two opposing viewpoints. The fact that there are similar official script transformation phenomena in the characters used in the states makes some researchers believe in the universality of the official script transformation. Nevertheless, researchers who hold the opposite view usually emphasize another fact that the Qin and Han official script was developed based on Qin characters for the purpose of unifying the written symbols used across the country and define only this process as the official script transformation. Zhao Ping'an 赵平安 said, "The conclusion that the official script transformation is unique to the Qin characters is obtained by the backwards-deduction method.[9] Given that the State of Qin ended the Warring States Period and replaced the other six states' characters with its own characters during the process of annexing, the official script used in the unified country reigned by the Qin Dynasty (221–207 BCE) is naturally regarded as a successor of the Qin writing system."[10] Wang Zhiping 王志平 and Dong Kun 董琨 also point out in "Research on Characters Used in Bamboo and Silk Manuscript" 简帛文献文字研究 that the reason we have a clearer understanding of the evolutionary history of the official script now is the excavation of a large number of Qin documents. Tang Lan 唐兰 who holds that "the simplified or cursive character forms appearing in all the six states' writing systems are early experimental official-script forms" is correct about the beginning time of the official script transformation, which is the Warring States Period (475–221 BCE). Nevertheless, the logic of his judgment about the source of the standard official-script characters is not rigorous enough. Nowadays, academic circles generally accept this view: the popular-form characters transformed from standard-character forms for convenient writing by the people of the Qin state constitute the foundation for the establishment of the official script.[11] There is not enough evidence to show that the transformed characters of the six states are also the source of the Qin and Han official script, but it is a fact that the six states' characters underwent a similar official script transformation. Researchers, who insist that the official script transformation is unique to the Qin characters because the official script evolves from Qin characters, make such a mistake: they do not strictly distinguish the two concepts, namely the official script and the official script transformation. These two concepts are related to each other, but they discuss issues of different natures. The official script transformation describes a widespread trend of transforming characters in all the states in the late Warring States Period, but the official script defined a writing font developed from Qin characters. Therefore, it is wrong to deny the universality of the official script transformation because of the fact that the six state's transformed characters failed to be handed down. Transformed Qin characters are mainly simplified characters, and similar simplification phenomena also occurred in the characters of the six states. If the State of Qin had failed to unify the country, the characters of different states would have also been simplified. Such changes are systematic changes in the entire Chinese writing system and would not be influenced by geographical differences. Just as Qiu Xigui 裘锡圭 said, "During the Warring States Period (475–221 BCE), popular-form characters of the six states look very much like the official-script characters. Typical examples are those simple and squarish characters appearing on the Chu-state bamboo and silk manuscripts (Guo Moruo 郭沫若: "The Dialectical Development of Ancient Chinese Characters" 古代文字之辩证的发展, *Chinese Archaeology* 考古学报, 1972, issue 3, p. 8). In pottery inscriptions of the State of Qi, the component 大 is written as *da* 大 (big) in the character 杏, and the component 木 is written as *mu* 木 (wood) in the character *tang* 棠 (a kind of flowering tree). Similar simplification methods are also used to transform some seal-script characters into official-script ones. Even if the State of Qin had failed to unify China, the characters of the six states would have also gradually gained new fonts that are similar to the official script."[12] So, all types of Chinese characters used amid the Warring States Period experienced a common development process, as they shared the same origin, and their users and their environment did not change fundamentally. Although there were some character differences caused by geographical differences, the writing system remained consistent across the country.

The replacement of pictographic lines and dots with simplified character strokes is a phenomenon observed in every state's character system. It is appropriate to name this change the official script transformation: this term refers to a transformation towards stroke-structured characters of the entire Chinese writing system, although its name comes from the Qin and Han official script. To some extent, the official script is an important symbol. Just as Wang Ning 王宁 said in *A Summary of Chinese Philology* 汉字学概要, "The replacement of the seal script with the official script is a great leap in the development of Chinese characters. It ends the complicated Archaic writing system based on depictions of images and starts the New-Style Chinese writing system. In view of its significance, this replacement is given a special name—the official script transformation—in Chinese philology."[13] Such a replacement happened not only in the Qin state but also in the six states, so it is unnecessary to use two terms to name the same phenomenon. Besides, the term "the official script transformation" is widely recognised, and it will be difficult for new terms to be accepted.

The above-mentioned controversy over the official script transformation came with many unearthed Warring-States-Period manuscripts. It involves a deeper understanding of the official script transformation regarding its nature and causes.

II. The Nature and Cause of the Official Script Transformation

Chinese characters are the writing symbols of the Chinese language. Logically speaking, their creation shall be based on the language, to be more specific, the sounds and/or the meanings of Chinese words. However, it was very difficult to build such a writing system from scratch. First, the composition of the Chinese language needs to be clearly and accurately analysed. Second, efforts must be exerted to popularise and learn the new writing symbols. For convenience and efficiency, existing pictographs and pictorial marks were somehow adopted and given new functions in the creation of early Chinese characters. Characters created in this way were widely accepted by people who got used to expressing feelings and communicating ideas with drawings and pictorial symbols. At that time, when people relied on pictures to communicate and could easily acquire information from drawings, creating characters with drawings to record the language was probably just the people's collective consciousness. These pictographic characters were collected by some people at a certain time, forming the initial aggregation of Chinese characters.

Just like the ancient writing symbols used by many ethnic minorities of China, early Chinese characters could not offer a systematic approach to fully recording the Chinese language. To improve this function, the existing early character forms were not enough, and new characters had to be created.

As the judgement that the development of pictorial written symbols led to the creation of Chinese characters is widely recognised, many questions arise. Are the pottery carvings in the Neolithic Age Chinese characters? Are the inscriptions on some bronze objects Chinese characters or pictures? The answers to such questions are related to the nature and causes of the official script transformation. Early Chinese characters depicted images but as written symbols recording the Chinese language, they should have represented the basic elements of language instead of just images. The appearance of early Chinese characters had its historical rationality, but this conflict would inevitably lead to the transition from pictographs to phonetic-semantic symbols or the official script transformation, especially when the development of society put high requirements for the Chinese writing system. This is the nature and cause of the official script transformation.

III. The Duration of the Official Script Transformation

Researchers generally believe that the official script transformation began in the middle or late Warring States Period (475–221 BCE), but Zhao Ping'an put forward a more accurate statement. He holds that the official script transformation started in the middle Warring States Period because he regards some cursive forms of Qin characters as archaic-official-script characters and advances the time of establishing the official script.[14] To determine the starting time of the official script transformation, it is necessary to take into consideration the following two issues:

(1) The differences caused by different writing instruments; and
(2) The number and the transformation degree of transformed characters.

Regarding the first issue, there are squarish turnings and simplified strokes in the carved Chinese characters, whose appearance is caused by the inconvenience of using a carving knife to create curvy lines instead of any transformation of characters. For instance, in the Shang-Dynasty (ca. 1600–1046 BCE) oracle-bone inscriptions, *si* 巳 (child) is also carved as 󰀀 and *mu* 木 (wood) is carved as 󰀁.

As to the second issue, researchers need to be as careful as possible when determining the transformation degree of characters. Up to now, all the studies on the character forms created through the official script transformation in the middle Warring States Period have been based on characters carved on weapons. Whether those character forms can be used as evidence for the official script transformation still needs to be considered. Given the studies on the bronze inscriptions of the Warring States Period, it is more appropriate to conclude that the official script transformation began in the late Warring States Period. Qiu Xigui 裘錫圭 arrives at the same conclusion in his book *A Summary of Chinese Philology* 文字学概要.

The ending time of the official script transformation is also a controversial issue. "When determining the ending time of the official script transformation, it is essential to first clarify what official script we are talking about. Is it the archaic official script, the *fen* official script, or the new official script? This problem has not been solved so far. The transformation into the archaic official script ended in the Warring States Period (475–221 BCE), that into the *fen* official script concluded in the Western Han Dynasty (206–8 BCE), and that into the new official script was completed during the Sui (581–618) and Tang (618–907) dynasties. My viewpoint is that it ended in the Sui (581–618) and Tang (618–907) dynasties," noted Lu Xixing 陆锡兴.[15]

"Researchers tend to think that the official script transformation was completed in the Han Dynasty (206 BCE–220 CE). This misunderstanding is caused by an inadequate understanding of the new official script. Different from the seal script, the official script has a broad connotation. It includes not only the *fen* official script used in the Han Dynasty (202 BCE–220 CE) but also the new official script, namely the regular script used after the Han Dynasty. The evolution from the Qin official script to the Han official script is just half of the official script transformation. The other half is the evolution from the *fen* official script to the regular script, which lasted from the last years of the Han Dynasty to the Tang Dynasty (618–907)."[16]

Zhao Ping'an observed, "The regular-script transformation is, to some extent, a continuation of the official script transformation, but they are two different concepts."[17]

Some researchers also hold such a viewpoint: in terms of character composition, the official script transformation divides the evolution of Chinese characters into two stages, namely the first stage featuring seal-script characters created based on images and the second stage boasting phonetic-semantic characters such as those belonging to the official script and the other script types created after it. Qi Gong 启功 said, "We notice that the character-like symbols on unearthed potteries from the Dawenkou Culture (ca. 4100–2600 BCE) as well as the surviving ancient Chinese fonts and small-seal characters all feature curved strokes and roundish shapes. Characters on the roughly inscribed decree slabs of the Qin Dynasty (221–207 BCE), however, begin appearing squarish, characterized by straight strokes and square corners. On the Qin-Dynasty slabs bearing the imperial laws, we can see even more straight strokes and squarish shapes, which indicate the creation of a new-style writing system that is still in use today. Therefore, we have a reason to name the character fonts created before and after the emergence of the new-style writing system seal-script fonts and official-script fonts, respectively. The regular-script fonts and Song typeface we use now are all evolved from the official-script fonts."[18] Tang Lan further pointed out that the great difference between ancient Chinese characters and modern and contemporary Chinese characters was that the former featured seal-script fonts and the latter boasted official-script fonts or cursive script fonts.[19]

Chen Mengjia 陈梦家 described the seal script as a witness to the end of ancient characters and the official script as a pioneer of modern and contemporary characters.[20] Archaeological evidence shows that many character variants appearing in Dunhuang documents and stele inscriptions of different dynasties have their origins in Qin and Han manuscripts, so there is some truth in Lu Xixing's view. Nevertheless, he might wrongly equate the official script transformation with the official-regular character system. The official script transformation is a process of transforming or replacing seal script characters. In this sense, this transformation process was completed in the Eastern Han Dynasty (25–220), as characters used back then had little seal-script features. The second evolution stage of the Chinese character lasts from the official script transformation to the establishment of currently used Chinese characters. During this stage, the transformation of the characters is guided by two rules: carrying our multitype modification and pursuing structural balance. The former highlights innovation and the replacement of the old system with a new system, leading to the creation of various new character forms. The latter emphasizes the perfection of the character system, leading to the removal or survival of various component variants. These two rules are embodied throughout the evolution stage: in the beginning, it is the multitype modification that plays a more significant role, and after that, more importance is attached to structural balance. To be more specific, the period from the official script transformation to the Eastern Han Dynasty (25–220) features the complete removal of seal-script elements in the writing system and the creation of new character forms and the principles for convenient writing. Although this period does not remove all the variants, it does decrease their number remarkably and prevent the creation of new variants. Since the Three Kingdoms (220–280), the adjustments and improvements made to the writing system are just intended to enhance its systematicity and increase its maturity. Given this, I agree with Zhao Ping'an about the ending time of the official script transformation, which is in the last years of the Eastern Han Dynasty.

IV. The Official Script Transformation and the Popular-Form Characters

Researchers generally agree that it was the official script transformation that led to the creation of many popular-form characters. "The Emergence of the Popular-Form Characters from the Perspective of the Official Script Transformation" 从隶变看俗字的产生 by Zhao Liwei 赵立伟 contains such a statement: "While simplifying the Chinese characters for convenient writing, the official script transformation somehow processed the various components and modifications into many popular-form characters."[21] "Types and Causes of the Popular-Form Characters Used in the Han-Dynasty Stele Inscriptions" 汉碑俗字的类型及其成因探析 by Jing Xuefa 井学法 points out that the official script transformation is the cause of the emergence of many popular-form characters in the Han-Dynasty stele inscriptions,[22] and Jing Xuefa clearly has mistaken many of the official-script transformed characters for popular-form characters, which is not in line with the reality of the evolution of Chinese characters. The official script transformation is a spontaneous process of replacing the pictographic seal-script character system with a new system of phonetic-semantic symbols. As it is a natural process, there are different types of modifications made to the original character forms, and sometimes a character component may be modified into different forms. Such modifications are aimed to create standard-form characters instead of popular-form ones, and the various new character forms created through them are experimental forms tried out in practice in the creation of standard-form characters. Character variants created in this way can be regarded as standard-character forms, and they are essentially different from popular-form characters that are simplified standard-form characters used for informal occasions. The fact that such character variants appear in lots of ancient classics, formal documents and famous calligraphy works can prove this viewpoint. The wrong view that characters created through the official script transformation are popular-form characters is not just a misunderstanding of the development history of Chinese characters but also a betrayal of a sinological tradition.

Libian 隶变, the Chinese term for the official script transformation, firstly appeared in *Wujing Wenzi* 五经文字 (Characters in the Five Classics), a book written by a Tang-Dynasty scholar named Zhang Can 张参. In the book, the author uses three terms to describe font changes: *libian* 隶变 (characters restructured through the official script transformation), *lisheng* 隶省 (characters simplified through the official script transformation), and *su* 俗 (popular-form characters). *Libian* characters include the following:

- *Ao* 奥 (the southwest corner of a house): a combination of *mian* 宀 (roofed room), *mi* 米 (rice), and *da* 大 (big). Because of the official script transformation, this character begins featuring the component *da* 大 (big), which also has a phonetic function in the composition of this character.[23]
- *Guang* 兊 (light) and *guang* 光 (light): the former is included in *Shuowen Jiezi* 说文解字 (An Explication of Written Characters), and the latter is a *libian* character.[24]
- *Pei* 紴 (reins) and *pei* 轡 (reins): the former is included in *Shuowen Jiezi* 说文解字, and the latter is a *libian* character.[25]

- *Yong* 饔 (cooked food) and *yong* 饗 (cooked food): the former is included in *Shuowen Jiezi*, and the latter is a *libian* character.²⁶
- *Tie* 飻 (greedy for food) and *tie* 饕 (greedy for food): the former is included in *Shuowen Jiezi*, and the latter is a *libian* character.²⁷
- *Wu* 霚 (fog), *wu* 雺 (fog) and *wu* 霧 (fog): the first character form is included in *Shuowen Jiezi*; the second character form is a big-seal-script form; the third is a *libian* character.²⁸
- *Sang* 𠅰 (to perish) and *sang* 喪 (to perish): the former is included in *Shuowen Jiezi*, and the latter is a *libian* character.²⁹
- *Xian* 㢸 (bowstring) and *xian* 弦 (bowstring): the former is included in *Shuowen Jiezi*, and the latter is a *libian* character.³⁰
- *Ning* 甯 (to prefer) and *ning* 寍 (to prefer): the former is included in *Shuowen Jiezi*, and the latter is a *libian* character.³¹

In Zhang Can's book, the following characters are referred to as *lisheng* characters:

- *Ben* 本 (root of a plant) and *ben* 夲 (root of a plant): the former is included and explained as a combination of *mu* 木 (wood) and *yi* 一 (one) in *Shuowen Jiezi*, and the latter is a *lisheng* character.³²
- *Yao* 㨊 (to swing) and *yao* 摇 (to swing): the former is included and explained as a combination of *rou* 肉 (flesh) and *fou* 缶 (earthen jar with big belly and small mouth) in *Shuowen Jiezi*, and the latter is a *lisheng* character.³³
- *Kuo* 捪 (to tie) and *kuo* 括 (to tie): the former is included in *Shuowen Jiezi*, and the latter is a *lisheng* character.³⁴
- *Zan* 赞 (to introduce) and *zan* 贊 (to introduce): the former is included in *Shuowen Jiezi*, and the latter is a *lisheng* character.³⁵
- *Han* 厈 (cliff) and *han* 厂 (cliff): the former is included in *Shuowen Jiezi*, and the latter is a *lisheng* character.³⁶
- *E* 启 (a strategic location) and *e* 厄 (a strategic location): the former is included in *Shuowen Jiezi*, and the latter is a *lisheng* character.³⁷
- *Yu* 䬩 (feast) and *yu* 飫 (feast): the former is included in *Shuowen Jiezi*, and the latter is a *lisheng* character.³⁸

The book also explains some popular-form characters:

- *Yang* 扬 (to lift): the name of a prefecture, whose popular form, a wrong form, features the radical *mu* 木 (wood).³⁹
- *Jiao* 徼 (to go on a tour of inspection): its popular form 僥 is a wrong form.⁴⁰
- *Bei* 悖 (be contradictory to): its popular form 勃 is a wrong form.⁴¹
- *Duo* 墮 (degenerate): its popular form 隳, which is also regarded as a popular form of *sui* 隋 (residual meat), is a non-standard form.⁴²
- *Jian* 姦 (adultery): its popular form 奸 is a wrong form.⁴³
- *Ji* 繼 (to continue): its popular form 继 is a non-standard form.⁴⁴
- *Chu* 處 (stop): the standard form of this character is a combination of *zhi* 夊 (end) and *ji* 几 (a thing to sit on), and its popular form 處 is a non-standard form.⁴⁵

Evidently, in *Wujing Wenzi* 五经文字 (Characters in the Five Classics), *libian* 隶变 (characters that are restructured through the official script transformation), *lisheng* 隶省 (characters that are simplified through the official script transformation), and *su* 俗 (popular-form characters) are strictly distinguished, and only *libian* and *lisheng* characters are regarded as standard-character forms created through the official script transformation. In fact, the author of the book writes out his criteria for choosing standard-character forms in the preface of the book.

"I mainly refer to *Shuowen Jiezi* to grasp the six means of creating Chinese characters. As to the characters not included in *Shuowen Jiezi*, I look them up in *Zilin* 字林 (A Collection of Characters). When I find that some archaic character forms are difficult for me and other scholars to explain and have to refer to the remaining parts of *Shijing* 石经 (Stele Inscriptions), I will also refer to *Jingdian Shiwen* 经典释文 (Interpretations of Classics) and dare not make arbitrary inferences." He clearly regarded the *lisheng* character forms recorded in *Jingdian Shiwen* as standard as those included in *Shuowen Jiezi*, *Zilin*, and *Shijing*.[46]

Notes

1 The original Chinese version was published in *Journal of Jinan University-Philosophy and Social Science Edition* 暨南学报（哲学社会科学版）, 2011, issue 3.
2 姜宝昌：《文字学教程》，第782页，济南：山东教育出版社，1987.
 Jiang Baochang: *A Course in Philology*, p. 782, Jinan: Shandong Educational Press, 1987.
3 赵平安：《隶变纵横谈》，载《历史教学》，1992（8）.
 Zhao Ping'an: "On the Official Script Transformation", *History Teaching*, 1992 (8).
4 唐兰：《中国文字学》，第165页，上海：上海古籍出版社，1979.
 Tang Lan: *Chinese Philology*, p. 165, Shanghai: Shanghai Classics Publishing House, 1979.
5 唐兰：《中国文字学》，第152页，上海：上海古籍出版社，1979.
 Tang Lan: *Chinese Philology*, p. 152, Shanghai: Shanghai Classics Publishing House, 1979.
6 饶宗颐：《楚帛书之书法艺术》，见饶宗颐、曾宪通：《楚地出土文献三种研究》，第342页，北京：中华书局，1993
 Rao Zongyi: "The Calligraphic Art of Chu-State Silk Manuscripts", Rao Zongyi and Zeng Xiantong: *Three Types of Unearthed Chu-State Documents*, p. 342, Beijing: Zhonghua Book Company, 1993.
7 郭沫若：《古代文字之辩证的发展》，载《考古》，1972（3）.
 Guo Moruo: "The Dialectical Development of Ancient Chinese Characters", *Archaeology*, 1972 (3).
8 姜亮夫：《古文字学》，第60页，杭州：浙江人民出版社，1984.
 Jiang Liangfu: *Ancient Chinese Philology*, p. 60, Hangzhou: Zhejiang People's Publishing House, 1984.
9 赵平安：《隶变研究》，第6页，保定：河北大学出版社，2009.
 Zhao Ping'an: *The Study on the Official Script Transformation*, p. 6, Baoding: Hebei University Publishing House, 2009.
10 赵平安：《隶变研究》，第7页，保定：河北大学出版社，2009.
 Zhao Ping'an: *The Study on the Official Script Transformation*, p. 7, Baoding: Hebei University Publishing House, 2009.
11 王志平、董琨：《简帛文献文字研究》，见简帛文献语言研究课题组，《简帛文献语言研究》，第215页，北京：社会科学文献出版社，2009.
 Wang Zhiping and Dong Kun: "Research on Characters Used in Bamboo and Silk Manuscript", Bamboo and Silk Manuscripts Research Group: *Research on the Language Used in Bamboo and Silk Manuscripts*, p. 215, Beijing: Social Sciences Academic Press, 2009.

12 裘锡圭：《文字学概要》，第 69 页，北京：商务印书馆，1988.
Qiu Xigui: *A Summary of Chinese Philology*, p. 69, Beijing: The Commercial Press, 1988.
13 王宁主编：《汉字学概要》，第 53 页，北京：北京师范大学出版社，2001.
Wang Ning, ed.: *A Summary of Chinese Philology*, p. 53, Beijing: Beijing Normal University Press, 2001.
14 赵平安：《隶变研究》，第 9 页，保定：河北大学出版社，2009.
Zhao Ping'an: *The Study on the Official Script Transformation*, p. 9, Baoding: Hebei University Publishing House, 2009.
15 陆锡兴：《隶变是一个文字发展阶段》，载《历史教学》，1992（9）
Lu Xixing: "The Official Script Transformation: A Stage of Development of Chinese Characters", *History Teaching*, 1992 (9).
16 陆锡兴：《唐代的文字规范和楷体正字的形成》，载《语文建设》，1992（6）
Lu Xixing: "The Formation of the Tang Dynasty's Writing Norms and Regular-Script Characters", *Language Planning*, 1992 (6).
17 赵平安：《隶变研究》，第 10 页，保定：河北大学出版社，2009.
Zhao Ping'an: *The Study on the Official Script Transformation*, p. 10, Baoding: Hebei University Publishing House, 2009.
18 启功：《古代字体论稿》，第 27–28 页，北京：文物出版社，1999.
Qi Gong: *Discussion on Ancient Chinese Character Fonts*, pp. 27–28, Beijing: Cultural Relics Press, 1999.
19 唐兰：《中国文字学》，第 163 页，上海：上海古籍出版社，1979.
Tang Lan: *Chinese Philology*, p. 163, Shanghai: Shanghai Classics Publishing House, 1979.
20 陈梦家：《中国文字学》，第 165 页，北京：中华书局，2006.
Chen Mengjia: *Chinese Palaeography*, p. 165, Beijing: Zhonghua Book Company, 2006.
21 赵立伟：《从隶变看俗字的产生》，载《聊城大学学报(社会科学版)》，2004(5) .
Zhao Liwei: "The Emergence of the Popular-Form Characters from the Perspective of the Official Script Transformation", *Journal of Liaocheng University (Social Sciences Edition)*, 2004 (5).
22 井学法：《汉碑俗字的类型及其成因探析》，载《文化学刊》，2010(2) .
Jing Xuefa: "Types and Causes of the Popular-Form Characters Used in the Han-Dynasty Stele Inscriptions", *Culture Journal*, 2010 (2).
23 张参：《五经文字》卷上，文渊阁四库全书本.
Zhang Can: *Characters in the Five Classics (Vol. 1), Siku Quanshu (Wenyuange Edition)*, Shanghai: Shanghai Classics Publishing House, 2003.
24 张参：《五经文字》卷中，文渊阁四库全书本.
Zhang Can: *Characters in the Five Classics (Vol. 2), Siku Quanshu (Wenyuange Edition)*, Shanghai: Shanghai Classics Publishing House, 2003.
25 张参：《五经文字》卷下，文渊阁四库全书本.
Zhang Can: *Characters in the Five Classics (Vol. 3), Siku Quanshu (Wenyuange Edition)*, Shanghai: Shanghai Classics Publishing House, 2003.
26 张参：《五经文字》卷下，文渊阁四库全书本.
Zhang Can: *Characters in the Five Classics (Vol. 3), Siku Quanshu (Wenyuange Edition)*, Shanghai: Shanghai Classics Publishing House, 2003.
27 张参：《五经文字》卷下，文渊阁四库全书本.
Zhang Can: *Characters in the Five Classics (Vol. 3), Siku Quanshu (Wenyuange Edition)*, Shanghai: Shanghai Classics Publishing House, 2003.
28 张参：《五经文字》卷下，文渊阁四库全书本.
Zhang Can: *Characters in the Five Classics (Vol. 3), Siku Quanshu (Wenyuange Edition)*, Shanghai: Shanghai Classics Publishing House, 2003.
29 张参：《五经文字》卷下，文渊阁四库全书本.
Zhang Can: *Characters in the Five Classics (Vol. 3), Siku Quanshu (Wenyuange Edition)*, Shanghai: Shanghai Classics Publishing House, 2003.
30 张参：《五经文字》卷下，文渊阁四库全书本.
Zhang Can: *Characters in the Five Classics (Vol. 3), Siku Quanshu (Wenyuange Edition)*, Shanghai: Shanghai Classics Publishing House, 2003.

31 张参：《五经文字》卷下，文渊阁四库全书本.
Zhang Can: *Characters in the Five Classics (Vol. 3), Siku Quanshu (Wenyuange Edition)*, Shanghai: Shanghai Classics Publishing House, 2003.
32 张参：《五经文字》卷上，文渊阁四库全书本.
Zhang Can: *Characters in the Five Classics (Vol. 1), Siku Quanshu (Wenyuange Edition)*, Shanghai: Shanghai Classics Publishing House, 2003.
33 张参：《五经文字》卷上，文渊阁四库全书本.
Zhang Can: *Characters in the Five Classics (Vol. 1), Siku Quanshu (Wenyuange Edition)*, Shanghai: Shanghai Classics Publishing House, 2003.
34 张参：《五经文字》卷上，文渊阁四库全书本.
Zhang Can: *Characters in the Five Classics (Vol. 1), Siku Quanshu (Wenyuange Edition)*, Shanghai: Shanghai Classics Publishing House, 2003.
35 张参：《五经文字》卷上，文渊阁四库全书本.
Zhang Can: *Characters in the Five Classics (Vol. 1), Siku Quanshu (Wenyuange Edition)*, Shanghai: Shanghai Classics Publishing House, 2003.
36 张参：《五经文字》卷中，文渊阁四库全书本.
Zhang Can: *Characters in the Five Classics (Vol. 2), Siku Quanshu (Wenyuange Edition)*, Shanghai: Shanghai Classics Publishing House, 2003.
37 张参：《五经文字》卷中，文渊阁四库全书本.
Zhang Can: *Characters in the Five Classics (Vol. 2), Siku Quanshu (Wenyuange Edition)*, Shanghai: Shanghai Classics Publishing House, 2003.
38 张参：《五经文字》卷下，文渊阁四库全书本。
Zhang Can: *Characters in the Five Classics (Vol. 3), Siku Quanshu (Wenyuange Edition)*, Shanghai: Shanghai Classics Publishing House, 2003.
39 张参：《五经文字》卷上，文渊阁四库全书本.
Zhang Can: *Characters in the Five Classics (Vol. 1), Siku Quanshu (Wenyuange Edition)*, Shanghai: Shanghai Classics Publishing House, 2003.
40 张参：《五经文字》卷上，文渊阁四库全书本.
Zhang Can: *Characters in the Five Classics (Vol. 1), Siku Quanshu (Wenyuange Edition)*, Shanghai: Shanghai Classics Publishing House, 2003.
41 张参：《五经文字》卷中，文渊阁四库全书本.
Zhang Can: *Characters in the Five Classics (Vol. 2), Siku Quanshu (Wenyuange Edition)*, Shanghai: Shanghai Classics Publishing House, 2003.
42 张参：《五经文字》卷中，文渊阁四库全书本.
Zhang Can: *Characters in the Five Classics (Vol. 2), Siku Quanshu (Wenyuange Edition)*, Shanghai: Shanghai Classics Publishing House, 2003.
43 张参：《五经文字》卷下，文渊阁四库全书本.
Zhang Can: *Characters in the Five Classics (Vol. 3), Siku Quanshu (Wenyuange Edition)*, Shanghai: Shanghai Classics Publishing House, 2003.
44 张参：《五经文字》卷下，文渊阁四库全书本.
Zhang Can: *Characters in the Five Classics (Vol. 3), Siku Quanshu (Wenyuange Edition)*, Shanghai: Shanghai Classics Publishing House, 2003.
45 张参：《五经文字》卷下，文渊阁四库全书本.
Zhang Can: *Characters in the Five Classics (Vol. 3), Siku Quanshu (Wenyuange Edition)*, Shanghai: Shanghai Classics Publishing House, 2003.
46 张参：《五经文字·序》，文渊阁四库全书本.
Zhang Can: *Characters in the Five Classics (Preface), Siku Quanshu (Wenyuange Edition)*, Shanghai: Shanghai Classics Publishing House, 2003.

10 Sense Relations Among Same-Origin Chinese Characters (Words)[1]

I. The Essence of the Sense Relations Among Same-Origin Characters

Traditional-style analyses and views of same-origin or homologous Chinese characters are based on character meanings, which, in most cases, refer to 义位 or meanings (sememes). The terms used for such analyses, such as *yitong* 义同 (meaning sameness), *yijin* 义近 (meaning similarity), *yitong* 义通 (meaning interchangeability), are vaguely defined, causing troubles for researchers. In general, this analysis method has five major disadvantages.

(I) The traditional-style analysis method can lead to confusion in distinguishing the synchronic and diachronic systems. Character meanings or sememes are generated for communication at a given point in time as the smallest units of meaning and are thus defined by a certain synchronic system. Nevertheless, throughout the evolution of the Chinese language, the meanings of characters have undergone changes, resulting in the phenomenon where the same sememe may be expressed by characters of different origins. Take several characters that are included in *Shuowen Jiezi* 说文解字 (An Explication of Written Characters) as examples. "Head tilt" is the sememe for characters *qing* 顷 (the head tilt) and *po* 颇 (the head tilt), which are different in pronunciation and origin. In contrast, *cong* 囱 (window) and *cong* 葱 (scallions) have common ancestry but completely different sememes. Simply put, same-origin characters are defined from a diachronic point of view, and they do not necessarily have the same or similar sememes. Given this, it's impossible to determine the origins of characters based on sememes.

(II) The traditional-style analysis method can lead to randomness in determining sense relations. This kind of randomness is very likely to happen. As a sememe is a combination of semes (or semantic features), there are many possible ways to build connections between sememes through semes.

(III) The traditional-style analysis method can cause errors in determining homologous relations. When the determination of homologous relations is based on the sameness or similarity of character meanings (sememes), the conclusions and rules drawn may seriously distort the historical facts. This will cause errors in the determination of homologous relations.

(IV) The traditional-style analysis method cannot distinguish *yitong* 义通 (meaning interchangeability) phenomena caused by coincidences from those caused by a common ancestry of characters. Generally, *yitong* phenomenon is common among same-origin characters. Nevertheless, given the extensiveness of sense relations, the fact that character pronunciations are composed of a limited number of syllables, and the natural evolution of character meanings and pronunciations, *yitong* phenomena can also be caused by coincidences. There may be characters that have similar pronunciations and/or meanings but different ancestries. Similarities in pronunciation and meaning are a necessary, rather than a sufficient, condition, for homologous relations. The statement made by Wang Li 王力 in *Homologous Characters* 同源词典 is a typical example of determining homologous relations based on similarities in pronunciation and meaning: "Characters with the same pronunciation and similar meanings, those with the same meaning and similar pronunciation, and those with similar pronunciations and meanings are same-origin characters." This definition cannot exclude non-homologous characters that have similar meanings and pronunciations.

(V) The traditional-style analysis method may sometimes create confusion regarding the interchangeability of same-origin characters and loans. Loans are one of the six methods used to create Chinese characters, where an existing character or character component is used as a phonetic component to form a new character that has no sense relation with the original. On the other hand, interchangeability exists only among characters of the same origin. It can be challenging to determine homologous relations based on sememes as such relationships are not always reflected in the meaning of the characters. As a result, homologous relations are frequently confused with loans.

To sum up, extrapolating homologous relationships in accordance with character meanings (sememes) will lead to various inevitable problems, and it is impossible to reveal real homologous relations through character meanings. What is the essence of the sense relations among homologous characters? This study finds out that it is the relations among semes (or semantic features).

Youwen 右文 theory is an important theory about same-origin characters. It argues that characters with the same right-placed component that has both phonetic and semantic functions have certain sense relations and homologous relations. This theory should be given enough attention because it avoids problems, such as vague definitions and randomness in determining sense relations, and succeeds in revealing some real homologous relations. This theory has not been thoroughly expounded upon or written into a book, but its analysis method and examples are enough to prove the scientific nature of this theory.

A typical set of examples includes *gou* 鉤 (hook), *qu* 鞠 (yoke), *gou* 刞 (sickle), *gou* 筍 (a basket trap for fish), *gou* 痀 (a hunchback), and *gou* 朐 (dried meat), which are defined as homologous characters in *Wenshi Dictionary of Homologous Characters* and *Dictionary of Homologous Characters*.

> *Gou* 鉤 (hook) is arranged under the radical *ju* 句 (bent) and explained as a combination of *jin* 金 (metal) and *ju* 句 (bent) that also serves as a phonetic component in *Shuowen Jiezi* 说文解字. Duan Yucai 段玉裁 (1735–1815) annotated this explanation: "Weapons, such as *gouxiang* 鉤镶, *wugou* 吴鉤, and diaogou 钓鉤 (a weapon), are made of metal, so the character *gou* 鉤 (hook) features the radical *jin* 金 (metal)."

- *Gou* 笱 (a basket trap for fish) is arranged under the radical *ju* 句 (bent) and explained as a combination of *zhu* 竹 (bamboo) and *ju* 句 (bent) that also serves as a phonetic component in *Shuowen Jiezi*.
- *Qu* 軥 (yoke) is arranged under the radical *che* 车 (vehicle) and explained as a combination of *che* 车 (vehicle) and a phonetic component *ju* 句 (bent) in *Shuowen Jiezi*. Duan Yucai 段玉裁 further pointed out that this character referred to the wooden bar or frame by which two horses are joined at their necks for pulling a carriage.
- *Gou* 刉 (sickle) is arranged under the radical *dao* 刀 (knife) and explained as a combination of *dao* 刀 (knife) and a phonetic component *ju* 句 (bent) in *Shuowen Jiezi*. Duan Yucai 段玉裁 thought that *gou* 刉 (sickle) could be written alternatively as *gou* 鉤 (hook).
- *Gou* 朐 (dried meat) is arranged under the radical *rou* 肉 (flesh) and explained as a combination of *rou* 肉 (flesh) and a phonetic component *ju* 句 (bent) in *Shuowen Jiezi*. In a note made to *Gongyang Zhuan* 公羊传 (Gongyang's Commentary on The Spring and Autumn Annals), He Xiu (129–182) said that crooked dried meat is named *gou* 朐 (dried meat) and uncrooked dried meat is referred to as *ting* 脡 (strips of dried meat).
- *Gou* 痀 (a hunchback) is arranged under the radical and explained as a combination of *guang* 广 (wide) and a phonetic component *ju* 句 (bent).

The analysis of the sense relations among the six characters is shown in the table below.

Table 10.1 Analysis of Sense Relations Among Same-Origin Chinese Characters

Characters Semes		Gou 鉤 (hook)	Qu 軥 (yoke)	Gou 刉 (sickle)	Gou 笱 (a basket trap for fish)	Gou 痀 (a hunchback)	Gou 朐 (dried meat)
(Material)	Jin 金 (metal)	+	−	+	−	−	−
	Mu 木 (wood)	−	+	−	−	−	−
	Zhu 竹 (bamboo)	−	−	−	+	−	−
	Gurou 肉 (flesh and bone)	−	−	−	−	+	+

Sense Relations Among Same-Origin Chinese Characters (Words)   163

Characters Semes		Gou 鈎 (hook)	Qu 軥 (yoke)	Gou 刉 (sickle)	Gou 笱 (a basket trap for fish)	Gou 佝 (a hunchback)	Gou 朐 (dried meat)
(Function)	Hanging things	+	–	–	–	–	–
	Riding a horse	–	+	–	–	–	–
	Fishing	–	–	–	+	–	–
	Food	–	–	–	–	–	+
	Reaping	–	–	+	–	–	–
(Shape)	Bended	+	+	+	+	+	+

As shown in the table above, these six characters probably share the same ancestry as they share the seme, "to bend". Their homologous relations are embodied in their seme relations.

Huang Chengji 黄承吉 (1771–1842) further improved the *youwen* 右文 theory. He pointed out that some characters that have the same right-placed component, similar pronunciations, and different phonetic components also have certain sense relations and homologous relations. His view further illustrated that homologous relations were manifested as seme relations. He gave a set of examples: *rui* 鋭 (awn), *ji* 蒍 (little grass), *hui* 嘒 (small voice), *hui* 槥 (small crude coffin), *wei* 鏏 (a small tripod cauldron), *ji* 虮 (lice), and *ji* 叽 (to take a little food).

- *Rui* 鋭 (awn) is arranged under the radical *jin* 金 (metal) and explained as a combination of *jin* 金 (metal) and a phonetic component *dui* 兌 (happy) in *Shuowen Jiezi*. Its big-seal-script form is written as 劂. Du Yu 杜預 (222–285) adopted this explanation when he made a note on a line in *Zuo Zhuan* 左传 (Zuo's Commentary on The Spring and Autumn Annals). The original line reads, "且吾以玉賈罪，不亦鋭乎？ (This jade, a trivial object, will bring sins upon us. It's not worth it.), while he explained the character *rui* 鋭 as "trivial".
- *Ji* 蒍 (little grass) is arranged under the radical *cao* 艸 (herbage) and explained as a combination of *cao* 艸 (herbage) and a phonetic component *jue* 劂 (to sculpture) in *Shuowen Jiezi*.
- *Hui* 嘒 (small voice) is arranged under the radical *kou* 口 (mouth) and explained as a combination of *kou* 口 (mouth) and a phonetic component *hui* 彗 (broom) in *Shuowen Jiezi*. In *Shi Jing* 诗经 (The Book of Songs), there is such a line: "嘒彼小星" (Small are those starlets).
- *Hui* 槥 (small crude coffin) is arranged under the radical *mu* 木 (wood) and explained as a combination of *mu* 木 (wood) and a phonetic component *hui* 彗 (broom) in *Shuowen Jiezi*. Duan Yucai 段玉裁 explained the characters "棺椟" that *Shuowen Jiezi* used to define the character: "*du* 椟 meant cabinet, and *guandu* 棺椟 meant small coffin." The character appears in *Han Shu* 汉书 (The History of the Han Dynasty): "令士卒从军死者为槥" (The remains of every dead soldier are kept in a small coffin). Ying Shao 应劭 (ca. 153–196) noted, "*Hui* 槥 means small coffins, which are currently called *du* 椟."

- *Wei* 鏏 (a small tripod cauldron) is arranged under the radical *jin* 金 (metal) and explained as a combination of *jin* 金 (metal) and a phonetic component *hui* 彗 (broom) in *Shuowen Jiezi*. The character appears in *Huainanzi* 淮南子 (Master Huainan): "水火相憎，鏏在其间，五味以和" (Fire and water are incompatible, but *wei* 鏏 enables them to work together harmoniously to cook good meals). Gao You 高诱, an Eastern-Han-Dynasty (25–220) scholar noted that *wei* 鏏 is a small-sized tripod cauldron used for cooking.
- *Ji* 叽 (to take a little food) is arranged under the radical *kou* 口 (mouth) and explained as a combination of *kou* 口 (mouth) and a phonetic component *ji* 几 (a thing to sit on) in *Shuowen Jiezi*.
- *Ji* 虮 (lice) is arranged under the radical *chong* 虫 (worm/insect) and explained as a combination of *chong* 虫 (worm/insect) and a phonetic component *ji* 几 (a thing to sit on).

The homologous relations of the seven characters listed above are determined by the fact that they share the same "small/little".

Since Huang Chengji 黄承吉 (1771–1842), almost every sinologist has discussed same-origin characters. Unfortunately, given the limited understanding of the sense relations among characters and the neglect of the importance of character compositional structures, their theories often suffer from vagueness and randomness. For instance, Wang Niansun 王念孙 (1744–1832) related the character *da* 大 to many other characters in *Shi Da* 释大 (Probing into the Meanings of *Da* 大). There is a great amount of vagueness and arbitrariness in the definitions of these relations. Other sinologists, such as Ruan Yuan 阮元 (1764–1849), Hao Yixing 郝懿行 (1757–1825), Qian Yi 钱绎 (1770–1855), Liu Shipei 刘师培 (1884–1919), Liang Qichao 梁启超 (1873–1929), and Liu Ze 刘赜 (1891–1978) made similar mistakes. Nevertheless, their research also provides some useful insight into the sense relations among same-origin characters.

Wang Niansun 王念孙 (1744–1832) discovered that the characters *ling* 霝 (drops of rain), *ling* 棂 (window lattice), ling 軨 (lattice work on panels of a carriage), *ling* 笭 (bamboo screen), *cong* 葱 (scallions), *chuang* 窗 (window), *ling* 欞 (window lattice), *ling* 舲 (small boat with windows), and *long* 笼 (cage-like basket) all related to the seme "cavity".[2] Liu Shipei 刘师培 (1884–1919) observed that characters featuring the same phonetic component often share similarities in *yixiang* 义象 or meaning. He pointed out that early Chinese characters were created through the combination of components, and similar-meaning characters often featured the same phonetic component that often had some semantic function. He concluded that characters containing components, such as *jia* 叚 (loan), *jian* 开 (even level), *lao* 劳 (to work hard), *rong* 戎 (weapons), and *jing* 京 (artificial mound) imply a state of being important, notable, or distinguished; that characters containing *zhui* 叕 (to connect) and *qu* 屈 (to bend) suggest a state of being short; and that characters containing components such as *shao* 少 (inadequate), *dao* 刀 (knife), *wan* 宛 (to bend), and *mie* 蔑 (slight) imply a state of being small or trivial.[3] Shen Jianshi 沈兼士 (1887–1947) erroneously explained that the term *yixiang* 义象 proposed by Liu Shipei was equivalent to the term *yilei* 义类 used in the book

Sense Relations Among Same-Origin Chinese Characters (Words)   165

Shi Ming 释名 (Explanations of Names).[4] The concept of *yilei* 义类 is defined according to a single character, but the term *yixiang* 义象 proposed by Liu Shipei 刘师培 actually refers to the phonetic and semantic functions of characters with the same pronunciation.

In the preface of *Wenshi Dictionary of Homologous Characters*, Zhang Taiyan 章太炎 (1869–1936) explicitly points out that the sense relations among same-origin characters are embodied in semes. He said, "The sense relation between the homologous characters *jiang* 绛 (deep red) and *yao* 轺 (a light horse cart) is reflected only on the seme that describes the scale, namely, deep and light."

So, sense relations among same-origin characters, including both semantic-phonetic and non-semantic-phonetic characters, are embodied by semes. Although previous sinologists did not succeed in revealing the essence of these relations, they came very close to it when studying same-origin characters and their relations.

II. Core Semes and Rules Governing the Multiplication of Homologous Characters

American structural linguistics holds that different languages divide and classify things in the objective world, which is a continuous system, in their own specific ways. Such division and classification are embodied in the grouping of homologous phenomena of words and expressions, which also shows how speakers of different languages differ in their perception of the world. In discussing the naming of things, Xun Zi 荀子 (313–238 BCE) noted, "How do we identify similarities and differences? It is determined by our senses of knowing the world. When we sense similarities in things, we name them in similar ways."[5]

What Xun Zi (313–238 BCE) said is also applicable to the analysis of same-origin Chinese characters. People's initial naming of things is not based on the analysis of the essence or nature of things but on their superficial and intuitive understanding of things. Zhang Taiyan 章太炎 (1869–1936) said, "Things have different origins, and so do characters. For instance, *lan* 蓝 (indigo plant) is originally named *cong* 葱 (scallions), and the name *cu* 鼀 (toad) originates from *chuo* 𪚥 (a kind of blue-colour, four-legged animal). They do not necessarily belong to the same category of plant or animal but share similarities in appearance. This phenomenon is common in the names of animals and plants."[6] Liu Shipei 刘师培 (1884–1919) said, "In primitive times, people did not have the ability to distinguish things clearly, so they distinguished things only by appearance."[7] For example, the following groups of homologous characters, which describe things of different natures and have a common seme "round shape": *hun* 棞 (whole piece of log or unbroken firewood), *qun* 囷 (round-shaped storage bin for grain), *jun* 菌 (mushroom), *hun* 圂 (round pigsty), *huan* 寏 (courtyard fence), *xun* 紃 (round-shaped cord), *bei* 杯 (cup), *xuan* 䥧 (round stove), *huan* 环 (ring), *wan* 丸 (pellet), *zhi* 卮 (round wine container), *yuan* 圆 (round), *guo* 果 (fruit), *zhi* 𦄣 (knot), and *wan* 丸/𠃬 (the pellets spit out by eagles). The things described by these Chinese characters are not of the same category, but given their similarity, the characters used to name them come from the same origin and thus have similar pronunciations.

Objects and phenomena exhibit distinct qualities and may also share common attributes. "Big" and "small" are two attributes with opposing meanings, but they are both part of the larger category of scale. These attributes form a systematic network, a unity of opposing forces that accounts for the vast range of variations in the objective world. Semes are the units of meaning that people use to articulate these attributes. The objects and phenomena are interconnected, and so are the semes used to describe them. The semes that play a decisive role in sense relations among homologous characters are core semes.

Objects and phenomena are interconnected and possess multiple attributes. Naming them involves identifying a particular type of sense relation and characteristic that reflects people's experience and perception of the world. When people group a set of objects or phenomena based on analogies with other objects or phenomena and assign them names, they create a core seme for a group of homologous characters.

Core semes (or core semantic features) play a decisive role in the multiplication of characters. A core seme of a group of same-origin characters describes their common semantic feature. For instance, "bent" is the sore seme for *gou* 鉤 (hook), *qu* 軥 (yoke), *gou* 刡 (sickle), *gou* 笱 (a basket trap for fish), *gou* 痀 (a hunchback), and *gou* 胊 (dried meat), and "trivial" is the core seme for *rui* 锐 (awn), *hui* 嘒 (small voice), and *ji* 虮 (lice). As a core seme summarizes the common semantic feature of a group of characters, it is often an adjective or a descriptive verb. Zhang Taiyan (1869–1936) described the situation in the following words: "Things in the world share similarities."[8] Core semes do not affect the usage of characters and the development of their semantic functions. They just play a role in defining the meanings of these characters, but they are not explicitly expressed sometimes. For instance, "many" is the core seme for *san* 三 (three/many) and *sen* 森 (full of trees/many), which have been listed as similar-sounding characters since ancient times. Nevertheless, the fact that they share a seme does not prevent them from differing in meaning or sememe. *Shuowen Jiezi* explains *san* 三 as the number three, implying the ways of heaven, earth, and people. Ancient Chinese people regarded the number three as an important notation in mathematics and used it to express the idea of "many". This usage appears in *Laozi* 老子 (The Philosophy of Laozi): "The Tao produced One; One produced Two; Two produced Three; Three produced All things (一生二，二生三，三生万物)." It also appears in *Shuowen Jiezi*: the pictographic form of *you* 又, which means a hand, depicts a three-fingered hand, which is an imaginary number, not a real one (手之列多不过三也). Nevertheless, there is no such meaning when *san* 三 is used as a number. As to *sen* 森 (full of trees/many), *Shuowen Jiezi* explains it as a combination of *lin* 林 (woods) and *mu* 木 (wood), describing a place full of trees. A prose collected in *Wen Xuan* 文选 (Anthology of Poems and Proses) uses the character to convey the meaning "many": "many deities followed behind (百神森其备从兮)". Sometimes, characters featuring the same meaning (sememe) may derive from different core semes.

The characters *yan* 嫣 (tall) and *ting* 侹 (tall) are typical examples. These two words are included in *Shuowen Jiezi*, and, in many cases, they can be used interchangeably. Nonetheless, the core seme of *yan* 嫣 (tall) is "extend", and that of *ting*

Sense Relations Among Same-Origin Chinese Characters (Words) 167

侹 (tall) is "vertical". The former shares a common seme with *yan* 延 (be on a long journey), *dan* 诞 (a long sigh), and *yan* 傿 (to raise prices), and the latter shares a common seme with *ting* 珽 (jade tablet), *ting* 梃 (a stalk), *xing* 鋞 (a kind of wine utensil), and *xing* 娙 (tall and beautiful). The great difference between the pronunciation of these two characters also implies their difference in origin.

People sense that some things and phenomena are connected or coexist, which is reflected in the interconnectedness of some core semes and the fact that a group of homologous characters may have more than one core semes that are related to one another. These core semes provide opportunities for the development of character derivation and the formation of more homologous characters. For example, the core semes "bright" and "white", which describe two objective phenomena that often occur simultaneously, are often combined in the formation of homologous characters. According to *Shuowen Jiezi*, the character *gao* 杲 means "bright", and *Guangya* 广雅 (Guangya Dictionary) explains *gaogao* 杲杲 as "white". *Shuowen Jiezi* shows that *hao* 皓 describes the rising sun, and in Duan Yucai's 段玉裁 notes, it can also be used to refer to the whitest and brightest colour. *Shuowen Jiezi* uses *haogan* 皓旰 to define the character *hao* 暭 (brilliant), and, according to Duan Yucai, *haogan* 皓旰 describes whiteness and brightness. The word *haohao* 暭暭 is explained as "white" in *Guangya* 广雅, and *jiao* 皦 (bright white) is explained as a word used to describe white-colour jade in *Shuowen Jiezi*. The ancient dictionary *Fangyan* 方言 (Dialects) points out that *jiao* 皦 means bright, and *Shuowen Jiezi* includes characters, such as *he* 翯 (glistening plumage), *he* 睢 (clear and pure white feather), *hao* 灏 (soybean milk), *gao* 缟 (white raw silk), and *xu* 旭 (rising sun). Among the abovementioned characters, there are characters derived from the seme "bright", such as *gao* 杲 (bright), *hao* 皓 (luminous), *hao* 暭 (brilliant), *xu* 旭 (rising sun), and those derived from the seme "white", such as *he* 翯 (glistening plumage), *hao* 灏 (soybean milk), and *gao* 缟 (white raw silk). They all have similar pronunciations, which indicates that "bright" and "white" are two core semes derived under the same pronunciation. In conclusion, these characters share the same origin.

III. Examples of Sense Relation Among Same-Origin Characters

Sense relations among same-origin characters are determined by semes (or semantic features). A group of homologous characters share a common core seme, and core semes are also interconnected with one another. Four groups of homologous characters are analysed below to further illustrate this point.

(I) The three interconnected core semes, "circular movement", "extension", and "continuity", determine the homologous relations of *gen* 亘 (continuous extension), *yuan* 𧺆 (a farming system featuring the rotation of land), *xuan* 咺 (non-stop crying of a child), *heng* 恒 (permanent), *yuan* 爰 (to lead on to), *yuan* 轅/辕 (shafts of a cart), *yuan* 渊 (whirling water), and *yuan* 开 (whirling water).

From the perspective of its movement direction, a vortex is often a forward extension. Inspired by their observation of various naturally formed vortices, the ancient

Chinese people thought of "circular movement", "extension", and "continuity" as coexisting phenomena and made them three interconnected core semes in the language.

The State of Jin invented the *yuantian* 爰田 system where farmland was divided into upper, middle, and lower grades, and peasants took turns cultivating the land. To describe such a rotation operation, people back then created the character *yuan* 爰 (a farming system featuring the rotation of land) through the combination of *zou* 走 (go) and *gen* 亙 (continuous extension): the former was used to convey the meaning of "operation", and the latter to refer to the rotation. The character component *gen* 亙 is a combination of *er* 二 (two/twice) and *hui* 回 (turn around), and Duan Yucai 段玉裁 noted that both *gen* 亙 and *hui* 回 describe a circular movement. In other words, *gen* 亙 features a core seme, the "circular movement", as does *yuan* 爰. The word *yuantian* 爰田 can also be written as *yuantian* 爰田, and the character *yuan* 爰 (to lead on to) is included in *Shuowen Jiezi*. The book explains the character as a combination of *biao* 爫 (an object falling into a fixed place) and *kui* 亏 (deficient) and a term used to refer to the shaft of a cart in the seal script. According to Duan Yucai 段玉裁, in the big seal script, only this character can be used to refer to the shaft of a cart. Appearing much later than *yuan* 爰, *yuan* 轅 still keeps the core seme of the character "extension". The fact that *yuantian* 爰田 and *yuantian* 爰田 can be used interchangeably reflects that the core seme "circular movement" and "extension" are closely related. Another pair of characters *yuan* 淵 (whirling water) and *yuan* 遛 (walking) also shows the connection between the two core semes, and the core seme "circular movement" is expressed through the phonetic and semantic components of *yuan* 淵 (whirling water). Apart from the seme "extension", the core seme "circular movement" is closely related to "continuity". The composition of *heng* 恆 (permanent) is a typical example: the core seme of the character is "continuity", and that of its component *zhou* 舟 (boat) is "circular movement". *Shuowen Jiezi* points out that the character *heng* 恆 (permanent), a combination of *zhou* 舟 (boat), and *er* 二 (two/twice), describes the scene of paddling a boat. *Heng* 死, the archaic form of *heng* 恆, features the radical *yue* 月 (moon), which is often used to express permanence. There is such an expression in *Shi Jing* 诗经 (The Book of Songs): "as permanent as the moon (如月之恒)". Given this, it is reasonable to infer that the core seme of *heng* 恆 is "continuity". Interestingly, the core seme of *zhou* 舟 (boat), is "circular movement". This point can be proved by the records in *Shuowen Jiezi*: "The character *zhou* 舟 (boat) implies the circular movement, and the character *chuan* 船 (ship/vessel) implies the act of following; *ban* 般 describes the rotation of a boat." The book also uses the word *zhouxuan* 舟旋 to describe a circular movement. The phonetic and semantic component *gen* 亙 (continuous extension) of *heng* 恆 (permanent) keeps its core seme "continuity" in the composition of other characters. *Xuan* 咺 (non-stop crying of a child) is a typical example.

(II) The three interconnected core semes "circular movement", "circle", and "bent" determine the homologous relations of *yuan* 圓 (circle), *huan* 环 (ring), *xuan* 槫 (round food trays), *juan* 卷 (roll up), *quan* 圈 (to circle), *xuan* 旋 (revolve), *huan* 还 (return), *xuan* 漩 (a whirlpool), *yuan* 㤹 (to use lacquer and ashes to make pellets), *guan* 筦 (bamboo bobbins used to wind silk threads), *guan* 莞 (a kind of aquatic herb/mats made of the herb), and *wan* 丸 (pellet).

The seme "circular movement" depicts a dynamic process, and semes "circle" and "bent" depict static statuses. The character *yuan* 圓 (circle) originally means celestial bodies, but it is often used to express the state of being rotated. There is such a sentence in *Kongzi Jiayu* 孔子家语 (Teachings of Confucius): "There is a waterfall that is about 50 meters long and a huge whirlpool with a radius about 40 kilometres (有悬水三十仞，圓流九十里)." The character *juan* 卷 (roll up) originally means the act of bending one's knees, but it is widely used to describe the act of rolling something into a tube. In *Shi Jing* 诗经, there are such poetic lines: "My heart will not change easily; it is not a pebble that can be rolled back and forth nor a mat that can be rolled up (我心匪石，不可转也，我心匪席，不可卷也)."

Originally, the character *quan* 圈 refers to livestock fences. Gradually, its meaning is changed to "to circle". *Li ji* 礼记 (The Book of Rites) contains such sentences: Those people are walking in a circle at a brisk pace in small steps, looking like a herd of chained pigs; they barely lift their feet off the ground, and the fluttering hems of their clothes look like water waves (圈豚行，不举足，齐如流)." Zheng Xuan (127–200) noted that the character *quan* 圈 used here means "to circle". *Shuowen Jiezi* puts the character *xuan* 旋 (revolve) under the radical *yan* 㫃 (flags flying) and explains the character as the act of spinning a flagpole. Duan Yucai 段玉裁 agreed with the book as to the original meaning of the character, but he pointed out that its meaning expanded in use. *Erya* 尔雅 (Erya Dictionary) equals *xuan* 旋 (revolve) to *huan* 还 (return), and *Zilin* 字林 (A Collection of Characters) explains *xuan* 旋 (revolve) with the character *hui* 回 (turn around). All the three characters describe a process that repeats itself or goes round and round. *Shuowen Jiezi* arranges the character *xuan* 漩 (revolve) under the radical *shui* 水 (water) and explains it as a combination of *shui* 水 (water) and a simplified phonetic component *xuan* 旋 (revolve). Duan Yucai further pointed out that the character refers to a huge whirlpool that sucks boats and ships in just as what is described in *Jiangfu* 江赋 (Ode to the River)."

Evidently, *xuan* 旋 (revolve) and *xuan* 漩 (a whirlpool) are homologous characters that share the core seme "circular movement", but not all the characters that share the same semantic and phonetic right-placed component express the same core seme. For instance, the character *xuan* 镟 (round stove) gets its pronunciation from *xuan* 旋 (revolve), and its core seme is "circle", which is closely related to "circular movement". Another character featuring the core seme "circular movement" is *huan* 睘 (round). *Shuowen Jiezi* puts this character under the radical *mu* 目 (eye) and explains it as a combination of *mu* 目 (eye) and a phonetic component *yuan* 袁 (long), describing the act of widening one's eyes in shock. This character appears in *Shi Jing* 诗经: "I walk alone in anxiety (独行睘睘)." The word *huanhuan* 睘睘 describes a situation in which a person has nothing to rely on and keeps looking in all directions in horror.

Interestingly, three characters *yuan* 圜 (circle), *huan* 环 (ring), and *xuan* 槶 (round food trays), which sound like *huan* 睘 (round), share the core seme "circle" instead of "circular movement", which is the core seme of *huan* 睘 (round). The same thing happened to another group of similar-sounding characters consisting of *yuan* 坃 (to use lacquer and ashes to make pellets), *guan* 筦 (bamboo bobbins used to wind silk threads), and *guan* 莞 (a kind of aquatic herb/mats made of the herb). *Yuan* 坃 is arranged under that radical *tu* 土 (soil) and explained in the book *Shuowen Jiezi* as the act of using lacquer and ashes to make pellets (以桼和灰丸而鬓也). According to Duan Yucai 段玉裁, the character *wan* 丸 (pellet) appearing in the explanation is closely related to *yuan* 圜 (circle). *Shuowen Jiezi* puts the character *guan* 筦 (bamboo bobbins used to wind silk threads) under the radical *zhu* 竹 (bamboo) and equals it to *fu* 箁 (spinning tools made of bamboo). Duan Yucai points out that *yan* 筵 (bamboo mat), *guan* 筦 (bamboo bobbins used to wind silk threads), and *fu* 箁 (spinning tools made of bamboo) originally refers to the same thing, which is a spinning wheel, and lists the names of this tool in different dialects. The character *guan* 莞 (a kind of aquatic herb/mats made of the herb) is arranged under the radical *cao* 艹 (herbage) in *Shuowen Jiezi*, and, according to Duan Yucai, the herbs have round stems. Given this, the core seme of the character is "circle". The characters *juan* 桊 (a small ring threaded into the nose of a bull), *huan* 豢 (feed pig with grains in sty), *quan* 觠 (curved horns), and *juan* 卷 (roll up) share the same phonetic component *juan* 龹. Nevertheless, the first two feature the core seme "circle", and the last two share the core seme "bent". The characters *yuan* 夗 (to lie on your side with your hips and knees bent), *wan* 盌 (small basin), and *wan* 宛 (to bend) sound similar. Nonetheless, the core seme of *yuan* 夗 is "circular movement", and that of *wan* 盌 and *wan* 宛 (to bend) is "bent".

(III) The two core semes "circular movement" and "quickness and benefits" determine the homologous relations of *juan* 獧 (rash), *xuan* 儇 (quick in mind), and *xuan* 趡 (rapid).

The character *xuan* 旋 (revolve) has an extended meaning of "immediately". This usage appears in *Hou Han Shu* 后汉书 (The History of the Han Dynasty): "卓既杀琼、邲，旋亦悔之", which roughly translates to, "Dong Zhuo regretted immediately after executing Qiong and Bi." The character *huan* 还 (return) also has an extended meaning: "quick". For example, there is such a line in *Shi Jing* 诗经 (The Book of Songs): "子之还兮，遭我乎猫之间兮", which roughly translates to, "The man that I met while hunting in the valley was really quick." This usage also appears in *Han Shu* 汉书 (The History of the Han Dynasty): "此皆可使还至而立有效者也 (The Dynasty needed measures that could make a difference immediately)." It should be noted that the character 还 should be read as *xuan* 旋 (revolve) when this meaning is adopted. Apart from this case, *huan* 还 (return) is often equated to another character *fu* 复 (repeat) and features the core seme "circular movement". The core seme of the character *yuan* 圜 (circle) is also

Sense Relations Among Same-Origin Chinese Characters (Words) 171

"circular movement", and characters that share the same phonetic component *huan* ageas (round) with it also have the meaning "fast/quick". Such characters include *xuan* 趨 (rapid), *juan* 獧 (rash), and *xuan* 儇 (quick in mind). The character *xuan* 儇 is explained as "smart" in *Shuowen Jiezi* and used to refer to the cleverness and the benefits brought by it in *Shi Jing* 诗经 and *Xun Zi* 荀子 (The Philosophy of Xun Zi). The ancient Chinese people regarded quickness as a sign of cleverness and slowness as a sign of stupidity. They usually associated "benefits" and "cleverness" to "quickness". Therefore, the core seme of these character is summarised as "quickness and benefits".

(IV) Given the relations among the core semes "circular movement" and "circle" are associates with abundance, multiplicity, and largeness, the following characters are homologous characters: *yun* 云 (clouds), *hui* 洄 (an eddy), *hun* 混 (torrent), and *hun* 浑 (surging sounds).

The abovementioned core semes are linked together for a reason: naturally formed vortices require a large amount of airflow or running water, and thus expressions regarding these natural phenomena are closely linked to one another. *Shuowen Jiezi* specifically points out that the pictographic form of the character *yun* 云 (clouds) depicts a circular movement apart from naming its component 雨, and *Shi Jing* also has a minor court hymn containing the words "昏姻孔云" (great relationships with relatives). This shows that in addition to its core seme "circular movement", the character also conveys the meaning "greatness". Besides suggesting the greatness in quality, it is also used to express "a great amount" in *Shi Jing*: "齐子归止，其从如云" (When she returned her home, she was followed by a large entourage). The character *hui* 洄 (an eddy) has an extended meaning "chaos". In accordance with *Erya* 尔雅 (Erya Dictionary), the word *huihui* 洄洄 is equivalent to *hun* 惛 (muddled/bewildered). The character *hun* 混 (torrent), which is arranged under the radical *shui* 水 (water) in *Shuowen Jiezi*, has an extended meaning: rotation. This usage appears in *Huainanzi* 淮南子 (Master Huainan): "混然而往", which is explained by Gao You (an Eastern-Han-Dynasty scholar) as "taking a turn and walking in the opposite direction". It has another extended meaning: "being unable to distinguish right from wrong". For example, in *Xun Zi* (The Philosophy of Xun Zi), there is such a sentence: "使天下混然不知是非治乱之所存者，有人矣" (Some people are trying to confuse people, making them unable to tell right from wrong). Yang Liang, the Tang-Dynasty sinologist, also pointed out such a usage. The original meaning of the character *hun* 浑 is "surging sounds", as explained in *Shuowen Jiezi*. *Xun Zi* contains such a sentence: "财货浑浑如泉源" (A flood of money and commodities came in). Its core seme is "undivided state". Relevant evidence can be found in *Fangyan* 方言 (Dialects) and *Jin Shu* 晋书 (The History of the Jin Dynasty). *Jin Shu* contains a chapter about the famous scholar Wang Rong (234–305), which reads: "尝且山涛为璞玉浑金" (Wang Rong regarded Shan Tao as a beautiful jade without carving and unrefined gold).

IV. Conclusion

Chinese homologous characters are characters that conform to a certain pattern of phonetic proximity and share the same or interconnected core semes.

Sense relations among homologous characters reflect how people perceive the world. Traditional-style studies on same-origin characters reached a bottleneck because they always evolved around vaguely defined meanings or sememes and neglected that semes determine the sense relations among homologous characters. Such relations are caused by the similarities, differences, and interconnections of core semes. To investigate the deep structures of the Chinese language within the context of its complex historical and cultural backgrounds, it is imperative for researchers to acquire a profound comprehension of this notion, all while avoiding the influence of superficial phenomena.

Notes

1 The original Chinese version was first published in *Academic Voice* 学术之声 (issue 3), which is a supplement to *Journal of Beijing Normal University*, by the School of Chinese Language and Literature of Beijing Normal University in August 1990.
2 王念孙：《广雅疏证》卷三，第 99 页，北京：中华书局，1983.
Wang Niansun: *Annotations to Guangya* (Vol. 3), p. 99, Beijing: Zhonghua Book Company, 1983.
3 刘师培：《左盦集》卷四，第 17 页，宁武南氏校印本，1936.
Liu Shipei: *Works of Liu Shipei* (Vol. 4), p. 17, published by Ningwu Nanshi, 1936.
4 沈兼士：《沈兼士学术论文集》，第 259 页，北京：中华书局，1986.
Shen Jianshi: *Academic Papers of Shen Jianshi*, p. 259, Beijing: Zhonghua Book Company, 1986.
5 王先谦：《荀子集解·正名篇》，《诸子集成》第 2 册，第 276 页，上海：上海书店，1986.
Wang Xianqian: "Works of Pre-Qin Scholars", *Annotations to the Works of Xunzi* (Vol. 2), p. 276, Shanghai: Shanghai Bookstore Publishing House, 1986.
6 章太炎：《文始·序》，《章氏丛书》第二册，第 4 页，江苏：广陵古籍刊印社，1981.
Zhang Taiyan: "Wenshi Dictionary of Homologous Characters", *Works of Zhang Taiyan* (Vol. 2), p. 4, Jiangsu: Guangling Ancient Books Printing House, 1981.
7 刘师培：《小学发微补》，《刘申叔先生遗书》卷十一，第 10 页，宁武南氏校印本，1936.
Liu Shipei: "Works by Liu Shenshu", *Supplements to Minor Studies* (Vol. 10), p. 10, published by Ningwu Nanshi, 1936.
8 章太炎：《语言缘起说》，《章氏丛书》第十四册，第 36 页，江苏：广陵古籍刊印社，1981.
Zhang Taiyan: "The Origin of the Language", *Works of Zhang Taiyan* (Vol. 14), p. 36, Jiangsu: Guangling Ancient Books Printing House, 1981.

11 Three Issues Regarding the Currently Used Chinese Characters[1]

I. Functional Classification of Components

There are two aspects to discussing the composition of Chinese characters: components and compositional structures. Character components are combined in different ways, or different compositional structures, to form characters. In general, character components can be divided into the following three categories: semantic components, phonetic components, and marks. Semantic components are related to the meanings of characters, and phonetic components, to the pronunciations of characters. As to marks, they are usually defined as components that have no semantic or phonetic functions in the composition of characters. The confirmation of marks is a subject worth discussing. Sometimes, the so-called marks, such as *ri* 日 (sun) and *xin* 心 (heart), also have semantic functions, as in the characters *qing* 晴 (cloudless) and *yi* 意 (idea). In *Modern Chinese* 现代汉语, Qian Nairong 钱乃荣 puts forward such a view: "The classification of components should be determined according to their roles in the composition of characters, which means that a component may be put into different categories in different situations."

(1) *ri* 日 (sun), *xin* 心 (heart), *chong* 虫 (worm/insect), *shan* 山 (hill), *men* 门 (door), and *tu* 土 (soil)
(2) *qing* 晴 (cloudless), *yi* 意 (idea), *yi* 蚁 (ants), *yi* 屹 (towering), *shan* 闪 (to peek out from behind a door), and *chen* 尘 (dust)

The characters listed in the first (1) row are single-component characters. Their components are marks that have nothing to do with their pronunciations or meanings. However, in the characters listed in the second (2) row, these marks become semantic components. Su Peicheng, in *Outline of Modern Chinese Philology*, comments on this phenomenon as follows. "Components, such as *ri* 日 (sun) and *yue* 月 (moon), are marks when used independently, but they convey meanings related to the sun, light, or shade when used as radicals of multi-component characters, such as *qing* 晴 (cloudless), *ming* 明 (light), *dan* 旦 (daybreak), *hun* 昏 (dusk), *shai* 晒 (exposed to the sun), *hui* 晖 (light), *chen* 晨 (early morning), and *an* 暗 (dim). There is no contradiction between the two phenomena. The single-component character *ri* 日 (sun) is regarded as a mark because its current form is not pictographic enough, but this character has its meaning and pronunciation. When used as a radical, *ri* 日 retains the original pronunciation and meaning of the character to varying degrees."

Yang Runlu 杨润陆 also points out this phenomenon in *The General Theory of Modern Chinese Philology* 现代汉字学通论: "Single-component characters, such as *li* 力 (capability), *gong* 工 (work), and *tu* 土 (soil), are marks, but they become semantic components when they are used as radicals in multiple-component characters, such as *gong* 功 (achievement), *qiao* 巧 (ingenious), and *di* 地 (ground)."

The abovementioned views are not necessarily correct. They ignore the historical process by which these single-component characters were transformed from pictographs to non-pictographic characters. There is also a logical fallacy. Those marks, such as *ri* 日 (sun), retain their meanings either when used alone or in combination with other components. It seems unreasonable to define them as both marks and semantic components. The semantic-compound character *cong* 从 (follow) is also a typical example. In this case, only *ren* 人 is involved in the composition of the character, and the two *ren* 人 components rely on each other to explain themselves. If the character is regarded as a combination of 人 marks whose forms have nothing to do with pronunciations or meanings, how can these characters be explained as one person following another? Furthermore, the function of *ren* 人 (person) clearly does not depend on its usage: whether used alone as a single-component character or as part of a multicomponent character, it is an ideograph. So, there is no physical or functional difference between *ren* 人 (person) and the component *ren* 人 (person) in *cong* 从 (follow) or between *ri* 日 (sun) and the component *ri* 日 (sun) in *qing* 晴 (cloudless). There is no need to name them marks when they serve as single-component characters and semantic components when they appear in multicomponent characters. To thoroughly understand this issue, it is necessary to grasp the nature of the evolution of Chinese characters: Chinese characters evolve from pictographs into phonetic-semantic symbols. Early Chinese characters were created to depict images, and it was difficult to have uniform standards for describing images. As a result, early characters and character companions generally had no standard forms. For example, when depicting a person in a character, there might be uncertainty about whether to omit the head or the feet, and whether to depict the person sitting, kneeling, or standing. The pictographic forms of *ni* 逆 (meet head-on) differ from one another in terms of component usage: they may feature component *zhi* 止 (toe), 彳, or *chuo* 辵 (walking). Such phenomena are very common in oracle-bone inscriptions: although pictographs cannot depict things as realistically as sketches or paintings, their essence is still pictorial symbols. This feature of pictographs causes two problems: (1) the low writing speed and (2) the difficulties in reading and understanding.

These shortcomings determine the primitiveness of early Chinese characters. When Chinese characters were transformed from pictographs into phonetic-semantic symbols, their forms were gradually simplified for convenient writing. Because characters were widely used for communication, this transformation process was long. When pictographs were transformed into sub-pictographs, such as the bronze-inscription characters and the characters used in the Warring States Period

(475–221 BCE), the forms of characters could hardly evoke images of things. The pictographic features of the characters were further reduced in the small-seal script and completely removed during the official script transformation, which marked that Archaic pictographs were transformed into New-Style phonetic-semantic symbols. Despite the changes in forms, a tradition of Chinese characters has been preserved: certain shapes in the writing system still have certain pronunciations and meanings. This is because pictographic characters were generally transformed into phonetic-semantic symbols, not some marks. For the same reason, it is incorrect to name the transformed, non-photographic components, such as those found in the characters *cong* 从 (follow) and *qing* 晴 (cloudless), as marks.

It is worth noting that the above analysis does not negate the fact that there are marks among the components of currently used Chinese characters. For example, the component in the middle of the character *han* 寒 (cold) is a mark. This mark is an irregular mixture of *mang* 茻 (tufted grass) and *ren* 人 (person), which has no correspondence with the ancient forms at all, and it has no phonetic or semantic functions. Due to the changes in pronunciation, the phonetic component *gong* 工 (work) of the character *gang* 缸 (vat) can no longer accurately represent the pronunciation of the character, and thus becomes a mark.

Based on the above analysis, character components are divided into four categories in this study, namely: *cifu* 词符 (word symbols), semantic components, phonetic components, and marks. The term *cifu*, or word symbols, refers to components that can function independently as characters (one-character words) and convey both the meaning and pronunciation of a word.

II. Classification of Semantic Components Used in Semantic-Phonetic Characters

How do semantic components in semantic-phonetic characters express meanings? Or, how is it possible to define the sense relations between semantic-phonetic characters and their semantic components? At present, there are only general and imprecise answers to this question, such as "semantic-phonetic characters and their semantic components being directly or indirectly related". In fact, this question is of considerable importance and needs to be solved through systematic and comprehensive analysis. The solution to the problem is related to the nature and creation basis of currently used Chinese characters, the functions of semantic components, and the studies of Chinese characters and culture. A preliminary analysis of this issue is contained in the following paragraphs, and the analysis is based on the 7,000 characters included in the "List of Frequently Used Characters in Modern Chinese".

(I) Principles of the Analysis

1. This study is based on the standard interpretations of semantic-phonetic characters and those of their semantic components published in *The Modern Chinese Dictionary* (revised in July 1996).

176 *Three Issues Regarding the Currently Used Chinese Characters*

2. Characters in binome words and reduplicated words, which serve as syllables, are treated as independent characters in the analysis. For instance, the two characters in the binome word *chaya* 嵖岈 (name of a mountain in Henan province) are analysed as independent characters featuring the semantic component *shan* 山 (hill). The characters in the reduplicated word *daodao* 忉忉 (worried) are analysed as independent characters featuring the semantic component *xin* 忄 (heart).
3. The analysis acknowledges the fact that some semantic components have already developed into category names. *Shou* 扌 (hand) is regarded as a category name for characters describing human body movements, such as *kang* 抗 (resist) and *dou* 抖 (quiver). The component *quan* 犭 (dog) has become a category name for characters that denote animal names, such as *ma* 犸 (mammoth), *bei* 狈 (a legendary beast), and *pao* 狍 (roe deer).
4. The analysis considers the fact that some semantic components reflect some ideas of the ancient Chinese people, which are deemed wrong from today's point of view. For instance, the ancient Chinese people used the semantic component *yu* 玉 (precious stone) in *manao* 玛瑙 (agate) because they considered agate to be jade, which is now considered to be a misclassification.

(II) Types of Sense Relations between Semantic-Phonetic Characters and Their Semantic Components

1. Synonymy

Synonymy is a sense relation between semantic-phonetic characters and their semantic components where they have the same or similar meanings.

For instance, *ba* 爸 (father) is synonymous with its semantic component *fu* 父 (father), and *ji* 肌 (muscle) is synonymous with its semantic component *yue* 月/肉 (flesh). The component *xiang* 香 (fragrance) has the same meaning as the character *fu* 馥 (fragrance).

2. Homogeneity

Homogeneity is a sense relation where a group of semantic-phonetic characters share a common semantic component that acts as a classification category for their common characteristics.

The characters *yi* 议 (discuss), *lun* 论 (discourse), *ping* 评 (comment), *zha* 诈 (swindle), and *ju* 讵 (an interjection used to express surprise) all feature the component *yan* 讠 (speak), which is a simplified form of *yan* 言 (speak). The characters *si* 汜 (name of a river), *cha* 汊 (a branching stream), *yuan* 沅 (name of a river), *mian* 沔 (name of a river), *feng* 沣 (name of a river), *si* 泗 (name of a river), and *bi* 沘 (name of a river) all share the common component *shui* 氵 (water).

3. Inclusion

Inclusion is a sense relation between semantic-phonetic characters and their semantic components where the characters describe specific aspects of the objects or concepts represented by their semantic components.

Three Issues Regarding the Currently Used Chinese Characters 177

The character *nai* 奶 (women's breasts) describes a part of *nv* 女 (woman/girl), which is its semantic component. The character *dai* 轪 (iron cap covered on the hub of a cart) describes a part of *che* 车 (cart).

4. *Deeds and Doers*

Deeds and Doers is a sense relation where a group of semantic-phonetic characters that describe actions or deeds share a common semantic component that indicates the doer of the action.

The characters *dian* 佃 (to rent farmland from a landlord), *ren* 任 (to assign someone to a post), *zhang* 仗 (battle), *zuo* 佐 (assist), *si* 伺 (to inspect and wait), and *you* 佑 (protect) all share the same component *ren* 亻 (person) that indicates the doer of these deeds. The characters *ai* 嗳 (interjection), *tu* 吐 (spit), *yao* 吆 (cry out), *diao* 叼 (hold in the mouth), *ding* 叮 (sting), *ming* 鸣 (chirp), *e* 呃 (interjection used to express exclamation or reminder), *bi* 吡 (slander), and *yi* 呓 (speak in one's sleep) are all related to mouth movements and share the component *kou* 口 (mouth).

5. *People, Things, and Their Conditions*

People, Things, and Their Conditions is a sense relation where semantic-phonetic characters that describe the conditions of a person or a thing share a common semantic component that indicates the person or thing itself.

The characters *ding* 仃 (lonely), *chen* 伧 (vulgar person), *pi* 伾 (mighty), *zhong* 仲 (the second eldest brother), and *lun* 伦 (human relations) describe a characteristic or status of a person, which is represented by their common semantic component *ren* 亻 (person). The characters *xiong* 洶 (turbulent), *cang* 沧 (dark green), *yun* 沄 (turbulent), *xi* 汐 (night tides), *li* 沥 (trickle), and *gou* 沟 (narrow waterway) describe the state of water, which is represented by their common semantic component *shui* 氵 (water).

6. *Objects and Their Materials*

Objects and Their Materials is a type of sense relation wherein a group of semantic-phonetic characters used to name objects share a common semantic component that denotes the material substance from which the object is made.

The character *wan* 纨 (fine silk) features the semantic component *si* 纟 (silk), and the characters *zhang* 杖 (walking stick), *wu* 杌 (a square stool), *cha* 杈 (pitchfork), and *cai* 材 (timber) all share the semantic component *mu* 木 (wood). The component *jin* 钅 (metal) appears in characters, such as *luo* 锣 (gong), *chui* 锤 (hammer), *guo* 锅 (cooking-pot), and *ding* 钉 (nail).

7. *Actions and Tools*

Actions and Tools is a sense relation where semantic-phonetic characters used to describe actions share a semantic component indicating the tool involved.

The character *gu* 锢 (fill up cracks with molten metal) features the semantic component *jin* 钅 (metal), and *ren* 纫 (to thread a needle) features the semantic component *si* 纟 (silk). The semantic component *shui* 氵 (water) is shared by the characters *mu* 沐 (to wash one's hair), *tai* 汰 (to wash out), and *ou* 沤 (to soak).

8. Actions and Action Targets

Actions and Action Targets is a sense relation in which a group of semantic-phonetic characters denoting actions share a common semantic component denoting the target of the actions.

The character *ji* 汲 (to draw water from well) features the semantic component *shui* 氵 (water), and the character *ren* 轫 (a block that keeps a wheel of a vehicle from moving) has the semantic component *che* 车 (vehicle).

9. Adjectives and Typical Examples

Adjectives and Typical Examples is a sense relation where a group of semantic-phonetic characters describe the attributes of an object through their shared semantic components, which represent the object itself.

The one-character adjective *xian* 纤 (delicate) features the semantic component *si* 纟 (silk), and another one-character adjective *ren* 韧 (resilient) has the semantic component *wei* 韦 (tanned leather). The semantic component *mi* 米 (rice) appears in a series of one-character adjectives: *jing* 精 (refined), which originally means "polished rice"; *cu* 粗 (crude), which originally means "unpolished rice"; *cu* 粹 (pure), which is originally used to refer to "pure rice"; *cao* 糙 (rough), whose original meaning is "brown rice"; and *nian* 粘 (sticky), which originally means "paste made of rice".

10. Events and the Places of Occurrence

Events and the Places of Occurrence is a sense relation where semantic-phonetic characters denoting events share semantic components used to indicate the places where these events occur.

The characters *chen* 沉 (sinking), *mo* 没 (submerging), and *lun* 沦 (rippling) all feature the semantic component shui 氵 (water).

11. Actions and Places of Occurrence

Actions and Places of Occurrence is a sense relation where semantic-phonetic characters denoting actions share semantic components used to indicate the places where these actions occur.

The following characters, including *du* 渡 (ferry someone through), *she* 涉 (to wade), *qiu* 泅 (to float), *yong* 泳 (to swim), and *yu* 渔 (fishing), all feature the semantic component *shui* 氵 (water), as all these actions take place in rivers, seas, and other bodies of water.

III. The Determination and Classification of Phonetic Components of Semantic-Phonetic Character

(I) Criteria for Determining Pronunciation Similarity

The pronunciations discussed in this part refer to the way in which a Chinese character or character component is currently pronounced, excluding its ancient pronunciations. This is a common practice in studies on the pronunciations of Chinese characters. However, there is no consensus among researchers on the criteria for determining pronunciation similarity. Some researchers hold that if one of the following seven criteria is met, pronunciation similarity can be confirmed: two characters (including character components) sharing the same (1) *pinyin* initials, finals, and tones; (2) initials and finals; (3) initials and tones; (4) finals and tones; (5) initials; (6) finals; or (7) tones can be regarded as homophonic characters. This is the most lenient standard. Some researchers adopt relatively strict standards and accept only three or six of the abovementioned criteria, and some believe that the most rigorous research approach shall accept only the first (1) criterion. In this study, both the first (1) and second (2) criteria are adopted in determining pronunciation similarity. To be more specific, in this study, components are regarded as phonetic components of semantic-phonetic characters only when they meet one of the following three criteria:

(a) sharing the same Chinese *pinyin* initials, finals, and tones with the semantic-phonetic characters;
(b) sharing the same initials and finals with the semantic-phonetic characters; and
(c) sharing the same main vowels and final vowels or consonants in the finals.

There is usually no dispute over the above-listed criteria (a) and (b), but criterion (c) needs further explanation. Simply put, criterion (c) refers to a situation where the component and the character rhyme properly. This is taken as a criterion for the following four reasons:

(1) The history of semantic-phonetic characters shows that not all semantic-phonetic characters are created with phonetic components that are pronounced identically and that most semantic-phonetic characters just rhyme with their phonetic components.
(2) The phenomenon mentioned in (1) was widely accepted in the ancient research literature and embodied in the compilation of ancient dictionaries.

180 *Three Issues Regarding the Currently Used Chinese Characters*

(3) The phenomenon mentioned in (1) is still widespread among currently used Chinese characters, and such phenomena with historical reasons should not be ignored.
(4) By rhyming with semantic-phonetic characters, phonetic components can also realise their function of expressing character pronunciations.

(II) Multi-Pronunciation Phonetic Components

There are two types of multi-pronunciation components: (1) multi-pronunciation characters used as single-pronunciation phonetic components; (2) multi-pronunciation characters used as multi-pronunciation phonetic components.

For example, 车, as a character, has two pronunciations: *che* and *ju*, but as a phonetic component, it is pronounced only as *che*: *chē* 伡 (boat engine) and *chē* 砗 (a kind of mollusc). The character 孛 is pronounced as *bei* or *bo*, and it is also a multi-pronunciation phonetic component: *bèi* 悖 (be contradictory to), *bó* 勃 (vigorous), *bó* 脖 (neck), *bó* 鹁 (a kind of bird), *bó* 醇 (strong fragrance), *bō* 饽 (a kind of pasta), and *bō* 哱 (a kind of bird).

(III) Character and Non-Character Phonetic Components

Phonetic components can be divided into two types according to whether they can be used independently as Chinese characters. Character phonetic components can be used as characters. For example, the character *feng* 风 (wind) serves as a phonetic component in the character *feng* 枫 (maple tree). Non-character phonetic components cannot be used in this way. Typical examples are *liao* 尞 (fuel used for worship ceremonies) and *ye* 枼 (flat pieces of wood), which cannot be used as characters today. Among the 7,000 characters included in the "List of Frequently Used Characters in Modern Chinese", there are 12 characters featuring the phonetic component *liao* 尞: *liao* 獠 (to hunt), *liao* 僚 (official), *liao* 撩 (to put in order), *liao* 獠 (to hunt), *liao* 缭 (to wind round), *liao* 镣 (fetters), *liao* 潦 (rainy), *liao* 寮 (small window), *liao* 嘹 (resonant), *liao* 燎 (set afire), *liao* 鹩 (wren), and *liao* 鹩 (wren). The nine characters featuring the phonetic component *ye* 枼 include *dié* 堞 (battlements), *dié* 碟 (small dish), *dié* 蝶 (butterfly), *dié* 谍 (spy), *xiè* 渫 (dredge), *dié* 喋 (talk endlessly), *dié* 牒 (writing slip), *dié* 喋 (talk endlessly), and *dié* 鲽 (flatfish). Among the nine characters, only *xiè* 渫 (dredge) is pronounced differently. This phenomenon is called phonetic variation, and 枼 in 渫 is thus referred to as a phonetic component variant, which also meets the criteria mentioned in part (I). There are more than 90 non-character phonetic components in the "List of Frequently Used Characters in Modern Chinese".

(IV) Phonetic Component Variants

Semantic-phonetic characters featuring phonetic component variants described in part (II) are referred to as semantic-phonetic character variants.

In the "List of Frequently Used Characters in Modern Chinese", there are 12 semantic-phonetic characters featuring the phonetic component *xu* 需 (await). Among them, there are 10 semantic-phonetic characters pronounced as *rú* and two semantic-phonetic character variants pronounced as *nuò*: *rú* 儒 (scholar server), *rú* 蠕 (squirm), *rú* 薷 (an edible fungus), *rú* 嚅 (talk indistinctly and falteringly), *rú* 濡 (name of a river), *rú* 孺 (child), *rú* 襦 (jacket), *rú* 蕦 (an edible fungus), *rú* 颥 (the temporal bone), *rú* 臑 (upper limbs), *nuò* 懦 (cowardly), and *nuò* 糯 (glutinous rice).

Among the 13 semantic-phonetic characters featuring the phonetic component *ta* 它 (worm) in the "List of Frequently Used Characters in Modern Chinese", there are 12 semantic-phonetic characters pronounced as *tuó* and one semantic-phonetic character variant pronounced as *shé*: *tuó* 陀 (uneven), *tuó* 驼 (camel), *tuó* 鸵 (ostrich), *tuó* 沱 (tributary), *tuó* 佗 (a load), *tuó* 跎 (to carry on the back), *tuó* 砣 (a stone roller), *tuó* 坨 (lump), *tuó* 酡 (to be flushed with wine), *tuó* 柁 (girder), *tuó* 舵 (helm), *tuó* 铊 (short spear) and *shé* 蛇 (snake).

They are 96 phonetic component variants in the "List of Frequently-Used Characters in Modern Chinese".

Note

1 The original Chinese version was published in *Applied Linguistics* 语言文字应用, 2005, issue 2.

References

[1] Dictionary Editorial Office, Institute of Linguistics of the Chinese Academy of Social Sciences: *The Modern Chinese Dictionary (Revised Edition)*, Beijing: The Commercial Press, 1996.
[2] Language and Culture Press: *Language Specification Manual (Revised and Updated Edition)*, Beijing: Language and Culture Press, 1993.
[3] Qian Nairong et al.: *Modern Chinese*, Beijing: Higher Educational Press, 1990.
[4] Su Peicheng: *Outline of Modern Chinese Philology*, Beijing: Peking University Press, 1994.
[5] Su Peicheng: *References for Studies on Modern Chinese Characters*, Beijing: Peking University Press, 2001.
[6] Yang Runlu: *The General Theory of Modern Chinese Philology*, Beijing: Great Wall Publishing House, 2000.

12 Analysis Methods Used in Studies of Characters on Unearthed Texts[1]

I. Characters in Ancient Texts and Ancient Character Books

Studies of ancient Chinese characters are usually based on two types of materials: ancient texts and ancient character books. The former refers to ancient books, articles, documents, and account books, in which characters appear in specific contexts. The latter refers to various kinds of ancient dictionaries, character tables, and character lists, which record only characters and sort them by the number of strokes or by phonetics. Ancient character books, such as *Leibian* 类编 (Leibian Character Book), *Yupian* 玉篇 (Chinese dictionary compiled by Gu Yewang in the 6th century), and *Jiyun* 集韵 (Jiyun Rhyming Dictionary), collect Chinese characters used in different time periods and organize them according to certain rules. The compilation of such character books often involved the transcription of contents from previous character books. Ancient character books are rarely cited in studies on the history of Chinese characters for the following three reasons:

(1) Ancient character books tend to set standards for character forms and include only regular-script forms instead of the widely used forms, thus being inadequate in reflecting the history of Chinese characters.
(2) Ancient character books usually do not include all the character forms in use, especially character variants, which results in the loss of research clues regarding the evolution of character forms and meanings.
(3) The contents of ancient character books often overlap with one another, making it hard to determine which historical periods the character forms belong to. Problems such as inaccurate character forms and unreasonable arrangement also appear in modern and contemporary character tables and character lists. For instance, there are more than 110 obvious errors or inaccurate descriptions in *Table of Qin, Han, Wei, and Jin Official-Script Characters*, published by Sichuan Lexicographical Publishing House.

So, as shown by all the errors mentioned above, character books cannot provide reliable information for the statistics and investigation of the studies on the history of Chinese characters.

Analysis Methods Used on Unearthed Texts 183

Table 12.1 Mistaken Copies of Characters from Silk Manuscripts Unearthed in Mawangdui

Original Form		Mistaken Form	
	Laozi 老子 (The Philosophy of Laozi), manuscript A, line 325		*Table of Qin, Han, Wei, and Jin Official-Script Characters*, page 95
	Laozi 老子 (The Philosophy of Laozi), line 233		*Table of Qin, Han, Wei, and Jin Official-Script Characters*, page 214
	Chunqiu Shiyu 春秋事语 (Events of the Spring and Autumn Period), line 94		*Table of Qin, Han, Wei, and Jin Official-Script Characters*, page 901
	Laozi 老子 (The Philosophy of Laozi), manuscript B, line 229 (part 1)		*Table of Qin, Han, Wei, and Jin Official-Script Characters*, page 866
	Laozi 老子 (The Philosophy of Laozi), manuscript B, line 22 (part 2)		*Table of Qin, Han, Wei, and Jin Official-Script Characters*, page 845
	Laozi 老子 (The Philosophy of Laozi), manuscript A, line 13		*Table of Qin, Han, Wei, and Jin Official-Script Characters*, page 760
	Zhanguo Zonghengjia Shu 战国纵横家书 (Political Strategists of the Warring States Period), line 248		*Table of Qin, Han, Wei, and Jin Official-Script Characters*, page 739
	Laozi 老子 (The Philosophy of Laozi), manuscript B, line 78 (part 1)		*Table of Qin, Han, Wei, and Jin Official-Script Characters*, page 675
	Chunqiu Shiyu 春秋事语 (Events of the Spring and Autumn Period), line 8		*Table of Qin, Han, Wei, and Jin Official-Script Characters*, page 514
	Laozi 老子 (The Philosophy of Laozi), manuscript A, line 115		*Table of Qin, Han, Wei, and Jin Official-Script Characters*, page 511
	Chunqiu Shiyu 春秋事语 (Events of the Spring and Autumn Period), line 95		*Table of Qin, Han, Wei, and Jin Official-Script Characters*, page 446
	Chunqiu Shiyu 春秋事语 (Events of the Spring and Autumn Period), line 13		*Table of Qin, Han, Wei, and Jin Official-Script Characters*, page 403
	Zhanguo Zonghengjia Shu 战国纵横家书 (Political Strategists of the Warring States Period), line 217		*Table of Qin, Han, Wei, and Jin Official-Script Characters*, page 214

The existing ancient texts are divided into two categories: handed-down texts and unearthed texts. The former mainly exist in printed versions now and thus do not include character forms used to create or transcript the texts. The latter can provide reliable materials for studies on the history of Chinese characters since the age of their creation can be accurately judged.

As mentioned above, characters appear in contexts in these ancient texts. Therefore, it is possible to analyse both the forms and meanings of characters based on text analyses and the use of summary tables to summarise the character forms appearing in these texts. Such texts provide reliable materials for the systematic analysis of character forms and meanings.

II. Character Analysis

(I) Similarities and Differences in Character Samples

The study of unearthed texts is complicated by the fact that they primarily consist of manuscripts, and writers often exhibit varying writing habits, resulting in multiple possible variations for a given character. For the convenience of analysis, the characters collected are referred to as character samples, which are combinations of their form and meaning (semantic function), and the analysis of character samples centres on comparing and contrasting their similarities and differences in both form and meaning. Character samples are firstly divided into different categories according to their different meanings or semantic functions. After that, a group of synonymous character samples is further classified according to their differences in form.

There are same-form synonymous character samples, such as ▨, which appear three times in the 66th line and once in the 71st, 88th, and 92nd lines of *Chunqiu Shiyu* 春秋事语 (Events of the Spring and Autumn Period), a silk manuscript unearthed from the Mawangdui Han Tombs.

Due to changes in writing habits and the evolution of characters, there are differently written synonymous character samples, such as those appearing in the following parts of the silk manuscripts unearthed from Mawangdui Han Tombs: ▨ and ▨, respectively, in the 409th and 372nd lines of the silk-manuscript copy (part A) of *Laozi* 老子 (The Philosophy of Laozi); ▨ in the 75th line of *Chunqiu Shiyu* 春秋事语; ▨ and ▨, respectively, in the 183rd and 150th lines of *Zhanguo Zonghengjia Shu* 战国纵横家书 (Political Strategists of the Warring States Period), and ▨ in the 122nd line of the silk-manuscript copy (part B) of *Laozi* 老子.

They are also differently structured synonymous character samples, and typical examples could be found in the following parts of the silk manuscripts unearthed from the Mawangdui Han Tombs: the 121st and 51st lines of the silk-manuscript copy (part A) of *Laozi* 老子; the 224th line of the silk-manuscript copy (part B) of *Laozi* 老子 (The Philosophy of Laozi).

The non-synonymous character samples are also classified in the above way: there are same-form non-synonymous character samples, differently written non-synonymous character samples, and differently structured non-synonymous character samples.

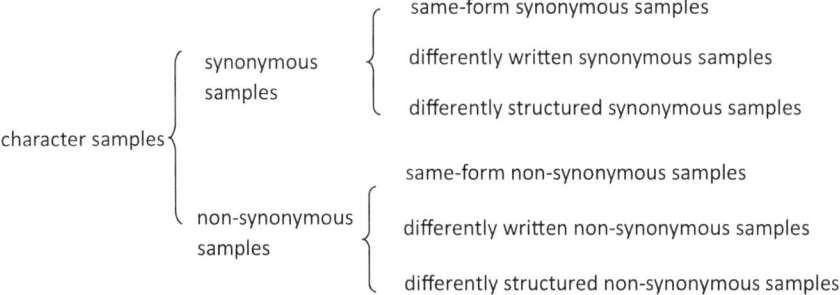

Figure 12.1 Classification of Character Samples Based on Functions and Forms

Same-form synonymous character samples appear repeatedly in the texts involved, while differently structured non-synonymous character samples and differently written non-synonymous character samples are considered distinct characters. For example, *wu* 𠂉 (无, negative) and *xian* 𠂔 (先, previous) are differently written non-synonymous characters.

In the analysis, *wu* 𠂉 and *wu* 𣥂 (无, negative) shall be grouped into the set of variants of *wu* 无, and *xian* 𠂔 and *xian* 𣥂 (先, previous) shall be grouped into the set of variants of *xian* 先. Therefore, in the analysis of a set of variants of the same character, the focus shall be placed on differently written synonymous character samples, differently structured synonymous character samples, and same-form non-synonymous character samples. These three types of character samples are referred to as differently written variants, differently structured variants, and homographs.

(II) Differently Written Variants, Differently Structured Variants, and Homographs

Differently written variants are the results of the evolution of Chinese characters or different writing habits. For these reasons, a character used in ancient texts often has several differently written variants, such as 𠀎, 𠀍, and 𠀌, which appear in the 331st, 369th, and 293rd lines of the silk-manuscript copy (part A) of *Laozi* 老子 (The Philosophy of Laozi), and those appearing in the 293rd line of the silk-manuscript copy (part A) of *Laozi* 老子, 𠀌 appearing in the 69th line of *Chunqiu Shiyu* 春秋事语, and 𠀍 appearing in the 136th line of the silk-manuscript copy (part B) of *Laozi* 老子. In the analysis, a standard form should be chosen for each character from its various variants, while considering all the variants as the same character.

The choice of a standard form is based on the following ideas. When the writing system was in a process of change and did not reach a stable state, there was naturally a plethora of variants for a character. These variations were, however, only temporary phenomena. When the stable state was reached, the number of variants per character tended to decrease to only one, and the forms other than this selected form (sometimes, the selected form would be altered a little) would be abolished. Therefore, such a selected form or its predecessor became the standard form of the character. It is worth noting that variants appearing during the transitional phase or prior to the stable state possessed theoretically equivalent status, but in practice, were distinguished by differences in their capacity to convey the intended meaning, character form and structure, and ease of writing, among other factors. A variant that offered advantages in semantic function and structure was more likely to be designated as the standard form.

Different writing systems used in different periods proposed different requirements for character forms. The oracle-bone script needed characters to be as pictographic as possible. The small-seal script highlighted the importance of standard forms and the integration of form and meaning. The establishment of the official script was realised through the replacement of various lines and dots with simplified strokes and the modification or abolishment of seldom-used or pictographic characters. For example, 夲 and 畕 were, respectively, modified into *fu* 夫 (man) and 丠 during this process. Both the small-seal script and the official script pursued regularity in character forms, but it was the official script that made a step further in this respect: to pursue regularity in character forms, the official script even allowed a decrease in the characters' ideographic function.

In this study, the determination of early official-script standard-character forms follows two principles: (1) a standard-character form selected shall have its origin in the small-seal script; (2) a standard-character form selected shall be built reasonably with standardised character components. The second (2) principle refers to the rules governing the character composition system of the official script. These two principles are also applicable to the selection of standard-character components and standard-character morphs (character morphs: the smallest units of Chinese characters, which have independent structural characteristics and compositional functions and cannot be further broken down), which are differentiated in their capacity to function independently as characters.

What needs to be clarified is that the standard forms mentioned above are selected for a certain range of texts instead of for a script or a writing system. If the character samples do not cover all the character forms used in a script or writing system, the standard forms selected out of them shall not be regarded as the standards for the script or writing system.

Differently structured variants include three types:

(1) Differently structured variants feature different character components. Typical examples include *sun* 损 (impair) and 敹 (impair), *cha* 察 (examine) and 詧 (examine), and *que* 卻 (retreat) and 御 (retreat).
(2) Differently structured variants feature the same character components combined in different ways, such as *jing* 静 (motionless) and 靖 (motionless), *ling* 軨 (lattice work on panels of a carriage) and 軨 (lattice work on panels of a carriage), *du* 妒 (envious) and 妬 (envious), and *xu* 怴 (be puzzled) and *huo* 惑 (be puzzled). In this type of differently structured variants, the change in the combinations of components does not make any change to the meanings of the characters. As there are no hierarchical relations among the components of such a character and its differently structured variants, these components

can be combined in different ways without harming the character's compositional structure or semantic function. If the original compositional structure and semantic function of a character is affected through an arbitrary modification (such as changing the orientation of a component), the character variant created through such modification shall be regarded as a differently written variant instead of a differently structured variant. Arbitrarily modified character forms usually caused confusion in the writing system, so it was hard for such character forms to be popularised and passed down. Such arbitrarily modified characters include 孞 (standardly written as 命), which appears in the 331st line of the silk-manuscript copy (part A) of *Laozi* 老子 (The Philosophy of Laozi), and 𣪘 (standardly written as 殷), which appears in the 86th line of the silk-manuscript copy (part B) of *Laozi* 老子.

(3) Differently structured variants created through the simplification of the original character forms. Typical examples include *jue* 爵 (peerage) and 𠈱 (peerage), *you* 憂 (mourning), and 𢝊 (mourning), 屈 (to bend) and *qu* 屈 (to bend), and *gu* 穀 (paper mulberry) and 㲁 (paper mulberry). *Shuowen Jiezi* 说文解字 (An Explication of Written Characters) also regards such simplified character forms as differently structured variants of the original character forms. For example, character 爑 (burned) is arranged under radical *huo* 火 (fire) and explained as a combination of *huo* 火 (fire) and phonetic component *za* 雥 (a flock of birds) in the book, and the book also points out that it has a simplified form *jiao* 焦 (burned). Character *rong* 融 (smoke from kitchen chimneys) is explained as a simplified form of the big-seal-script character 𧢴 and a combination of *ge* 鬲 (separate) and phonetic component *chong* 蟲 (insect) in the book. As to the calligraphic simplification made to characters (mainly to strokes instead of structures), they can be regarded as differently written characters theoretically, and they are essentially personalised and artistic treatments of character forms. So, to distinguish between differently structured variants and differently written variants, it is a must to find out whether the changes made to the original forms are aimed at strokes or character components. Differently structured characters involve changes made to character morphs and their combinations.

Nevertheless, differently written characters involve changes only made to strokes. Character *shi* 施 (flag waving) is written simply as 也 in silk manuscripts. As 㫃 is a character morph that cannot be further broken down and the removed part 方 is just a combination of strokes, this simplified form shall be regarded as a differently written variant of *shi* 施. Character *ma* 馬 (horse) can be written simply as 馬 by removing a dot from the original form, so the latter is a differently written variant of the former.

It is noteworthy to mention that this study considers differently structured variants as individual characters in its character statistics.

Homographs refer to same-form non-synonymous character samples, whose emergence is the result of coincidence formed in the natural evolution process of Chinese characters, i.e., different characters evolving into the same form. For instance, the characters *rou* 肉 (flesh) and *yue* 月 (flesh) are written as 肉 in silk manuscripts from the Mawangdui Han Tombs, and characters *wu* 无 (negative) and *xian* 先 (previous) are written as 㐬 in the manuscripts. Character *fen* 分 (divide) is sometimes written as ⿰, which is also the then-used form of *jie* 介 (armour), in the manuscripts. It is worth noting that the homographic relations discussed here exist among both standard-form and variant-form characters.

In the character statistics of this study, the homographs are counted as individual characters.

(III)   Character Morphs, Character Morphemes, and Character Components

Based on the similarities and differences in character samples, characters in ancient texts are sorted into different radical categories of a character list. The choice of the radicals and the arrangement order of characters in each radical category follow the examples set by *Shuowen Jiezi* 说文解字. As to the characters that are not included in the book, they are arranged under corresponding radicals and ranked after the characters that are included in the book. It should be noted that some characters in this character list may differ from one another in only a few strokes, such as a dot or a line, but they are still included in this list as such small differences are also results of the evolution of Chinese characters.

Character morphs are the smallest components of characters: they are physical forms representing some morphemes or meanings and cannot be further broken down. A list of character morphs is generated after splitting characters into morphs and merging the morphs that have the same structural and compositional functions, which makes it possible to count the number of character morphs.

Character morphemes are conveyed through character morphs that are classified into different types in accordance with their different compositional functions. In other words, a character morpheme is a meaning or a linguistic unit expressed by a group of character morphs that have the same compositional function. In the studies on the composition system of Chinese characters, this term is widely used to refer to the smallest units of the compositional structure of a character.

From the above description, in comparison with character morphs, character morphemes do not have certain physical forms. This reflects such a reality: a group of character morphs that convey the same character morpheme are originally descriptions of the same image, which may vary because of personal writing habits, the evolution of Chinese characters, and the changes in character components and their combination. For these reasons, there are character morphs conveying the same meaning but having different physical forms. It should be noted that different from a traditionally defined morpheme, a character morpheme can be expressed concretely through the choice of a standard-form character morph.

In a similar way that a standard-character form is chosen, a standard-character morph is chosen from a group of character morphs that convey the same character morpheme to visualise the character morpheme, and the unchosen character morphs are regarded as character morpheme variants.

Character morphemes can be divided into two types according to whether they can be used as Chinese characters independently, namely free character morphemes

Analysis Methods Used on Unearthed Texts 189

and bound character morphemes. The former is combinations of physical forms and meanings, equivalent to characters, and the latter can only serve as parts of characters.

Character components are basic units of the composition system of Chinese characters. There are monomorphemic components and poly-morphemic components. For instance, the two components that make up the character *ti* 缇 (orange red) include a poly-morphemic phonetic component *shi* 是 (right), which is a combination of *ri* 日 (sun) and *zheng* 正 (proper), and a monomorphemic component *si* 糸 (silk), which cannot be further broken up. Similar-looking monomorphemic components, such as *xue* 血 (blood) and *min* 皿 (shallow containers), belong to two different types; the former is a free monomorphemic component that can be used independently as a character, and the latter, a bound monomorphemic component that can be used only as a part of a character.

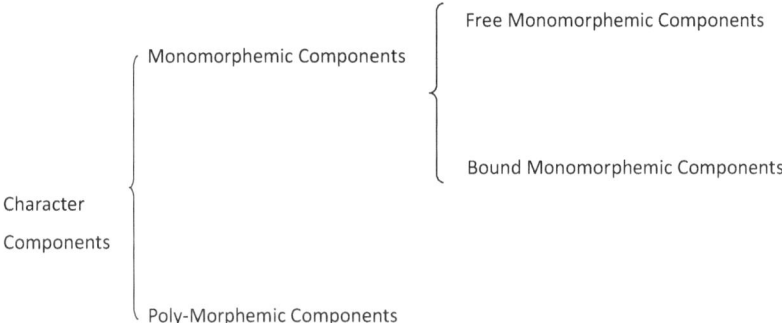

Figure 12.2 Classification of Character Components

(IV) Monomorphemic Characters and Poly-Morphemic Characters (014)

Given the differences in the number of character morphemes contained in characters, the characters can be divided into monomorphemic and poly-morphemic characters.

Sometimes, it is very difficult to distinguish between the two given the difficulty in determining character morphemes. Due to the evolution of Chinese characters, a previously monomorphemic character may develop into a multicomponent character, and a previously multicomponent character may develop into a monomorphemic character. To determine whether a character is a free-character morpheme or a combination of bound-character morphemes, it is necessary to first find out the historical period to which it belongs.

III. Character Component Analysis

Character components analysed here include only level-1 components, excluding the subcomponents at the lower levels. The determination of such components is based on their compositional functions and pictographic origins.

As Chinese characters are created through combinations of physical forms that convey meaning, they can be broken up into character components. The analytical process is described through the following examples.

(1) 𠂤 is the early oracle-bone-script form (*Houshang* 后上 9.7) of *shu* 蜀 (name of an ancient state). The character's current form 蜀, early oracle-bone-script form 𠂤, and small-seal-script form 蜀 have similar upper parts and semi-enclosed structures in the lower parts. The only difference is that the current form and the small-seal-script form have the component *chong* 虫 (worms and insects) inside their semi-enclosed structures. Given this, the character *shu* 蜀 is usually broken up into two components: 罒 and *chong* 虫. The only exception is the official-script form of this character, 蜀, which is broken up into *rou* 肉 (rump) and *mu* 目 (eye). In the official-script form, the lower part of the character is changed into 肉, and the replacement of 肉 with *rou* 肉 (rump) also appears in other characters transformed during the establishment of the script, such as *yu* 禹 (the reputed founder of the Xia Dynasty), *wan* 萬 (scorpion), *yu* 禺 (a kind of monkey), *li* 离 (Chinese oriole), and *qin* 禽 (fowl). This example shows that, before analysing Chinese character components, you must determine the historical period to which the Chinese characters belong.

(2) Character *yi* 疑 (doubt) is written as 疑, 疑, or 疑 in the silk manuscripts from the Mawangdui Han Tombs (locations of the three-character forms: the 32nd line of *Zhanguo Zonghengjia Shu* 战国纵横家书, the 139th line of the silk-manuscript copy (part A) of *Laozi* 老子, and the 58th line of *Chunqiu Shiyu* 春秋事语). The 止, which appears in all the three characters is a cursive form of *zhi* 止 (toe), and the 矣, which appears in all three looks similar to 矣, which is a part of the character's small-seal-script form and also appears in other small-seal-script characters, such as 疑, *yi* 疑 (doubt), and *yi* 肄 (study). *Shuowen Jiezi* 说文解字 regards *yi* 肄 (study) as a character variant and thus does not give any explanation for it. In the book, the character 疑 (unsettled) is explained as a combination of *dian* 匕 (change) and a phonetic component 矣, which was originally written as *shi* 矢 (arrow), and *yi* 疑 (doubt) is explained as a combination of *zi* 子 (son), *zhi* 止 (toe), *bi* 匕 (spoon) and *shi* 矢 (arrow), which is a phonetic component. There is some controversy over the arrangement of these two characters: instead of being arranged under the radical *shi* 矢 (arrow), these two characters are arranged, respectively, under the radical *bi* 匕 (spoon) and *zi* 子 (son) in the book. Xu Kai 徐锴 (920–974) held that the radical of *yi* 疑 (doubt) should be *shi* 矢 (arrow). Duan Yucai 段玉裁 (1735–1815) supported the arrangement made by *Shuowen Jiezi* but pointed out that *zhi* 止 (toe) was the phonetic component and 疑 was a simplified form of the character. To further analyse this issue, it is necessary to study the character's earlier forms. In the oracle-bone script, the character is usually written as 疑 (*houxia* 后下24.4), 疑 (*qian* 前 7.36.2), or 疑 (*qian* 前5.42.2), which depict an indecisive person who walks with a walking stick and keeps looking around. Sometimes, the depiction excluded the walking stick or included 彳 to indicate a road. Later, the character is transformed into 疑 in the small-seal script: the pictographic line depicting the walking stick is changed into *bi* 匕 (spoon), which is a phenomenon also happening in the transformation of the character *lao* 老 (old). The component 矣 is kept in the seal-script

and official-script forms of *yi* 疑 (doubt), and, apart from it, *zhi* 止 (toe) and *zi* 子 (son) also appear in these two forms. The bronze-inscription forms of *yi* 疑 (doubt) include the following: 🈶 on Boyifu Gui Container (伯疑父簋), and 🈶 on Qishiyi Zhi Container (齐史疑觯). Compared with the seal-script and official-script forms, these forms feature the addition of a phonetic component *niu* 牛 (cattle) and a semantic component *chuo* 辵 (walking). Some researchers believe that the seal-script and official-script forms are created through simplification of the bronze-inscription form, and some argue that the component *zi* 子 (son) appearing in the seal-script and official-script forms is a miswritten form of the component *niu* 牛 (cattle) appearing in the bronze-inscription forms. All the above analysis and facts show that 🈶 is a single-component pictograph, and 🈶 is its variant.

Component samples are sorted out in the following two ways in this study: a group of identical component samples are counted as one component sample, and a group of very similar component samples are classified into one type. Differently written samples of a component can be extracted from a group of differently written character samples. The analysis process is illustrated by the following example. The four character variants, namely 🈶 in the 191st line of the silk-manuscript copy (part A) of *Laozi* 老子, 🈶 and 🈶 in the 264th and 3rd lines of *Zhanguo Zonghengjia Shu* 战国纵横家书, and 🈶 in the 163rd line of the silk-manuscript copy (part B) of *Laozi* 老子, consist of two components *ren* 人 (person) and *yan* 言 (speak). The *ren* 人 component is written in the same way (亻) in the first three variants, and thus these three component samples are counted as one component sample. Therefore, the *ren* 人 component of the character has two differently written samples: 亻 and 𣥂. As to the component *yan* 言 (speak), it is written in four different ways in the four character variants. Therefore, the *yan* 言 (speak) of the character has four differently written component samples: 言, 言, 吾, and 吉.

For the convenience of analysis, components need standard forms that are selected according to the rules mentioned in "(II) Character Analysis". In the case of the *ren* 人 component, the more common 亻 makes the standard form and 𣥂 is its variant. 言 is generally regarded as the standard form of *yan* 言 (speak), and the other three 言, 吾, 吉 are its variants. Sometimes, differently written component samples can also be extracted from character samples that have no obvious connections in meaning or structure. For instance, two differently written samples of the same component 孑 and 子 can be extracted from *li* 李 (李 plum or a surname) in the 279th line of the silk-manuscript copy (part A) of *Laozi* 老子 and *sun* 孙 (孙, grandchild) in the 197th line of *Zhanguo Zonghengjia Shu* 战国纵横家书. Competent samples can be divided according to their functions, and same-function different-form components are referred to as differently structured components, which are mainly extracted from differently structured character variants. Typical examples include *bi* 敝 (worn-out) and 敝, which are extracted from 弊 and 弊, and *ji* 祭 (worship) and 祭, which are extracted from 察 and *cha* 察 (to examine). Competent samples can be divided according to their physical forms, and same-form different-function components are referred to as unified-form components: in silk manuscripts from the Mawangdui Han Tombs, the components *yun* 勻 (equal), *zhou* 舟 (boat), *zhao* 爪 (nails), and *rou* 肉 (flesh) all appear in the form 🈶, and the components *zhi* 之

192 *Analysis Methods Used on Unearthed Texts*

(grow), *shi* 士, *tu* 土 (soil) (gentleman), *ren* 壬 (carry on a shoulder pole), *feng* 丰 (luxuriant), and *da* 大 (big) all appear in the form 乂. These findings are of great value to the studies of the history and evolution of Chinese characters. What needs to be added is that in the development of Chinese characters, a character sometimes may also develop into two characters.

In silk manuscripts from the Mawangdui Han Tombs, such same-origin characters or character components are used interchangeably. Typical examples include 夂, 夊, ta 它 (worm), and ye 也 (also), which should be put in the same category.

IV. Morphemic Analysis

Apart from morphemes conveyed through monomorphemic characters and monomorphemic character components, morphemes need to be extracted from poly-morphemic character components. The morphemic breakdown of a character component is like the process of breaking down a character into components: both physical forms and functions shall be taken into consideration.

There are three types of character morphemes: morphemes conveyed by monomorphemic characters, those conveyed by monomorphemic character components, and those extracted from poly-morphemic components. Same-form and same-function morpheme samples are counted as one morpheme, and same-function morpheme samples that have different forms are grouped into the same category. Among morpheme samples of a category, the one conveyed by a monomorphemic character is usually regarded as the standard form, and other morpheme samples in the category are regarded as variants. Same-form morphemes that have different functions are referred to as unified-form morphemes.

In the morphemic analysis of characters, researchers often encounter special phenomena that should be handled in accordance with certain principles. The following paragraphs illustrate these principles with examples from silk manuscripts from the Mawangdui Han Tombs.

(1) The Handling of Pictographic Forms

It is difficult to determine whether a pictographic character is a monomorphemic or poly-morphemic character because usually both interpretations can be accepted. The various changes happening in the evolution of Chinese characters further increase the complexity of this issue.

A typical example is the controversy over the character *yuan* 元 (head). Some researchers argue that it is a poly-morphemic character as its oracle-bone script consists of *er* 二 (two/twice) and *ren* 人 (person), and some researchers who regard the bronze-script-form of the character as the first standardised form of the character hold that it is a monomorphemic character. To avoid such controversy, it is necessary to take into consideration the evolution of Chinese characters and the systematic features of the Chinese character composition system when conducting a morphemic analysis of a character. The morphemic analysis of the character *zhu* 主 (master) can offer some useful insight into this point. *Shuowen Jiezi* 说文

解字 incorrectly explains the character *zhu* 主 (whose small-seal-script form is 壴) as a combination of phonetic component 丶 and pictographic component 王, and the book even mistakes the component 丶 as an individual character. Such wrong explanations may be influenced by some features of small-seal script or by its own wrong interpretation of character *pou* 音 (to spit out). Character *pou* 音 (to spit out) is a variant of *fou* 否 (negative), and it is probably transformed from a variant of *fou* 否. Character *fou* 否 has variants because *bu* 不 (no/not) can be otherwise written as *mu* 木 (wood) or other forms in the pictographic scripts. Nevertheless, as the small-seal script does not allow such variants, *Shuowen Jiezi* reinterprets *pou* 音 (to spit out) and *zhu* 主 (master) as characters featuring the component 丶. (丶 also appears in bronze inscriptions but doesn't necessarily have the same function as it does in *pou* 音 and *zhu* 主.) Such explanations seem reasonable in *Shuowen Jiezi* 说文解字, since the book also regards 丶 as a character. Unfortunately, 丶 does not exist as an independent character in the silk manuscripts. As mentioned above, *pou* 音 (to spit out) is probably a variant of *fou* 否 and does not need to be broken up in the way mentioned in *Shuowen Jiezi* (for the relevant reasoning and textual research process, please refer to Part (IV) below). Therefore, there is no reason to break up *zhu* 主 (master) in the same way. So, whether characters like *zhu* 主 (master) should be regarded as monomorphemic or poly-morphemic characters is determined by the scripts or writing systems they belong to. For example, in the writing system embodied by the silk manuscripts, *zhu* 主 (master) can be regarded as a combination of two bound morphemes, and it can also be regarded as a monomorphemic character or a free character morpheme.

There is such a rule in the evolution of Chinese characters: complicated-looking single-component pictographic characters are simplified in a systematic way, producing multicomponent characters whose components and subcomponents are organised in hierarchical structures. Evidence of this simplification can be observed in the silk manuscripts; however, at times, such simplification results in seemingly meaningless forms due to the disregard of certain universal rules concerning the physical forms of characters. For instance, *niao* 䲕 (鸟, long-tailed bird), which is a simplified form, consists of two parts *zi* 自 (nose) and *yan* 焉 (焉, a kind of bird), but there is no systematic simplification rules embodied hereof. Under such circumstances, the identification of character morphemes or the distinction between monomorphemic and poly-morphemic characters shall follow two steps: (1) determining the applicability of the character form involved; and (2) checking its composition. Only a very common and reasonably composed character form is defined as a poly-morphemic character. Otherwise, it shall be defined as a monomorphemic character. These steps are illustrated by the following examples:

In the silk-manuscript copy (part A) of *Laozi* 老子, the character *shu* 蜀 (蜀, name of an ancient state) includes a part *zhi* 之 (grow), and so do another two-character forms interpreted as *zhuo* 浊 (name of a river) and *du* 独 (lonely). The fact shows that, in a certain period, the part *zhi* 之 (grow) is a component widely used to build character and 蜀 was a standard-form character. The part *zhi* 之, which shall be regarded as a character component, is different from the two parts of *niao* 䲕 (鸟, long-tailed bird): the latter cannot be used to build characters other than *niao* 䲕

(鸟, long-tailed bird). Therefore, niao 鳥 (鸟, long-tailed bird) cannot be broken up into components and shall be regarded as a single-component or monomorphemic character. The two steps described above are inspired by *Shuowen Jiezi* 说文解字. In the book, characters are usually broken up into widely applicable components, and characters and character components that cannot be analysed in this way are defined as pictographic characters. For example, in the book, *qin* 禽 (fowl) is arranged under the radical *rou* 凶 (rump) and explained as a combination of a pictographic component *rou* 凶 (rump) and a phonetic component *jin* 今 (now), but *shun* 舜 (herbage), which cannot be broken up into widely used components, is explained as a pictographic character containing a part *chuan* 舛 (run counter) that indicates its pronunciation.

Pictographic variants of a pictographic character may differ from one another in terms of complexity, and such differences may be caused by the lack of regularity in the pictographic writing system (such as *shou* 首 and *shou* 百, which means "head", and 𠫓 and 㔾, which are upside-down versions of *zi* 子 that means "son") or interchangeable modifications (such as 艸 and 芔, 十 and 甲, and 井 and 丼). Compared with the simpler variants, the more complex variants just have extra pictographic parts that are used to add details to the image depiction. Therefore, pictographic variants of the same character, which have the same meaning or semantic function, shall be counted as one character morpheme. To be more specific, only a group of monomorphemic pictographs that have the same meeting can be counted as a character morpheme. The reason that *ren* 刃 (knife edge) and *dao* 刀 (knife) are counted as two morphemes is that these two monomorphemic pictographs have different meanings or semantic functions. 乁, the archaic form of character *ji* 及 (overtake) in Three-Script Stele Inscriptions (三体石经) and its seal-script form 綊 are also counted as two morphemes that have the same meaning, but the seal-script form is a poly-morphemic character consisting of components *ren* 人 (person) and *you* 又 (again). Therefore, these two forms cannot be counted as one morpheme.

(II) The Handling of Cursive Forms

Cursive forms are essentially different from their original forms, and thus are regarded as monomorphemic characters. The character *duo* 朵 (cluster of flowers), whose small-seal-script form is 朮, is written as 朵 in the silk manuscripts. The character *yi* 矣 (particle of completed action), whose small-seal-script form is 瑞, is written as 矣 in the silk manuscripts.

(III) The Handling of Single-Component Ideographs

Character morphemes are extracted from character components, and single-component characters are monomorphemic characters. Some single-component ideographs seem to be composed of two components, such as *ben* 本 (root of a plant), *mo* 末 (end), *zhu* 朱 (vermilion), *ren* 刃 (knife edge), and *yi* 亦 (armpits). Nevertheless, they are not monomorphemic characters. The character *ren* 刃 (knife edge) is created by adding a dot to the pictographic character *dao* 刀 (knife), but the dot is

Analysis Methods Used on Unearthed Texts 195

not an independent morpheme: it is used to mark the position of the knife blade. Similarly, the two dots in *yi* 亦 (armpits) are used to mark the position of armpits, and the remaining part of the character is *da* 大 (big), a pictographic form depicting the front side of a person. The dot in *xue* 血 (blood) describes the shape of blood droplets, and the horizontal lines in *gan* 甘 (delicious) and *fu* 夫 (man) represent food in the mouth and a hairpin used only by adult men, respectively.

Simply put, single-component ideographs are combinations of strokes instead of those of morphemes. For comparison, here are a few examples of characters created through the combination of morphemes. The component *mu* 木 (wood), when combined with the component *tian* 田 (cropland), yields the character *guo* 果 (fruit); while in combination with the component *rou* 肉 (flesh), it forms the character *wei* 胃 (stomach). These components differ from the strokes in single-component ideographs, as they possess both independent meanings and distinct forms. In contrast, the meanings of strokes in single-component ideographs are lost when separated from the other strokes within the character.

(IV) The Handling of Forms with Meaningless Stroke Addition

Forms with meaningless stroke addition refer to forms that have a few meaninglessly added strokes in comparison with their original forms: they are usually regarded as variants. Therefore, 丰 is deemed to be a variant of *feng* 丰 (luxuriant), and 灻 is a variant of *yan* 炎 (flame). Such variants also widely exist in the written materials dating back to the Warring States Period (475–221 BCE) and even earlier periods: the characters that have a long horizontal line at the top often have variants featuring the addition of a dot or a short horizontal line above the top horizontal lines.

Table 12.2 Examples of Stroke Additions

Characters	Zheng 正 (proper)	Xin 辛 (crime)	Bi 帀 (silks) and shi 師 (division)	Ke 可 (approve)	Dai 百 (hundred)	Bu 不 (no/not)
Forms without a short horizontal line	[image]	[image]	[image]	[image]	[image]	[image]
	The treaty of alliance unearthed at Houma (侯马盟书)	*Houshang* 18.3	Shi Gui Container (师簋)	The Chu-state silk manuscripts (楚帛书)	Mian Plate (免盘)	The Chu-state bamboo slips unearthed at Baoshan (包山楚简)
Forms containing a short horizontal line	[image]	[image]	[image]	[image]	[image]	[image]

(Continued)

Table 12.2 (Continued)

Characters	Zheng 正 (proper)	Xin 辛 (crime)	Bi 币 (silks) and shi 师 (division)	Ke 可 (approve)	Bai 百 (hundred)	Bu 不 (no/not)
	The treaty of alliance unearthed at Houma (侯马盟书)	Jia 甲 2282	The tripod caldron made for Cai Taishi, a high-ranking official (蔡太师鼎)	The Chu-state silk manuscripts	The tripod caldron made for Yu (禹鼎)	The Chu-state bamboo slips unearthed at Baoshan (包山楚简)

Many variants created through the addition of meaningless strokes are included and explained in *Shuowen Jiezi* 说文解字. For instance, the book includes not only the seal-script form of *zheng* 正 (proper), but also its variant featuring the addition of a short horizontal line, which is explained as an archaic form of the character. On the contrary, the form of *di* 帝 (supreme ruler), featuring the addition of a short horizontal line is explained as the seal-script form of the character, but the one without the addition is regarded as the archaic form in the book. Such variants are a common phenomenon in the silk manuscripts: such a variant maintains the meaning of the original-form character, so they are not regarded as two different characters. The book *Shuowen Jiezi* 说文解字 makes a mistake in this respect, it does not reasonably analyse *bu* 不 (no/not) and 丕. When explaining character *fou* 否 (negative), the book arranges the character under the radical *kou* 口 (mouth) and the radical *bu* 不 (no/not) and interprets it as a combination of *kou* 口 (mouth) in both explanations. When explaining another character *pou* 咅 (to spit out), it explains this character as a combination of 丶 and a phonetic component *fou* 否 (negative). Nevertheless, *fou* 否 (negative) and *pou* 咅 (to spit out) are two forms of the same character: *pou* 咅 probably evolves from an early variant of *fou* 否 since the component *bu* 不 (no/not) can be otherwise written as *mu* 木 (wood) or 丕 in the writing system of the Warring States Period (475–221 BCE) and in the oracle-bone script and bronze inscriptions. Besides, there are only two characters featuring the radical 丶 in *Shuowen Jiezi*: *pou* 咅 (to spit out) and *zhu* 主 (master). As *zhu* 主 (master) is proven to be a monomorphemic pictograph, 丶 cannot stand alone as a character or character component that has an independent meaning. A lot of evidence can be found in the silk manuscripts to prove the interchangeability between *pou* 咅 (to spit out) and *fou* 否 (negative). For instance, it is *pou* 咅 that appears in character *bei* 倍 (back towards) in *Zhanguo Zonghengjia Shu* 战国纵横家书, but in the silk-manuscript copy (part A) of *Laozi* 老子, the component *pou* 咅 in the character is replaced by *fou* 否. The phenomenon also happens to another character *bu* 部 (an ancient place).

It is worth noting that a morphemic analysis of variants caused by the addition of meaningless strokes needs to consider the different development stages of these variants. In the silk manuscripts, as such a variant maintains the meaning and function of its standard form, they are counted as one morpheme. Nevertheless, if such a variant begins to convey other meaning(s) and thus develops into another character in some stage of its development, it becomes a new morpheme.

Another noteworthy issue is that there are three types of stroke addition: one type is related to morphs and morphemes (as mentioned above), and the other two types affect the forms of character or level-1-character components. Take the character *bao* 保 (to carry on one's back) as an example. Its oracle-bone-script form ᛞ (appearing in *qian* 前 5.27.2) usually depicts a person carrying a child (*zi* 子) on the back, but sometimes, the character is also written as ᛞ (appearing in *tan* 探 300) including a stroke ノ. As to the explanation of the stroke, Wu Dacheng 吴大澂 (1835–1902) pointed out that it depicted swaddling clothes in his book *Shuowen Jiliu Bu* 说文吉籀补 (Additional Remarks to *Shuowen Jiezi*'s Explanations to Seal-Script Characters). In addition to mentioning this view of Wu Dacheng 吴大澂, Lin Yiguang 林义光 (?–1932) added in his book *Wen Yuan* 文源 (The Origin of Characters) that the stroke was caused by a disconnection of a stroke combination in ᛞ, a variant of the character. He also noted that neither of these views was proven correct. In *Yinxu Wenzi Ji* 殷虚文字记 (Explanations to Shang-Dynasty Characters), Tang Lan 唐兰 (1901–1979) observed that this stroke was added for aesthetic purposes after the character was made into a left-right structured character. As characters *bao* 保 (to carry on one's back) and *yu* 毓 (give birth to) both consisted of components *ren* 人 (person) and *zi* 子 in the oracle-bone structure, they had to be differently structured to distinguish them from each other. Therefore, *bao* 保 was made a left-right-structured character, and *yu* 毓 became an up-down-structured character. Tang Lan 唐兰 added that, to further improve the form ᛞ aesthetically, another stroke was added to make the form ᛞ. Tang Lan 唐兰 made this correct judgment because he noticed that the addition of strokes was used only for aesthetic purposes instead of semantic purposes: the addition of strokes affects only the form of character *bao* 保 not its character components or morphemes. A similar addition of strokes happens to character *nu* 奴 (slave). In the silk manuscripts, character *nu* 怒 (rage) is written as ᛞ (*Zhanguo Zonghengjia Shu* 战国纵横家书), and *nu* 奴 (slave) is written as ᛞ [the silk-manuscript copy (part A) of Laozi 老子] or ᛞ (*Zhanguo Zonghengjia Shu* 战国纵横家书). The added stroke 八 does not appear in *nu* 怒, or its components *nv* 女 (woman/girl), *cha* 又 (prong). It is added to *nu* 奴 (slave).

(V) The Handling of Differentiated Forms

The characters used in the silk manuscripts are early-form official-script characters, and there are still many variant forms and unstandardised modified forms in the writing system at that time. This issue shall be taken into consideration in the morphemic analysis. The well-established morphemes do not need to be further broken down, such as 大, 六, gong 廾 (two hands) and 不 (these four morphemes evolve from ᛞ) in the characters *feng* 奉 (offer), *nong* 弄 (play around with), *jie* 戒 (guard against), *bing* 兵 (troops), *ju* 具 (prepare), *gong* 共 (together), *qi* 弃 (throw away), bao 暴 (expose to the sun), *tai* 泰 (slippery), *ju* 舉 (raise), *shun* 舜 (a legendary Chinese ruler), and *dian* 奠 (pay respect). As to the differentiated forms, they need to be broken up into morphemes, such as *jiu* 丩 (to join or connect the vine) and *you* 又 (again) extracted from *cheng* 丞 (assist) and *yi* 畁 (odd).

(VI) The Handling of Symbols

Symbols refer to fully transformed characters or character components, which have no pictographic or ideographic functions. Symbols originate from two distinct approaches.

(1) Replacement: pictographic and ideographic forms are replaced by similar-looking symbols. The evolution processes of the following characters can provide some useful insight into this point. The early form of *zhen* 朕 (pronoun 'I') includes a component 灷 (关). This component is written as ⽊ in the silk manuscripts: its upper part 山 is a variant of *huo* 火 (fire), and this variant is commonly seen in the bronze inscriptions; 卄 is transformed from 収. The early form of *juan* 卷 (roll up) features a phonetic component 关 (关), and this component is replaced by 关, which is transformed from 关. The character *zhe* 者 (this) evolves from 煮 to 耂 and then to 耂. The original form of *lao* 老 (old) has a component 耂 that depicts a long-haired person, and in the silk scripts, this component is replaced by 耂 since they look very much like.

(2) Evolution: some symbols are the results of the evolution of the writing system and the influence of other forms. The upper part of the character *jin* 晉 (enter) is written as 㚚 or 㚚 in oracle-bone and bronze inscriptions and as 㚚 or 㚚 in the silk manuscripts. During this natural evolution process, it gradually becomes a symbol without pictographic or ideographic functions. 夲, the lower part of the character 夲 is written as *fu* 夫 (man), which is a change that occurs under the influence of the character *fu* 夫 (man). In this character, the component does not have any ideographic function, either.

Some forms are regarded as symbols for neither of the two abovementioned reasons. They become symbols when some stroke changes affect their pictographic or ideographic functions. For instance, 变 (change), which is a combination of *pu* 攴 (tap) and a phonetic component *bing* 丙 (third), is written as *geng* 更 (change) in the silk manuscripts, and *Shuowen Jiezi* 说文解字 treats it as a symbol and does not break it up in the corresponding interpretation. There is another character treated in this way in the book: *ge* 革 (leather). The book explains that this character is an inheritance of its pictographic form, which can be broken up into *sanshi* 三十 (thirty) and a phonetic component 口. This explanation implies that the pictographic form of the character can be broken up into components, but its seal-script-form cannot be understood in this way.

Symbols in Chinese characters were created with the establishment of the official script because the script broke with tradition by allowing characters to become semantic and phonetic symbols. Later, the symbols were inherited by the regular script.

When identifying symbols in silk manuscripts, there is another issue to consider: the influence of personal writing habits. To be more specific, when judging a symbol in the silk manuscripts, it is essential to determine whether it was created by the writer's habit or by the systematic changes in the writing system. Only those caused by the latter and were widely used in the mature official script shall be defined as symbols. Unfortunately, it is impossible to make such a judgment based on the silk manuscripts alone. Therefore, when identifying symbols in the silk manuscripts, the character forms in the mature official and regular scripts are also used as references.

Note

1 The original Chinese version was published in *Yuyan Lunji* 语言论集 (vol. 4) by Yuyan Lunji Editorial Office of the School of Liberal Arts of Renmin University of China, China Minzu University Press, in October 1999.

13 A Study on Characters from Bamboo Slips and Silk Manuscripts[1]

The unearthed bamboo slips and silk manuscripts (hereinafter collectively referred to as the Manuscripts) discussed hereof date back to the Warring States Period (475–221 BCE), the Qin Dynasty (221–207 BCE), the Han Dynasty (206 BCE–220 CE), and the Three Kingdoms (220–280) (hereinafter collectively referred to as the Period).

The Manuscripts are credible sources for research into the original appearance of Chinese characters for the following two reasons. First, this Period marked a transition from Archaic to New-Style characters, with drastic changes in character composition and usage. Second, these Manuscripts were written by different individuals, offering various personalized writing styles. Researchers have revealed that functional division and reorganisation of characters during the Period led to the creation of many New-Style characters found in later documents, including the so-called characters in popular form and erroneous characters, even many currently used Chinese characters. Therefore, a systematic study on characters used in the Manuscripts can fill the gap in the study of the development Chinese characters, not only helping to clarify the development trajectory of character forms and usage, but also making it easier to analyse the causes, mechanism, and rules of the development, which cannot be resolved by studying the forms of characters used after the Period only.

Up to date, only very rough descriptions are provided to characters used in the Manuscripts. Therefore, a systematic sorting and study of these characters will offer a comprehensive understanding of the nature and classification of them, which will contribute to more detailed and clearer interpretation and annotation of the Manuscripts.

One of the difficulties in studying bamboo slips and silk manuscripts lies in interpreting characters. However, no matter how complex characters are, there should be established rules to follow, such as which characters can be interchangeable and that can be borrowed from. In recent years, bamboo slips and silk manuscripts have been the subject of concentrated research. As a result, a large amount of research achievements was available, making it possible for systematically sorting and study. If existing research results are applied in thorough sorting and study of those characters, existing data and patterns of character usage will become explicit, thus making the study of many unsorted or unearthed documents much

DOI: 10.4324/9781032622965-13

smoother. Furthermore, duplication of interpenetration and annotation will also be avoided. In the end, the study of bamboo slips and silk manuscripts will be taken to a higher level.

The sorting and study of characters from bamboo slips and silk manuscripts are of great significance for the compilation of reference books. Preliminary statistics show that there are over 300 characters in the Guodian Chu-State Bamboo Slips whose form and structure are not included in the regular scripts section of the Great Chinese Dictionary,[2] and there are more than six times as many interchangeable characters in such documents from the Qin and Han dynasties as in classic books from ancient times.[3] Due to the complexity of characters used in bamboo slips and silk manuscripts, the existing annotations are incomplete, together with mistakes and omissions. In addition, these materials are scattered all around. Therefore, it is difficult to directly cite them for the compilation of reference books. The sorting and study work will provide systematic data for the revision of existing large reference books and the compilation of new ones.

The character-usage issue includes two levels. First, how many individual characters are used and how these characters are used. Second, what should be the focus of the research? The second level is mainly manifested by the relationship between character form and ideographic function, which can be roughly divided into six aspects: differently written characters, differently structured characters, phonetic loan characters, homophonous interchangeable characters, homograph, and interchangeable characters with similar forms.

I. Differently Written Characters

In 1993, Professor Wang Ning 王宁, my thesis adviser, introduced the concepts and terms of "differently written characters" and "differently structured characters" when guiding me in writing my doctoral dissertation, "A Research on the Composition System of Chinese Characters in the Silk Manuscripts from Mawangdui Han Tombs" 马王堆帛书汉字构形系统研究. Under his guidance, I conducted a detailed analysis of the differently written characters and differently structured characters in the silk manuscripts.

Differently written characters refer to variations of the same character that were generated due to irregularities in writing and character form evolution. "Writing" here refers to individual differences. For the same character, different people wrote it in different styles, resulting in a variety of forms. The existence of these variations is temporary and individualistic. Another writing change is governed by trends of the characters from the system. Although this change also originates from and is expressed as individual writing, it reflects the changes in the entire character system and has a certain regularity, which is not temporary but will continue for a long time and eventually replace the original character form. Therefore, it is an important factor in the development and evolution of Chinese characters and can be called the irregular evolution of character form.

Differently written characters vary in the strokes, mainly in changes in stroke position, stroke length, stroke curvature, stroke addition and subtraction, and stroke splitting and merging. It is very important to distinguish differently written characters separately because the development of Chinese character scripts, such as the official script, running script, regular script, etc., is basically a variation of written forms of characters, and should be analysed comparatively from the stroke level rather than other aspects such as structure or components.

Differently written characters are a basic phenomenon in handwritten texts and are very common in oracle-bone scripts, bronze inscriptions, and especially in bamboo slips and silk manuscripts. However, in the era of printed documents, differently written characters almost disappear and only very few exist in printed materials. Therefore, the concept of differently written characters is only emphasized along with the large-scale unearthed bamboo-slip and silk manuscripts.

II. Differently Structured Characters

Differently structured characters refer to characters with different structures but the same function. The so-called same function means that the phonetic-semantic functions represented by the character are the same, while the different structures include the following situations:

(I) Differently Structured Characters Featuring Different Components

1. Different Components Combined in the Same Way

In the silk manuscripts from Mawangdui Han Tombs and bamboo slips from Yinqueshan Han Tombs, *dong* 勭 (to act) is used to represent *dong* 動 (to act) in following sentences: "而民生生, 勭皆之死地之十有三" (One-third of people are those who originally could have had a good life, but choose to lead themselves to self-destructive path.),[4] "勭静不时胃(谓)之逆,生杀不当胃(谓)之暴"[5] (Behaviour that is inappropriate for the occasion is called a reversal, and decisions that are inappropriate for life and death are called brutality.) and "勭如雷神(电),起如蛋(飞)鸟"[6] (swift as lightning, rising like a bird). Such use was certified by *Jiyun* 集韵 (Jiyun Rhyming Dictionary) that *dong* 動 (to act) can also be written as 勭 (to act).[7] These two characters are interchangeable in terms of phonetic components, and their compositions belong to semantic-phonetic combinations.

Gou 詢 (blame) is used to represent *gou* 诟 (scold) in "受邦之詢, 是胃(谓)社稷之主"[8] (Only those who can withstand the slander directed at their nation and who allow citizens to provide criticism can become the leader.) and "受国之詢, 是胃(谓)社稷之主"[9] (Only those who can withstand the slander directed at their country and who allow citizens to provide criticism can become the leader.). *Gou* 詢 (blame) is the differently structured character of *gou* 诟 (scold). According to *Shuowen Jiezi* 说文解字 (An Explication of Written Characters), *gou* 詢 (blame) can also be written as *gou* 诟 (scold), with *ju* 句 (sentence), serving as its semantic component, and their phonetic components are interchangeable.[10] In "戴营袙抱一, 能毋离乎? "[11] (Can the human body, mind, and soul blend together in such a way that they never separate?), po 祏 (soul) is used to represent po 魄 (soul). In handed-down works, po 祏 (soul) is written as po 魄(soul). Po 祏 (soul) consists of the semantic component shi 示 (manifest) and phonetic components bai 白 (white), while po 魄 (soul) consists of the semantic component gui 鬼 (ghost) and phonetic components bai 白(white).

2. *Different Components Combined in Different Ways*

Although the character ye 野 (field) was found in the silk manuscripts from Mawangdui Han Tombs, it was written as ye 埜 (field) in Chu-State bamboo slips. The former is a semantic-phonetic character, while the latter is a compound-ideograph one. In "是必为福，非必为㴙"[12] (Correct cognition is a blessing, while incorrect cognition is a disaster.) and "祸㴙废立，如竟(影)之隋(随)刑(形)"[13] (Prosperity and decline are like shadow following form.), zai 㴙 (disaster) is used to represent zai 灾 (disaster), with the former being a semantic-phonetic character, and the latter is a compound-ideograph character. In "贵富而驕，自遗咎也"[14] (If one becomes arrogant after getting rich, he or she will make mistakes.) and "贵富而骄，自遗咎也"[15] (If one becomes arrogant after getting rich, he or she will make mistakes.) and "[尊]而不骄，共(恭)也"[16] (To be humble means to respect but not to be arrogant.), jiao 驕 (arrogant) is used to represent jiao 骄 (arrogant), with the former being compound-ideograph character and the latter being semantic-phonetic character.

3. *Adding or Reducing Components*

In the silk manuscripts from Mawangdui Han Tombs, some characters were used to represent others by adding a component. Que 卻 (but) is used to represent que 却 (but) by adding the radical 彳, as in text "御军之日，无伐齐、外齐焉"[17] (The agreed date for withdrawing and attacking the Qin army is essentially for punishing and isolating the State of Qi.). Some characters were used to represent others by omission of some components. For example, ba 朝 (chief of feudal princes) is used to represent ba 霸 (chief of feudal princes) in "朝主积甲士而正(征)不备(服)"[18] (The chief lord accumulates military power to conquer vassal states that do not obey.) and "朝者臣，名臣也"[19] (to have a chief lord as the minister). Jue 时 (peerage) is used to represent jue 爵 (peerage) in "德之贵也，夫莫之时而恒自然也"[20] (The dignity of morality is not based on titles but determined by the essence of the relationship between morality and material things.). Gu 稟 (grain) is used to represent gu 榖 (paper mulberry) in text "天下之所恶，唯孤寡不稟，而王公以自名也"[21] (What humans detest are being "alone" and "not having grain," yet lords and nobles use these terms to refer to themselves.) and "夫是以侯王自胃(谓)孤寡不稟"[22] (The lords and kings call themselves as the lonely sovereign.). Ai 发 (love) is used to represent you 憂 (worry) in "终日号而不发，和之至也"[23] (Being able to cry out loudly all day without getting hoarse is because one's blood is gentle and reached the extreme.).

204 *A Study on Characters from Bamboo Slips and Silk Manuscripts*

(II) *Differently Structured Characters Featuring Same Components*

Some characters have the same components but are positioned differently. Such cases were also found in the silk manuscripts from Mawangdui Han Tombs. In texts, "然臣亦见其必可也。猶贠不知变事以功(攻)宋也"[24] (I also believe that it can be done. However, I am still unsure of how to overcome the changing circumstances in order to successfully conquer Song.) and "简之为言也猷贺(加)，大而罕者"[25] (It is admirable to simplify the speech, and its rarity makes it more valuable,), *you* 猶 (particularly) and *you* 猷 (particularly) have the same components that are positioned differently. In, "守怨之本，养乱之亚"[26] (Conserving the causes for trouble and nurturing the seeds of chaos lead to unrest.), "故必贵而以贱为本，必高矣而以下为亚"[27] and "故必贵以贱为本，必高矣而以下为圲"[28] (Poverty and lowliness are the foundation of nobility, while the lower class forms the basis for the upper class.), *ji* 亚 (foundation) and *ji* 圲 (foundation) are both used to represent 基, while the former adopts an up-down structure and the latter a left-right structure. In, "少则得，多则惑"[29] (When we have less, we gain clarity; when we have more, it becomes confusing.) and "无好无亚(恶)，上用口口而民不糜(迷)惐"[30] (The wise follow the laws of the universe, without bias towards good or evil. When rulers employ such individuals, the people will not become misguided or confused.), *huo* 惑 (be puzzled) and *yu* 惐 (be puzzled) are differently structured characters with same components, and so are *an* 案 (stool) and *an* 桉 (eucalyptus) in, "故大道废，案有仁义"[31] (Therefore, when the great law is abandoned, how can there be benevolence and righteousness?) and "慎桉其众，以隋(随)天地之从"[32] (Strictly stabilise one's followers, and obey the laws of nature and the universe.).

III. Phonetic Loan Characters

Phonetic loan characters refer to those that are borrowed based on phonetic identity, similarity, or transfer, without any semantic connection. In some cases, the term "phonetic loan characters" is synonymous with the commonly used term "borrowed characters", but the meaning of "borrowed" varies depending on the context.

To illustrate, the earliest definition and examples of "borrowed characters" were given by Xu Shen 许慎 (ca. 58–147) in *Shuowen Jiezi*. In the Preface, he wrote: "A borrowed character has no original of its own; it is used to represent a meaning according to its pronunciation. *Ling* 令 (to demand) and *zhang* 长 (chief) are two examples."[33] However, the term of "borrowed characters" in *Shuowen Jiezi* is fundamentally different from what we now commonly refer to. This distinction was already noted by scholars in the Qing Dynasty. Nevertheless, many writings today still fail to distinguish between them.

When many works discuss the "borrowed characters" in *Shuowen Jiezi*, they express that Xu Shen's definition of "borrowed characters" is correct, but the examples of *ling* 令 (to demand) and *zhang* 长 (chief) are improper. In fact, Xu Shen's definition includes extended meanings, as explained by Duan Yucai 段玉

裁 (1735–1815, a Qing-Dynasty sinologist) in his *Shuowen Jiezi Zhu* 说文解字注 (Notes to *Shuowen Jiezi*): "To borrow means to rely on; it refers to something with phonetic similarity. Thus, for all things that have no corresponding characters, they can be given a character through phonetic loan. For example, people in Han Dynasty call *xianling* 县令 (a county magistrate) as *xianzhang* 县长, where *ling* 令 (to demand) is used for officials governing over 10,000 households, and *zhang* 长 (chief) is used for officials governing less than 10,000 households. The original meaning of *ling* 令 (to demand) was to issue orders, while the original meaning of *zhang* 长 (chief) was to be long-standing. Neither *xianling* 县令 (a county magistrate) nor *xianzhang* 县长 (a county magistrate) originally had corresponding character, but they were given one based on their extended meanings of issuing orders and being long-standing, respectively. This is what is meant by borrowing."[34]

The main text of *Shuowen Jiezi* also elaborates on the concept of borrowed characters, as seen in the entry for radical *xi* 西 (west): "*xi* 西 (west) refers to the bird in the nest, hence the character is pictographic. Birds perch in the nest when the sun sets in the west, so the character *xi* 西 (west) is used to represent the west. The character *qi* 栖 (to perch) is a substitute of *xi* 西 (west), consisting of the components *mu* 木 (wood) and *qi* 妻 (wife)."[35] That's why the character *xi* 西 (west), which originally means bird's nest, was borrowed to represent the west.[36]

Similarly, *Shuowen Jiezi* interprets that the character *lai* 来 (to come) originally meant "auspicious grain", but because auspicious grain comes from the sky, the character was borrowed to represent "coming". Regardless of whether the extended meanings discussed in *Shuowen Jiezi* are reasonable or not, based on Xu Shen's understanding of Chinese characters, the fact is that *xi* 西 (west), *lai* 来 (to come), *ling* 令 (to demand) and *zhang* 长 (chief) are characters whose forms were borrowed to represent their extended meanings. Therefore, they are considered borrowed characters.

Why does *Shuowen Jiezi* treat the extended meaning of a character as borrowing? This could be answered by its understanding of the nature of Chinese characters. Different from other dictionaries, *Shuowen Jiezi* has an analysis of the character form for which only one meaning is provided. Xu Shen believed that Chinese characters were constructed based on meanings of the components, and the form and meaning of a character were unified. Therefore, the character form is interpretable and has only one corresponding meaning. Since a certain character form is created based on a certain meaning, this form corresponds to only this meaning instead of any others. When it is used to represent other meanings (whether or not they are related to the original meaning), it means that this character form is borrowed by other meanings, and it is called a borrowed character.

Although some scholars have argued that there may be some semantic connection between borrowed characters and their original meanings, it is generally accepted that borrowed characters have no semantic connection and are borrowed solely based on their phonetic similarity. Therefore, even though the term "borrowed characters" has been used throughout history and in different works, its meaning has varied depending on the context. We should neither simply dismiss *Shuowen Jiezi* as erroneous according to modern theories nor blindly follow ancient rules. Instead, under the premise of a clear understanding of the evolution of the meaning of "borrowed character" in ancient and modern times, we should establish its specific content in accordance with a better interpretation of Chinese characters. Whether there is a semantic connection reflects two completely different usages of Chinese characters, which should be distinguished.

Phonetic loan characters are those that have no semantic relationship but are phonetically identical or like the original one. The relationship of the character forms is not a concern in phonetic loan characters. Nevertheless, some character forms belong to the derivation category. For example, one character is created based on another character's form. Generally, there was no such character before so an existing character was borrowed, and then additional parts were added or replaced on this basis to produce a new character. Let's take *wei* 胃 (stomach) and *wei* 谓 (to speak) to illustrate such character formation. *Wei* 胃 (stomach) originally meant "grain storage" as explained in *Shuowen Jiezi*.[37] Later, it was borrowed to mean "to speak", and the *yan* 言 (speech) component was added to create the derived character *wei* 谓 (to speak). In the Chu-State bamboo slips of the Warring States Period, *wei* 谓 (to speak) was not yet seen, and *wei* 胃 (stomach) was used instead. In Chu-State bamboo slips unearthed at Guodian, there were sentences "目而知之胃之进之"[38] (The eyes can tell if the food has entered the stomach.) and "何胃六德"[39] (What can be called the Six Virtues?) and "是胃重基"[40] (This can be seen as virtuous deeds.). The Qin bamboo slips unearthed at Shuihudi and silk manuscripts from Mawangdui Han Tombs adopt both *wei* 胃 (stomach) and *wei* 谓 (to speak).

As for another type of borrowed character, when the original character is borrowed to mean something else, additional components are added or replaced based on the original character to create a new regular character. Consider *chang* 常 (often) and *shang* 裳 (long skirt), for example. The original meaning of *chang* 常 (often) was "lower garment" as explained in *Shuowen Jiezi*.[41] Sentences containing *chang* 常 (often) were found as in "缇襌便常一" (one orange-colour long skirt)"[42] from the bamboo slips in Mawangdui Han Tomb and in "利以裁(制)衣常 (convenient for making tops and skirts)"[43] from the Qin bamboo slips unearthed at Shuihudi. *Chang* 常 (often) was also borrowed to mean "constancy", and then the semantic component was replaced to create the derived character *shang* 裳 (long skirt). When 常 no longer represents the meaning of clothing, *chang* 常 (often) and *shang* 裳 (long skirt) become phonetic loan characters.

IV. Homophonous Interchangeable Characters

Homophonous Interchangeable Characters refer to those that can be used interchangeably because they have a historical relationship in meaning and are phonetically similar or identical. In essence, they are newly derived characters that have undergone semantic extension. For a certain period, both the new and old characters were used interchangeably. Each Chinese character represents several meanings, which can be broadly classified into three categories: the original meaning, the extended meaning, and the borrowed meaning. The extended meaning is formed by semantic extension, while the borrowed meaning is formed by borrowing characters. Such method was adopted by the Chinese to save writing symbols and reduce the difficulty in writing and reading. However, if the polysemy of a character is allowed to develop without control, it will also increase the difficulty of distinguishing meanings. Therefore, new characters have been derived to share some of the original characters' functions.

Derived characters are those that are created based on the original characters' form, mainly by adding components and changing components, to share the original characters' meaning. Therefore, there is a historical relationship in forms between derived characters and original ones, and they share similar or identical pronunciations. Among them, some derived characters that share borrowed meanings form new borrowing relationships, so they are classified as phonetic loan characters. Some homophonous common characters are developed through the distribution of semantic functions of characters that were originally differently written or differently structured characters but become homophonous interchangeable characters later. The following are some of the ways that homophonous interchangeable characters with form relationship are produced.

(I) Differently Written Characters Assuming Different Functions

By establishing forms that were resulted from differently written manners of the same character as different characters, the meanings that were originally represented by one character are distributed. For example, from the character forms in the silk manuscripts from Mawangdui Han Tombs, zhen 阵 (formation) was originally a variant form of *chen* 陈 (to display), but later it shared the meaning of "battle array".[44]

(II) Adding Components

Such usage can be explained by *qiao* 乔 (tall) and *jiao* 憍 (be haughty). *Qiao* 乔 means "high and curved" in *Shuowen Jiezi*.[45] Later, it is extended to mean "arrogant". The Chu bamboo slips unearthed from Guodian adopted *jiao* 骄 (arrogant) instead of *qiao* 乔 (tall). Later, the component *xin* 心 (heart) was added to *qiao* 乔 (tall) because arrogance is a psychological activity. Thus, the character *jiao* 憍 (be haughty) was derived, which was used to specifically represent arrogance. It can be found in the Chu bamboo slips unearthed from Baoshan and the Tomb of Marquis Yi of Zeng State. Another example is *wo* 我 (myself) and *yi* 義 (righteousness). *Wo* 我 (myself) is defined as "myself" in *Shuowen Jiezi*[46], and it is extended to refer to appearance and justice. While, when composed of *wo* 我 (myself) and *yang* 羊 (sheep and goats), *yi* 義 (righteousness) means "the appearance of myself" in *Shuowen Jiezi*.[47] *Wo* 我 (myself) is its phonetic component. In the Chu bamboo slips unearthed in Guodian, *wo* 我 (myself) and *yi* 義 (righteousness) were used interchangeably when they referred to the meaning of "justice". The following sentences, "爱亲忘贤，仁而未義也；尊贤遗亲，我而未仁也"[48] (Loving one's family but forgetting the righteousness is not true benevolence; honouring the righteousness but neglecting one's family is not true kindness.), "仁生于人，我生于道"⁴⁹ (Benevolence is born in humans, while righteousness is born from the law of universe.), and "不我而加诸己，弗受也"⁵⁰ (I will not accept it if the king is to enforce something unrighteous on me), are evidence of their derivative relationship.

(III) Changing Components

In *Shuowen Jiezi*, *chang* 嘗 (to taste) was interpreted as "taste with the mouth". With *zhi* 旨 (delicious) as its semantic component and *shang* 尚 (still/yet/even) as its phonetic component, the original meaning of this character is to taste.⁵¹ It extended to refer to the autumn sacrifice later.

Erya 尔雅 (Erya Dictionary) says "秋祭曰嘗" (the autumn sacrifice is called 嘗). Guo Pu 郭璞 (276–324) explained, "*chang* 嘗 (to taste) means tasting new grains".⁵² *Baihu Tongyi* 白虎通义 (Standard Explanations to Classics Made at Baihu Taoist Temple) says, "秋曰嘗者，新谷熟，嘗之"⁵³ (*chang* 嘗 (to taste) in autumn refers to tasting new grains when they are ripe). Later, the character *shi* 示 (manifest) was used instead of *zhi* 旨 (delicious) to indicate the change in meaning, and the new character *chang* 裳 (to taste) was derived to represent the autumn sacrifice. It can be found in Chu bamboo slips unearthed in Baoshan, Wangshan, and Jiudian. In the Guodian Chu bamboo slips, *chang* 裳 (to taste) was used to express *tianchang* 天常 (the law of the universe), *dachang* 大常 (true nature), and the meaning "long-lasting". It is a borrowed character probably because it adopted the radical *shi* 示 (manifest) as its semantic component.

V. Homographs

Homographs refer to characters that are identical in form but different in meaning. Although their forms are superficially identical, their composition intentions are mostly different. For most of the homographs that were used in bamboo slips and silk manuscripts from the same era, only part of their forms was identical, and the characters whose forms were totally identical are very few. In the silk manuscripts from Mawangdui Han Tombs, *jin* 仅 (only/merely) is an alternative form of *you* 佑 (to bless and protect) as in sentences "天仅而弗戒，天官地一也"⁵⁴ (If possessing the "blessing of heaven" does not make Chi You fearful, what can be done if both heaven and earth are assisting him?) and "子勿言仅，交为之备" (You can forget about talking about things like "blessing of heaven" for now. What we need is unity and cooperation to prepare for defence.).

According to *Zheng Zi Tong* 正字通 (Proper Forms of Characters), *jin* 仅 (only/merely) is also an alternative form of *fu* 付 (hand over).⁵⁵ Similarly, in the text "执大象，[天下]住，住而不害，安平大"⁵⁶ (One who masters the "Great Law" will be followed, admired, and sought after by people from all over the world, and they will not hinder each other but turn to him. Thus, everyone is peaceful and secure.), in silk manuscripts from Mawangdui Han Tombs, *zhu* 住 (to reside) is a variant form of the character *wang* 往 (to depart for). In the Qin and Han dynasties, the component 彳 was often written as 亻, such as *yi* 役 (labour) written as *yi* 伇 (labour), and *jing* 径 (footpath) as *jing* 俓 (footpath).

VI. Interchangeable Characters with Similar Forms

In *Jing Yi Shu Wen* 经义述闻 (Commentaries on Classical Works), Wang Yinzhi 王引之 (1766–1834) discussed the issue of erroneous forms, stating that many characters in the classics were prone to errors due to their form similarity. By making corrections, the meaning of the text can be clarified and understood.[57] He gave over 250 examples of such errors, such as mistaking *fu* 夫 (man) for *shi* 矢 (arrow) due to their form similarity, mistaking *jie* 介 (armour) for *fen* 分 (divide), *zuo* 左 (left) for *you* 右 (right), and so on.

Of course, some of the examples given by Wang fall under the category of exchangeable characters, such as *shi* 事 (government post) and *shi* 史 (history), *qing* 卿 (high official) and *xiang* 乡 (township), *yi* 義 (righteousness), and *wo* 我 (myself), etc. Theoretically speaking, some form errors are accidental, while most are caused by two reasons. One is that the characters are easily confused and often mixed up unconsciously. The other is that the confusion has become a habit, and then people intentionally mix them up. Mr. Li Ling 李零 (1948–) said, "We cannot ascribe all form errors to low educational levels or accidental negligence. In some cases, errors are repeated in Chu bamboo slips because they were accepted by the writing and reading habits of that time, becoming a consensus that mistakes are accepted as correct. This is different from the general concept of 'erroneous characters'."[58] In this statement, he refers to the second reason. The latter is more likely to become popular, and thus it is worth summarizing and defining it as "interchangeable characters with similar forms". However, because we have access to only a small part of the bamboo slips and silk manuscripts, it is sometimes difficult to distinguish between accidental and intentional errors, so they should be summarised uniformly. Due to the continuous revision during transmission and printing in various dynasties, the phenomenon of interchangeable characters with similar forms in classical literature is not too common. The errors described by Wang Yinzhi mostly relate to the mixed use of seal and clerical scripts, so he finally said, "to understand the true characters, one must trace them back to their original forms in seal scripts and official scripts, otherwise, it is impossible to correct them."

Interchangeable characters with similar forms are common in bamboo-slip and silk manuscripts. For example, in slips 236, 239, 243, 245, and 247 from the Chu-State bamboo slips unearthed at Baoshan, the character *nai* 柰 (how) in the sentence "*wu you nai* 毋又(有)柰" is an erroneous form of *sui* 祟 (evildoing). In the Chu-State Silk Manuscript of the Warring States Period, *yi* 弋 (hunt with bow and arrow) was written as *ge* 戈 (dagger-axe).[59] In the Chu-State bamboo slips unearthed in Guodian, all *yi* 弋 (hunt with bow and arrow) are written as *ge* 戈 (dagger-axe), such as in "*nai yi qi xiao* 乃弋其孝", "*nai yi qi chen* 乃弋其臣", "*chu yi bing ge* 出弋兵革" and "*jin zhi yi yu zhi zhe, wei nian bu yi* 今之弋于直者，未年不弋". In Han bamboo slips unearthed in Zhangjiashan, *luo* 络 (to wind) was regarded as *ji* 级 (level/rank/grade) in "夺其将爵一络"[60] (Strip him of one rank of his generalship.), but *ji* 级 (level/rank/grade) was taken as *luo* 络 (to wind) in "*si lian: yi ji si qiu lian* 丝练：以级丝求练" from the *Suanshu Shu* 算数书 (Book of Mathematics).[61]

Interchangeable characters with similar forms are sometimes one way, that is, only one character can be used as another. Sometimes they are two way, that is, one character can be used as another and vice versa.

When it comes to character usage, geographical and temporal factors need to be considered. Different regions or periods may have different habits and rules for character usage. For example, in the Chu Bamboo Slips Unearthed in Guodian, the character *gu* 谷 (valley) is used for *yu* 欲 (to want), and *yu* 浴 (bathe) is used for *gu* 谷 (valley). In later literature, the character *fu* 辅 (assistant) is used in *fuzhu* "辅助" (to assist), while in Chu-State bamboo slips from the Warring States Period, the character *fu* 楠 (a shrub) was borrowed to refer to *fu* 辅 (assistant).

Notes

1 The original Chinese version was published in *Journal of Northwest University* 西北大学学报 in 2008 (issue 3).
2 见陈伟武：《郭店楚简中所无之字》，《中国文字研究》第三辑，南宁：广西教育出版社，2002.
   Chen Weiwu: "Characters Not Included in the Great Chinese Dictionary in Chu Bamboo Slips Unearthed in Guodian", *Research on Chinese Characters* (Vol. 3), Nanning: Guangxi Education Publishing House, 2002.
3 见钱玄：《秦汉帛书简牍中的通假字》，载《南京师院学报》，1980（3）.
   Qian Xuan: "Exchangeable Characters in Bamboo Slips and Silk Manuscripts from Qin and Han Dynasties", *Journal of Nanjing Normal College*, 1980 (3).
4 国家文物局古文献研究室：《马王堆汉墓帛书》（壹），第 4 页，北京：文物出版社，1980.
   Research Office of Ancient Documents, National Cultural Heritage Administration: *Silk Manuscripts Unearthed from Mawangdui Han Tombs* (Vol. 1), p. 4, Beijing: Cultural Relics Press, 1980.
5 国家文物局古文献研究室：《马王堆汉墓帛书》（壹），第 52 页，北京：文物出版社，1980.
   Research Office of Ancient Documents, National Cultural Heritage Administration: *Silk Manuscripts Unearthed from Mawangdui Han Tombs* (Vol. 1), p. 52, Beijing: Cultural Relics Press, 1980.
6 银雀山汉墓竹简整理小组：《银雀山汉墓竹简》（壹），第 136 页，北京：文物出版社，1985.
   The Group for Sorting Bamboo Slips from Yinqueshan Han Tomb: *Bamboo Slips from Yinqueshan Han Tombs* (Vol. 1), p. 136, Beijing: Cultural Relics Press, 1985.
7 （宋）丁度等：《集韵》，第 301 页，上海：上海古籍出版社，1985.
   Ding Du et al. (Song Dynasty): *Jiyun* 集韵 (Jiyun Rhyming Dictionary), p. 301, Shanghai: Shanghai Classics Publishing House, 1985.
8 国家文物局古文献研究室：《马王堆汉墓帛书》（壹），第 7 页，北京：文物出版社，1980.
   Research Office of Ancient Documents, National Cultural Heritage Administration: *Silk Manuscripts Unearthed from Mawangdui Han Tombs* (Vol. 1), p. 7, Beijing: Cultural Relics Press, 1980.
9 国家文物局古文献研究室：《马王堆汉墓帛书》（壹），第 93 页，北京：文物出版社，1980.
   Research Office of Ancient Documents, National Cultural Heritage Administration: *Silk Manuscripts Unearthed From Mawangdui Han Tombs* (Vol. 1), p. 93. Beijing: Cultural Relics Press, 1980.

10 王贵元：《说文解字校笺》，第 106 页，上海：学林出版社，2002。
Wang Guiyuan: *Proofreading Notes to Shuowen Jiezi*, p. 106, Shanghai: Academia Press, 2002.
11 国家文物局古文献研究室：《马王堆汉墓帛书》（壹），第 95 页，北京：文物出版社，1980。
Research Office of Ancient Documents, National Cultural Heritage Administration: *Silk Manuscripts Unearthed From Mawangdui Han Tombs* (Vol. 1), p. 95. Beijing: Cultural Relics Press, 1980.
12 国家文物局古文献研究室：《马王堆汉墓帛书》（壹），第 58 页，北京：文物出版社，1980。
Research Office of Ancient Documents, National Cultural Heritage Administration: *Silk Manuscripts Unearthed from Mawangdui Han Tombs* (Vol. 1), p. 58, Beijing: Cultural Relics Press, 1980.
13 国家文物局古文献研究室：《马王堆汉墓帛书》（壹），第 58 页，北京：文物出版社，1980。
Research Office of Ancient Documents, National Cultural Heritage Administration: *Silk Manuscripts Unearthed from Mawangdui Han Tombs* (Vol. 1), p. 58, Beijing: Cultural Relics Press, 1980.
14 国家文物局古文献研究室：《马王堆汉墓帛书》（壹），第 10 页，北京：文物出版社，1980。
Research Office of Ancient Documents, National Cultural Heritage Administration: *Silk Manuscripts Unearthed from Mawangdui Han Tombs* (Vol. 1), p. 10, Beijing: Cultural Relics Press, 1980.
15 国家文物局古文献研究室：《马王堆汉墓帛书》（壹），第 95 页，北京：文物出版社，1980。
Research Office of Ancient Documents, National Cultural Heritage Administration: *Silk Manuscripts Unearthed from Mawangdui Han Tombs* (Vol. 1), p. 95, Beijing: Cultural Relics Press, 1980.
16 国家文物局古文献研究室：《马王堆汉墓帛书》（壹），第 18 页，北京：文物出版社，1980。
Research Office of Ancient Documents, National Cultural Heritage Administration: *Silk Manuscripts Unearthed from Mawangdui Han Tombs* (Vol. 1), p. 18, Beijing: Cultural Relics Press, 1980.
17 马王堆汉墓帛书整理小组：《马王堆汉墓帛书》（叁），第 40 页，北京：文物出版社，1978。
The Group for Sorting Silk Manuscripts Unearthed from Mawangdui Han Tombs: *Silk Manuscripts Unearthed from Mawangdui Han Tombs* (Vol. 3), p. 40, Beijing: Cultural Relics Press, 1978.
18 国家文物局古文献研究室：《马王堆汉墓帛书》（壹），第 50 页，北京：文物出版社，1980。
Research Office of Ancient Documents, National Cultural Heritage Administration: *Silk Manuscripts Unearthed from Mawangdui Han Tombs* (Vol. 1), p. 50, Beijing: Cultural Relics Press, 1980.
19 国家文物局古文献研究室：《马王堆汉墓帛书》（壹），第 81 页，北京：文物出版社，1980。
Research Office of Ancient Documents, National Cultural Heritage Administration: *Silk Manuscripts Unearthed from Mawangdui Han Tombs* (Vol. 1), p. 81, Beijing: Cultural Relics Press, 1980.
20 国家文物局古文献研究室：《马王堆汉墓帛书》（壹），第 4 页，北京：文物出版社，1980。
Research Office of Ancient Documents, National Cultural Heritage Administration: *Silk Manuscripts Unearthed from Mawangdui Han Tombs* (Vol. 1), p. 4, Beijing: Cultural Relics Press, 1980.
21 国家文物局古文献研究室：《马王堆汉墓帛书》（壹），第 3 页，北京：文物出版社，1980。

Research Office of Ancient Documents, National Cultural Heritage Administration: *Silk Manuscripts Unearthed from Mawangdui Han Tombs* (Vol. 1), p. 3, Beijing: Cultural Relics Press, 1980.
22 国家文物局古文献研究室：《马王堆汉墓帛书》（壹），第 81 页，北京：文物出版社，1980.
Research Office of Ancient Documents, National Cultural Heritage Administration: *Silk Manuscripts Unearthed from Mawangdui Han Tombs* (Vol. 1), p. 81, Beijing: Cultural Relics Press, 1980.
23 国家文物局古文献研究室：《马王堆汉墓帛书》（壹），第 4 页，北京：文物出版社，1980.
Research Office of Ancient Documents, National Cultural Heritage Administration: *Silk Manuscripts Unearthed from Mawangdui Han Tombs* (Vol. 1), p. 4, Beijing: Cultural Relics Press, 1980.
24 马王堆汉墓帛书整理小组：《马王堆汉墓帛书》（叁），第 61 页，北京：文物出版社，1978.
Research Office of Ancient Documents, National Cultural Heritage Administration: *Silk Manuscripts Unearthed from Mawangdui Han Tombs* (Vol. 3), p. 61, Beijing: Cultural Relics Press, 1980.
25 国家文物局古文献研究室：《马王堆汉墓帛书》（壹），第 18 页，北京：文物出版社，1980.
Research Office of Ancient Documents, National Cultural Heritage Administration: *Silk Manuscripts Unearthed from Mawangdui Han Tombs* (Vol. 1), p. 18, Beijing: Cultural Relics Press, 1980.
26 国家文物局古文献研究室：《马王堆汉墓帛书》（壹），第 51 页，北京：文物出版社，1980.
Research Office of Ancient Documents, National Cultural Heritage Administration: *Silk Manuscripts Unearthed from Mawangdui Han Tombs* (Vol. 1), p. 51, Beijing: Cultural Relics Press, 1980.
27 国家文物局古文献研究室：《马王堆汉墓帛书》（壹），第 3 页，北京：文物出版社，1980.
Research Office of Ancient Documents, National Cultural Heritage Administration: *Silk Manuscripts Unearthed from Mawangdui Han Tombs* (Vol. 1), p. 3, Beijing: Cultural Relics Press, 1980.
28 国家文物局古文献研究室：《马王堆汉墓帛书》（壹），第 89 页，北京：文物出版社，1980.
Research Office of Ancient Documents, National Cultural Heritage Administration: *Silk Manuscripts Unearthed from Mawangdui Han Tombs* (Vol. 1), p. 89, Beijing: Cultural Relics Press, 1980.
29 国家文物局古文献研究室：《马王堆汉墓帛书》（壹），第 12 页，北京：文物出版社，1980.
Research Office of Ancient Documents, National Cultural Heritage Administration: *Silk Manuscripts Unearthed from Mawangdui Han Tombs* (Vol. 1), p. 12, Beijing: Cultural Relics Press, 1980.
30 国家文物局古文献研究室：《马王堆汉墓帛书》（壹），第 87 页，北京：文物出版社，1980.
Research Office of Ancient Documents, National Cultural Heritage Administration: *Silk Manuscripts Unearthed from Mawangdui Han Tombs* (Vol. 1), p. 87, Beijing: Cultural Relics Press, 1980.
31 国家文物局古文献研究室：《马王堆汉墓帛书》（壹），第 11 页，北京：文物出版社，1980.
Research Office of Ancient Documents, National Cultural Heritage Administration: *Silk Manuscripts Unearthed from Mawangdui Han Tombs* (Vol. 1), p. 11, Beijing: Cultural Relics Press, 1980.

32 国家文物局古文献研究室：《马王堆汉墓帛书》（壹），第 79 页，北京：文物出版社，1980.
Research Office of Ancient Documents, National Cultural Heritage Administration: *Silk Manuscripts Unearthed from Mawangdui Han Tombs* (Vol. 1), p. 79, Beijing: Cultural Relics Press, 1980.
33 王贵元：《说文解字校笺》，第 661 页，上海：学林出版社，2002.
Wang Guiyuan: *Proofreading Notes to Shuowen Jiezi*, p. 661, Shanghai: Academia Press, 2002.
34 （清）段玉裁：《说文解字注》，第 756 页，上海：上海古籍出版社，1981.
Duan Yucai (Qing Dynasty): *Notes to Shuowen Jiezi*, p. 756, Shanghai: Shanghai Classics Publishing House, 1981.
35 王贵元：《说文解字校笺》，第 515 页，上海：学林出版社，2002.
Wang Guiyuan: *Proofreading Notes to Shuowen Jiezi*, p. 515, Shanghai: Academia Press, 2002.
36 王贵元：《说文解字校笺》，第 79 页，上海：学林出版社，2002.
Wang Guiyuan: *Proofreading Notes to Shuowen Jiezi*, p. 79, Shanghai: Academia Press, 2002.
37 王贵元：《说文解字校笺》，第 170 页，上海：学林出版社，2002.
Wang Guiyuan: *Proofreading Notes to Shuowen Jiezi*, p. 170, Shanghai: Academia Press, 2002.
38 荆门市博物馆：《郭店楚墓竹简》，第 151 页，北京：文物出版社，1998。为印刷方便，释文有时用通行字，下同.
Jingmen Municipal Museum: *The Guodian Chu-State Slips*, p. 151, Beijing: Cultural Relics Press, 1998. The interpretations sometimes adopt interchangeable characters for the convenience of printing. Same below.
39 荆门市博物馆：《郭店楚墓竹简》，第 187 页，北京：文物出版社，1998。
Jingmen Municipal Museum: *The Guodian Chu-State Slips*, p. 187, Beijing: Cultural Relics Press, 1998.
40 荆门市博物馆：《郭店楚墓竹简》，第 217 页，北京：文物出版社，1998.
Jingmen Municipal Museum: *The Guodian Chu-State Slips*, p. 217, Beijing: Cultural Relics Press, 1998.
41 王贵元：《说文解字校笺》，第 319 页，上海：学林出版社，2002.
Wang Guiyuan: *Proofreading Notes to Shuowen Jiezi*, p. 319, Shanghai: Academia Press, 2002.
42 湖南省博物馆、湖南省文物考古研究所：《长沙马王堆二、三号汉墓》，第 73 页，北京：文物出版社，2004.
Hunan Museum and Hunan Archaeological: *No. 2 and No. 3 Mawangdui Han Tombs*, p. 73, Beijing: Cultural Relics Press, 2004.
43 睡虎地秦墓竹简整理小组：《睡虎地秦墓竹简》，第 238 页，北京：文物出版社，1990.
The Group for Sorting Qin Bamboo Slips Unearthed at Shuihudi: *Qin Bamboo Slips Unearthed at Shuihudi*, p. 238, Beijing: Cultural Relics Press, 1990.
44 详王贵元：《汉墓帛书字形辨析三则》，《中国语文》，1996（4）.
Wang Guiyuan: "Three Principles on Distinguishing Character Forms of the Silk Manuscripts from Han Tombs", *Studies of the Chinese Language*, 1996 (4).
45 王贵元：《说文解字校笺》，第 440 页，上海：学林出版社，2002.
Wang Guiyuan: *Proofreading Notes to Shuowen Jiezi*, p. 440, Shanghai: Academia Press, 2002.
46 王贵元：《说文解字校笺》，第 559 页，上海：学林出版社，2002。
Wang Guiyuan: *Proofreading Notes to Shuowen Jiezi*, p. 559, Shanghai: Academia Press, 2002.
47 王贵元：《说文解字校笺》，第 559 页，上海：学林出版社，2002.
Wang Guiyuan: *Proofreading Notes to Shuowen Jiezi*, p. 559, Shanghai: Academia Press, 2002.

48 荆门市博物馆：《郭店楚墓竹简》，第 157 页，北京：文物出版社，1998。
Jingmen Municipal Museum: *The Guodian Chu-State Slips*, p. 157, Beijing: Cultural Relics Press, 1998.
49 荆门市博物馆：《郭店楚墓竹简》，第 194 页，北京：文物出版社，1998。
Jingmen Municipal Museum: *The Guodian Chu-State Slips*, p. 209, Beijing: Cultural Relics Press, 1998.
50 荆门市博物馆：《郭店楚墓竹简》，第 209 页，北京：文物出版社，1998。
Jingmen Municipal Museum: *The Guodian Chu-State Slips*, p. 209, Beijing: Cultural Relics Press, 1998.
51 王贵元：《说文解字校笺》，第 198 页，上海：学林出版社，2002.
Wang Guiyuan: *Proofreading Notes to Shuowen Jiezi*, p. 198, Shanghai: Academia Press, 2002.
52 周祖谟：《尔雅校笺》，第 84 页，南京：江苏教育出版社，1984.
Zhou Zumo: *Proofreading Notes to Erya*, p. 84, Nanjing: Jiangsu Education Publishing House, 1984.
53 《续修四库全书》编委会：《续修四库全书》1142 册，第 79 页，上海：上海古籍出版社，2003.
Compiling Committee for Continuous Compiling of Si Ku Quan Shu: *Continuous Compiling of Si Ku Quan Shu (Complete Library in the Four Branches of Literature)* (Vol. 1142), p. 79, Shanghai: Shanghai Classics Publishing House, 2003.
54 国家文物局古文献研究室：《马王堆汉墓帛书》（壹），第 67 页，北京：文物出版社，1980.
Research Office of Ancient Documents, National Cultural Heritage Administration: *Silk Manuscripts Unearthed from Mawangdui Han Tombs* (Vol. 1), p. 67, Beijing: Cultural Relics Press, 1980.
55 四库全书存目丛书编撰委员会：《四库全书存目丛书》经 197，第 79 页，济南：齐鲁书社，1997.
Compiling Committee for Series of Index to Si Ku Quan Shu: *Series of Index to Si Ku Quan Shu* (Vol. 197), p. 79, Jinan: Shandong Qilu Press, 1997.
56 国家文物局古文献研究室：《马王堆汉墓帛书》（壹），第 13 页，北京：文物出版社，1980.
Research Office of Ancient Documents, National Cultural Heritage Administration: *Silk Manuscripts Unearthed from Mawangdui Han Tombs* (Vol. 1), p. 13, Beijing: Cultural Relics Press, 1980.
57 （清）王引之：《经义述闻》，第 778 页，南京：江苏古籍出版社，1985.
Wang Yinzhi (Qing Dynasty): *Commentaries on Classical Works*, p. 778, Nanjing: Jiangsu Classics Publishing House, 1985.
58 李零：《郭店楚简校读记》，第 193 页，北京：北京大学出版社，2002.
Li Ling: *Proofreading of Chu-state Bamboo Slips Unearthed in Guodian*, p. 193, Beijing: Peking University Press, 2002.
59 详李家浩：《著名中年语言学家自选集•李家浩卷》，安徽教育出版社，2002.
Li Jiahao: *Selected Works of Famous Middle-aged Linguistics: The Volume of Li Jiahao*, Hefei: Anhui Education Publishing House, 2002.
60 张家山二四七号汉墓竹简整理小组：《张家山汉墓竹简（二四七号墓）》，第 152 页，北京：文物出版社，2001.
The Group for Sorting Bamboo Slips in No. 247 Han Tomb in Zhangjiashan: *Han Bamboo Slips Unearthed in Zhangjiashan (No. 247)*, p. 152, Beijing: Cultural Relics Press, 2001.
61 张家山二四七号汉墓竹简整理小组：《张家山汉墓竹简（二四七号墓）》，第 259 页，北京：文物出版社，2001.
The Group for Sorting Bamboo Slips in No. 247 Han Tomb in Zhangjiashan: *Han Bamboo Slips Unearthed in Zhangjiashan (No. 247)*, p. 259, Beijing: Cultural Relics Press, 2001.

14 Discussion on the Original Meaning of *Wu* 物[1]

The original meaning of a Chinese character directly explains the form of the character and serves as the origin of the character's extended meanings that are developed in the actual use of language by highlighting and enhancing a feature or quality of the original meaning. It is worth noting that the original meaning is not some archaic definition of a character, which is no longer in everyday use. Both the original meaning and extended meanings of a character are put into daily use, and it takes effort to distinguish a character's original meaning from its extended meanings. The original and extended meanings of a character are inherently corelated: the features or qualities of an original meaning are separately embodied in its group of extended meanings. Therefore, it is possible to detect the origin of an extended meaning in the original meaning and to identify the original meaning by discovering commonality of a group of extended meanings. Given this, the study on a character's original meaning shall adhere to such a principle: the identification of the original meaning must be based on the system analysis of a group of meanings instead of isolated analyses of character meanings to prevent biased conclusions. Such biased conclusions are not uncommon in previous studies on the original meaning of the character *wu* 物.

Possible original meanings of *wu* 物 include the following: (1) a varicoloured ox[2]; (2) the flag of a district[3]; and (3) the character *li* "犁" (to plough).[4]

When it means a varicoloured ox, *wu* 物 is in fact a combination of two components *wu* 勿 (red-white flag) and *niu* 牛 (ox/cattle). In oracle-bone scripts, there were many multiple-component phenomena, such as *huangyin* 黄尹 as "𦫻", *huangniu* 黄牛 as "𤘘". *Wu* 物 was sometimes written as "𤘟". In such scripts, *wu* 勿 (red-white flag) and *niu* 牛 (ox/cattle) were often in succession, with *wu* 勿 (red-white flag) occasionally at the end of the previous line and *niu* 牛 (ox/cattle) at the beginning of the next. In addition, there were also such phrases as *wuma* 勿马, *wumu* 勿牡, *wupin* 勿牝, *wushang* 勿牢, etc. Obviously, *wuniu* 勿牛 is a phrase rather than a single character.[5]

Which one is the correct original meaning of *wu* 物, "the flag of a district" or "the character li '犁' (to plough)"? The answer depends on which one can best fit the rules of extension and encompass all meanings of the character being discussed. As any characteristic of the original meaning or the object it represents would lead to an extended meaning, the list of extended meanings from different original meanings varied, corresponding to the differences among original meanings or among objects they represent. As a result, only the original meaning from which the extended meanings derived can completely encompass a meaning list.

According to early documents, *wu* 物 had the following extended meanings:

(1) Class:
Wu 物 was explained as "class" by both Du Yu 杜预 (222–285) and Wei Zhao 韦昭 (204–273) when it appeared in expressions, like *yan yi zhi wu* 言以知物 (to speak and know its class) and *shi you qi wu* 事有其物 (everything belongs to a class) from *Zuo Zhuan* 左传 (Zuo's Commentary on The Spring and Autumn Annals), and *ru cao mu zhi chan ye, ge yi qi wu* 如草木之产也，各以其物 (Like the growth of plants and trees, each gathering in its own class.) in *Guo Yu* 国语 (Discourses on Governance of the District).

(2) Colour:
Wu 物 was interpreted as "colour" by Zheng Xuan 郑玄 (127–200) and Wei Zhao 韦昭 (204–273) when in expressions, such as *yong quan wu* 用牷物 (use animals with pure colour) and *yi wu yun zhi wu* 以五云之物 (clouds with various colours) from *Zhou Li* 周礼 (Rites of the Zhou Dynasty), and *mao yi shi wu* 毛以示物 (the colour of the wool) from *Guo Yu*.

(3) All things on earth:
Wu 物 was interpreted as "all things on earth" as in expressions *wu ye zhe, da gong ming ye* 物也者，大共名也 (*wu* "物" is the largest shared name of all things on earth) by Xun Zi 荀子 (313–238 BCE, a Confucian philosopher) in his works *Zheng Ming* 正名 (Rectification of Names), and in *hun yuan yun wu* 浑元运物 (heaven and earth make all things move and change) from a prose entitled *You Tong Fu* 幽通赋 by Ban Gu 班固 (ca. 32–92).

(4) Matter or thing:
Du Yu 杜预 (222–285) interpreted *wu* 物 as "matter or thing" as in *jian yi guan er san wu cheng* 建一官而三物成 (three matters were solved by establishing one post) and in *suo wei 'yong yong zhi zhi' zhe, wei ci wu ye fu* 所谓'庸庸祇祇'者，谓此物也夫？ (This is probably the matter that is meant by the "usable and respectful" in *Zhou Shu* 周书 (Book of the (Northern) Zhou)). Likewise, Zheng Xuan 郑玄 (127–200) noted that *wu* 物 referred to "matter or thing" in *xing yi wu er san shan jie de zhe, wei shi zi er yi* 行一物而三善皆得者，唯世子而已 (Only the crown prince can get three good results from doing one thing.) from *Li ji* 礼记 (The Book of Rites).

(5) Observe and choose:
When *wu* 物 was used in *wu tu fang* 物土方 (to choose a place for soil excavation) from *Zuo Zhuan* and in *wu zhi ke yi feng yi zhe* 物之可以封邑者 (to choose places where settlements can be built) from *Zhou Li* 周礼 (Rites of the Zhou Dynasty), Du Yu 杜预 (222–285) and Zheng Xuan 郑玄 (127–200) interpreted it as "observe and choose".

First, let's talk about the original meaning of *wu* 物 as "the flag of a district".

According to *Zhou Li* 周礼 (Rites of the Zhou Dynasty), nine kinds of flags were used to distinguish the ranks of officials and soldiers in pre-Qin kingdoms. As recorded in Notes to *Zuo Zhuan* 左传, *bai guan zun bei bu tong, suo jian ge you qi wu* 百官尊卑不同，所建各有其物 (Officials are different in ranks, and each has his own flag.) and *bai guan xiang wu er dong, jun zheng bu jie er bei* 百官象物而动，军政不戒而备 (With the flags of the officials moving, the military and political affairs are prepared without warning), *wu* 物 was one kind of the nine flags. Du Yu 杜预 (222–285) further extended the meaning of *wu* 物 to "class". *Wu* 物 implied the meaning of "class" when it referred to flags because flags were used to classify people at different ranks. In addition, the abovementioned nine flags were different in images or colours. The flags that *wu* 物 represented didn't have any image but were characterized by mixing two colours of red and white in various manners to distinguish people at the same rank. Therefore, the meaning of *wu* 物 was also extended to "colour", and the meaning of *wan wu* 万物 (all things on earth) was extended to "all colours". As stated in ancient documents, the ancients would use colours to represent concrete subjects. *Zuo Zhuan* 左传 (Zuo's Commentary on the Spring and Autumn Annals) recorded that *wu se bi xiang, zhao qi wu ye* 五色比象，昭其物也 (The images of five colours were used to represent different objects.), which was interpreted by 杜预 (222–285) and Kong Yingda 孔颖达 (574–648) that five basic colours of the vehicles, clothing, or equipment represented the four cardinal directions, and the space between the sky and the earth showed that they were meaningful objects. Then, *wu* 物 was extended to "object" or "thing", and *wan wu* 万物 to "all objects". Besides, *wu* 物 was also interpreted as "observe and choose", which was derived from its use in *bai guan xiang wu er dong* 百官象物而动 (officials moving with the flags). In ancient times, flags were essential in commanding warfare because officers and soldiers had to observe the change of flags to decide what actions they should take. That's how the meaning of "observe and choose" came from. The distinction between *shi* 事 (thing) and *wu* 物 (object or thing) was not very clear in ancient times and was often collectively referred to as *wu* 物, which was certified by *Li ji* 礼记 (The Book of Rites) "诚者物之终始" (Sincerity is the start of everything.).

According to Zheng Xuan 郑玄 (127–200), *wu* 物 here referred to all things on earth and was an alternative of *shi* 事. All in all, we can conclude that "flag of a district" is the original meaning of *wu* 物, and it is able to encompass all its extended meanings in accordance with the law of extension.

Now, let's discuss whether "to plough" is an original meaning of *wu* 物.

In an agrarian society, because *li* 犁 (to plough) was everyone's primary concern, it was possible to extend "to plough" to all things on earth. Nevertheless, natural things already existed long before ploughing, and "man-powered" ploughing existed even before oxen ploughing. Therefore, it is rather far-fetched to say, "Oxen plough is the origin of all things on earth", and it is also quite unlikely to relate other meanings of *wu* 物 to "to plough". Therefore, a conclusion can be made that the original meaning of *wu* 物 is "the flag of the district".

Although *wu* 勿 was shaped like a knife ploughing the ground in oracle-bone scripts, such as "⸺" or "⸺", the character was always used in front of animal names as a modifier, such as *wuniu* 勿牛 (varicoloured cows), *wuma* 勿马 (varicoloured horses), *wumu* 勿牡 (varicoloured male animals), and *wupin* 勿牝 (varicoloured female animals), proving that the original meaning of *wu* 勿 was not "to plough". "A knife ploughing the ground" was its form intention, but its meaning was "varicoloured", i.e., the colour of the tilled land. With weeds and grain stalks in the land, its colour became variegated. The form and meaning intentions of *wu* 勿 were like those of *hei* 黑 (black). The seal-script form of *hei* 黑 (black) was written as *zi* 鄨. *He* 嗮 is the ancient form of *cong* 囱 (chimney), which means "window of a stove". *Hei* 黑 consists of two components yan 炎 (flame) and 囧, and the latter is arranged above the former. The actual meaning of the character was the colour of smoke. Likewise, *wuniu* 勿牛 and *wuma* 勿马 in oracle-bone scripts referred to "varicoloured cow" and "varicoloured horse", respectively. Other colours of cows were also recorded in oracle-bone scripts, such as *huangniu* 黄牛 (yellow cow), *zhiniu* 戠牛 (yellow cow), *youniu* 幽牛 (dark cow), *bainiu* 白牛 (white cow), *jinniu* 堇牛 (violet cow), etc. Therefore, the interpretation of *wu* 物 as "varicoloured cow" was a result of mistakenly attributing the meaning of the phrase *wuniu* 勿牛 to *wu* 物.

The flag of a district was made of red-white cloth, which was also the colour of *wu* 勿. Therefore, the character *wu* 斻 was created to represent the flag. *Wu* 斻 had two components, *yan* 㫃 and *wu* 勿 and was pronounced same to *wu* 勿. In bronze inscriptions, *yan* 㫃 (the pictographic component of all characters representing the nine flags) was engraved as ⸺, and *niu* 牛 as ⸺. Because of the similarity of them, *wu* 斻 was later mistakenly written as *wu* 物. *Yan* 㫃 was substituted by *niu* 牛 by mistake. Such case was explained in *Shuowen Jiezi* 说文解字 (An Explication of Written Characters), which certified that many *wu* 物 used in documents should have been *wu* 斻. For example, in the following sentences and phrases, *za bo wei wu* 杂帛为物 (use red-white cloth as flags), *da fu shi jian wu* 大夫士建物 (senior officials use red-white flags), and *xiang sui zai wu* 乡遂载物 (township officials use red-white flags) from *Zhou Li*, *jing ge yi qi wu* 旌各以其物 (the shooters use their usual flags) and *wei ming ge yi qi wu* 为铭各以其物 (the deceased is inscribed with coloured cloth according to his identity) from *Yi li* 仪礼 (Annotations on the Book of Rites and Rituals), *wu* 物 was actually a variant of 斻. Gradually, *wu* 物 substituted for 斻, and that was the real birth story of *wu* 物. Therefore, its original meaning was, of course, the flag of a district.

The principle of exploring the original meaning by referring to the extended meaning list plays an indispensable role in obtaining the correct definition. Following this principle, various information about the original meaning can be obtained from the list of extended meanings. Furthermore, the approach and direction of the exploration process will be rectified.

Because of the existence of borrowed meanings, not all meanings of a character can be included in its list of extended meanings. As a result, it cannot be assumed that only the item that encompasses all the meanings of a character is the original meaning. Nevertheless, borrowed meanings are relatively rare, so they do not affect the application of this principle.

Notes

1 The original Chinese version was published in *Journal of Liaoning Educational Institute* 辽宁教育学院学报 in 1987 (issue 2).
2 王国维《观堂集林》卷六，商承祚《殷墟文字类编》"物"字条.
  Wang Guowei: *Guan Tang Ji Lin* (Vol. 6); Shang Chengzuo: *The Entry for the Character Wu* 物 from *A Book for the Characters Found at the Ruins of Yin*.
3 陆宗达、王宁：《训诂方法论》，第 83 页，北京：中国社会科学出版社，1983.
  Lu Zongda and Wang Ning: *Methodology on Philology*, p. 83, Beijing: China Social Sciences Press, 1983.
4 《郭沫若全集·考古编（一）》"释 勿"
  Interpretation of wu 勿 *and*, Archaeology Section from Guo Moruo's Complete Works (I).
5 详见《中国文字》第七卷"释物"
  "Interpretation of wu 物*", Chinese Characters*, Volume 7.

15 The Connotations of *Xie* 偕 in "Fish and Wine" from *Shi Jing*[1]

Collected in *Shi Jing* 诗经 (The Book of Songs), the Minor Court Hymns *Yu Li* 鱼丽 ("Fish and Wine") was usually sung at royal banquets.

(The 1st Stanza) How fish in the basket are fine! Yellow Cheek Carp and Snail Carp. Our host has wine. So delicious and abundant. 魚丽于罶，鲿鲨. 君子有酒，旨且多.
(The 2nd Stanza) How fish in the basket are fine! So many blackfish and breams. Our host has wine. So abundant and good it seems. 魚丽于罶，魴鲤. 君子有酒，多且旨.
(The 3rd Stanza) How fish in the basket are fine! So many carps and mudfish. Our host has wine. As delicious and much as you wish. 魚丽于罶，鰋鲤. 君子有酒，旨且有.
(The 4th Stanza) How abundant the food! So delicious and good! 物其多矣，维其嘉矣.
(The 5th Stanza) How delicious the food at hand! So much from the sea and the land! 物其旨矣，维其偕矣.
(The 6th Stanza) We love the food so abundant. For it is as delicious as we want. 物其有矣，维其时矣.
[Translator's Note: The translations of all the poems cited in this chapter from *Shi Jing* are adapted from the version translated by Xu Yuanchong 许渊冲 (1921–2021).]

As to the character *xie* 偕 used in the 5th Stanza from the above song, both Zheng Xuan 郑玄 (127–200) and Zhu Xi 朱熹 (1130–1200) interpreted it as "to be equal".[2] Nevertheless, Wang Yinzhi 王引之 (1766–1834), a famous scholar in the Qing Dynasty, interpreted it as "excellent" in his work *Jing Yi Shu Wen* 经义述闻 (Commentaries on Classical Works). Gao Heng 高亨 (1900–1986) adopted both interpretations and further elaborated the first one in his work *Shi Jing Jin Zhu* 诗经今注 (Annotations of the Book of Songs) as "to be harmonious" as in "the food looks harmonious with others".[3] These are all the interpretations of *xie* 偕 given so far, but none of them are suitable to be used in the interpretation of the above-shown lines. Besides, inversion in the poem and the phenomenon of synonym substitution add further complexity to this analysis.

DOI: 10.4324/9781032622965-15

According to Wen Yiduo 闻一多 (1899–1946), fish was always associated with happiness and well-being.[4] Such usage was evidenced by other songs that pictured the happiness of life in *Shi Jing* 诗经 (The Book of Songs) and other ancient Chinese poems. For example,

(The 1st Stanza) Fish among the seed. Heads happily swing. Our king in the capital. Drinking the wine with glee. 魚在在藻，有頒其首. 王在在镐，岂乐饮酒. 角在在藻，有莘其尾. 王在在镐，饮酒乐岂.

(The 2nd Stanza) Fish among the seed. Tails joyfully swing. Our king in the capital. Drinking the wine happily. 角在在藻，有莘其尾. 王在在镐，饮酒乐岂.
. . . . . .
(Translated from "Fish Among the Seed", a Minor Court Hymn of *Shi Jing*)

(The 1st Stanza) Southern fish fine, swim and fro. Our host has wine; guest drink and glow. 南有嘉魚，烝然罩罩. 君子有酒，嘉宾式燕以乐.

(The 2nd Stanza) Southern fish fine, swim all so free. Our host has wine; guest drink with glee. 南有嘉魚，烝然汕汕. 君子有酒，嘉宾式燕以衎.

((The 3rd Stanza) South wood is fine, and gourds are sweet. Our host has wine, with cheer guests meet. 南有樛木，甘瓠累之. 君子有酒，嘉宾式燕绥之.
. . . . . .
(Translated from Southern Fish Fine, a minor court hymn of *Shi Jing*)

Obviously, the initial sentences of the first three stanzas of "Fish and Wine" were used for association, which is one of the three main ways of expression in *Shi Jing* 诗经 and often uses an objective thing as metaphor to elicit for feelings and sensibilities or set off the theme. These lines have no necessary connection with the following sentence, and they are not the theme of this song. A Qing-Dynasty scholar named Ma Ruichen 马瑞辰 (1777–1853) pointed out that Zheng Xuan 郑玄 had mistakenly related "abundant and delicious" in the song to both fish and wine. He made it clear that they referred only to the wine.[5] Similarly, *liao mu* 樛木 (fine wood) in the 3rd stanza of "Southern Fish Fine" was used the same as fish in the abovementioned songs, a metaphor as a lead-in for the real subject of a song.

The last three stanzas of "Fish and Wine" were correlated with the last lines of the first three stanzas. The wine was so delicious and abundant that people began to require more kinds of food and hoped delicious food to be abundant and vice versa. As *wu* 物 (food) here was derived from wine, it referred to certain kind of food rather than many others. Therefore, it was obviously wrong to explain *xie* 偕 as "to be harmonious with others".

Inversion was a typical rhetorical device in *Shi Jing*. It was found in the first three (the 1st–3rd stanzas) and last three stanzas (the 4th–6th stanzas) of "Fish and Wine". For example, in the 1st–3rd stanzas, to express "delicious and abundant", the song used *zhi qie duo* 旨且多 (delicious and abundant) and *zhi qie you* 旨且有 (delicious and abundant) in the 1st and 3rd stanzas but *duo qie zhi*

多且旨 (abundant and delicious) in the 2nd stanza, where the rhetorical device is applied (according to Zhu Xi, both *you* 有 and *duo* 多 means abundant). In addition, another typical phenomenon in *Shi Jing* was a synonym substitution. As for the last three stanzas, Zheng Xuan already pointed out that *zhi* 旨 and *jia* 嘉 meant delicious. Later, Wang Yinzhi interpreted *shi* 时 and *jia* 嘉 as delicious when they referred to food. Therefore, *jia* 嘉, *zhi* 旨 and *shi* 时 were synonyms meaning delicious in this song. As explained above, the 5th stanza applies the device of inversion to realise its rhetorical intention. Since we have known that *you* 有 and *duo* 多 meant abundant, it is quite easy to conclude that *xie* 偕 is their synonym and meant "abundant", too.

Other songs in *Shi Jing* also proved that *xie* 偕 referred to "abundant", such as in *jiang fu kong jie* 降福孔皆 (abundant blessings for all) from *Feng Nian* 丰年 (Harvest), which was cited as *jiang fu kong xie* 降福孔偕 in *Zuo Zhuan* 左传 (Zuo's Commentary on the Spring and Autumn Annals). Chen Huan 陈奂 (1786–1863) agreed that *xie* 偕 and *jie* 皆 were substitutions.[6] Likewise, *jiang fu ji duo* 降福既多 and *jiang fu rang rang* 降福穰穰 were used in Eulogy of Lu and Eulogy of Zhou. Zhu Xi clarified that *rang* 穰 referred to abundant. A Pear Tree, a Minor Court Hymn, described how a family expected their members in the army to be back. The expected one didn't return although his army service was due. The more anxious his family were, the more urgent it was to know his fortune. Therefore, *bu shi xie zhi* 卜筮偕止 (fortune-telling activities became abundant). According to Gao Heng, *zhi* 止 was a modal particle.

In conclusion, if *xie* 偕 was interpreted as "excellent" as Wang Yinzhi did, it would be hard to understand the songs abovementioned and the rhetorical intention in *Shi Jing* were not considered.

Notes

1 The original Chinese version was published in *Journal of Northwest Normal University (Social Sciences)* 西北师大学报(社会科学版专辑) in June, 1999.
2 阮元：《十三经注疏》(上册), 第 417 页, 北京：中华书局, 1979 年影印本。
朱熹：《诗集传》, 第 109 页, 北京：中华书局, 1958.
Ruan Yuan: *Notes and Commentaries to Thirteen Classics Explanatory* (Vol. 1), p. 417, Beijing: Zhonghua Book Company, photocopy published in 1979. Zhu Xi: *Studies on the Book of Songs*, p. 109, Beijing: Zhonghua Book Company, 1958.
3 高亨：《诗经今注》, 第 236 页, 上海：上海古籍出版社, 1980.
Gao Heng: *Annotations of the Book of Songs*, p. 236, Shanghai: Shanghai Classics Publishing House, 1980.
4 闻一多：《神话与诗》, 第 117 页, 上海：古籍出版社, 1956.
Wen Yiduo: *Myth and Poetry*, p. 117, Shanghai: Shanghai Classics Publishing House, 1956.
5 《毛诗传笺通释》, 见《皇清经解续编》第 6 册.
"The Annotation on Mao Heng's Commentaries on the Book of Songs", see *The Sequels to the Notes to the Classics in Qing Dynasty, Volume 6.*
6 《诗毛诗传疏》, 见《皇清经解续编》第 7 册.
"The Annotation on Mao Heng's Commentaries on the Book of Songs", see *The Sequels to the Notes to the Classics in Qing Dynasty, Volume 6.*

16 An Evaluation of Different Versions of *Shuowen Jiezi*[1]

Shuowen Jiezi 说文解字 (An Explication of Written Characters) is the first Chinese dictionary that analyses characters' forms, meanings, and pronunciations. It is also the first Chinese philological work exploring the inherent connections among the forms, pronunciations, and meanings of Chinese characters. Nowadays, this book can still arouse the interest of many researchers while being widely used as a reference book for ancient character interpretation, dictionary compilation, and studies on Chinese history, philosophy, literature, and medical technology. Nevertheless, when conducting such research, researchers usually pay little attention to the different versions of the book and refer only to the most widely circulated version edited by the Qing-Dynasty sinologist 陈昌治 (1830–1896), which is known as *Chen Changzhi Yi Zhuan Yi Hang Ben* 陈昌治一篆一行本 (Chen Changzhi's One-Character-One-Volume Version). As to sinological studies on the book, they tend to refer to only Duan Yucai's 段玉裁 (1735–1815) *Shuowen Jiezi Zhu* 说文解字注 (Notes to *Shuowen Jiezi*). In fact, there are many versions of *Shuowen Jiezi* and sinological studies on the book, which date back to periods before the Song Dynasty (960–1279), and many of them have high academic value, especially those unearthed or discovered after the Qing Dynasty (1636–1912). Therefore, the works of Qing-Dynasty sinologists, including Duan Yucai 段玉裁, cannot completely make up for the deficiencies of the popular version of *Shuowen Jiezi*. The following is an evaluation of different versions of *Shuowen Jiezi* before the Song Dynasty (including the reprinted Song copies from the Qing Dynasty) and their adaptations.

I. Tang-Dynasty Manuscript Versions

The earliest surviving versions of *Shuowen Jiezi* are two manuscript versions dating back to the Tang Dynasty (618–907), both of which are incomplete. (These two manuscript versions can be individually or collectively referred to as *Tangxieben* hereinafter.)

(I) The Tang-Dynasty Manuscript Containing Entries Involving Radical **Mu** 木 *(Wood)*

There are 188 characters explained in this manuscript, which was originally owned by Zhang Renfa 张仁法, a Qing-Dynasty county magistrate. In 1863, Zhang Renfa

DOI: 10.4324/9781032622965-16

donated it to the famous Qing scholar Mo Youzhi 莫友芝 (1811–1871), who wrote *Tangxieben Shuowen Jiezi Mubu Jian Yi* 唐写本说文解字木部笺异 (Annotations to the Tang-Dynasty *Shuowen Jiezi* Manuscript Containing Entries Involving Radical *Mu* 木) to publish his research results on this manuscript. This book was later included in *Shuowen Jiezi Gulin* 说文解字诂林 (Explanation to *Shuowen Jiezi*). In his book *Wen Xue Ji* 问学集 (Essays of Zhou Zumo), Zhou Zumo 周祖谟 (1914–1995, a Chinese sinologist) includes photographs of the manuscript. This manuscript was probably written by someone in the middle of the Tang Dynasty. The paper of the manuscript is hard and yellow, and the calligraphy is exquisite. Judging from its content, its academic value is even higher than that of Xu Ka's 徐锴 (920–974) and Xu Xuan's 徐铉 (917–992) editions of *Shuowen Jiezi*. Its academic value can be proved through an analysis of the following examples that are taken from Chen Changzhi's one-character-one-volume version. Other examples discussed in this part are also taken from this edition.

1. *Ji* 楫 (oar) refers to *zhouzhuo* 舟櫂 (oar).

The character *zhao* 櫂 included in the explanation is proven to be an error through a comparative study with *Tangxieben*. (As Xu Kai's 徐锴 Edition of *Shuowen Jiezi* also adopts this explanation, it also contains such an error.) This character should be written as *zhuo* 擢 since there is no entry for 櫂 in *Tangxieben*. Character *zhuo* 擢 means "to pull". As *ji* 楫 (oar) is a tool for propelling a boat, it is reasonable for this character to appear in the word *zhouzhuo* 舟擢 (oar).

2. *You* 橚 (firewood) means "to kindle a fire by piling up wood".

This explanation also appears in Xu Kai's 徐锴 Edition of *Shuowen Jiezi*, but in *Tangxieben* 积火 (accumulating fine) is replaced by 积木 (piling up wood). According to Mo Youzhi's 莫友芝 *Tangxieben Shuowen Jiezi Mubu Jian Yi* 唐写本说文解字木部笺异 (Annotations to the Tang-Dynasty *Shuowen Jiezi* Manuscript Containing Entries Involving Radical *Mu* 木), *liao* 燎 (to kindle a fire) embodies the meaning of fire, so the use of '积火' in this interpretation is incorrect. There are other documents proving that it is 积木 instead of 积火 that should be used here. For example, *Yupian* 玉篇 (Chinese dictionary compiled by Gu Yewang in 6th century) defines *you* 橚 (firewood) as 积木燎以祭天 (to accumulate and burn wood as a sacrifice to the heavens). *Wujing Wenzi* 五经文字 (Characters in the Five Classics) also interprets it as 积木燎之 (to kindle a fire by piling up wood.)

3. *Zhi* 桎 (fetters) refers to shackles for feet, consisting of semantic component *mu* 木 (wood) and phonetic component *zhi* 至 (to reach).

In *Tangxieben*, the characters 足械也 (shackles for the feet) are followed by 所以质地, which is also included in Volume 13 and 84 of *Yiqiejing Yinyi* 一切经音义 (Explanations of All Sutras) by Huilin (736–820, a Tang-Dynasty monk and sinologist), Notes to "Handling Prisoners" from *Zhou Li* 周礼 (Rites of the Zhou

Dynasty) by Lu Deming 陆德明 (ca. 550–630), and Volume 644 of *Tai Ping Yu Lan* 太平御览 (Taiping Imperial Encyclopaedia). Therefore, "所以质地" should be added to the interpretation for this character.

4. *Xia* 柙 (wooden cage) is a fence used to keep tigers and rhinoceroses.

In *Tangxieben*, 以藏虎兕 (to keep tigers and rhinoceroses) is written as 可以盛藏虎兕 (to be used to keep tigers and rhinoceroses). It is the same as the quote in Volume 25 of *Tang Yun* 唐韵 (the Book of Tang Rhyme) and should be corrected accordingly.

5. *Jie* 楬 (marking stake) refers to *jiejie* 楬桀 (a marking stake), consisting of semantic components *mu* 木 (wood) and phonetic component *he* 曷 (what). *Chun Qiu Zhuan* 春秋传 (Commentaries on Spring and Autumn Annals) says, 士舆楬 (scholar-officials carried the coffin to show that they were not afraid of death).

In *Tangxieben*, *jiejie* 楬桀 is written as *jiezhu* 楬橥 (wooden pile). Both *Wuyin Yunpu* 五音韵谱 (The Book of Five-Note Rhyme) and *Yunhui* 韵会 (A Collection of Rhyme) use the same two characters to explain *jie* 楬. Volume 7 of Annotations to *Guangya* by Wang Niansun 王念孙 (1744–1832) also verifies the interpretation of *jiezhu* 楬橥 (wooden pile). Therefore, it can be concluded that 橥 is wrongly replaced by 桀 in some versions of *Shuowen Jiezi*. Besides, *Tangxieben* also shows that 士舆楬 (scholar-officials carried the coffin to express their determination) is an expression cited from *Zhou Li* 周礼 (Rites of the Zhou Dynasty) instead of *Chun Qiu Zhuan* 春秋传 (Commentaries on Spring and Autumn Annals).

6. *Fei* 棐 (to assist) is a synonym for *fu* 辅 (to assist), consisting of semantic component *mu* 木 (wood) and phonetic component *fei* 非 (violate).

This character is the last entry for radical *mu* 木 (wood) in Xu Xuan's 徐铉 edition of *Shuowen Jiezi*. As pointed out by Duan Yucai 段玉裁, this character has missed its old sequence. In *Tangxieben*, the entry of this character is placed between *gua* 栝 (the pointed end of an arrow) and *qi* 棊 (chess). This arrangement conforms to the character sequence rules in *Shuowen Jiezi*, so this arrangement should be the original one.

When Xu Xuan 徐铉 (916–991) and his co-workers revised *Shuowen Jiezi* in the Song Dynasty, many other editions and copies of the book were lost. As a result, the only book that could be used to collate Xu Xuan's Edition of *Shuowen Jiezi* was Xu Kai's 徐锴 Edition. These two editions differ from the original version of *Shuowen Jiezi* in format. When other books quote *Shuowen Jiezi*, they often quote only the definitions and interpretations of the characters. For these reasons, it is difficult to determine the original content of *Shuowen Jiezi*. Fortunately, *Tangxieben* provide a very reliable reference for relevant studies. For example, the character *cong* 从 (to follow) used in Xu Xuan's 徐铉 edition is written as *cong* 從

226 *An Evaluation of Different Versions of* Shuowen Jiezi

(to follow) in Xu Kai's 徐鍇 Edition and *Tangxieben*. The interpretation format of a character is "从A从B" (consisting of component A and component B) in Xu Xuan's 徐铉 Edition, but it is "從 AB" (composed of components A and B) in Xu Kai's 徐鍇 Edition and *Tangxieben*. The following table shows the differences of the three versions in interpreting same characters.

Table 16.1 The Three Versions' Explanations for 釪, 抙, 鎒, and 析

Examples	Xu Xuan's 徐铉 Edition	Xu Kai's 徐鍇 Edition	Tangxieben
hua 釪 (spade)	或从金从于	或從金于	或從金于
	Consisting of components *jin* 金 (metal) and *yu* 于 (go)		
pou 抙 (gather)	从木从手亦声	從木手手亦声	從木手手亦声
	Consisting of components *mu* 木 (wood) and *shou* 手 (hand), and *shou* is also the phonetic component		
nou 鎒 (weed)	或从金	或從金作	㧻或從金
	Featuring a radical *jin* 金 (metal)		
xi 析 (split wood)	破木也。一曰折也。从木从斤	破木。從木斤声。一曰折也	破木也。從木斤。一曰折
	Split wood. It is also written as *zhe* 折 (break), consisting of components *mu* 木 (wood) and *jin* 斤 (axe)		

(II) The Tang-Dynasty Manuscript Containing 12 Entries Involving Radical Kou 口 (Mouth)

The Second Tang-Dynasty Manuscript Containing 12 Characters, which was copied by Japanese scholars who studied in China in the Tang Dynasty. The original manuscript is kept in Japan. Zhou Zumo's 周祖谟 *Wen Xueji* includes a handwritten copy of this manuscript. Although this manuscript contains a few characters, it still has high academic value.

1. *Guo* 咼 (jaw) means 口戾不正 (an irregular mouth).

Ding Fubao's 丁福保 *Shuowen Jiezi Gulin* 说文解字诂林 (Explanation to *Shuowen Jiezi*) points out that the explanation for *guo* 咼 (口戾也: an irregular mouth) is cited by *Huilin Yinyi* 慧琳音义 (Hui Lin's Semantic and Phonetic Interpretations of All Sutras) (page 17 of Volume 24, page 26 of Volume 27, page 11 of Volume 66). In the book, Ding Fubao 丁福保 also expresses his doubts. "According to *Guangyun* 广韵 (a sinological work by Chen Pengyuan and Qiuyong in the Song Dynasty) and *Yupian* 玉篇 (Chinese dictionary compiled by Gu Yewang in 6th century), the character *li* 戾 can fully express the meaning of *buzheng* 不正 (irregualr), so why bother to say 不正 one more time in the interpretation "口戾不正"? His doubt is justified by *Tangxieben*, where the explanation for *guo* 咼 (jaw) is 口戾. As to the characters 不正 (irregular), they were probably a note to *li* 戾, which were mistakenly added to the text of *Shuowen Jiezi*.

2. *She* 舌 (tongue) means "to block the mouth", consisting of semantic component *kou* 口 (mouth), and phonetic component *jue* 毕 (short wooden stake) 毕 reads as *jue* 厥.

The three characters 毕音厥 (*jue* 毕 reads *jue* 厥) are probably from Xu Xuan's 徐铉 notes since Xu Kai's 徐锴 Edition says "毕古文厥字" (*jue* 毕 is the ancient form of *jue* 厥). Wang Niansun 王念孙 checked *Yupian* 玉篇 and *Guangyun* 广韵, finding that *jue* 毕 was the ancient form of *jue* 厥. Because both *Yupian* and *Guangyun* are based on *Shuowen Jiezi*, and *Tangxieben* also records that "毕 is the ancient form of 厥", therefore, 毕音厥 should be corrected into 毕古文厥.

3. *Sou* 嗾 means 使犬声 (to give vocal signals to a dog).

Xu Kai's 徐锴 Edition also explains *sou* 嗾 with 使犬声. *Tangxieben*, however, explains it as 使犬也. This explanation also appears in a note made by 陆德明 Lu Deming to *Zuo Zhuan* 左传 (Zuo's Commentary on the Spring and Autumn Annals). To interpret *sou* 嗾, *Yupian* quotes 秦晋冀陇谓使犬曰嗾 (People living in such places as Qin, Jin, Ji, and Long used *sou* 嗾 to describe the act of making a dog bark) from *Fangyan* 方言 (Dialects). Given the above analysis, the interpretation in *Tangxieben* should prevail.

4. *Fei* 吠 refers to the sound of a dog barking. It consists of two components: *quan* 犬 (dog) and *kou* 口 (mouth).

In terms of the annotation to *fei* 吠 (the sound of a dog barking), there are disputes on 从犬口 [composed of components of *quan* 犬 (dog) and *kou* 口 (mouth)]. Xu Kai 徐锴 interpreted it as 从口犬 [composed of components of *kou* 口 (mouth) and *quan* 犬 (dog)] and *Tangxieben* writes it as [(composed of a semantic component *kou* 口 (mouth) and a phonetic component *quan* 犬 (dog)]. Both Wang Yun 王筠 (1784–1854, a Qing-Dynasty sinologist) and 钱坫 Qian Dian (1744–1806, a Qing-Dynasty scholar) suspected that the character form of *fei* 吠 (the sound of a dog barking) was incorrect considering its form and meaning. They recommended that 吠 should belong to the radical of *quan* 犬 (dog) instead of the radical of *kou* 口 (mouth). Duan Yucai 段玉裁 argued that the original character form of *fei* 吠 (the sound of a dog barking) should be 㕟 as shown in *Zilin* 字林 (A Collection of Characters). For example, *Tai Xuan* 太玄 (the Supreme Mystery) says, "鸱鸠在林 㕟彼众经 (The scops owls are in the woods, and dogs are all barking at them.)." The most likely explanation for the above phenomenon is as follows: 从口犬声 [(composed of a semantic component *kou* 口 (mouth) and a phonetic component *quan* 犬 (dog)] in *Tangxieben* is indeed the original version of explanation since the replacement of *ba* 犮 (dog running) by *quan* 犬 (dog) occurs before the character being included in *Shuowen Jiezi*. When Xu Kai 徐锴 interpreted the character, he noted 或云从犬 (the character might be featuring component *quan* 犬). There must be a clerical error in this note, as the seal-script form of the character listed in the book already features component *quan* 犬. What he originally wanted to write should be 或云从犮 (the character might be featuring component *ba* 犮). In the official script, *ba* 犮 sometimes is also written as *quan* 犬. For instance, the character *ba* 拔 (pull) was written as "扌犬" in the silk manuscripts unearthed from Mawangdui Han Tombs.

In conclusion, the annotation to *fei* 吠 (the sound of a dog barking) originally should have been 从口犮声 [consisting of the semantic component of *kou* 口 (mouth) and phonetic component of *ba* 犮 (dog running)]. In later generations, the character *ba* 犮 (dog running) was mistakenly replaced by *quan* 犬 (dog) due to their similarity in forms, and thus the annotation was changed to 从口犬声 [(composed of a semantic component *kou* 口 (mouth) and a phonetic component *quan* 犬 (dog)]. Afterwards, later generations thought that 犬 was not an accurate phonetic component for the character, so they deleted the character *sheng* 声 (sound) and changed the annotation to "从口犬". Later, it was otherwise written as 从犬口.

II. Xu Kai's Edition

During the Southern Tang Dynasty (937–975), Xu Kai 徐锴 added his annotations to his hand-copied version of *Shuowen Jiezi*, compiling *Shuowen Jiezi Xizhuan* 说文解字系传 (The Annotations to *Shuowen Jiezi*) in 40 volumes, which is known as Xu Kai's Edition of *Shuowen Jiezi*. This book became incomplete in the Song Dynasty, and the current version of the book was based on a copy found by a Song-Dynasty official named Su Song 苏颂 (1020–1101), When the copy was discovered, its Volume 25 was missing, and the missing part was replenished based on Xu Xuan's 徐铉 Edition. This copy of Xu Kai's Edition contains Zhang Cili's 张次立 (a Song-Dynasty official) remarks, so sinologists in Qing Dynasty speculated that this copy might have many mistakes due to adaptions made by Zhang Cili. Despite that, this speculation cannot deny the fact that with the purpose of annotating *Shuowen Jiezi*, *Shuowen Jiezi Xizhuan* does not or seldom change the original text of *Shuowen Jiezi*. except for some notes recording the author's doubts about the original text of *Shuowen Jiezi*. In this sense, *Shuowen Jiezi Xizhuan* 说文解字系传 or Xu Kai's 徐鍇 Edition of *Shuowen Jiezi* is better than Xu Xuan's 徐铉 Edition. The analysis of the following examples can illustrate this point.

(1) *Xia* 祫 refers to a worship ceremony dedicated to ancestors consisting of two components: *shi* 示 (manifest) and *he* 合 (close).

从示合 [the components of *shi* 示 (manifest) and *he* 合 (close)] in Xu Kai's Edition is written as 从示合声 [having *shi* 示 (manifest) as its semantic component and *he* 合 (close) as its phonetic component]. Xu Kai's 徐锴 Edition was cited in Volume 97 of *Yiqiejing Yinyi* 一切经音义 by Huilin and Volume 17 of *Yunhui* 韵会. In his note to this explanation, Xu Kai suspected that the character's form should be explained as 从示合 [the combination of *shi* 示 (manifest) and *he* 合

(close)] instead of 从示合声" [having *shi* 示 (manifest) as its semantic component and *he* 合 (close) as its phonetic component], but he did not change the original text regardless of his suspicion. On the contrary, Xu Xuan's Edition deleted 声 from the original text because of Xu Kai's note and interpret this character as 从示合 [the components of *shi* 示 (manifest) and *he* 合 (close)].

(2) *Gang* 岡 means ridge of a hill.

Although other versions of *Shuowen Jiezi* use 山骨也 (the ridge of a hill), Xu Kai's Edition writes 山脊也 (the ridge of a hill). As *shanji* 山脊 (the ridge of a hill) is also used by *Shi Ming* 释名 (Explanations to Names), *Erya* 尔雅 (Erya Dictionary) and *Shi Jing* 诗经 (The Book of Songs), it is reasonable to say that 脊 is mistaken for 骨 in some versions of *Shuowen Jiezi*.

(3) 碌 is synonymous with *jun* 陖 (high and precipitous).

Jun 陖 (high and precipitous) is written as *duo* 陊 (fall) in Wang's Copy, Wang Zhong's Copy, Bao's Copy, and Ding's Copy, but it is written as *duo* 堕 (fall) in Xu Kai's Edition. Both *Tangxieben* and *Yupian* 玉篇 cite it as *duo* 堕 (fall). *Zhuanli Wanxiang Mingyi* 篆隶万象名义 (Dictionary of Seal- and Official-Script Characters) also adopts the same explanation as Xu Kai's Edition does, so this explanation adopted by Xu Kai is correct.

(4) *Bian* 揙 (to fight) is a synonym for *fu* 抚 (to touch gently)

This explanation is adopted by Wang's Copy, Wang Zhong's Copy, Huang's Copy Bao's Copy and Ding's Copy. Xu Kai's Edition explains the character as a synonym for *bo* 搏 (to fight). According to *Zhuanli Wanxiang Mingyi* 篆隶万象名义 and *Yupian* 玉篇, the character is synonymous with *bo* 搏 (to fight) instead of *fu* 抚 (to touch gently), so Xu Kai's explanation is correct.

The main drawback of Xu Kai's Edition is that it transcribes the original text of *Shuowen Jiezi* into characters commonly used in his time. In addition, many of the explanations in Xu Kai's Edition are the same as those in Confucian classics and relevant sinological studies, which makes people doubt that the explanations in Xu Kai's Edition have been modified based on some sinological studies.

III. Xu Xuan's Edition

(I) In the third year of the Yongxi reign (986) of Emperor Taizong of the Song Dynasty, Xu Kai's brother Xu Xuan 徐铉 and other scholars were ordered to proofread *Shuowen Jiezi*. This version of *Shuowen Jiezi*, edited by Xu Xuan and other scholars, is known as Xu Xuan's Edition of *Shuowen Jiezi*. In his report to the emperor, Xu Xuan said, "The seal script has been replaced by the official script for a long time, and all those who have copied and transmitted *Shuowen Jizi* are not the original authors. Thus, there are errors, omissions, and confusion that cannot be completely investigated in various versions of the book. We have collected and studied these versions, both official and private, to produce a corrected version." When Xu Xuan and his co-workers proofread and compiled *Shuowen Jiezi*, they referred to many surviving versions of the book. In addition to collating these versions, they also made the following changes to the original text of *Shuowen Jiezi*:

(1) 19 characters that appeared in the annotations and examples of *Shuowen Jiezi* but were not listed in the entries were added as entries;
(2) 402 characters that were not included in *Shuowen Jiezi* but were used in other classics or in social contexts were added to different radical sections in accordance with their radicals. Such entries were arranged as the last parts of relevant radical sections and titled "Newly Added Entries";
(3) Annotations were added, including corrections to the original text's explanations and character variants, and all the annotators signed their names as 臣铉等曰 on their annotations or indicated the names of other annotators, such as Xu Kai 徐锴 and Li Yangbing 李阳冰, when citing their annotations;
(4) The original text of *Shuowen Jiezi* did not provide *fanqie* 反切 phonetic notations [a traditional method of indicating the pronunciation of a Chinese character by using two other Chinese characters, the first having the same consonant as the given character and the second having the same vowel (with or without final nasal) and tone], but as from the Former Song Dynasty (420–479), scholars began to add phonetic notations to *Shuowen Jiezi*, the phonetic notations in different versions were not identical. Xu Xuan borrowed the phonetic system from *Tangyun* 唐韵 by Sun Mian 孙愐 (a Tang-Dynasty phonologist);
(5) The original *Shuowen Jiezi* had 14 volumes of text and one volume of preface, for a total of 15 volumes. Xu Xuan divided each volume into upper and lower sections, resulting in 30 total volumes; and
(6) The postscript of *Shuowen Jiezi* contains a table of contents for each volume and section. Xu Xuan followed the conventions of later books and added a separate table of contents before the text, which is called "*Shuowen Jiezi* Headings" 说文解字标目 in the current edition.

There are three surviving Song-Dynasty copies of Xu Xuan's Edition of *Shuowen Jiezi*.

1. Wang's Copy: the small-sized copy once owned by Wang Chang 王昶 (1725–1806) who lived in Qingpu, a county in Southern China.

This copy was used for reference when Duan Yicai 段玉裁 compiled *Jiguge Shuowen Ding* 汲古阁说文订 (Correction to *Shuowen Jiezi* at Jiguge). The original copy was later kept by the Iwasaki family's Shizuka Hall in Japan. It was borrowed for photocopying by the Hanfen Building in Shanghai, and this photocopy was included in Xuguyi Collection 续古逸丛书 (Xuguyi Series) and *Sibu Congkan* 四部丛刊 (the Collection of Confucian classics, history, philosophy, and literature). This copy was once collected and sealed by Ruan Yuan 阮元 (1764–1849,

a mid-Qing Dynasty official), and at the end of the book, Ruan Yuan wrote the following words. "In the summer of the second year of Jiaqing's reign (1797), Ruan Yuan used this copy to collate Jiguge Copy 汲古阁本 at the Hangzhou Academy. Mao Jin's 毛晋 copy was based on this one, and all errors in the copy were due to Mao's arbitrary changes."

2. Wang Zhong's Copy: the small-sized copy once owned by Wang Zhong 汪中 (1744–1794, a famous philosopher in the Qing Dynasty).

This copy features a postscript written by Ding Yan 丁晏 (1794–1876) in the 18th year of the Daoguang reign (1838). It was once acquired by Yang Shaohe 杨绍和 (1830–1875) who wrote an inscription, stating, "This is the Song copy that Tenghuaxie [the name of the studio of Elebu (1826–1900, an official in late Qing Dynasty)] Copy was based on." By comparing the two copies, we found many differences. There are imprints such as "Elebu Houyuezhai" (the Studio of Elebu named Haoyuezhai) and "Elebu Seal" inside, indicating that it was once owned by Elebu. Nonetheless, according to the preface of Elebu's Tenghuaxie Copy, the Song copy used by him was the one owned by Bao Xifen 鲍惜分 (ca. 1763–1807). Wang Zhong's Copy doesn't have Bao's imprint, so it is certain that Bao Xifen never owned this copy. Therefore, Elebu did not use this one for reference.

3. Huang's Copy: the copy with the imprint of 黄志淳 Huang Zhichun.

This is a copy with the imprint of 黄志淳 Huang Zhizhun. It is copied in seal script and red.

The abovementioned details seem to indicate that the three copies are made from the same master copy, but a comparative study of them denies this possibility. Despite their similarities, there are also differences. For example, the character *du* 毒 (poison) on page 1 of the lower section 1 is explained as 从中 [the semantic component is *che* 中 (grass)] in Wang Zhong's Copy, but the other two copies both explain it as 从山 [the semantic component is *shang* 山 (mountain)]. As to the character *qian* 芊 (lush) on page 9 of the lower section 1, Wang's Copy explains it as 千声 [the phonetic component is *qian* 千 (thousand)], while the other two copies both explain it as 子声 [the phonetic component is *zi* 子 (son)]. With respect to *sha* 篓 on page 2 of upper section 5, Wang Zhong's Copy writes 从女 [the semantic component is *nü* 女 (woman)] while the other two copies write 从妾 [the semantic component is 妾 (woman slave)]. As to the entry *he* 贺 (congratulation) on page 4 of the lower section 6, Wang's Copy writes 从礼 [the semantic component is *li* 礼 (offer sacrifice to gods)], while the other two copies both write "以礼" (with presents). In addition, there are also differences in the names of the editors, such as on page 6 of the lower section 1 of Wang Zhong's Copy, the editor is Zhan Derun 詹德润, while it is Shi 施 in Wang's Copy.

Given the above analysis, it is reasonable to say that the three copies are not made from the same copy and that the similarity in the names of the editors is probably because they were reproduced together as different versions.

Nevertheless, these three copies seem to have the same origin and a mutual transmission relationship. Among the three copies, Huang's Copy is more primitive, with more damaged and missing characters. Wang Zhong's Copy has a dignified and antique handwriting, while Wang's Copy is relatively crudely made. For example, under the entry *jiu* 赳 (valiant) on page 7 of the upper section 2, Huang's Copy has a blurry entry of *qiao* 鐈 (a tall tripod vessel), which looks like the character *jiao* 撟 (to correct) at first glance, while Wang's Copy corrects it to *jiao* 撟 (to correct). Under the entry *mao* 眊 (be blurred in eyesight) on page 1 of the upper section 4, Huang's Copy connects the lower horizontal line of *wang* 亡 (run away) with the top of the character *tang* 矘 (a lifeless, vacant stare), and Wang's Copy mistakes this clerical for character *er* 二 (two). These facts seem to suggest that Wang's Copy is based entirely or in part on Huang's Copy. The research on the editors shows that the earliest of the three copies was probably made in the early Southern Song Dynasty (1127–1279). Someone considered that it might be based on a Northern-Song copy according to naming conventions, but at present, there is no clear evidence to prove this statement. Simply put, all three copies have their strengths, and some examples are given below.

(1) *Chang* 伥 means madness. It consists of semantic component *ren* 人 (person) and phonetic component *chang* 长 (long). It is sometimes written as *shen* 什 (ten).

As to this entry, *shi* 什 (ten) is used in Ding's Copy, while *pu* 仆 (fall forward) is used in Wang's Copy, Wang Zhong's Copy, Huang's Copy, Bao's Copy, Xu Kai's Edition and *Zhuanli Wanxiang Mingyi* 篆隶万象名义. *Shuowen Erxu Qianyi* 说文二徐笺异 (The difference between Xu Kai and Xu Xuan's Editions of *Shuowen Jiezi*) by Tian Wuzhao 田吴炤 (1870–1926) explains this difference: *pu* 仆 (fall forward) means falling forward, which is semantically like *chang* 伥 (madness).

(2) *Zun* 傅 means converge. It consists of semantic component *ren* 人 (person) and phonetic component *zun* 尊 (wine vessel). *Shi Jing* 诗经 contains such a sentence: 傅沓背憎 (People talk affectionately when they are face to face, but when they stood back-to-back, they hate each other.).

As to this sentence 傅沓背憎, *Seng* 僧 (monk) is used in Ding's Copy, while it is written as *zeng* 憎 (hate) in Wang's Copy, Huang's Copy, and Minor Court Hymns from *Shi Jing* 诗经. As Zheng Xuan 郑玄 (127–200) interpreted *beizeng* 背憎 as people showed their hatred only in private, Wang's Copy and Huang's Copy are correct in this case.

(3) *Yu* 庾 refers to the water trough.

Cao 槽 (trough) is written as *cao* 漕 (transport by water) in Bao's Copy. *Cao* 漕 (transport by water) is used in Wang's Copy, *Tangxieben*, *Yupian* 玉篇, *Yunhui* 韵会, *Jiyun* 集韵, and *Leipian* 类篇. Therefore, Wang's Copy is correct in this case.

(4) *Yi* 睪 means to look at.

Mushi 目视 (look at) is written as *sishi* 司视 in Wang's Copy, which is the same in Ding's Copy and Xukai's Copy. *Wenxueji* 问学集 by Zhou Zumo 周祖谟 says, "司视 in Wang's Copy is correct." It is 伺视也 in *Zhuanli Wangxiang Mingyi*.

(7) *Lu* 戕 means "to rob".

Qiang 抢 (rob) is written as *qiang* 枪 (gun) in the three copies, and this form is also used in *Wuyin Yunpu* 五音韵谱 and Xu Kai's Edition. Therefore, this entry should be corrected accordingly.

(8) *Keng* 阬 means a door.

Men 门 (door) is written as *lang* 阆 (high) in the three copies, and this form is also used in Bao's Copy and Xu Kai's Edition. Therefore, this entry should be corrected accordingly. *Tangxieben* and *Yupian* 玉篇 cites it as *wen lang* 闻阆, while *Zhuanli Wanxiang Mingyi* 篆隶万象名义 cites it as *lang ye* 阆也 (a door).

(II) Mao Jin 毛晋 (1599–1659) and his son, Mao Yi 毛扆 (1640–1713), bought Xu Xuan's Edition, then carved and printed it. In this way, Xu Xuan's Edition was reprinted and published. Many later copies are based on Mao's Copy, which include Daxing Zhu Yun's Copy 大兴朱筠刻本, produced in the 38th year of Emperor Qianlong's reign [which the Shanghai Zhonghua Book Company's *Sibu Beiyao* 四部备要 (Complete collection of the Four Branches of Literature) is based on], and the Huainan Book Company's Copy 淮南书局刻本 in Emperor Guangxu's reign. Unfortunately, Mao's Copy made many changes to Xu Xuan's Edition based on the Xu Kai's Edition, resulting in a lot of errors, which were criticized by Qing-Dynasty scholars as "ignorant". During the Qing Dynasty, there were also three publishers who reprinted *Shuowen Jiezi* based on the Song copies.

1. Sun's Copy: The reprinted Song copy of *Shuowen Jiezi* that Sun Xingyan 孙星衍 (1753–1818) was published in the ninth year of Emperor Jiaqing's reign (1804).

This copy was included in Sun Xingyan's *Pingjing Guan Congshu* 平津馆丛书 (Pingjinguan series). In the preface, it is stated that the book is published in accordance with the Song copies, and any errors were not changed to preserve the originality. Sun's Copy retained the original format of the Song copies, with fewer errors, and is considered to be the most refined one among its counterparts. Many later copies of *Shuowen Jiezi* were based on Sun's Copy, such as Chen Changzhi's One-Character-One-Volume Version 陈昌治刻一篆一行本, carved in 1873, Gujing Jiehui Han Copy 古经解汇函本, carved by Yuedong Book Company in the same year, the Dongwu Pushi Reprint Copy 东吴浦氏本, carved in 1874, Hong's Copy carved in 1875, the copy by Shanghai Tongwen Book

Company in 1885, and the Pingjinguan Series published by Zhu Jirong 朱记荣 in Wu County in 1885.

2. Bao's Copy: The copy published by Elebu 额勒布 in the twelfth year of the Jiaqing reign (1807), which is based on a Song copy collected by Bao Xifen 鲍惜分.

This copy is also called Tenghuaxie Copy. The title page of this copy contains three lines that read "imitating the small-sized Song copy of *Shuowen Jiezi*," "engraved in the year of Dingmao (1807)," and "Tenghua Xie's collection." The preface of the copy was written by Elebu, stating that he found a Song copy of *Shuowen Jiezi* in Bao Xifen's collection, and that, after careful examination, there were no errors in the copy. He believed that the copy he found was a valuable treasure worth engraving and publishing. Bao's Copy has fewer errors and is on par with Sun's Copy. Li Zhizhong 李致忠 suggests that both Bao's and Sun's Copies were based on a Song copy in his *Songbanshu Xulu* 宋版书叙录 (Catalogue of Song Books). Nevertheless, a comparative study of the two copies reveals many differences, indicating that they have different origins. The Shanghai Commercial Press printed a facsimile of Bao's Copy. Although it is not stated in the book, some obvious errors in the original copy are corrected in this facsimile.

3. Ding's Copy: The reprinted Song copy that Ding Shaoshan 丁少山 compiled and published in the seventh year of the Emperor Guangxu's reign (1881), which is based on a collection of Jiguge.

The title page of this copy contains two lines that read "imitating the Song copies of *Shuowen Jiezi*" and "revised and annotated according to the old collection of Jiguge, completed in the winter of 1881". The book includes an introduction written by Pan Zuyin 藩祖荫 from Wu County. Ding Shaoshan 丁少山 was a famous scholar in the Qing Dynasty and a disciple of Xu Han 许瀚, who was proficient in calligraphy and sinological research. Xu Han had previously proofread Sun's Copy and Gui Fu's 桂馥 *Shuowen Jiezi Yizheng* 说文解字义证 (Proofs to *Shuowen Jiezi*). Ding's Copy, including Ding Shaoshan's notes to the text, with few changes made to the original text, are compared to Sun's and Bao's Copies. There is a note on the right column of the first page of the introduction that reads "a record of the revision and annotation", but unfortunately this part was not published. Sun's Copy, Bao's Copy, and Ding's Copy can also be used to locate and correct errors in the popular version of *Shuowen Jiezi*. The following example can be used to illustrate this point.

(1) *Que* 趚 means walking quickly or describes a state of walking, featuring the radical *zou* 走 (go).

Bao's Copy records *qiaoque* 趬趚 (walking quickly) as *queque* 趚趚, so do *Wuyin Yunpu* 五音韵谱 and Xu Kai's Edition. According to the convention of

Shuowen Jiezi, if it is written as *qiaoque* 趫趙 (walking quickly), 趙 should be the explanation for 趫, which shows that there must be some clerical error in this sentence. *Guangya* 广雅 (Guangya Dictionary) explains 趫趙 as to walk. Therefore, the original explanation in *Shuowen jiezi* should be "趫趙, 行也" (walking quickly or a state of walking), and the addition of 一日 must be a mistake.

(2) 逭, 兆也. *huan* 逭 means to escape.

In Bao's Copy and Ding's Copy, *zhao* 兆 (omen) was written as *tao* 逃 (to escape). *Erya* 尔雅 (Erya Dictionary) explains this character as 逭逃也 (逭 means to escape). This character appears in *Li ji* 礼记 (The Book of Rites): 自作孽不可以逭 (If you make a mistake, you cannot escape.). Zheng Xian's 郑玄 commentary says, "*huan* 逭 means to escape."

(3) *Jiu* 麔 refers to a female deer.

Pin 牝 (female bird or animal) in this entry was written as *mu* 牡 (male animal) in Bao's and Wang's Copies. *Erya* 尔雅 explains *mi* 麋 as a male deer. Yan Shigu 颜师古 (581–645) said that "A male deer is called *jiu* 麔" in his annotations to *Ji Jiu Pian* 急救篇 (a classic text that teaches common sense and character recognition). Given this, 牝 in this entry should be changed into 牡.

(4) *Yin* 蔭 refers to shaded ground.

In Ding's Copy, *di* 地 (ground) in the entry was written as *ye* 也 (also). *Shuowen Jiezi Judu* 说文解字句读 (Interpretations to *Shuowen Jiezi*) by Wang Yun 王筠 explains that "the character *di* 地 (ground) is probably a mistaken form for *ye* 也 (also). This equation is similar to that of 趐 and 是少.

(5) *Xi* 裼 means to take off one's top.

Bao's and Ding's Copies both write *tan* 袒 (strip oneself naked to the waist) as *dan* 但 (but), so do Wang Zhong's and Huang's Copies. Wang Yun 王筠 also uses *dan* 但 (but) for this entry according to Xu Kai's Edition. As *ren* 人 (people) is explained as 但裼也 (*dan* 但 means baring one's chest) in these copies, these two characters 袒 and 但 are interchangeable. Given this, the entry containing 但 is correct.

(6) *Dian* 澱 refers to sediment.

Ding's Copy writes *zi* 滋 as *yin* 垽, so do *Wuyin Yunpu* 五音韵谱, Xu Kai's Edition and *Liushugu* 六书故 (A sinological work compiled during the end of the

Song Dynasty and the beginning of the Yuan Dynasty), as 坙 is explained as *dian* 澱 (sediment) in these copies. Therefore, 坙 and 滋 (sediment) can be used interchangeably. The entry containing 坙 is correct.

(7) One 秅 equals 120 catties (a catty is approximately 500 g). One 秅 of rice equals 20 litre (unit of dry measure for grain) of millet, and one 秅 of wheat or broomcorn millet equals 16 and a half litres of millet.

Ding's Copy writes *sheng* 升 (litre) as *dou* 斗 (measure for measuring decalities of grain, one *dou* equals 10 litres), while Xu Kai's Edition writes it as *jin* 斤 (catty). 大半升 (half litre) was written as 大半升 (half litre) in Xu Kai's Edition but as 大半斗 (half *dou*) in Ding's Copy. Studies show that both *jin* 斤 (catty) and *sheng* 升 (litre) should have been *dou* 斗, whose official-script form is ▨ or 斗, which are easily confused with *jin* 斤 (catty) or *sheng* 升 (litre). Therefore, the original text should be "稻一秅，为粟二十斗；禾黍一秅，为粟十六斗大半斗" (One 秅 of rice equals 20 *dou* of millet, and one 秅 of wheat or broomcorn millet equals 16 and a half *dou* of millet). To further prove this interpretation, *can* 粲 (polished white rice) has the interpretation "稻重一秅，为粟二十斗" (Rice weighs one 秅, equals 20 *dou* of millet." And the character 糗 is explained as "粟重一，为十六斗大半斗" (one 秅 of wheat or millet equals 16 *dou* 斗 and a half."

IV. Adaptions of *Shuowen Jiezi*

(I) Shuowen Jiezi Yunpu 说文解字韵谱 *(Table of Rhymes of* Shuowen Jiezi, *usually referred to as* Yunpu 韵谱*)*

At the request of his brother Xu Xuan, Xu Kai compiled *Yunpu*, which consists of 10 volumes. The book rearranges the order of the original entries of *Shuowen Jiezi*, using the *fanqie* 反切 rhyme sequence formulated by Lu Fayan 陆法言 (562-?, a phonologist) as the framework for the arrangement. Each annotation in the book is limited to two or three characters, mostly citing *Shuowen Jiezi*, but sometimes using other sources. Later, Xu Xuan revised the book based on the *fanqie* sequence formulated by Li Zhou (a Tang-Dynasty phonologist) as well as adding newly discovered characters. The purpose of this book was mainly for ease of reference, but it also corrected some errors in Xu Xuan's Edition. This will be illustrated through the following examples.

(1) *Song* 訟 means *shuo* 说 (to speak).

Xu Kai's Edition has the same interpretation, while *Yunpu* 韵谱 interprets it as *song* 讼 (argue), which is consistent with Erya 尔雅 and Mao's commentary on *Shi Jing* 诗经. Volume 11 of Dai Dong's 戴侗 *Liu Shu Gu* 六书故 certifies that the Tang-Dynasty versions of *Shuowen Jiezi* also interpret it as *song* 讼 (song). Therefore, *Yunpu* 韵谱 is incorrect in this case.

(2) *Zang* 牂 (ewe) means *muyang* 牡羊 (a male sheep).

Yan Kejun 严可均 (1762–1842) thought that *mu* 牡 (a male animal) should have been *pin* 牝 (a female animal or bird). Volume 29 of *Chu Xue Ji* 初学记, Volume 902 of *Yu Lan* 御览, and *Yunhui* 韵会 are cited as sources for *pinang* 牝羊 (ewe). According to *Yunpu*, it should be *pinyang* 牝羊 (ewe). Therefore, Yan Kejun 严可均 is correct in this case.

(3) *Lei* 诔 means *shi* 謚 (to give a posthumous title).

In *Yunpu* 韵谱, *shi* 謚 (to give a posthumous title) is written as *shi* 谥 (to give a posthumous title). Wang Yun 王筠 and Niu Shuyu 钮树玉 (1760–1827) also use *shi* 谥 (to give a posthumous title) according to Xu Kai's Edition. *Yunpu* is correct in this case because *Shuowen Jiezi* does not include the character *shi* 謚 (to give a posthumous title). *Shuowen Jiezi Zhu* 说文解字注 by Duan Yucai 段玉裁 gives an explanation for *shi* 謚: "Various versions use 从言兮皿阙 [consisting of the components of *yan* 言 (speak), *xi* 兮 (how) and *min* 皿 (vessel)] to explain the composition of *shi* 謚, which was mistakenly changed by later generations. According to Monk Xuanying's 玄应 book on phonetics in Buddhist scriptures, *shi* 谥 means the deeds of a person. It is composed of semantic component *yan* 言 (speak) and phonetic component *yi* 益 (overflow). *Wujing Wenzi* 五经文字 says: *shi* 谥 is included in *Shuowen Jiezi*, while *shi* 謚 (to give a posthumous title) is included in *Zilin* 字林 (A Collection of Characters). *Zilin* defines *shi* 谥 (to give a posthumous title) as the sound of laughter. *Guangyun* 广韵 explains that *Shuowen Jiezi* uses 谥 for 謚. *Liushugu* 六书故 says, "The Tang-Dynasty versions of *Shuowen Jiezi* does not include '謚', but does include '谥', which means the deeds of a person." Based on these sources, there is no doubt that *Shuowen Jiezi* uses 谥. *Tangxieben* includes "谥" instead of "謚". Therefore, it is correct for *Yunpu* 韵谱 to use 谥.

(II) **Shuowen Jiezi Wuyin Yunpu** 说文解字五音韵谱 *(The Book of Five-Note Rhyme of* **Shuowen Jiezi***, usually referred to as* **Wuyin Yunpu** 五音韵谱*)*

During the Southern Song Dynasty, Li Tao 李焘 (1115–1184) and Jia Duanxiu 贾端修 referred to Xu Kai's *Shuowen Jiezi Yunpu* 说文解字韵谱 and compiled *Shuowen Jiezi Wuyin Yunpu* 说文解字五音韵谱, which consists of 12 volumes. The book reorganizes the 540 radicals of *Shuowen Jiezi* according to the rhyme order of *fanqie* 反切. The radical headers are arranged according to *Jiyun* 集韵 with *dong* 东 (east) as the first and *jia* 甲 (armour) as the last, while characters under the same radical are arranged according to the tonal order of the five natural tones of the Chinese language, which is a tonal language. *Wuyin Yunpu* 五音韵谱 also includes the newly discovered characters and characters added to *Shuowen Jiezi Yunpu* 说文解字韵谱 by Xu Xuan. According to the Ming-Dynasty copy of the book, carved by Chen Dake 陈大科 (1534–1601) in 1598 (the 26th year of the Emperor Wanli's reign), the title page contains four lines: "Based on the Song copies, revised and annotated"; "The true edition of *Shuowen Jiezi*"; "A collection of Jiguge"; and Chen Dake's note "Engraving *Shuowen Jiezi*". The original "*Shuowen Jiezi* Headings" was replaced with "*Shuowen Jiezi* Index". The index includes Xu Shen's 许慎 preface, Xu Chong's 许冲 preface, Xu Xuan's 徐铉 report to the emperor, and Yongxi's 雍熙 official document. Unlike *Shuowen Jiezi Yunpu*, this book directly copies the entries from Xu Xuan's Edition of *Shuowen Jiezi*, with occasional additions or omissions. Nonetheless, it mostly preserves the original entries of Xu Xuan's Edition. A comparative study shows that this book's explanations of characters are like those in Bao's Copy. This book was exceptionally popular during the Yuan and Ming dynasties because it was easy to use. Many people at that time were not even aware of the existence of Xu Xuan's Edition. It was only when Mao Jin 毛晋 (1599–1659) and his son printed Xu Xuan's Edition at the end of the Ming Dynasty that people started to depreciate the book. Nevertheless, the value of the book cannot be ignored with respect to the explanations of characters. Several examples are presented below.

(1) *Chang* 茛 (name of a plant) refers to 茛楚跳弋 (a type of plant used for making arrows).

Tiaoyi 跳弋 (name of a plant) is written as *yaoyi* 铫弋 (name of a plant) in *Wuyin Yunpu* 五音韵谱. *Erya* 尔雅 explains, *changchu* 长楚 is the name of *yaoyi* 铫芅 (name of a plant). Mao's commentary says, "*Changchu* 茛楚 (name of a plant) refers to *yaoyi* 铫弋 (name of a plant)." *Wuyin Yunpu* 五音韵谱 is correct in this case.

(2) *Jun* 菨 refers to *jingzao* 井藻 (water plants).

According to *Wuyin Yunpu* 五音韵谱, *jing* 井 (well) should have been *niu* 牛 (cow) in this explanation. Similarly, *Erya* 尔雅 records that *jun* 菨 is a type of big water plant. As explained by Wang Yun 王筠, when something is named after *niu* 牛 (cow) or *ma* 马 (horse), its size is very large.

(3) *Si* 薜 means a type of red flower, a combination of two components: *cao* 艹 (grass) and *si* 肆 (display).

Wuyin Yunpu 五音韵谱 has the character 声 after the character 肆: 从艹肆声 [a combination of semantic compoenent *cao* 艹 (grass) and phonetic component *si* 肆 (display)]. *Wuyin Yunpu*'s 五音韵谱 explanation is correct, and this entry should be corrected accordingly.

(4) 嗔 refers to 野人言之 (spoken by the common people)

As to 野人言之 (spoken by the common people) in this explanation, *Wuyin Yunpu* 五音韵谱 records it as 野人之言 (speech spoken by the common people), so do Ding's Copy and Xukai's Edition. Therefore, this entry should be corrected accordingly.

(5) *Lian* 鍊 refers to *yejin* 冶金 (smelt metal).

Although the explanation of *yejin* 冶金 (smelt metal) was adopted by many other versions of *Shuowen Jiezi*, *Wuyin Yunpu* 五音韵谱 interprets it as *zhijin* 治金, so do *Jiyun* 集韵 and *Yiqiejing Yinyi* 一切经音义, *Yupian* 玉篇, and *Zhuanli Wanxiang Mingyi* 篆隶万象名义. Duan Yucai's 段玉裁 *Shuowen Jeizi Zhu* 说文解字注 says, "*Lian* 湅 means to process silk; *lian* 練 means to process silk fabrics; *lian* 鍊 means to process metal. All mean purifying and refining, not just melting." Therefore, *Wuyin Yunpu* 五音韵谱 is probably right again in this case.

Note

1 The original Chinese version was published in *Journal of Ancient Books Collation and Studies* 古籍整理研究学刊 in 1999 (issue 6).

17 Four Misunderstandings about *Shuowen Jiezi*

As the most important ancient classic for studying Chinese characters, *Shuowen Jiezi* 说文解字 (An Explication of Written Characters) remains an essential reference book for the studies of the Chinese language and Chinese characters today. So far, research on *Shuowen Jiezi* is still a hot topic in linguistic and character studies. Nevertheless, as an in-depth, systematic research written in classical Chinese, this book does not read easily. Today, there are still various misunderstandings about some key issues discussed in the book, which often affect the teaching and learning of classical Chinese at all stages of education and related philological, sinological ad phonological studies. Therefore, these misunderstandings must be corrected.

I. Misunderstanding 1: *Shuowen Jiezi* Giving Wrong Examples in the Discussions of Borrowed Characters

In the preface to *Shuowen Jiezi*, there is a discussion on the definition of borrowed character. It states, "Borrowed characters originally have no character forms of their own and are based on their sounds to refer to things. For example, *ling* 令 and *zhang* 长." Regarding this viewpoint, the prevailing view is that this definition is very good, but the examples given are incorrect. Scholars who hold this view include both well-known older-generation and contemporary experts in the study of *Shuowen Jiezi*.

Tang Lan 唐兰 said, "Borrowed characters, theoretically speaking, are easy to understand. As Xu Shen 许慎 (ca. 58–147) said, 'They have no character forms of their own and are based on their sounds to refer to things.' Unfortunately, he cited the wrong examples. The two characters he cited, *ling* 令 (demand) and *zhang* 长 (elder), are examples for characters' extended meanings. They are definitely not borrowed characters."[1]

Yang Wuming 杨五铭 said, "Borrowed characters feature forms loaned from other characters that sound the same or similar. These characters are homophones or near-homophones. Xu Shen's 许慎 definition of borrowed characters is clear, but unfortunately, the examples of *ling* 令 (demand) and *zhang* 长 (elder) are not appropriate . . . *Ling* 令 (demand) and *zhang* 长 (elder) involve the issue of extended meanings. They are not suitable examples for borrowed characters."[2]

Zhong Ruxiong 钟如雄 said, "The principle of creating borrowed characters became easy to understand after Xu Shen 许慎 explained it in his work *Shuowen Jiezi*. Nevertheless, the examples Xu Shen 许慎 cited did not align with the principle, which led to various speculations and criticisms. Xu Shen's 许慎 definition of borrowed characters is accurate, but the examples given, namely *ling* 令 (demand) and *zhang* 长 (elder), appear to contradict to his own definition. This is because the original meaning of *ling* 令 (demand) is to issue an order, and its extended meaning is a county magistrate, while the original meaning of *zhang* 长 (elder) is to grow, and its extended meaning is a county official in charge. Using examples of extended meanings to demonstrate the principle of phonetic-borrowed characters inevitably leads to a counterproductive effect. Although this was probably not the original intention of Xu Shen's 许慎 argument, it should be viewed as his historical limitations as he might not have fully understood the difference between the development of extended meanings and the principles of creating borrowed characters at the time. Therefore, we cannot deny his principle of creating borrowed characters for his citation mistakes."[3]

Wang Yuren 王玉仁 said, "There are, indeed, problems with the examples Xu Shen 许慎 cited. He defined *ling* 令 (demand) as 'issuing orders' and *zhang* 长 (elder) as 'long-lasting,' which are actually [the] extended meanings of these characters. In oracle-bone inscriptions, *zhang* 长 (elder) depicts the image of a person with long hair, indicating an elderly person. It is quite natural for the character *ling* 令 (demand) to develop from 'issuing orders' to 'county magistrate' and *zhang* 长 (elder) from 'elderly' to 'county official in charge'. With such clear route of meaning development, it is quite clear that these two characters are examples for the extension of a character meaning, rather than for borrowed characters."[4]

Xu Shen 许慎 is the greatest philologist of the Han Dynasty, and his *Shuowen Jiezi* provides a detailed analysis of the meanings and forms of 9,353 Chinese characters. Given that his time period was not long after the Archaic Period of Chinese characters, his understanding of Chinese characters should be more profound than ours. As such, it is almost impossible to believe that such a philologist would cite two example characters incorrectly in the discussion of 12 borrowed characters. The only possibility is that our understandings of his definition on borrowed characters is flawed.

The biggest difference between *Shuowen Jiezi* and other dictionaries is twofold. Firstly, it provides just one meaning for each character, with only a few characters given multiple meanings. Secondly, it explains the composition of a character form in relation to its character meaning. From the establishment of the oracle-bone script of the Shang Dynasty (1066–046 BCE), Chinese characters had evolved into a stage where one character often has multiple meanings, and *Shuowen Jiezi* mainly explains the small-seal script used in the Qin Dynasty (221–207 BCE) when one character already corresponded to multiple meanings. So, why does *Shuowen Jiezi* provide only one meaning for each character, rather than multiple meanings? This is because Xu Shen 许慎 believed that Chinese character forms were created based on their meanings, and that their meanings and forms were unified. He expressed such views in the preface of *Shuowen Jiezi*: "The meaning can be obtained and explained through forms", and "Characters can be classified according to their different features in forms". On this premise that the form of a character is generated based on a specific meaning, the form can only represent the meaning it was formed for. If the form represents any other meaning, this phenomenon will be termed as borrowing. Therefore, the term of borrowing in *Shuowen Jiezi* refers to a character form representing any meaning other than the original meaning on which it was composed, including extended meanings. The only condition for borrowing is that the pronunciation should be the same or similar. From our point of view, the meanings of a character can be broadly divided into three types: the original meaning, extended meanings, and borrowed meanings, but this is not the case in *Shuowen Jiezi*. To get a clearer idea of the difference, please refer to the following chart.

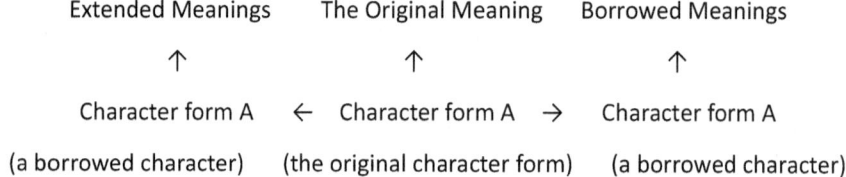

Figure 17.1 The Original Meaning and Extended and Borrowed Meanings

To understand the definition of borrowed characters in *Shuowen Jiezi*, we must first understand a term used in the book: *jiajie* 假借 (borrowing), which is a combination of two synonyms *jia* 假 (borrow) and *jie* 借 (borrow). There is a passage from *Zuo Zhuan* 左传 (Zuo's Commentary on The Spring and Autumn Annals) saying, "宫之奇谏假道" (Palace officials were using a borrowed path to give some unusual advice.). Therefore, *jiajie* 假借 (borrowing) refers to the use of a character for a meaning that is not its original meaning. *Shuowen Jiezi* not only discusses borrowing in the preface but also mentions it in the explanations of individual characters. The most typical example is the explanation of *wei* 韋 (tanned leather):

Wei 韋 means opposite or reverse. It consists of the radical *chuan* 舛 (run crisscross) and a phonetic component *kou* 口 (mouth). The skin of wild animals is used as leather straps, to bind and connect things in a crisscross pattern, hence the character is borrowed to mean leather.

When explaining borrowed characters, *Shuowen Jiezi* often uses the term *yiwei* 以为. Both 借以为 and 借用为 mean "borrowed as", and *yi* 以 is synonymous with *yong* 用 (use). *Shuowen Jiezi* often uses *yi* 以 as *yong* 用. Related examples are listed below.

(1) *Feng* 玤, a kind of stone inferior to jade used for making precious ornaments. It consists of semantic component *yu* 玉 (jade) and phonetic component *feng* 丰 (luxuriant).

The entry for radical *cao* 艸 (grass) says: "芧, 艸也。从艸，予声。可以为绳。" (*xu*芧, refers to a kind of plant. It is written with the semantic component of *cao* 艸 (grass) and pronounced as *yu* 予 (give). It refers to a kind of material that can be used to make ropes.

(2) *Bao* 苞 refers to a kind of plant. In Nanyang, it is used to make coarse shoes. It is composed of semantic component *cao* 艸 (grass) and phonetic component *bao* 包 "(wrap up)."

以为系璧 means "being used for making precious ornaments." 可以为绳 means "being used for making ropes," and 南阳以为麤履 means "being used for making coarse shoes in Nanyang."

The original meaning of *wei* 韋 is "opposite". After processing, animal skin can be used to bind things together. When bound, the leather strips are often opposite to each other, so the meaning conveyed through *wei* 韋 of "opposite" is borrowed to represent animal skins. Therefore, in *Shuowen Jiezi*, *wei* 韋 is explained as a borrowed character when it is used to represent animal skins, and the two meanings "opposite" and "animal skin" are related meanings, with the latter being an extended meaning. There are several characters like *wei* 韋 in *Shuowen Jiezi*.

(1) *Xi* 西 depicts a bird in its nest. The character takes its form from this image. As birds return to nests when the sun sets in the west, this character is borrowed to represent the west direction and thus has an extended meaning.

(2) *Lai* 来 is the name of the auspicious wheat that is said to have been given to the Kingdom Zhou by the deities. It looks like the shape of a bunch of wheat spikes. As it was a gift from the deities, it is borrowed to refer to the meaning "arrivals". 诒我来麰 from *Shi Jing* 诗经 (The Book of Songs) contains its original meaning, which means offering me the gift of wheat. As to the meaning "arrival", it is an extended meaning of the character. When the character is used to represent this meaning, it is a borrowed character.

(3) *Zhe* 耴 refers to an earlobe. It is a pictograph. *Chun Qiu Zhuan* 春秋传 (Commentaries on Spring and Autumn Annals) contains a sentence: 秦公子耴者，其耳下垂，故以为名 (The prince of Kingdom Qin, whose name was *zhe* 耴, had long earlobes. That's how he was named.).

The character *zhe* 耴 originally means earlobe. When it is used to name after the Qin prince who had large earlobes, it has an extended meaning and becomes a borrowed character.

(4) *Yao* 姚 is originally the name of the place where Shun 舜 (a legendary Chinese ruler) lived. Gradually, it was borrowed to be used as a surname. It consists of semantic component *nv* 女 (woman) and phonetic component *zhao* 兆 [a sign (in fortune telling)]. *Yao* 姚 as a surname is an extended meaning of the character. When the character is used to represent this meaning, it is a borrowed character.

The explanations of borrowed characters above show why *ling* 令 and *zhang* 长 are defined as borrowed characters in *Shuowen Jiezi*. They also prove that what the book describes as a borrowed character may instead be characters used to represent one of its own extended meanings.

This misunderstanding of *Shuowen Jiezi* is related to the evolution of the meaning of the term "borrowing". Many concepts and terms in traditional Chinese philology have different meanings in different periods, so the same term may have different meanings in different stages. Today, we use the term "borrowed characters" to refer to the homophones and near-homophones among Chinese characters. According to this definition, the examples for extended meanings in *Shuowen Jiezi* naturally do not meet the standard of borrowing. Therefore, the so-called errors in the examples for borrowed characters in *Shuowen Jiezi* are caused by our misunderstanding of how the term "borrowing" is used in the book.

II. Misunderstanding 2: "Borrowing" in *Shuowen Jiezi* Only Applying to One Situation: Characters Without Forms

Regarding the forms of borrowed characters, there are two types: those with their own character forms and those without their own character forms. The latter includes *qi* 其, which originally means sieve but is borrowed to represent he/she/it, a concept that does not have its own character form. On the other hand, borrowed characters that have their own character forms include *zao* 蚤 (flea), which is borrowed to mean *zao* 早 (early). *Zao* 早 (early) is the original character while *zao* 蚤 (flea) is a borrowed character having its own original form. Many scholars mistakenly believe that the borrowed characters in *Shuowen Jiezi* refer only to the former type of borrowing without original character forms. They call this type of borrowing "*Shuowen* Borrowing", *Liushu* Borrowing, or Character-Creation Borrowing. Meanwhile, they refer to borrowing with original character forms as Usage Borrowing. For example, Hong Chengyu 洪成玉, the editor-in-chief of *Ancient Chinese Language* 古代汉语, states, "The so-called borrowing in *Shuowen Jiezi* refers to the borrowing without original character forms. While *tongjia* 通假 (interchangeability of characters) refers to borrowing with original character forms. There is a distinction between the two. For instance, the interrogative pronoun *shu* 孰 (who) had no form of its own and later borrowed the form and pronunciation of *shu* 孰 [the ancient form of *shu* 熟 (ripe)]. This is what was referred to as borrowing in *Shuowen Jiezi*. Nonetheless, the characters for *zao* 蚤 (flea) and *zao* 早 (early) existed at the same time. In the past, when writing articles, people used character *zao* 蚤 (flea) instead of the rightful character *zao* 早 to express the meaning of 'early'. For example, there is such a sentence in *Shiji* 史记 (Records of the Grand Historian): 旦日不可不蚤自来谢项王 (On the morning of that day, he had to thank Xiang Yu.).[5] The case of *zao* 蚤 (flea) and *zao* 早 (early) are characters used interchangeably."

Huang Biyun 黄碧云 said, "Regarding characters that already have their own character forms but are borrowed because of similar or close pronunciation, they are actually wrongly written characters or mispronounced characters, not what Xu Shen referred to as borrowed characters."6

Chen Shunzhi 陈顺芝 observed, "Xu Shen 许慎 is very clear in defining the term of borrowed characters. It refers to the borrowing of characters when creating new characters, and does not include the borrowing of those that already have their own character forms."7

Nevertheless, these statements are inconsistent with the discussion of borrowing in the character explanations in *Shuowen Jiezi*. As already mentioned, the term often used to describe borrowing in character explanations is *yiwei* 以为 (used as), and similar terms includes *jieyiwei* 借以为 (borrowed to mean), *guyiwei* 故以为 (therefore used as), and *yinyiwei* 因以为 (for used as).8 *Shuowen Jiezi* uses these terms to describe both borrowed characters without their own original character forms, such as *wei* 韦 (tanned leather), *lai* 来 (arrival), and *yao* 姚 (surname), and those that already have their own character forms, such as those listed below.

(1) *Cao* 屮 originally means the growth of grass and trees. Its shape evokes the images of poles, stems, and branches. In ancient writing, it was used as *cao* 艸 (grass).

This entry explicitly points out that *cao* 屮 was borrowed to reprent the meaning of *cao* 艸 (grass) in ancient texts. This is an example of borrowing with its own character form. As Duan Yucai 段玉裁 explains, "When *Shuowen Jiezi* says that a character was used as another character in ancient times, it means that this is an example of borrowing, where a character is borrowed to represent another character with a similar pronunciation or meaning."9

(2) *Qian* 臤 means "firm", which consists of semantic component *you* 又 (again) and phonetic component *chen* 臣 (male slave). This character and its related characters all have *qian* 臤 (firm) as their radical. In ancient texts, it is sometimes used as the character *xian* 贤 (virtuous).

In ancient texts, *qian* 臤 (firm) is sometimes used as the character *xian* 贤 (virtuous). This is an example of borrowing, where the involved character has its own character form.

(3) *Yuan* 爰 means "to pull" and is composed of *biao* 爫 and *yu* 于 (go). In big-seal script, it was borrowed to represent the character *yuan* 辕 (shafts of a cart). This is an example of borrowing where the character involved has its own character form.
(4) *Ge* 哥 means "sound" and is composed of two component *ke* 可 (can). In ancient text, it was used as the character *ge* 謌 (slander).
(5) *Mian* 敽 means "to abandon", having *pu* 攴 (tap) as its semantic component and *shou* 𠷎 (long life) as its phonetic component. In *Zhou Shu* 周书 (The History of Zhou of the Northern Dynasties), it was used to represent the character *tao* 讨 (denounce). As Shi Jing writes "无我敽兮".

(6) *Kuai* 俫 means "to send". It has *ren* 人 (person) as its semantic component and *zhuan* 奊 (fire spark) as its phonetic component. This character was seen in 有侁氏以伊尹俫女 (Yiyin sent his daughter to get married.), which was a sentence said by Lü Buwei 吕不韦 (292–235 BCE). In ancient texts, it was used to represent the character *xun* 训 (instruct).
(7) *Qi* 诐 means "to dispute", having *yan* 言 (speak) as its semantic component and *pi* 皮 (skin) as its phonetic component. In ancient texts, it was used as the character *po* 颇 (oblique).
(8) *Kao* 丂 means "to release pent-up energy" and resembles the shape of being blocked by *yi* 一 (one) on top. In ancient texts, it was used to represent *kui* 丂 (be short of) or *qiao* 巧 (skillful).
(9) *Wan* 完 means "to complete" and has *mian* 宀 (roofed room) as its semantic component and *yuan* 元 (head) as its phonetic component. In ancient texts, it was used to represent the character *kuan* 宽 (wide).

Based on the analysis above, we can conclude that there are two types of borrowed characters in *Shuowen Jiezi:* those without their own character forms and those with their own character forms. Some scholars wrongly think that *Shuowen Jiezi* uses the term borrowed characters to refer only to those without their own character forms because the definition says "本无其字" (originally having no character form). This is caused by a misunderstanding of the four characters in the definition. *Shuowen Jiezi* states 本无其字 (originally having no character form) instead of 无其字 (having no character form), and there are subtle differences between these two expressions. 本无其字 (originally without its own character) in *Shuowen Jiezi* means that borrowing originated from the situation where there was an expression without a corresponding character, but with the development of the writing system, the expression might acquire its own form: a new character was created for the expression. When this character was created, the old, borrowed character used for the expression was probably still in use. As a result, the newly created character and the old, borrowed character could be used interchangeably. This explains why sometimes borrowing happens to a character that already has a form. To get a clear idea of the issue, please refer to the following chart.

Figure 17.2 Development of an Expression Without a Character Form

Wei 谓 (to say) is an example that originally had no character and later acquired one. In the beginning, it did not have its own character form and relied on another character, *wei* 胃, to express its meaning. *Wei* 胃 (stomach) was once borrowed to represent *wei* 谓 (to say). Typical examples are the Chu bamboo slips dating back to the Warring States Period. There are such sentences on the Chu Bamboo Slips Unearthed in Guodian: 目而知之胃之进之[10] (The eyes can tell if the food has entered the stomach.); 何胃六德 (What can be called the Six Virtues). On the Qin bamboo slips unearthed in Suihudi and silk manuscripts from Mawangdui Han Tombs, *wei* 胃 (stomach) *wei* 谓 (to say) are used interchangeably. According to existing materials, the character *wei* 谓 (to say) was probably created at the time when the Qin Dynasty unified China. Therefore, in the pre-Qin Periods, *wei* 谓 (to say) did not have its own character form and existed as 胃, but after the Qin Dynasty, the character form 谓 was created and 胃 became a borrowed character for a character that has its own form.

Another example is *jia* 袷 (lined garment), Before this character was created, *he* 合 (close) was used as its borrowed character. Therefore, before the middle of the Western Han Dynasty (202 BCE–8 CE), the character *he* 合 (close) was borrowed to represent it. For example, in a note to the expression 襜褕袷复褶袴裈 (many kinds of clothing) from *Ji Jiu Pian* 急就篇, Yan Shigu 颜师古 (581–645) said, "衣裳施里曰袷，褚之以绵曰复 [*qia* 袷 refers to a double-layered lined garment. When it is lined, it is called *fu* 复]. As shown below, many bamboo and wooden slips created prior to the middle of the Western Han Dynasty use the character *he* 合 to represent *qia* 袷.

青绮禅合衣，素掾 (Slip No. 350, from No. 3 Han-Dynasty of Mawangdui)
生绮禅合衣一，素掾 (Slip No. 357, from No. 3 Han-Dynasty of Mawangdui)
连紩合衣幭一 (Slip No. 358, from No. 3 Han-Dynasty of Mawangdui)
霜丸合衣一领 (Wood slip 1, from No. 2 Han-Dynasty Tomb in Yin Wan)
缥丸合衣一领 (Wood slip 12, from No. 6 Han-Dynasty Tomb in Yin Wan)
雪丸合衣，出□绛(绔)繟上禅衣各一领 (Wood slip from Han-Dynasty Tomb in Shiqi)
缥丸合衣一领 (Wood slip A, from Western Han-Dynasty Tomb in Xiguobao)
柑谷合衣一领 (Wood slip A, from Western Han-Dynasty Tomb in Xiguobao)

According to existing materials, the character *qia* 袷 first appeared on a wooden slip unearthed from No. 101 Han Tomb in Xupu, which contains the phrase "绿袷一领" (a green-lined garment). This tomb dates to 5 CE. From the analysis above, we can conclude that *qia* 袷 existed as *he* 合 prior to the middle of the Western Han Dynasty,[11] and, later, when the character 袷 was created, he 合 became a borrowed character for a character with its own character form.

The analysis above reveals the reason for the phenomenon of borrowing a character for the purpose of using it to represent another character that has its own form. In theory, there should be no need for a borrowed character if there was an available character form. The situation where a borrowed character used to represent another character that has its own form is often the result of the creation of a new character. It is worth noting that borrowed characters are different from wrongly used homophones.

In fact, Duan Yucai 段玉裁 gave a correct explanation for 本无其字 a long time ago, but this viewpoint was neglected by many researchers. Duan Yucai said,

248 *Four Misunderstandings about* Shuowen Jiezi

"A borrowed character used to express a new idea is not different from the one used to express the idea of another existing character. This is because, borrowing may occur before the invention of a new character for the idea. When this happens, both the old, borrowed form and the newly invented form are correct forms for the characters. Nevertheless, as time goes by, some old, borrowed [characters] will not be used anymore. These are the causes for the different types of borrowed characters."[12]

III. Misunderstanding 3: Criticizing *Shuowen Jiezi* by Comparing its Character Forms With Archaic Characters

The composition of Chinese characters has gone through a long period of evolution. The current form of a character may be very different from its Archaic form. It is precisely because Chinese characters can adapt to new social needs and constantly adjust their compositional system that they have become the only ancient writing system that has been used up to the present day. The evolution of their composition is divided into stages, and the interpretation of their forms must be changed accordingly. Nevertheless, people today lack understanding of this concept. As Li Guanghua 李光华 said, "*Shuowen Jiezi* mainly discusses Archaic, big-seal-script, and small-seal-script forms of characters. Many of them are used after the late Zhou Dynasty (1046–256 BCE). A period that is more than a thousand years away from the time when the oracle-bone script of the Shang Dynasty (1600–1046 BCE) was widely used. The characters changed a lot over these periods, and thus their Archaic forms are very different from even the ones used in the Warring States Period (475–221 BCE). Living in the Eastern Han Dynasty (25–220), Xu Shen 许慎 could neither see the unearthed oracle-bone scripts nor the bronze scripts from the early Zhou Dynasty. Therefore, his explanation of the character forms is inevitably prone to errors."[13]

That viewpoint is representative, and there is a glaring error in the point of view: the failure to realise the developmental and phased nature of the composition system of Chinese characters, which leads to criticism of the character form interpretations in *Shuowen Jiezi* by referring to such archaic characters as those used in oracle-bone and bronze inscriptions.

The development and evolution of Chinese character composition is a process of self-adjustment within its own system. For example, the character *diao* 吊 (hang) has undergone changes in its form from the oracle-bone-script form to the small-seal-script form, as shown in the following table:

Table 17.1 Changes in the Form of 吊

The Shang Dynasty (ca. 1600–1046 BCE)	The Western Zhou Dynasty (1046–771 BCE)	The Spring and Autumn Period (770–476 BCE)	The Warring States Period (475–221 BCE)	The Small-Seal Script

According to *Shuowen Jiezi*, *diao* 吊 means to ask about someone's end. It is composed of the radicals for *ren* 人 (person) and *gong* 弓 (bow). In ancient times, those who were buried were clothed thickly and thrown into the wild, so people had to use bows to fight against birds. In *Shuowen Jiezi*, the character form is explained as '从人弓'[composed of radical f 人 (person) and component *gong* 弓 (bow)]. This explanation applies specifically to the small-seal-script form, which indeed consists of the two components: 人 (person) and *gong* 弓 (bow). Nevertheless, this character has a different form before the Warring States Period when it was composed of radical *ren* 人 (person) and *zeng* 矰 (arrow with attached silk cord). According to *Shuowen Jiezi*, *zeng* 矰 means a tied-up arrow. It is composed of component *shi* 矢 (arrow) and phonetic component *ceng* 曾 (already). *Yupian* 玉篇 (Chinese dictionary compiled by Gu Yewang in the 6th century) describes *zeng* 矰 as "to tie or fasten to an arrow". A *zeng* 矰 (arrow with attached silk cord) is an attacking weapon that is tied with a rope, likely used to retrieve the weapon after an attack.

Diao 吊 is one of the forms of ancient funerals. *Zhou Yi* 周易 (The Book of Changes) records the earliest form of mourning in China. It says, "In ancient times, burials involved wrapping the body in thick clothes and straw and then leaving it in the wilderness without burying him it. There was no set mourning period." So the earliest form of mourning in fact involved wrapping the body in straw and throwing it into the wilderness, which is shown by the character *zang* 葬 (bury), a combination of three components, namely *mang* 茻 (grass), which symbolises grass, *si* 死, representing a corpse, and *yi* 一 (one), indicating a wooden board used to carry the body to the wilderness. In *Lüshi Chunqiu* 吕氏春秋 (Master Lü's Spring and Autumn Annals), it is written, "郑之富人有溺者，人得其死者，富人请赎之 (Among the wealthy people of Zheng, there was a drowning victim for whom someone found the body. The wealthy people sought to redeem the body)." *Zuo Zhuan* 左传 records that "白公奔山而缢，其徒微之。生拘白乞而问白公之死焉。对曰：'余知死所，而长者使余勿言 (Bai Gong fled to the mountains and hanged himself. His followers kept it secret. When Bai Ji was captured and asked about Bai Gong's death, he replied, 'I know where he died, but my elders have forbidden me from speaking.')." In the past, it was common to dispose of a body by leaving it in the wilderness for birds and beasts to devour. Nevertheless, with the emergence of the concept of soul, people began to view a dead body as a vessel of the soul, which was believed to be eternal. To protect the soul, people began to bury bodies instead of leaving them in the wilderness, showing their respect for the deceased and avoiding any potential calamities caused by angry spirits. Moreover, as the soul was considered immortal, family members were reluctant to allow the body to be damaged by wild animals. So, another custom developed, in which the deceased's relatives would bring a *zeng* 矰 (arrow with attached silk cord) to drive away birds and beasts from the dead body. This is what the character *diao* 吊 represents: stones and the like used to drive away birds and beasts, which had to be picked up again after being thrown, in case they were needed again. The rope could save them the trouble of picking things up. Protecting the body from birds and beasts is the origin of the mourning period for later generations. According to

Li Ji 礼记 (The Book of Rites), the mourning period for family members of the deceased lasted three months, five months, nine months, one year, or three years, depending on the closeness of the relationship to the deceased. Close relatives usually mourned for three years. There is such a sentence in *Yanzi Chunqiu* 晏子春秋 (Tales of Yanzi): "When his mother died, he buried her very deeply and mourned for three years, crying bitterly."

In *Wuyue Chunqiu* 吴越春秋 (History of the Southern States Wu and Yue), there is such a paragraph: "The crossbow was created based on the bow, the bow was created based on the string, and the string was invented by the filial sons of ancient times. . . . In ancient times, the people were simple and ate birds and beasts when they were hungry and drank dew when they were thirsty. When they died, they would be wrapped in white straw and thrown into the wilderness. Filial sons could not bear to see their parents being eaten by birds and beasts, so they made strings to protect them and prevent them from being harmed by birds and beasts." The record in *Wuyue Chunqiu* is consistent with the evolution of the characters' form in the pre-Warring States Period. According to the character form for 吊 before the Warring States Period, people carried projectiles and used bows and arrows, which was a further development. The small-seal-script form of the character *diao* 吊 represents the later state of development.

At the same time, replacing *zeng* 矰 (arrow with attached silk cord) with *gong* 弓 (bow) was also a requirement for further systematising Chinese character composition. *Zeng* 矰 (arrow with attached silk cord) appeared only in the character for *diao* 吊, and its ability to form characters was low. Using *gong* 弓 (bow) to represent *zeng* 矰 (arrow with attached silk cord) removed a seldomly used component, making the system more efficient and scientific. Character forms included in *Shuowen Jiezi* conform to the adjustment of Chinese character composition, and the book made new explanations for the changed character forms, which was reasonable. If we deem that *Shuowen Jiezi* is inaccurate[14] and argue that *diao* 吊 shall be composed of *ren* 人 (person) and *zeng* 矰 (arrow with attached silk cord) based on the pre-Warring States Period form, we will draw a conclusion that does not conform to historical facts.

Another example is the character *huang* 皇 (emperor). From the Shang-Dynasty form to the small-seal-script form, its change is shown in the table below:

Table 17.2 Changes in the Form of 皇

The Shang Dynasty (ca. 1600–1046 BCE)	The Western Zhou Dynasty (1046–771 BCE)	The Spring and Autumn Period (770–476 BCE)	The Warring States Period (475–221 BCE)	The Small-Seal Script
皇	皇	皇 皇	皇	皇

The form of *huang* 皇 (emperor) was a pictorial form, originally resembling a feather crown placed on a crown seat. During the Spring and Autumn Period, the crown seat was represented by two horizontal strokes or three horizontal strokes, but in the latter, a vertical stroke was added to the horizontal strokes. During the Warring States Period, the vertical stroke became shorter, and the crown seat evolved into the character *wang* 王 (king). In small-seal script, the top part of the crown evolved into the character *zi* 自 (self). Therefore, *Shuowen Jiezi* explains it as a compound ideograph. In the entry for *wang* 王 (king) from *Shuowen Jiezi*, it says "皇 means 'great'. It is made up of the component for *zi* 自 (self), which means 'beginning'. *Zi* 自 (self) is pronounced like *bi* 鼻 (nose), and people use *bizi* 鼻子 to mean 'first-born son'." The evolution of the character form for *huang* 皇 (emperor) from the Shang Dynasty to the small-seal-script form was also a deliberate transformation of the character-form system. Whether it was a feather crown or a crown seat, it was a low-frequency component of composition that appeared in only one character form. In the evolution from monomorphemic pictograph multiple-component characters, the upper part was developed into *zi* 自 (self), and the lower part was developed into *wang* 王 (king), becoming the small-seal-script form of the "自-王" combination. This not only eliminated the low-frequency components, but also produced a new compound-ideograph that conformed to the later rules of character composition. Therefore, we cannot assume that the small-seal-script form is an error, nor can we conclude that *Shuowen Jiezi*'s explanation of the character form is incorrect.

For example, the character *ni* 逆 (meet) underwent changes in its form during the Shang Dynasty, Western Zhou Dynasty, and the small-seal-script period, as shown in the following table.

Table 17.3 Changes in the Form of 逆

The Shang Dynasty (ca. 1600–1046 BCE)	The Western Zhou Dynasty (1046–771 BCE)	The Small-Seal Script
ꜗ 𣥩 𣥩	🖼 🖼	𨑨

Shuowen Jiezi explains that *ni* 逆 means to meet head-on and is composed of the radical for *chuo* 辵 (walk) and a phonetic component *ni* 屰 (meet head-on). In the eastern regions, *ni* 逆 (meet head-on) was used; while in the western regions, it was called *ying* 迎 (meet head-on). In oracle-bone scripts from the Shang Dynasty, there were three different forms of the character. The first form had an upper part resembling a person walking closer, with the lower part being the toes of the person facing the incoming person, representing the person welcoming. The second form was composed of the incoming person and the radical *chi* 彳 (walk slowly), which represents road, indicating the incoming person walking on a road. The third form represented the host welcoming a guest on the road. In Western Zhou bronze inscriptions, the first form was the same as the third oracle-bone script from the Shang Dynasty, while the second form was based on the pictograph of *xing* 行 (walk), which also represents a road. Both Shang and Western Zhou scripts were compound pictographs. The seal script form of *ni* 逆 (meet head-on) originated from the first form in Western Zhou bronze inscriptions. Nevertheless, on the one

252 *Four Misunderstandings about* Shuowen Jiezi

hand, the form representing the incoming person no longer resembled a person upside down. On the other hand, *chi* 彳 (walk slowly) and *zhi* 止 (stop) were combined to form a new semantic component, thus *ni* 逆 (meet head-on) had been transformed from a compound pictograph to a semantic-phonetic character by the small-seal-script period. Therefore, *Shuowen Jiezi*'s explanation that *ni* 逆 (meet head-on) is composed of the radical for *chuo* 辵 (walk) and phonetic component *ni* 屰 (meet head-on) is correct.

IV. Misunderstanding 4: Mistaking *Shuowen Jiezi*'s Explanations for Character Compositions for Interpretation of Character Meanings

There is a difference between the compositional interpretations and literal interpretations for characters in *Shuowen Jiezi*. The compositional interpretation deals with the concept behind the composition of a character, which involves using a certain form to represent its meaning. The literal interpretation refers to the specific meaning represented by the character. Whether these two interpretations can be unified or not depends on the characteristics of the character. If the character's meaning is concrete and singular, then its compositional interpretation is often consistent with its literal interpretation.

The character *guan* 盥 (to wash hands) in *Shuowen Jiezi* is a typical example. In ancient times, aristocrats would have someone else pour water from a ladle for them to wash their hands with and there would be a dish to catch the runoff. As shown in small-seal script, 盥 depicts the image of washing hands. With single and concrete meaning, this character has unified compositional interpretation and literal interpretation.

Another example is the character *xiang* 向. *Shuowen Jiezi* explains that it represents a north-facing window and is composed of the radical for *mian* 宀 (roofed room) and the radical for *kou* 口 (mouth). In *Shi Jing* 诗经, there is a line that goes, "塞向墐户" (Block the north-facing window with thorns.). The small-seal-script form of 向 takes the radical *mian* 宀 (roofed room) to indicate a house, while the *kou* 口 (mouth) inside represents the window. Therefore, its compositional interpretation is the same as its literal interpretation.

The process of creating a written character involves making an abstract concept concrete by finding a specific image to represent it. When a character has an abstract or broad meaning, the process of creating a character often involves reconciling different aspects of the concept into a single image. This can result in a character that does not entirely reflect the original meaning of the character it represents. To explain the unified relationship between the form and meaning of Chinese characters, *Shuowen Jiezi* often provides a compositional interpretation for a character rather than a literal interpretation. Mistaking these compositional interpretations for literal interpretations can lead to errors, so when providing explanations and annotations for *Shuowen Jiezi*, it is important to clarify the essence of its content.

For instance, character *qi* 齐 as explained in *Shuowen Jiezi* means *ping* 平 (level) and is depicted with the image of wheat or barley spikes growing on a level surface. Nevertheless, this definition cannot be found in any other literature, nor can it be possible since *Shuowen Jiezi* explains the character's composition, not its meaning. The original meaning of *qi* 齐 (level) is "even" or "level", which is an abstract concept that needed a visual representation in the form of a pictograph. To reflect the character's meaning, ancient people looked to the wheat fields where the plants grew evenly in height and used the image of the wheat to represent "level". In the small-seal script, *qi* 齐 (level) is written as 齊, while in the oracle-bone script, it is represented by the image of multiple wheat plants growing in a field. Besides this character, there are many similar examples.

For instance, Chinese characters composed of three identical components often convey the concept of "many," such as *zhong* 众 (crowd), which consists of three *ren* 人 (person) and *sen* 森, which uses three *mu* 木 (wood) to illustrate a forest. There is another character form consisting of three wheat plant images arranged in a triangular shape. These three images are combined to create a picture with perspective. Based on the analysis above, it is reasonable to say that the entry of *qi* 齐 (level) in *Shuowen Jiezi* as "the spikes of wheat growing on a level surface" is not appropriate, since this explanation does not capture the essence of the character's original meaning.[15] Instead, it should be understood as "using the image of wheat or barley spikes growing on a level surface to represent levelness".

Another example is *hei* 黑 (black). *Shuowen Jiezi* seems to explain it as the colour produced by smoking. Nevertheless, this definition cannot apply to other objects that are also black. In fact, *Shuowen Jiezi* only explains the character's composition rather than its literal meaning. *Hei* 黑 (black) is an abstract concept that needed a visual representation in the form of a pictograph. Ancient people looked to common household items for inspiration. The small-seal script for the character *hei* 黑 (black) is 黑, which composed of two components: the Archaic forms for *chuang* 窗 (window) and *yan* 炎 (the symbol for flames). In ancient times, people lived in cave dwellings that still exist in some Northern regions of China today. In the past, wood was used to start fires for both warmth and cooking, resulting in smoky environments within the cave dwellings. The small circular windows in these caves were the only escape for smoke, causing the people and their surroundings to be blackened by smoke. This was a common phenomenon in the cave dwellings, and thus the image of window and that of flame were combined to represent the colour black. Therefore, if we interpret the definition of *hei* 黑 (black) in *Shuowen Jiezi* as "the colour produced by smoking,"[16] it still does not give a proper explanation for the character's meaning. The accurate interpretation should be "using the colour produced by smoke to represent all shades of black".

Character *chen* 尘 (dust) is also a typical example, which is written as *cu* 麤 (rough) in traditional Chinese. In accordance with *Shuowen Jiezi*, it is explained as "when a group of deer run, they kick up soil". Here, the three *lu* 鹿 (deer) in *cu* 麤 (rough) represent a group of deer, and the definition is also based on a compositional interpretation. It means "using the image of a group of deer kicking up soil while running to represent dust and soil".

Notes

1 唐兰：《中国文字学》，第72页，上海：上海古籍出版社，1949.
   Tang Lan: *Chinese Philology*, p. 72, Shanghai: Shanghai Classics Publishing House, 1949.
2 杨五铭：《文字学》，第78页，长沙：湖南人民出版社，1986.
   Yang Wuming: *Chinese Philology*, p. 78, Changsha: Hunan People's Publishing House, 1986.
3 钟如雄：《说文解字论纲》（修订本），第109页，北京：中国社会科学出版社，2014.
   Zhong Ruxiong: *A Generalization of Shuowen Jiezi*, p. 109, Beijing: China Social Sciences Press, 2014.
4 王玉仁：《初步》，第90页，上海：学林出版社，2009.
   Academia PressWang Yuren: *Preliminary Discussion on Shuowen Jiezi*, p. 90, Shanghai: Academia Press, 2009.
5 洪成玉主编：《古代汉语》下册，第278页，北京：中华书局，1990.
   Hong Chengyu: *Ancient Chinese Language* (Vol. 2), p. 278, Beijing: Zhonghua Book Company, 1990.
6 黄碧云：《许慎"六书"释义辨证》，《说文学研究》第一辑，第142页，武汉：崇文书局，2004.
   Huang Biyun: "Analysis and Interpretation of Xu Shen 许慎's 'Liu Shu'", *Studies of Shuowen Jiezi* (Vol. 1), p. 142, Wuhan: Chongwen Press, 2004.
7 陈顺芝：《六书和汉字构形》，《说文学研究》第二辑，第347页，武汉：崇文书局，2006.
   Chen Shunzhi: "Six Means of Creating Chinese Characters and the Formation of Chinese Characters", *Studies of Shuowen Jiezi* (Vol. 2), p. 347, Wuhan: Chongwen Press, 2006.
8 详见萧璋：《文字训诂论集》，第141–158页，北京：语文出版社，1994.
   Xiao Zhang: *Collection of Essays on Textual Exegesis*, pp. 141–158, Beijing: Language & Culture Press, 1994.
9 段玉裁：《说文解字注》，第21页，上海：上海古籍出版社，1981.
   Duan Yucai: *Notes to Shuowen Jiezi*, pp. 21, Shanghai: Shanghai Classics Publishing House, 1981.
10 For convenience in printing, sometimes common characters are used in the *Shuowen Jiezi* explanations.
11 This conforms to the case of borrowing that having semantic relationship.
12 段玉裁《说文解字注》，第756页，上海：上海古籍出版社，1981.
   Duan Yucai: *Notes to Shuowen Jiezi*, pp. 756, Shanghai: Shanghai Classics Publishing House, 1981.
13 李光华：《与训诂语法论稿》，第77页，合肥：安徽大学出版社，2005.
   Li Guanghua: *'Shuowen' and Grammar of Interpretation*, p. 77, Hefei: Anhui University Press, 2005.
14 容庚：《宝蕴楼彝器图录》，第47页，北京：中华书局，2011.
   Rong Geng: *Catalogue of Yi Vessels in the Baoyun Building*, p. 47, Beijing: Zhonghua Book Company, 2011.
15 汤可敬：《说文解字今释》，第942页，岳麓书社，1997.
   Tang Kejing: *Contemparary Interpretation to Shuowen Jiezi*, p. 942, Changsha: Yue Lu Book Company, 1997.
16 汤可敬：《说文解字今释》，第1395页，岳麓书社，1997.
   Tang Kejing: *Contemparary Interpretation to Shuowen Jiezi*, p. 1395, Changsha: Yue Lu Book Company, 1997.

18 New Proofs of *Shuowen Jiezi*[1]

Archaeological data do great benefit to the study and help sort out the handed down ancient books. Recent years have witnessed my focus on the unearthed documents and written materials; the character forms that appear on these unearthed documents and materials provide proof for the interpretation of character forms in *Shuowen Jiezi* 说文解字 (An Explication of Written Characters). Several examples are illustrated as follows.

I. *Fei* 吠 (Bark)

Shuowen Jiezi 说文解字 explains this character as a combination of *quan* 犬 (dog) and *kou* 口 (mouth) and points out that *kou* 口 is its radical. (吠，犬鸣也。从犬口。)

The following five existing ancient copies of the book also use 从犬口 [a combination of *quan* 犬 (dog) and *kou* 口 (mouth)] to explain the composition of the character.

(1) 孙星衍平津馆丛书原刻大徐本: the earliest block-printed copy of *Shuowen Jiezi* [Xu Xuan's 徐铉 (917–992) edition] collected by a Qing-Dynasty scholar named Sun Xingyan 孙星衍 (1753–1818);
(2) 王昶所藏宋刻元修大徐本: a Yuan-Dynasty (1271–1368) edited version of a Song-Dynasty (960–1279) block-printed copy of *Shuowen Jiezi* [Xu Xuan's 徐铉 edition], which is collected by Wang Chang 王昶 (1725–1806);
(3) 汪中所藏丁晏跋宋刻元修大徐本: a Yuan-Dynasty edited version of a Song-Dynasty block-printed copy of *Shuowen Jiezi* [Xu Xuan's 徐铉 edition], which contains an epilogue by Ding Yan 丁晏 (1794–1875) and is a collection of Wang Zhong 汪中 (1744–1794);
(4) 丁少山仿刻汲古阁旧藏宋监本大徐本: Ding Shaoshan's 丁少山 reprinted copy of *Shuowen Jiezi* [Xu Xuan's 徐铉 edition] that was a collection of the Song-Dynasty Imperial College;
(5) 黄志淳藏宋刻元修大徐本: a Yuan-Dynasty edited version of a Song-Dynasty block-printed copy of *Shuowen Jiezi* [Xu Xuan's 徐铉 edition], which is collected by 黄志淳 Huang Zhichun.

One existing ancient copy of the book uses 从口犬 [a combination of *kou* 口 (mouth) and *quan* 犬 (dog)] to explain the composition of the character. This copy is named 藤花榭本小徐本: the Tenghuaxie version *Shuowen Jiezi* [Xu Kai's 徐鍇 (920–974) edition].

The Tang-Dynasty Manuscript Version of *Shuowen Jiezi* uses 从口犬声 [a combination of *kou* 口 (mouth) and phonetic component *quan* 犬 (dog)] to describe the composition of the character.

In *Shuowen Shili* 说文释例 (Illustrations of Examples from *Shuowen Jiezi*), Wang Yun 王筠 (1784–1854) points out that as *fei* 吠 (bark), a combination of *kou* 口 (mouth) and *quan* 犬 (dog) and *ming* 鸣 (cry of bird or animal), a combination of *kou* 口 (mouth) and *niao* 鸟 (bird) have similar compositional structures, they should have similarities in the selection of their radicals. He holds that as *ming* 鸣 is arranged under radical 鸟 in *Shuowen Jiezi*, *fei* 吠 shall be arranged under radical *quan* 犬 instead of radical *kou* 口. A Qing-Dynasty scholar Qian Dian 钱坫 (1744–1806) expresses support for this view in his book *Shuowen Jiezi Zhequan* 说文解字斠诠 (Commentary on *Shuowen Jiezi*). Taking into consideration the compiling format and the form and connotation of character *fei* 吠, Wang Yun's 王筠 analysis does make sense. If the arrangement of *fei* 吠 under radical *kou* 口 is indeed wrong, it is probably due to some mistake made in the copying of the book. It is most likely that component 犬 in this character is originally written as 犮. In the silk manuscripts unearthed from Mawangdui Han Tombs, the character 拔 is sometimes written as 扷. Jn *Shuowen Jiezi Zhu* 说文解字注 (Notes to *Shuowen Jiezi*), Duan Yucai 段玉裁 (1735–1815) explains that character *fei* 吠, which is a semantic-phonetic character, is written as 吠 in *Zilin* 字林 (A Collection of Characters) and that this form appears in *Taixuan* 太玄 (Supreme Mystery): "鸱鸠在林, 吠 彼众经 (The scops owls are in the woods, and dogs are all barking at them)." Xu Kai's 徐鍇 (920–974) Edition of *Shuowen Jiezi* contains such a statement in the explanation of the character: "或云从犬 (some form of the character features component *quan* 犬)." This is an obvious mistake since the standard form of the character in this edition is *fei* 吠, which features the component *quan* 犬. Given this, there must be some mistake in the statement 或云从犬, and the most likely explanation is that the statement should originally be 或云从 犮.

Given the above analysis, it can be inferred that the original text used to explain the character in Xu Kai's 徐鍇 (920–974) Edition of *Shuowen Jiezi* and *Shuowen Jiezi* is 从口 犮声 (the Tang-Dynasty Manuscript Version of *Shuowen Jiezi*) and that the standard seal-script form of the character shall be 吠. The text 从口犬, which is used to explain the character in Xu Kai's 徐鍇 (920–974) edition] and the Tenghuaxie version of *Shuowen Jiezi* [Xu Kai's 徐鍇 (920–974) edition] is a result of the deletion of character *sheng* 声 (pronunciation). The reason for the deletion is probably that 犬 cannot express the pronunciation of the character as 犮 does. Because of this deletion, the explanation of character *fei* 吠 does not highlight its phonetic component anymore. Give this, 从口犬 can also be rewritten as 从犬口.

II. *Du* 妒 (Envious)

Shuowen Jiezi 说文解字 explains this character as a combination of *nv* 女 (woman/girl) and *hu* 户 (door) and points out that the former is its radical and the latter is its phonetic component. (妒, 妇妒夫也。从女, 户声。)

In *Shuowen Jiaoyi* 说文校议 (Proofreading Remarks on *Shuowen Jiezi*), Yan Kenjun 严可均 (1762–1843) refutes a view expressed in *Wujing Wenzi* 五经文字 (Characters in the Five Classics). *Wujing Wenzi* 五经文字 holds that *du* 妒 (envious) is the standard form of the character and 妬 is the wrong form, but Yan Kenjun 严可均 believes that, in comparison with *shi* 石 (stone), *hu* 户 (door) is a more reasonable component of the character since it has both phonetic and semantic functions. He argues that the combination of *nv* 女 (woman/girl) and *hu* 户 (door) may imply the causes of jealousy: in a polygamous marriage, when the husband always comes to the door of his favourite wife, other wives will become envious. Interestingly, Duan Yucai 段玉裁 expresses a completely opposite view in *Shuowen Jiezi Zhu* 说文解字注: he holds that 妬 is the standard form of the character. He agrees that, in his time, 妒 is the standard form of the character, featuring the phonetic component *hu* 户 but points out that *shi* 石 can also serve as a phonetic component in this character just as it does in *zhe* 柘 (a thorny tree), *tuo* 橐 (a sack), *du* 蠹 (moth), Duan Yucai's 段玉裁 viewpoint is consistent with the facts. Relevant archaeological evidence includes the following: Qin-Dynasty (221–207 BCE) bamboo slips unearthed at Shuihudi, which contain 40,000 plus characters; the silk manuscripts unearthed from Mawangdui Han Tombs, which date back to the Western Han Dynasty (202–220 BCE) and contains more than 120,000 characters. Both documents contain the character form *du* 妬 instead of *du* 妒. Therefore, the form listed in *Shuowen Jiezi* should be *du* 妬 instead of *du* 妒.

III. *Zui* 辠 (Guilt)

Shuowen Jiezi 说文解字 explains that this character is modified into *zui* 罪 (guilt) under the command of Emperor Qin Shi Huang (the first Emperor of the Qin Dynasty) because the character's original form is like *huang* 皇 (superior ruler). 186

The following archaeological evidence supports this claim. On the bamboo slips unearthed from No.11 Tomb at Shuihudi, Yunmeng County, Hubei Province in 1975, which date back to the late Warring State Period (475–221 BCE) and early Qin Dynasty (221–207 BCE), there is no character *zui* 辠, but there is character *zui* 罪. Contrary to this, there is no character *zui* 罪 but there is character *zui* 辠 on the bamboo slips unearthed from the No.6 Tomb at Longgang, Yunmeng County, in 1989, which date back to the late Qin Dynasty. These archaeological discoveries show that the modification of *zui* 辠 into *zui* 罪 was carried out after Emperor Qin Shi Huang unified China and chose the word *huangdi* 皇帝 (emperor) as his own address.

IV. *Dui* 對 (Reply)

Shuowen Jiezi 说文解字 explains the character as a combination of *zhuo* 丵 (thick grass), *kou* 口 (mouth), and *cun* 寸 (very short). It points out that Liu Heng 刘恒 (203–157 BCE), Emperor Wendi of Han, modified the form by replacing component *kou* 口 (mouth) with component *shi* 士 (gentleman) to express his disapproval of wordy, insincere replies.

    This record is supported by the following archaeological evidence. Among the silk manuscripts unearthed from Mawangdui Han Tombs, the silk-manuscript copy (part A) of *Laozi* 老子 (The Philosophy of Laozi) and the collected version of its missing and scattered part are written by one person. The fact that the writer does not avoid the name of Liu Bang 刘邦 (256–195 BCE), Emperor Gaozu of Han, and that of his Empress Lü Zhi 吕雉 (?–180 BCE) indicates that these manuscripts were written during the early period of the reign of Liu Bang 刘邦, namely from 206 to 195 BCE. For the same reason, the silk-manuscript copy of *Chunqiu Shiyu* 春秋事语 (Events of the Spring and Autumn Period) is believed to be written at about the same time, probably around 200 BCE. As the manuscript of *Zhanguo Zonghengjia Shu* 战国纵横家书 (Political Strategists of the Warring States Period) avoids the name of Liu Bang 刘邦 as a taboo, it is reasonable to believe that this manuscript was written in the early period of the reign of Liu Ying 刘盈 (195–188 BCE), Emperor Huidi of Han, namely around 195 BCE. In these three manuscripts that date back to the periods before Liu Heng 刘恒 (203–157 BCE), Emperor Wendi of Han, came to the throne, the form *dui* 對 is not replaced by *dui* 對 This form appears in the following places: the 278th line of the silk-manuscript copy (part A) of *Laozi* 老子 and the collected version of *Laozi*'s missing and scattered part; the 87th line of *Chunqiu Shiyu* 春秋事语; and the 289th line of *Zhanguo Zonghengjia Shu* 战国纵横家书.

    In the silk-manuscript copy (part B) of *Laozi* 老子 (The Philosophy of Laozi) and the collected version of its missing and scattered part, which was written during the reign of Liu Heng 刘恒 (179–167 BCE) by one person, *dui* 對 is replaced by *dui* 對. This discovery coincides with the statement that it was Liu Heng 刘恒 who modified the character.

    It is worth noting that *dui* 對 is not a character form created by Liu Heng 刘恒: this form first appears in bronze inscriptions. Zhao Mingcheng 赵明诚 (1081–1129) discussed this issue in his book *Jinshi Lu* 金石录 (Bronze and Stele Inscriptions). "對, which features the component *shi* 士 (gentleman) instead of the component *kou* 口 (mouth), is widely used in bronze inscriptions. It was probably the standard form of the character in the big-seal script. The replacement of *shi* 士 (gentleman) by *kou* 口 (mouth) was perhaps carried out by Li Si 李斯 (?–208 BCE), and Emperor Wendi of Han just restored the old form."

V. Che 赾 (to Resist)

Shuowen Jiezi 说文解字 explains the character as a combination of *zou* 走 (go) and a simplified phonetic component 庐.

    Both Xu Xuan's 徐铉 and Xu Kai's 徐锴 editions adopt this explanation of the character's compositional structure, but their explanations differ in the details. Xu Kai's 徐锴 edition points out that the character's standard seal-script form is 趩, which features the original form of the phonetic component 庐. This character form appears in the Qin bamboo slips unearthed at Shuihudi and the silk manuscripts from Mawangdui Han Tombs. Xu Xuan's 徐铉 edition gives the standard official-script form of the character, which is 赾. As *chi* 斥 is the big-seal-script form of 厂, which sounds different from the character, Xu Xuan 徐铉 could only explain the component 斥 as a simplified form of the phonetic component 屵.

VI. *Qin* 秦 (a feudal state)

As the land of the Qin State is suitable for planting millet, *Shuowen Jiezi* 说文解字 defined *he* 禾 (millet) as its radical and explains the character as a combination of *he* 禾 (millet) and a simplified component *chong* 舂 (grind grains in mortar). The book also points out that the big-seal-script form of the character is 𥣬, which is a combination of *li* 秝 (excessively thin) and a simplified component *chong* 舂.

In accordance with *Shuowen Jiezi* 说文解字, the upper part of *qin* 秦/𥣬 is a simplified form of *chong* 舂. Compared with its original form *chong* 舂, the simplified component form lacks the part *jiu* 臼 (mortar). This statement is consistent with archaeological discoveries. Of all the cultural relics discovered so far, there are several items showing how the character *qin* 秦/𥣬 was written before the Qin Dynasty.

(1) Shi You Gui Container (师酉簋) contains the character seemingly featuring the original form *chong* 舂, but the part *jiu* 臼 is incomplete.

(2) Shanghai Museum purchased four tripod cauldrons and two *gui* containers from the cultural relic market of Hong Kong in 1993, and then discovered that these bronzes were unearthed from the Qin Tombs at Mount Dabaozi, Li County, Gansu Province. Among them, No. 1 and No. 2 Qingong Gui Containers (秦公簋一, 秦公簋二) bear the character featuring the combination of *li* 秝 and *chong* 舂. These discoveries show that the upper part of *qin* 秦 is indeed a simplified form of *chong* 舂.

Note

1 The original Chinese version was published in *Research In Ancient Chinese Language* 古汉语研究 in 1999 (issue 3).

19 Mutual Confirmation Between Zhangjiashan Han-Dynasty Bamboo Slips and *Shuowen Jiezi*

Supplement to Proofreading Notes to *Shuowen Jiezii*[1]

After my work *Proofreading Notes to Shuowen Jiezi* 说文解字校笺 was published, I read the newly published Bamboo Slips Unearthed from Han Tomb in Zhangjiashan 张家山汉墓竹简(二四七号墓) and gained a lot from it. My doubt for years was dispelled, and I realised there were some mistakes in my book. As it was too late correct them in the book, I wrote this article as supplement and hope that other researchers can provide additional input on this topic or correct any misunderstanding.

(1) *Man* 缦 (plain silk), according to *Shuowen Jiezi* 说文解字 (An Explication of Written Characters), means plain silk and consists of two components *si* 糸 *(silk) and man* 曼 (long), the latter serving as a phonetic component. These is such a sentence in *Han Lü* 汉律 (Law of Han): 赐衣者缦表白里 (Robes bestowed on officials were made of plain silk and white lining.).

It is written in Bamboo Slips Unearthed from Han Tombs in Zhangjiashan that "robes bestowed on officials should be measured around 20 meters long and about 1.34 meters wide, with 1.67-meter *yuan* 缘 (hem) and 1.5 kilograms of *xu* 絮 (floss); *ru* 襦 (short jacket) should be measured about 6.67 meters long and 66.67 centimetres wide, with about 3.3 meter-hem and 1.5-kilogram floss; *ku* 绔 (袴) (silk trousers) should be measured about 6.67 meters long and 33.34 centimetre wide and equipped with floss weighing 0.75 kilograms; *qin* 衾 (quilt) should be measured about 16.67 meters long and 66.67 centimetres wide, with 6.67-meter and 2-meter hems and 5.5-kilograms floss. Robes of Officials above *Wu Daifu* 五大夫 (ancient Chinese official title) feature brocade coating and that of officials below *Gongcheng* 公乘 (ancient Chinese official title) feature silk coating, and the lining of all of them are made of silk. Robes of officials below *Sikou* 司寇 (ancient Chinese official title) feature fabric coating and lining." "There also was one kind of official robes made of silk and about 20 meters long and 1.34 meters wide and silk fabric (lining), without needing floss." Cites in *Shuowen Jiezi* are sketchy. According to Bamboo Slips Unearthed from Han Tombs, the robes bestowed on officials differ in fabric, not colours. Therefore, "*bai* 白 (white)" in *Shuowen Jiezi* could be misused as "*bo* 帛 (silk)".

(2) According to *Shuowen Jiezi*, *wei* 威 (power), referring to *gu* 姑 (husband's mother), consists of two components *nv* 女 (women/girls) and *xu* 戌 (11th terrestrial branch). There is a sentence in *Han Lü* 汉律 (Law of Han): "妇告威姑" (A woman made a claim against her husband's mother.).

Wei 威 refers to a husband's mother, and *gong* 公 refers to a husband's father in the sentence: "子告父母，妇告威公，奴婢告主、主父母妻子，勿听而弃告者市" (The claims made by son against their parents, a woman against her husband's father and mother, maid-servants against their master or master's parents or wife, will be rejected by the officials, and the plaintiff will be executed.), according to Bamboo Slips Unearthed from the Han Tombs in Zhangjiashan. Therefore, *weigong* 威公 corresponds with "parents". However, it doesn't make sense that "*weigu* 威姑" in *Shuowen Jiezi* refer only to a husband's mother. According to bamboo slips unearthed from Han Tombs, "*gu* 姑" in the "*weigu* 威姑" should be changed to "*gong* 公". *Li ji* 礼记 (The Book of Rites) wrote, "子事父母......妇事舅姑" (Sons attend upon their parents . . . a woman attend upon her parents-in-law.)", which could also serve as the proof.

(3) According to *Shuowen Jiezi*, *Zhi* 䅣 means bran grinded from wheat, consisting of *mai* 麦 (wheat) and *shang* 商 (commerce), the latter serving as the phonetic component. There is a sentence in *Shuowen Jiezi*: "十斤为三斗" (Five kilograms of wheat can produce three *dou* 斗 (a unit of weight; one-tenth of one *shi*) of bran).

According to *Suanshu Shu* 算数书 (Book of Mathematics) of the Bamboo Slips Unearthed from the Han Tombs in Zhangjiashan and Bamboo Slips Unearthed from Qin Tombs in Shuihudi 睡虎地秦墓竹简, "麦十斗，[为] 䅣三斗" (ten *dou* 斗 (a unit of weight; one-tenth of one *shi*) of wheat could produce three *dou* 斗 of *zhi* 䅣 (bran grinded from wheat)). So, "*jin* 斤" in "十斤为三斗" in *Shuowen Jiezi* is a mistake for "*dou* 斗", which is because "*dou* 斗" in the official script is sometimes shaped like "*jin* 斤".

(4) According to *Shuowen Jiezi*, one *shi* 䄷 (a unit of weight, one *shi* equals to 60 kilograms) of collected crops can produce twenty *dou* 斗 (a unit of weight; one-tenth of one *shi*) of *su* 粟 (grain), or ten-*dou mi* 米 (rice), the process of which is known as *hui* 毇 (husk rice), or six-and-half-*dou can* 粲 (polished rice)."

However, the Bamboo Slips Unearthed from Qin Tombs in Shuihudi says: "One *shi* 䄷 of collected crops can produce twenty-*dou su* 粟 (grain) and can be processed into ten-*dou mi* 米 (rice); and ten *dou* of *can* 粲 (polished rice) can be processed into six-and-half-*dou huimi* 毇(殼)米." The notes of Bamboo Slips Unearthed from Qin Tombs in Shuihudi reckon that the description about *can* 粲 in *Shuowen Jiezi* should be revised according to the bamboo slips. We used to think that *hui* 毇 and *can* 粲 are interchangeable in *Shuowen Jiezi*. Now, with the unearthing of the Zhangjiashan Han-Dynasty Bamboo Slips, we finally know it is not the fact. *Suanshu Shu* 算数书 (Book of Mathematics), of the Bamboo Slips Unearthed from the Han Tombs in Zhangjiashan, says, "王程曰：稻禾一石为粟廿斗，舂之为米十斗，为毇(殼)粲米六斗泰(大)半斗" (Wang Cheng 王程 said that 'one *shi* 石 (a unit of weight, one *shi* equals to 60 kilograms) of collected crops can produce twenty-*dou su* 粟 (grain) and can be processed into ten-*dou mi* 米 (rice) or pestled into six-and-half-*dou can* 粲 (polished rice)). The note in the Bamboo Slips Unearthed from Han Tomb in Zhangjiashan explained, "According to *Cang Lü* 仓律 (Law of Granary), '*can* 粲' in the bamboo slips is a redundant character due to misprinting or miscopying." Now, we can see that this note is incorrect. In fact, the statement in Bamboo Slips Unearthed from Han Tomb in Zhangjiashan and *Shuowen Jiezi* means the same thing, except that the sentence in the bamboo slips should read as "王程曰：稻禾一石，为粟廿斗，舂之为米十斗为毇(殼)，粲米六斗泰(大)半斗". Thus, we have reason to suspect that "*can* 粲" and "*hui* 毇(殼)" were misused as interchangeable characters in the Bamboo Slips Unearthed from Qin Tombs in Shuihudi.

(5) *Shi* 秅 (a unit of weight) in *Shuowen Jiezi* is a unit of weight, equalling 60 kilograms. *Shuowen Jiezi* says, "稻一秅，为粟二十升。禾黍一秅，为粟十六升大半升" (one *shi* of collected crops can produce twenty *sheng* 升 (a unit of weight; one-tenth of *dou*) of *su* 粟 (grain), and one-*shi* millet can produce grain weighing sixteen *sheng* 升 and a half).

Scholars of the Qing Dynasty have pointed out that the *sheng* 升 in the previous paragraph is mistaken for *dou* 斗. The Bamboo Slips Unearthed from Qin Tombs in Shuihudi shows that "one *shi* 石 (a unit of weight, one *shi* equals to 60 kilograms) of collected crops can produce twenty *dou* of *su* 粟 (grain)", which proved that what scholars of the Qing Dynasty said is correct. There is similar proof in the *Suanshu Shu* 算数书 (Book of Mathematics) of the Bamboo Slips Unearthed from the Han Tombs in Zhangjiashan.

(6) According to *Shuowen Jiezi*, one *shi* of *su* 粟 (grain) is equal to sixteen and a half *dou* of grain and can be processed into one *hu* 斛 (a unit of weight and equals to some five or ten *dou*) of *li* 糲 (coarse rice).

The note in *Suanshu Shu* 算数书 (Book of Mathematics) of the Bamboo Slips Unearthed from the Han Tombs in Zhangjiashan indicated that "禾黍一石，为粟十六斗泰(大)半斗，舂之为糲米一石" (one *shi* 石 (a unit of weight, one *shi* equals to 60 kilograms) of collected crops can produce sixteen and half *dou* 斗 of *su* 粟 (grain) or be pestled into one *shi* 石 of *li* 糲 (coarse rice). According to this text and the note of "*shi* 秅" in *Shuowen Jiezi* (see above), "*shi* 秅" in "粟重一秅"

(one *shi* of *su* 粟 (grain)) in *Shuowen Jiezi* should be the weight of the collected crops instead of *su* 粟 (grain), as "*heshu* 禾黍" and "*daohe* 稻禾" refer to crops while "*su* 粟" refers to unhusked rice or grains. Perhaps, the sentence in *Shuowen Jiezi* should read as "粟，重一柘为十六斗太半斗，舂为米一斛曰糳 (one *shi* of *su* 粟 (grain) is equal to sixteen and a half *dou* of grain and can be processed into one *hu* 斛 (a unit of weight and equals to some five or ten *dou*) of *li* 糲 (coarse rice))", and "重一柘" and refers to the weight of *heshu* 禾黍 (crops) instead of *su* 粟 (grain). Wang Yun 王筠 (1784–1854) pointed out in *Shuowen Jiezi Judu* 说文解字句读 (Interpretations to *Shuowen Jiezi*), "The sentence should be revised as '禾黍重一柘，为粟十六斗太半斗 (one *shi* of *heshu* 禾黍 (crops) can be processed into sixteen and a half *dou* of *su* 粟 (grain))' according to the interpretation of *shi* 柘."

(7) *Hui* 毇 in *Shuowen Jiezi* means to pound or grind one *hu* 斛 (a unit of weight and equals some five or ten *dou*) of rice into eight *dou* of polished rice."
"*Zuo* 糳 means to pound one *hu* 斛 (a unit of weight and equals to some five or ten *dou*) of *li* 糲 (coarse rice) into nine *dou* of polished rice."

In the Qing Dynasty, works such as *Shuowen Jiezi Jiaolu* 说文解字校录 by Niu Shuyu 钮树玉 (1760–1827), *Shuowen Jiaoyi* 说文校议 by Yan Zhangfu 严章福 (date of birth and death is unknown), *Shuowen Jiezi Zhu* 说文解字注 (Notes to *Shuowen Jiezi*) by Duan Yucai 段玉裁 (1735–1815), and *Shuowen Jiezi Yizheng* 说文解字义证 by Gui Fu 桂馥 (1736–1805) all thought that "*badou* 八斗" in "毇，米一斛舂为八斗也 (the process of pounding or grinding one *hu* of rice into eight *dou* of polished rice is known as *hui* 毇)" should be corrected to "*jiudou* 九斗", and "*jiudou* 九斗" in "糳，糲米一斛舂为九斗曰糳 (*zuo* 糳 means to pound one *hu* of *li* 糲 (coarse rice) into nine *dou* of polished rice)" should be corrected to "*badou* 八斗". The contemporary works, such as *Shuowen Jiezi Yuezhu* 说文解字约注 and *Shuowen Jiezi Jinshi* 说文解字今释, all agreed with it. However, according to "糲米一石为糳(糳)米九斗，九[斗]为毇(毇)米八斗" (one *shi* of *li* 糲 (coarse rice) can be processed into nine *dou* of *zuo* 糳(糳), which can be further processed into eight *dou* of *huimi* 毇(毇)米) in Bamboo Slips Unearthed from Qin Tombs in Shuihudi and "糲米一石为糳米九斗，糳米[九]斗为毇(毇)米八斗" (one *shi* of *li* 糲 (coarse rice) can be processed into nine *dou* of *zuo* 糳, which can be further processed into eight *dou* of *huimi* 毇(毇)米) in Bamboo Slips Unearthed from the Han Tombs in Zhangjiashan, we can see that the relevant description in *Shuowen Jiezi* is correct. Besides, in Xu Kai's edition, there is a character "*li* 糲" before "*mi* 米" in "米一斛舂为八斗也", and the same character could be found in *Liushu Gu* 六书故 (A linguistic work compiled by Dai Dong, a scholar, during the end of the Song Dynasty). The unearthed bamboo slips further proved it.

(9) *Bai* 粺 in *Shuowen Jiezi* refers to polished rice.

According to *Suanshu Shu* 算数书 (Book of Mathematics) of the Bamboo Slips Unearthed from the Han Tombs in Zhangjiashan, the sentences "米十为粺九，为

毁(毇)八 (ten units of *mi* 米 (rice) can be processed into nine units of *bai* 粺 (polished rice) or eight units of *hui* 毀(毇) (husked rice)" and "米少半升为毁(毇)米十五分升之四 (one-third *sheng* of *mi* 米 (rice) can be processed into four-fifteenth *sheng* of *hui* 毀(毇) (husked rice))", shows that "*bai* 粺" and "*hui* 毀" are two different things, which is consistent with the description in *Jiuzhang Suanshu* 九章算术 (Nine Chapters on the Mathematical Art). Thus, I think "*hui* 毀" in "粺，毀也" in *Shuowen Jiezi* should be "*zuo* 繫".

(9) According to *Shuowen Jiezi*, *ye* 擪 means to use a finger to press.

The note in *Shuowen Tongxun Dingsheng* 说文通训定声 (An Explanatory Book of Phonetic Sounds) by Zhu Junsheng 朱骏声 (1788–1858) said, "'*yizhi* 一指 (a finger)' should be corrected to '*yizhi* 以指 (use fingers)'". In Bamboo Slips Unearthed from the Han Tombs in Zhangjiashan, the sentence "失欲口不合，引之，两手奉其颐，以两拇指口中擪" (To fix a dislocated jaw, one needs to hold the jaw with both hands and put both thumbs into the mouth to press mandible.) shows that *ye* 擪 means to use fingers to press something instead of "one finger", which proved that Zhu Junsheng's note is correct.

(10) According to *Shuowen Jiezi*, it was stipulated in *Weilv* 尉律 that "学僮十七已上，始试。讽籀书九千字，乃得为吏。又以八体试之，郡移太史并课，最者以为尚书史" (Students who are seventeen years old or above have right to take the examination. People with ability to read and write nine thousand words could secure an official position. Eight writing styles serve as the test, and *Junxian* 郡县 (official position in ancient China) and *Taishi* 太史 (official position in ancient China) shared lessons. The best among them would be appointed as Chief of Secretariat 尚书史 (Official position in ancient China).).

However, it was written in *Han Shu* 汉书 (The History of the Han Dynasty) that "汉兴，萧何草律，亦著其法曰：'太史试学童，能讽书九千字以上，乃得为史。又以六体试之。课最者，以为尚书御史、史书令史" (Xiao He 萧何 enacted the law that *Taishi* 太史 is responsible for testing students, who with ability to read and write nine thousand words or more could serve as *shi* 史 (an official title in ancient China), and six writing styles are in included in test as well. And the best performer could be appointed as *shangshu yushi* 尚书御史 and *shishu lingshi* 史书令史). "*Fengzhou* 讽籀 (read aloud)" and "*weili* 为吏" in *Shuowen Jiezi* was written as "*feng* 讽" and "*weishi* 为史" in *Han Shu* 汉书 (The History of the Han Dynasty), respectively. According to the description, "试史学童以十五篇，能风(讽)书五千字以上，乃得为史。有(又)以八体试之，郡移其八体课大史，大史诵课，取最一人以为其县令史，殿者勿以为史。三岁壹并课，取最一人以为尚书卒史 (a student who can recite over 5000 characters from *Shizhoupian* (early school primer in great seal script) could serve as *shi* 史 (an official title in ancient China), and the student who is ranked first in the eight-writing-style test could serve as *lingshi* 令史 (an official title in ancient China) and the student who ranked the last wouldn't obtain the title of *shi*. After a term of three years, the best student could serve as *zushi* 卒史 (an official title in ancient China) for the minister)" in Bamboo Slips Unearthed from Han Tomb in Zhangjiashan, we can see that the use of "*feng* 讽" and "*weishi* 为史" in *Han Shu* 汉书 (The History of the Han Dynasty) is correct.

Note

1 The original Chinese version was published in *Research in Ancient Chinese Language* 古汉语研究 in 2004 (issue 2).

References

[1] The Group for Sorting Qin Bamboo Slips Unearthed at Shuihudi: *Qin Bamboo Slips Unearthed at Shuihudi*, Beijing: Cultural Relics Press, 1990.
[2] Xu Shen: *Shuowen Jiezi*, Beijing: Zhonghua Book Company, 1963.
[3] Wang Guiyuan: *Proofreading Notes to Shuowen Jiezi*, Shanghai: Academia Press, 2002.
[4] The Group for Sorting Bamboo Slips in No. 247 Han Tomb in Zhangjiashan: *Han Bamboo Slips Unearthed in Zhangjiashan (No. 247)*, Beijing: Cultural Relics Press, 2001.

20 A New Study on the Explanations of *Shuowen Jiezi*[1]

I.

The existing versions of *Shuowen Jiezi* 说文解字 (An Explication of Written Characters) uses 守备者 (defender) to explain the character *shou* 獸 and point out that it is a combination of *shou* 兽 (defender) and *quan* 犬 (dog). They define *shou* 兽 (defender) as the radical of the character.

As to the explanation of character *shou* 獸, annotators of various ages are divided: some say the character refers to domestic beasts, such as Xu Hao 徐灏 (1810–1879) and Wang Yun 王筠 (1784–1854); some, such as Yang Shuda 杨树达 (1885–1956), hold that it is probably the original form of *shou* 狩 (hunting). Xu Hao's 徐灏 *Shuowen Jiezi Zhujian* 说文解字注笺 (Notes to *Shuowen Jiezi*) gives the following explanation: "Since beasts may normally be used for preventing people from harms, and be good at standing sentinel, they are called as defenders." In his *Shuowen Jiezi Judu* 说文解字句读 (Interpretations to *Shuowen Jiezi*), Wang Yun 王筠 says, "Dogs can keep sentry. In this sense, the character shall be arranged under radical 犬 (dog), but the fact is that it is arranged under radical *shou* 兽 (defender). This arrangement seems to show that the character refers to beasts that are primarily used to serve human beings' needs." In his *Jiweju Xiaoshu Shulin* 积微居小学述林 (Dissertations on Chinese Characters in Many-A-Little Residence), Yang Shuda 杨树达 annotates that the character 獸 might be the original form of *shou* 狩 (hunting). Yang Shuda's 杨树达 view is echoed by *Great Chinese Dictionary* 汉语大字典. In the dictionary, the first meaning of *shou* 獸 is "hunting". In *Shuowen Jiezi* 说文解字, before the entry of *shou* 獸, there is the entry of *shou* 兽, which explains that *shou* 兽 is synonymous with *chan* 犝 (domestic animals). Nevertheless, the entry of *shou* 獸 does not contain any content indicating that this character is used to refer to beasts. Given that *Shuowen Jiezi*'s explanation does not denote beasts, Xu Kai's 徐锴 (920–974) edition of *Shuowen Jiezi* uses 守备也 (to stand sentry) to explain character *shou* 獸. *Jingdian Shiwen* 经典释文 (Textual Explanations of Classics and Canons) adopts this explanation and adds that there is another saying about the meaning of the character: "Among all animals, those with two feet are called *qin* 禽 (fowl), and those with four feet, *shou* 獸." Given the above analysis, it is reasonable to infer that the explanation of *shou* 獸 in the original version of *Shuowen Jiezi* should be 守备也 (to stand sentry) instead of 守备者

(defender). *Guangya* 广雅 (Guangya Dictionary) and *Xilin Yinyi* 希麟音义 (Pronunciation and Meaning by Xilin) use 守也 (to guard) to explain character *shou* 獸. Although many research results suggest that *shou* 獸 means *shou* 守 (guarding), it is difficult to find evidence from passed-down ancient written materials to support this viewpoint. Fortunately, many unearthed Chu-State Bamboo Slips provide evidence to support this view. Relevant evidence is sorted out as follows:

(1) Virtuous men, therefore, should be experienced and knowledgeable, and they shall guard the truth they found. [No. 38 slip of Guodian Chu Bamboo Slips · *Zi Yi* (郭店楚简·缁衣)].
(2) Once withdrawing one's internal awareness from without, one should turn the state into a normal and constantly keep it within by an engrossed way. [No. 24 slip of Guodian Chu Bamboo Slips · the copy (part A) of the Philosophy of *Laozi* (郭店楚简·老子甲本)].
(3) Diverse thoughts as one might adhere to, just like a room filled with gems of all kinds, it is impossible to keep all of them. [No. 38 slip of Guodian Chu Bamboo Slips · the copy (part A) of the Philosophy of *Laozi* (郭店楚简·老子甲本)].
(4) We should, thereupon, unite the people with good faith. [No. 1 slip of *Chu-State Bamboo Slips of the Warring States Period: A Collection of Shanghai Museum · Cong Zheng* (Part A) (上海博物馆藏战国楚竹书·从政甲)]
(5) The ways are intangible, and it will be satisfactory to a great extent for one to keep one of the ways. [No. 43 slip of Guodian Chu Bamboo Slips · *Liu De* (郭店楚简·六德)].
(6) If people of high social position could follow the principle of the ways in their governance, the people will naturally submit themselves to their authority. [No. 18 and No. 19 slips of Guodian Chu Bamboo Slips · the copy (part A) of the Philosophy of *Laozi* (郭店楚简·老子甲本)]

The examples set out above not only support the view that the explanation of *shou* 獸 in the original version of *Shuowen Jiezi* should be 守备也 (to stand sentry) instead of 守备者 (defender), but also prove that the explanation made by *Shuowen Jiezi* is based on documentary evidence.

II.

In the existing versions of *Shuowen Jiezi* 说文解字, the character *wei* 㣲 is regarded as a synonym for *miao* 妙 (fine) and explained as a combination of radical *ren* 人 (person), a component *pu* 攴 (tap), and a simplified phonetic component *qi* 豈 (how).

Some sinologists questioned this explanation, saying that the character is a synonym for *miao* 眇 (trivial) instead of *miao* 妙 (fine). This view can be found in the following books: Duan Yucai's 段玉裁 (1735–1815) *Shuowen Jiezi Zhu* 说文解字注 (Notes to *Shuowen Jiezi*), Yan Kejun's 严可均 (1672–1843) *Shuowen Jiezi Jiaoyi* 说文校议 (Proofreading Remarks on *Shuowen Jiezi*), and Wang Yun's 王

筠 (1784–1854) *Shuowen Jiezi Judu* 说文解字句读 (Interpretations to *Shuowen Jiezi*). Duan Yucai 段玉裁 said, "凡古言㱁 妙者，即今之微妙字。眇者，小也，引伸为凡细之偁。 The character *miao* 眇 (trivial) in the explanation of 㱁 has been falsified as 妙 (fine) by some copies of *Shuowen Jiezi*; hence, I correct them here and now. The ancient word 㱁 妙 is equivalent to the currently used word *weimiao* 微妙 (delicacy). The meaning of *miao* 眇 (trivial) can be extended, and it can be used to imply delicacy." His views are very influential and widely cited. Since the character *wei* 㱁 is regarded as a synonym for *miao* 妙 (beautiful) in all the existing editions of *Shuowen Jiezi,* many researchers still firmly support this view. However, this view is not adopted in *Guangyun* 广韵 (a linguistic work by Chen Pengyuan and Qiuyong in the Song Dynasty), *Wen Xuan* 文选 (Anthology of Poems and Proses), and *Zhuanli Wanxiang Mingyi* 篆隶万象名义 (Dictionary of Seal- and Official-Script Characters), as the relevant researchers argued that there was not enough evidence to support this view. *Guangya* 广雅 (Guangya Dictionary) does not agree with this view either. It annotates: "*miao* 妙 means *hao* 好 (good)." It was impossible to determine which point of view was correct in the past because the then-available handed-down ancient books could not provide any reliable evidence. Now, the unearthed Chu bamboo slips testify that *wei* 㱁 is indeed a synonym for *miao* 妙 (fine). Relevant examples from the unearthed bamboo slips include the following:

(1) To bear a son, he must be more seemly than others. [No. 35 slip of the Bamboo Slips unearthed from the No.5 and No.6 Tombs at Jiudian (九店楚简)]
(2) People all over the world know that what makes one appear beautiful is none other than another ill-looking one. [No. 15 slip of Guodian Chu Bamboo Slips · the copy (part A) of the Philosophy of *Laozi* (郭店楚简·老子甲本)]
(3) He favours the good-looking while rejecting the unsightly. [No. 3 slip of *Chu-State Bamboo Slips of the Warring States Period: A Collection of Shanghai Museum ·Xi Zhe Jun Lao* (上海博物馆藏战国楚竹书·昔者君老)]
(4) Virtuous men are not only clear about what people deem is beautiful, but also hold that they know people should stay committed to their conviction. [No. 38 slip of Guodian Chu Bamboo Slips · *Liu De* (郭店楚简·六德)]

III.

Xu Xuan's 徐铉 (917–992) edition of *Shuowen Jiezi* 说文解字 explains character *zun* 墫 (dance) with the following Chinese sentence：墫，舞也. In the book, the character *zun* 墫 (dance) is explained as a synonym for *wu* 舞 (dance) and a combination of radical *shi* 士 (man) and phonetic component *zun* 尊 (respect). To explain the usage of this character, the book quotes a line from *Shi Jing* 诗经 (The Book of Songs): 墫墫舞我 (Elegantly, I dance).

Wang Niansun 王念孙 (1744–1832) says in his *Wangshi Du Shuowen Ji* 王氏读说文记 (Wang Niansun's Notes to *Shuowen Jiezi*), "*Shuowen Jiezi Xizhuan* 说文解字系传 (The Explanation to *Shuowen Jiezi*) annotates that '*zun* 墫 means dance, with a radical *shi* 士 (man) and reading as that of *zun* 尊 (respect)'. It also points out that, in accordance with *Zhou Li* 周礼 (Rites of the Zhou Dynasty), this character is used to describe *shiwu* 士舞, which is a dance performed by men. *Jingdian Shiwen* 经典释文 (Textual Explanations of Classics and Canons) adopts this view and explains *zun* 墫 as *shiwu* 士舞 (a dance performed by men). This view can prove the rationality of the radical *shi* 士 (man), and *shiwu* 士舞 is probably the original explanation of *zun* 墫 (dance)." This seemingly reasonable analysis by Wang Niansun 王念孙 was not adopted by other sinologists. Zhang Shunhui's 张舜徽 (1911–1992) *Shuowen Jiezi Yuezhu* 说文解字约注 (Notes for *Shuowen Jiezi*) and Tang Kejing's 汤可敬 (1940–?), *Shuowen Jiezi Jinshi* 说文解字今释 (New Explanations on *Shuowen Jiezi*) still explain the character as *wu* 舞 (dance) instead of *shiwu* 士舞 (a dance performed by men).

In fact, Wang Niansun's 王念孙 viewpoint is probably correct. To explain this, it is a must to first explain two marks, namely the repetition mark and the pronoun mark, which are widely used in the manuscripts dating back to the Warring States Period (475–221 BCE) and the Qin (221–207 BCE) and Han (206 BCE–220 CE) dynasties and in Dunhuang Rolls (paper or silk rolls found in Dunhuang, Gansu province, China). The repetition mark is used to indicate that the character above/before it is to be repeated. (The ancient Chinese was often written vertically and from right to left). The pronoun mark is used to represent a component of the character appearing besides it, and this component can also serve as a character. The repetition mark appears in the following unearthed ancient manuscripts:

(1) Guodian Chu Bamboo Slips · the copy (part A) of the Philosophy of *Laozi* (郭店楚简·老子甲本): 智(知)之者弗言=之者弗智(知), which is equal to 智(知)之者弗言言之者弗智(知) (Those knowing it do not air their views whereas those airing their views do not know it).
(2) Guodian Chu Bamboo Slips · *Zi Yi* (郭店楚简·缁衣): 上帝板=下民卒担(瘅), which is 上帝板板下民卒担(瘅) (When the ruling governors behave against the well-established ways, the broad mass will be cursed with all sufferings).
(3) Guodian Chu Bamboo Slips · *Liu De* (郭店楚简·六德): "古(故)夫=妇=父=子=君=臣=, which is equivalent to 古(故)夫夫妇妇父父子子君君臣臣" (In the past, a husband deported as a husband should do, and a wife as a wife should do; a father as a father; a son as a son; a monarch as a monarch; an official as an official).
(4) Bamboo Slips Unearthed from the Qin Tombs in Shuihudi · *Xiao Lü* (睡虎地秦墓竹简·效律): 官嗇夫免县令=人效其官, which is 官嗇夫免县令令人效其官 (As the official Qiangfu was dismissed from his office, the county head ordered personnel to audit his government office).

The pronoun mark can be found in the following unearthed ancient manuscripts:

(1) *Chu-States Bamboo Slips of the Warring States Period: A Collection of Shanghai Museum · Confucius's Theory on Poetry* (上海博物馆藏战国楚竹书·孔子诗论): 孔=曰此命也夫, which is 孔子曰此命也夫. (Confucius asked, "Is this also what Providence has foreordained?")

(2) *Chu-States Bamboo Slips of the Warring States Period: A Collection of Shanghai Museum · Zi Gao* (上海博物馆藏战国楚竹书·子羔): 子羔昏(问)于孔=曰, which is 子羔昏(问)于孔子曰 (Zigao asks Confucius).
(3) *Chu Bamboo Slips Unearthed in Guodian · Zi Yi* (郭店楚简·缁衣): 吾夫=共(恭)且俭, which is 吾大夫共(恭)且俭 (We high-ranking officials lead a frugal and reverent life).
(4) *Bamboo Slips from the Yinqueshan Han Tombs · Sun Bing's Art of War* (银雀山汉墓竹简·孙膑兵法): 都夫=孰为不识事, which is 都大夫孰为不识事. (Among our leading generals, who are the ones inferior in the art of war?)

The repetition mark can be found in an unearthed Tang-Dynasty (618–907) manuscript of *Shuowen Jiezi* (唐写本《说文》木部残卷), which mainly contains entries arranged under the radical *mu* 木 (wood). In all the following entries, the repetition mark "=" is used to indicate that the character above/before it is to be repeated.

(1) 槶，=㓒(槶㓒)，裛器也。从木，威声。(The character *wei* 槶 means *weiyu* 槶㓒, (portable indoor toilet), consisting of the radical *mu* 木 (wood) and a phonetic component *wei* 威 (power).)
(2) 栙，=双也 (栙双也)。从木，夅声。读若鸿。(The character *jiang* 栙 means *jiangshuang* 栙双 (sails made of bamboo mats), consisting of the radical *mu* 木 (wood) and a phonetic component *jiang* 夅 (to descend).)
(3) 梱，=斗(梱斗)，可以射鼠。从木，固声。(The character *gu* 梱 means *gudou* 梱斗 (an appliance used for shooting rats), consisting of the radical *mu* 木 (wood) and a phonetic component *gu* 固 (to solidify).)
(4) 枥，=撕(枥撕)，柙指也。从木，历声。(The character *li* 枥 is equivalent to *lixi* 枥撕 (a cage used for keeping a beast in), consisting of the radical *mu* 木 (wood) and a phonetic component *li* 历.)

This unearthed manuscript proves that handwritten copies of *Shuowen Jiezi* before the Tang Dynasty probably contain repetition and pronoun marks. Nevertheless, the Song-Dynasty (960–1279) block-printed copies of *Shuowen Jiezi* [Xu Kai's 徐锴 (920–974) or Xu Xuan's 徐铉 (917–992) edition] do not contain such marks. The most likely explanation is Xu Kai 徐锴 and Xu Xuan 徐铉 probably replaced the marks with characters in the process of editing the book. In such a process, it was impossible to avoid problems, such as clerical errors and misreadings. Given this analysis, it is reasonable to speculate that, in the original version of *Shuowen Jiezi*, the Chinese sentence used to explain the character *zun* 墫 (dance) is 墫=舞也, which contains a pronoun mark representing *shi* 士 (man). This sentence 墫士舞也 can be translated as "*zun* 墫 means a dance performed by men", which coincides with Wang Niansun's 王念孙 viewpoint about *zun* 墫. Xu Xuan 徐铉 might have neglected the mark "=" in 墫=舞也, so he misread the sentence as 墫舞也. Given this, he explained *zun* 墫 as a synonym for *wu* 舞 (dance). Xu Kai 徐锴 probably understood the mark as a repetition mark, so he misread the sentence as 墫墫舞也.

IV.

In the existing versions of *Shuowen Jiezi* 说文解字, *ti* 替 (to replace) is explained as a synonym from *fei* 废 (to abolish) and a combination of *bing* 竝 (to combine) and a phonetic component *bai* 白 (white). The explanation (替废也一偏下也从竝白声) contains four characters, 一偏下也, which causes controversies.

Qing-Dynasty (1636–1912) scholars offered two explanations for 一偏下也:

(1) some such as Yan Kejun 严可均 and Duan Yucai 段玉裁 argue that 一偏下也 indicates another meaning of the character *ti* 替 (to replace); and

(2) Some, including Xu Hao 徐灏 and Wang Yun 王筠), hold that 一偏下也 is a supplementary explanation for *fei* 废 (to abolish). In *Shuowen Jiezi Jiaoyi* 说文校议 (Proofreading Remarks on *Shuowen Jiezi*), Yan Kejun 严可均 observes that there may be some scribal error in the explanation of *ti* 替. To be more specific, he thinks 废也一偏下也 should be 废也。一曰偏下也 [It (character *ti* 替) means "to abolish", or one side falling]. Duan Yucai 段玉裁 annotates in his *Shuowen Jiezi Zhu* 说文解字注 (Notes to *Shuowen Jiezi*) that 一偏下也 indicates another meaning of the character. Xu Hao 徐灏 annotates in his *Shuowen Jiezi Zhujian* 说文解字注笺 (Notes to *Shuowen Jiezi*) that there is some clerical error in the explanation of *ti* 替, and the original sentence should be 一偏下之废也. In *Shuowen Jiezi Judu* 说文解字句读 (Interpretations to *Shuowen Jiezi*), Wang Yun (王筠) says, "Character *ti* 替 is a synonym for *fei* 废 (to abolish) in accordance with *Erya* 尔雅 (Erya Dictionary). The character *ti* 替 means to invariably abolish and be no longer to be restored in *Shi Jing* 诗经 (The Book of Songs) and *Zuo Zhuan* 左传 (Zuo's Commentary on the Spring and Autumn Annals): 勿替引之 (Never abolish this ceremony and carry it on forever, and you will enjoy welfare and be blessed); 王替隗氏 (The king abolished Huai's 'regime' as well as others). Xu Shen 许慎 (ca. 58–147) added 一偏下 to the explanation of the character *ti* 替 probably because he thought that *fei* 废 (to abolish) and *ti* 替 (to replace) did not mean exactly the same thing. In this sense, 一偏下 is used for supplementary explanation 一偏下 probably describes such a situation: one side collapses though, another side fails to collapse."

Professor Liu Zhao (刘钊) put forward a new explanation for 一偏下. He points out in his article, "A Talk on the Significance of Archaeological Data for the Study of Shuowen," 谈考古资料在〈说文〉研究中的重要性 that "一偏下" means "one placed a little lower than the other" and describes the structure of the character *ti* 替. He also uses a citation from *Huilin Yin Yi* 慧林音义 (Explanations for Pronunciation and Meaning from Monk Huilin) to support his point of view: 废也。两并立，一偏下曰替 [It (character *ti* 替) means "to abolish". It consists of two characters *li* 立 (stand) arranged side by side, and one of the characters is placed a little lower than the other one.]. This viewpoint is also supported by archaeological evidence. The forms of *ti* 替 that appear in oracle-bone inscriptions and on the tripod cauldron of the Zhongshan King fit this description: ᝰ [two characters *li* 立 (stand) arranged side by side, and one of the characters is placed a little lower than the other one].

Unfortunately, Professor Liu Zhao's explanation is not completely in line with the description in *Shuowen Jiezi*: the seal-script form of *ti* 替 included in the book is 替, whose upper part is two *li* 立 (stand) arranged side by side but on the same horizontal level. The most likely explanation for this is as follows:

(1) The original seal-script form of *ti* 替 included in *Shuowen Jiezi* should be 替, whose upper part was two *li* 立 (stand) arranged side by side but on different horizontal levels.

(2) 一偏下 (one placed a little lower than the other) described 立立 (*ti* 替). 立立 appears earlier than 替, and 替 is a combination of 立立 and a phonetic component 白 that is a variant of *zi* 自 meaning nose. The addition of such a phonetic component is a common phenomenon in the evolution of Chinese characters.

(3) The character form 替 gradually developed into 替. This change was probably caused by evolutionary reasons that made characters decreasingly pictographic. It could also be caused by some clerical errors.

(4) Due to the change described in (3), 一偏下 (one placed a little lower than the other) stopped making any sense in the explanation of *ti* 替, so the explanation was modified and reinterpreted. A possible modified version of the explanation is 废也两并立一偏下也白声 [It (*ti* 替) is synonymous with *fei* 废 (to abolish), consisting of two *li* 立 (stand) arranged side by side but on different horizontal levels and reading as *zi* 白].

Note

1 The original Chinese version was published in the 3rd Volume of the *Study of Shuowen Jiezi* 说文学研究 by Jiangxi Education Press in June 2008。

References

[1] Xu Shen: *Shuowen Jiezi*, Beijing: Zhonghua Book Company, 1963.
[2] Jingmen Museum: *Bamboo Slips Unearthed from Chu Tombs in Guodian*, Beijing: Cultural Relics Press, 1998.
[3] Ma Chengyuan: *Chu-States Bamboo Slips of the Warring States Period: A Collection of Shanghai Museum* (Vol. 1), Shanghai: Shanghai Classics Publishing House, 2001.
[4] Ma Chengyuan: *Chu-States Bamboo Slips of the Warring States Period: A Collection of Shanghai Museum* (Vol. 2), Shanghai: Shanghai Classics Publishing House, 2002.
[5] Ma Chengyuan: *Chu Books Written on Bamboo Slips Preserved in Shanghai Museum* (Vol. 3), Shanghai: Shanghai Classics Publishing House, 2003.

21 Mutual Corroboration Between *Shuowen Jiezi* and Chu-State Bamboo Slips[1]

In theory, *Shuowen Jiezi* 说文解字 (An Explication of Written Characters) and unearthed Chu-State bamboo slips can be used to corroborate each other. The former discusses Chinese characters used in the manuscripts and bronze inscriptions of the Warring States Period (475–221 BCE), and the latter dates to this period. A comparative study also finds 120-plus common characters between the two. As *Shuowen Jiezi* has been handed down as hand-copied books for years, it is not surprising to find scribal errors in the existing copies of the book. Given this, this study takes unearthed Chu-State bamboo slips as a reliable reference to modify some scribal errors in *Shuowen Jiezi*.

I.

Shuowen Jiezi 说文解字 explains character *jun* 㕁 (君, monarch) as a combination of radical *kou* 口 (mouth) and component *yin* 尹 (administer) and points out that its archaic form is 㕁, which depicts a sitting monarch.

The archaic form listed in the book is questionable because in the Chu-State bamboo slips collected by Shanghai Museum (hereinafter referred to as the SH Chu Slips), the character is written as 㕁, a combination of 尹 (尹 administer) and *kou* 口 (mouth). Please refer to the following bamboo slips for the use of the two forms:

- Slip 4 of the 2nd Volume of the SH Chu Slips: 㕁 (君)卒, 大(太)子乃亡闻、亡圣(听), which means, "when the monarch passed away, the crown prince turned a deaf ear to distractive information (since he devoted himself to silent mourning)".
- Slip 22 of the 1st Volume of the SH Chu Slips: 《诗》员(云)㕁 (君)子好逑, which means, "*Shi Jing* 诗经 (The Book of Songs) says that a gentleman would like to marry a good girl".
- Slip 64 of Chu Bamboo Slips Unearthed in Guodian (*liude* 六德): 生民斯必又(有)夫妇、父子、 㕁(君)臣, which approximately means, "interpersonal relations can be divided into husband-wife, father-son, monarch-servant relations".

DOI: 10.4324/9781032622965-21

- Slip 8 of Chu Bamboo Slips Unearthed in Guodian: 出而为命(令)𠃌(尹)，遇楚庄也, which approximately means, "served as a high-ranking administer for Zhuanggong of Chu".

The archaic form of *jun* 👤 (君, monarch) listed in *Shuowen Jiezi* clearly differs from the form 👤 used in the Chu slips in the middle part. This difference is probably caused by the missing or accidental damage of certain stroke parts during the circulation of the book.

II.

In *Shuowen Jiezi* 说文解字, the character *gao* 👤 (诰, imperial mandate) is explained as a combination of radical *yan* 言 (speak) and component *gao* 告 (tell), with its archaic form being 👤.

The archive form of the character listed in the book, which is probably wrong, contains three components: the left-placed *yue* 月 (flesh), the right-placed *you* 又 (again), and the middle part *yan* 言 (speak). Nevertheless, this is not the case in unearthed Chu-State bamboo slips. Slip 15 of the 1st Volume of the SH Chu Slips contains such an imperial mandate "《康亯(诰)》员(云)：敬明乃罚", which can be roughly translated as "the monarch says that it is a must to discriminate between rewards and punishments". Slip 38 of Chu Bamboo Slips Unearthed in Guodian (*cheng zhi wen zhi* 成之闻之) contains another imperial mandate "《康亯(诰)》曰：不还大暊", which means, "non-compliance with the laws". The character 亯 can also be written as 👤, a combination of *yan* 言 (speak) and *gong* 廾 (two hands). In comparison with 亯, this form shares more similarities with 👤, but this does not negate the fact that 👤 is a wrong form probably caused by miscopying.

III.

Shuowen Jiezi 说文解字 explains that the character *you* 👤 (友, friend) is a combination of two components: *you* 又 (again) and has two archaic forms, 👤 and 👤.

The first form 👤 appears in the following slips: "一𦫶(友)罢𦫶绘纂又盍，一长羽翣" on Slip 2–019 of the Chu-State Bamboo Slips Unearthed in Xinyang City, Henan Province and "二𦫶(友)□屯又盍，四宫□" on Slip 2–024 of the Chu-State Bamboo Slips Unearthed in Xinyang. The character can also be written as 👤, which is a combination of the form 👤 and *bi* 白 (鼻, nose), such as on Slip 6 of Chu Bamboo Slips Unearthed in Guodian (*yu cong san* 语丛三): 👤(友)，君臣之道也. On Slip 87 of Chu Bamboo Slips Unearthed in Guodian (*yu cong yi* 语丛一), there is such a sentence 君臣、朋👤(友)，丌(其)罢(择)者也 (the monarch-servant relations and friendships are based on mutual choices). Slip 29–30 of Chu Bamboo Slips Unearthed in Guodian (*liude* 六德) bears this sentence: 为宗族𢼛朋友，不为朋友𢼛宗族. 👤 can also be written as 👤, which looks like 👤, the second archaic form of *you* 👤 (友, friend). Given that 👤 is a combination of *you* 双 (友, friend) and *bi* 鼻 (nose) and that 👤 is a combination of *yu* 羽 (feather) and *bi* 鼻 (nose), 👤 is probably a wrong form caused by the miscopying of *you* 双 for *yu* 羽.

IV.

When explaining the character *jian* 臤 (臤, hard), *Shuowen Jiezi* 说文解字 points out that it is a combination of *you* 又 (again) and phonetic component *chen* 臣 (male slave), and that it is an archaic form of character *xian* 贤 (virtuous).

In all unearthed Chu-State silk manuscripts and bamboo slips found so far, 臤 is used as *xian* 贤 (virtuous), and it is not a variant of *xian* 贤. The following slips are evidence:

- Slip 21 of Chu Bamboo Slips Unearthed in Guodian (*tang yu zhi dao* 唐虞之道): 受(授)臤(贤)则民举教而化乎道 (If the throne was bestowed to a virtuous person, people would pursue noble characters).
- Slip 35 of Chu Bamboo Slips Unearthed in Guodian (*zi yi* 缁衣): 亓(其) 上(等) 尊臤(贤)，义也 (It is righteous to respect virtuous people).
- Slip 17 of Chu Bamboo Slips Unearthed in Guodian (*tang wu xing* 五行): 大人不新(亲)亓(其)所臤(贤) (People in power do not approach virtuous people).
- Slip 52–53 of Chu Bamboo Slips Unearthed in Guodian (*yu cong san* 语丛三): 善日过我，我日过善，贤者唯其止也以异 (If others treat me with kindness, I will return the kindness, only that what virtuous people can achieve is different).
- Slip 10 of the 1st Volume of the SH Chu Slips: 童而皆贤于其初者也 (At last, they all became better than they first were).

It is worth noting that the book, *A Collection of Chu-State Characters*,[2] mistakes *qian* 掔 (掔, leash) as *xian* 贤 (virtuous). In accordance with *Longkan Shoujian* 龙龛手鉴 (Longkan Shoujian Word Book), 掔 is a popular form of *qian* 掔 (leash). There is a lot of literature to support this view. *Jiyun* 集韵 (Jiyun Rhyming Dictionary) contains such an entry "掔，牵也" (*qian* 掔 means "leash"). The character also appears in *Shi Ji* 史记 (Records of the Historian): 楚王入自皇门，郑襄公肉袒掔羊以迎 (The king of Chu State entered through the royal gate, and Xianggong of Zheng came out with bared torso, holding a goat on a leash to welcome him.). Slip 16 of Chu Bamboo Slips Unearthed in Guodian (*cheng zhi wen zhi* 成之闻之) bears the following characters: 可御也，而不可掔也 (can be managed instead of being kept on a leash).

V.

Shuowen Jiezi 说文解字 explains *xian* 閒 (gap) as a combination of radical *men* 门 (door) and component *yue* 月 (moon) and names 閞 as its archaic form.

Nevertheless, in unearthed Chu manuscripts, the character has several archaic forms. Slip 6 of the 2nd Volume of the SH Chu Slips (*rong cheng shi* 容成氏) bears the following character: 昔尧凥于丹府与藋陵之▮ (situated between Danfu and Diaoling). ▮ is 閒 (閒). The character is written as ▮ on Slip 9 of the 2nd Volume of the SH Chu Slips (*rong cheng shi* 容成氏): 会才(在) 天地之▮，而橐(包) 才(在)四海之内 (between sky and earth and surrounded by the four seas). Slip 220 of Baoshan Chu-State Bamboo Slips contains the following characters: ▮ (恒)占(贞)吉，庚辛又▮. On this slip, 列 (閒) is written in a simplified form ▮, which looks similar to the inside part of 閞, the archaic form *xian* 閒 (gap) mentioned in *Shuowen Jiezi*. In his book, *Shuowen Jiezi Zhu* 说文解字注 (Notes to *Shuowen Jiezi*), Duan Yucai 段玉裁 (1735–1815) observed that the character had many wrong archaic forms and that its standard form should be a combination of *men* 门 (door) and *wai* 外 (outside). He held that *Shuowen Jiezi* made this mistake because the author neglected that *xi* 夕 (sunset) and *yue* 月 (moon) could be used interchangeably in unearthed Chu-State bamboo slips and gave character 死 as an example. 死 is the archaic form of *heng* 恆 (constant) that originally featured component *yue* 月 (moon), which could be proved by a line from *Shi Jing* 诗经: 如月之恆 (as constant as the moon).

VI.

Shuowen Jiezi 说文解字 points out that the character *fa* 灋 (法, law) consists of three components: *zhi* 廌 (unicorn), *shui* 水 (water), and *qu* 去 (remove). *Shui* 水 means water: as the surface of water always remains flat, this component is used here as a metaphor that courts should stay impartial. The radical *zhi* 廌 (unicorn) originally refers to a legendary animal that enforces laws, and *qu* 去 (remove) indicates that the law is a tool to remove injustice. The book also points out that 佱 is the character's archaic form.

Nevertheless, the Chu-State bamboo slips do not contain such an archaic form. For instance, Slip 14 of the 1st Volume of the SH Chu Slips (*zi yi* 缁衣) contains the following characters: 隹(惟)作五疟之型(刑)曰㦸(法) (executing five kinds of cruel torture to enforce the laws). Xu Kai 徐锴 (920–974) and Wang Yun 王筠 (1784–1854) believed that the character 㦸 is a combination of *ji* 亼 (to assemble) and *zheng* 正 (proper), but the standard form of the character should be 佱, a combination of *quan* 全 (pure jade) and *zheng* 正 (proper). The form 㦸 is probably a result of stroke simplification: the bottom horizontal line of *quan* 全 is merged with the top and bottom horizontal lines of *zheng* 正.

VII.

Shuowen Jiezi 说文解字 explains that the character *jin* 近 (近 approach) consists of component *jin* 斤 (a tool for cutting trees) and radical *chuo* 辵 (walking), a combination of 彳 and *zhi* 止 (toe). 岂 is listed as the character's archaic form in the book.

The character is written as 㡿(近) on Slip 18 and Slip 34 of the 1st Volume of the SH Chu Slips (*xing qing lun* 性情论): 哀、乐，亓(其)眚(性)相㡿(近)也 (sadness and happiness are feelings of the similar nature, Slip 18); 㤅(爱)颣(类)七，唯眚(性) 㤅(爱)为近息(仁) (Slip 34, among the seven types of love, the love for nature is the one closest to the concept of *ren* 仁). Another form of the character 㡿 (近) appears on Slip 36 of Chu Bamboo Slips Unearthed in Guodian (*xing zi ming chu* 性自命出): 从丌(其)所为，㡿(近)旻(得)之壴(矣)，which can be approximately translated "learning through practice is easier (than directly learning the theory)". All these forms are composed of an up-placed component *jin* 斤 (a tool for cutting trees) and a down-placed component *zhi* 止 (toe). These two components appear in , the archaic form of the character *jin* 近 (approach) in *Shuowen Jiezi*, but they are combined in the opposite way. In fact, there are only a few characters featuring an up-placed component *zhi* 止 (toe) in unearthed Chu-State slips. Character *zu* 族 (arrowhead) is written as on Slip 14 of Chu Bamboo Slips Unearthed in Guodian (*yu cong san* 语丛三), and *you* 遊 (roam) is written as on Slip 51 of Chu Bamboo Slips Unearthed in Guodian (*yu cong san* 语丛三). In the form , there is a component *yan* 㫃 (flags flying), which looks like *zhi* 止 (toe). Character *qi* 旂 (flag) is written as on Zhugong He Bell (邾公釛钟) and as on the Dun Container of Qihou (齐侯敦), which feature the same components and compositional structure of . The above analysis reveals that is the archaic form of *qi* 旂 (flag). The reason *Shuowen Jiezi* defines it as the archaic form of *jin* 近 (approach) is that the author probably regarded *qi* 旂 as a loaned character used to express the idea of *jin* 近.

VIII.

In *Shuowen Jiezi* 说文解字, the character *song* (讼argue) is explained as a combination of *yan* 言 (speak) and phonetic component *gong* 公 (just). , a combination of radical *yan* 言 (speak) and component *gu* 谷 (valley) is explained as the archaic form of *song* 讼.

Slip 22 of the 2nd Volume of the SH Chu Slips (*rong cheng shi* 容成氏) contains the following characters: (禹) 乃(建)鼓于廷，(以)为民之又(有) (讼)告者(鼓)焉 (Yu erected a big drum in the court for the people to take a claim or disagreement to court). Character (the official-script form of 讼) derives from (讼), whose right-placed component is *gu* 谷 (valley) but written in a simplified way that makes this component look similar to *qu* 去(leave). Such simplification also occurs to other characters: , the standard seal-script form of *rong* 容 (contain), features component *gu* 谷 (valley), but the character can also be written as featuring component *gong* 公 (just). This phenomenon is caused by the interchangeability of these two phonetic components.

IX.

Shuowen Jiezi 说文解字 explains the character *you* (游, flag streamer) as a combination of radical *yan* 㫃 (flags flying) and component *qiu* 汓 (swim), and as its archaic form.

Slip 12 of the 2nd Volume of the SH Chu Slips (*zi gao* 子羔) bears the following characters: 又(有) (邰)是(氏)之女也，(遊)于串咎之内 (the daughter of the Youtai clan wander among chuan jiu). The character also appears on Slip 188 of Baoshan Chu-State Bamboo Slips: 壬晨(辰)，上猊邑人周乔㒓，(遊)郞、痙亚夫. On Slip 51 of Chu Bamboo Slips Unearthed in Guodian (*yu cong san* 语丛三), the character is written as : 急(仁)，(遊)于 (艺). Both forms consist of components *chuo* 辵 (walking) and *liu* 斿 (wander). The archaic form mentioned in *Shuowen Jiezi* also contains component *chuo* 辵.

X.

In *Shuowen Jiezi* 说文解字, the character *lv* 旅 (旅, a 500-man troop) is described as a combination of radical *yan* 㫃 (flags flying) and component *cong* 从 (follow), and 㫃 is listed as its archaic form.

This archaic form is questionable because, in Chu-State bamboo slips, the form of 㫃 is written as 遷, a combination of *chuo* 辵 (walking), and the archaic form of *lv* 旅, which consists of *yan* 㫃 (flags flying) and *cong* 从 (follow). Slip 4 of Baoshan Chu-State Bamboo Slips contains the following characters: 遷(遷)易(阳)公吕(以)楚帀(师)遷(后)鄚奠(郑)之戠(岁). Slip 119 of the Bamboo Slips Unearthed from the Tomb of Marquis Yi of the Zeng State bear the following: 遷(旅)公三蠶(乘)迻(路)车.

XI.

When discussing the character *zhi* 旨 (delicious), *Shuowen Jiezi* 说文解字 defines it as a combination of *gan* 甘 (delicious) and phonetic component *bi* 匕 (spoon) and points out that 𦥔 is its archaic form.

Slip 26 of Chu-State Bamboo Slips Unearthed in Guodian (*zun de yi* 尊德义) contains such a sentence: 不吕(以)旨(嗜)谷(欲)𡧅(害)亓(其)义 (Do not jeopardize one's morality for hobbies and desires.). In the sentence, *zhi* 旨 is written as 𦥔, which differs from 𦥔 in the upper part: the former's upper part seems to be a mirror-image of that of the latter. The character can also be written as 𦥔 on Slip 10 of Chu-State Bamboo Slips Unearthed in Guodian (*zi yi* 缁衣): 晉(资)夆(冬)𦥔(旨)(祁)沧(寒)，少(小)民亦佳(惟)日悁(怨) (In cold winter, the people only complain about the weather.). The component *gan* 甘 (delicious) is simplified into *kou* 口 (mouth) in this form. As to the archaic form of *zhi* 旨, Duan Yucai 段玉裁 (1735–1815) thought that it should be a combination of *qian* 千 (thousand) and *gan* 甘 (delicious). This view is wrong, according to the unearthed Chu-State slips. In these slips, character *qian* 千 is written as 𠂉, which is different from the component *bi* 匕 (spoon). Apart from appearing in character *zhi*, component *bi* 匕 (spoon) also appears in character *zhou* 卓 (distinguished) in the unearthed Chu-State slips. There is no possibility of confusing these two components. Slip 17 of the 1st Volume of the SH Chu Slips (*zi yi* 缁衣) contains the following sentence: 古(故)言则虑丌(其)所冬(终)，行则旨(稽)丌(其)所蔽(敝) (Consider the consequences of speeches and deeds.). In this sentence, character *zhi* 旨 is written as 𦥔: a combination of *kou* 口 (mouth) and *bi* 匕 (spoon). Given the above analysis, it is reasonable to conclude that the up-placed components in these two forms of *zhi* 旨 in the Chu-State Bamboo Slips are variants of *bi* 匕.

XII.

According to *Shuowen Jiezi* 说文解字, *rong* 容 (contain) consists of radical *mian* 宀 (roofed room) and component *gu* 谷 (valley), and its archaic form 容 features radical *gong* 公 (just).

The character is written as 🅾 on Slip 109 of Chu-State Bamboo Slips Unearthed in Guodian (*yu cong yi* 语丛一) and Slip 24 of Chu-State Bamboo Slips Unearthed in Guodian (*yu cong yi* 语丛二)：啓(号)牙(邪)🅾(容)牙(邪)，夫丌(其)行者；尔 (肆)生于易，🅾(容)生于尔(肆). This shows that the archaic form 🅾 listed in *Shuowen Jiezi* is not correct.

XIII.

Shuowen Jiezi 说文解字 states that *zheng* 徵 (徵, summon) is a combination of radical *ren* 壬 (carry on a shoulder pole) and a simplified form of *wei* 微 (walk clandestinely), means "summoning the ones who live in a lower class but are brilliant". The book lists 徵 as the character's archaic form.

The character can be written in several different ways in the unearthed Chu-State bamboo slips. On Slip 41 of the 2nd Volume of the SH Chu-State Slips (*rong cheng shi* 容成氏), there is such a sentence: 汤于是虐(乎) 徵(徵)九州之帀(师) (Tang summoned the troops of the country). Slip 22 of Chu-State Bamboo Slips Unearthed in Guodian (*xing zi ming chu* 性自命出) contains the following characters: 帀帛，所呂 (以)为信与徵(徵)也 (silk and money were used for treatment). In comparison with the archaic form 徵 listed in *Shuowen Jiezi*, these two forms also feature components *kou* 口 (mouth) and *yan* 言 (speak) but lack component *pu* 攵 (tap). These two forms are possibly two simplified forms of 徵. In comparison with the standard-seal script 徵 listed in *Shuowen Jiezi*, the two archaic forms are a combination of a phonetic component *lu* 艫 (prow of boat) and another component *kou* 口 (mouth), except that *ren* 壬 (carry on a shoulder pole) in the lower part of *lu* 艫 is replaced by *sheng* 升 (litre).

XIV.

In accordance with *Shuowen Jiezi* 说文解字, 捧 (to kneel and touch the ground with the forehead) is a combination of radical *shou* 手 (hand) and component 𣎵, and the character currently known as *bai* 拜 is originally written as 𢫶.

Slip 21 of Chu-State Bamboo Slips Unearthed in Guodian (*xing zi ming chu* 性自命出) contains the following characters: 𢫶(拜)，所呂(以)口口口. Considering that the original text is incomplete, this discovery can be used as evidence to prove that the archaic form 𢫶 listed in *Shuowen Jiezi* is correct.

XV.

Shuowen Jiezi 说文解字 defines *zhi* 㥄 (直, vertical) as a combination of radical *hao* ㄴ (mysterious) and another two components *shi* 十 (ten) and *mu* 目 (eye) and points out that 㥄 is the character's archaic form.

The character is written as 㥄, which is a combination of *zhi* 直 (vertical) and *mu* 木 (wood), in unearthed Chu-State slips. Slip 2 of the 1st Volume of the SH Chu-State Slips (*zi yi* 缁衣) and Slip 3 of Chu-State Bamboo Slips Unearthed in Guodian (*zi yi* 缁衣) contain two similar sentences: 静龏(恭)尔立(位)， 䚻(好)是

正𥄂(直) and 情(靖)共尔立(位)，好氏(是)貞(正)𥄂(直)，which means "treating your responsibility seriously and maintaining good virtue". Slip 34 of Chu-State Bamboo Slips Unearthed in Guodian (*wu xing* 五行) bears the following characters: 訬(辯)肰(然)而正行之，𥄂(直)也 (distinguish right from wrong and take the right path). *Shuowen Jiezi* 说文解字 included other characters consisting of *zhi* 直 (vertical). According to the book, character *sheng* 省 (examine) has a standard-seal-script form 𣈵 and an archaic form 𥄙, and character *mu* 睦 (harmonious) has a standard-seal-script form 睦 and an archaic form 𦣝. Based on the above analysis, there is reason to believe that the common component shared by these characters, which bears a resemblance to *jiong* 囧 (brilliant), is in fact component *mu* 目 (eye).

XVI.

In *Shuowen Jiezi* 说文解字, *guan* 観 (观, observe) is described as a combination of *xian* 见 (appear) and *guan* 雚 (a heron), and 𥊝, which includes the component *jiong* 囧 (brilliant), is defined as the archaic form of the character.

Nevertheless, in unearthed Chu-State slips, the character is written as 𥊝, a combination of *mu* 目 (eye) and phonetic component *guan* 雚 (a heron). Evidence can be found on Slip 3 of the 1st Volume of the SH Chu-State Slips (*kongzi shilun* 孔子诗论) and Slip 25 of Chu-State Bamboo Slips Unearthed in Guodian (*xing zi ming chu* 性自命出)： 邦风，丌(其)内(纳)勿(物)也，專(溥)𥊝(观)人谷(俗)安(焉) (when examining the customs of a country, it is necessary to consider all aspects); 𥊝 (观)《杢(賮)》、《武》，則齐女(如)也异 疢(斯)复(作). In conclusion, *Shuowen Jiezi* gives a wrong archaic form for *guan* 観 (观, observe): the part in 𥊝 is component *mu* 目 (eye) instead of *jiong* 囧 (brilliant). For analysis, please refer to XVI.

Notes

1 The original Chinese version was published in *Research on Chinese Characters* 中国文字研究 in 2008, as the second issue of its 11 of the year by Elephant Press.
2 李守奎：《楚文字编》，第 847 页，上海：华东师范大学出版社，2003.
Li Shoukui: *A Collection of Chu-State Characters*, p. 847, Shanghai: East China Normal University Press, 2003.

References

[1] Henan Institute of Cultural Relics: *Chu-State Tombs at Xinyang*, Beijing: Cultural Relics Press, 1986.
[3] Hubei Provincial Museum: *The Tomb of Marquis Yi of the Zeng State*, Beijing: Cultural Relics Press, 1989.
[2] Hubei Jingsha Railway Archaeological Team: *Baoshan Chu-State Bamboo Slips*, Beijing: Cultural Relics Press, 1991.
[4] Jingmen Municipal Museum: *Guodian Chu-State Bamboo Slips*, Beijing: Cultural Relics Press, 1998.
[6] Ma Chengyuan, ed.: *Chu-State Bamboo Slips of the Warring States Period: A Collection of Shanghai Museum* (Vol. 1), Shanghai: Shanghai Classics Publishing House, 2001.
[6] Ma Chengyuan, ed.: *Chu-State Bamboo Slips of the Warring States Period: A Collection of Shanghai Museum* (Vol. 1), Shanghai: Shanghai Classics Publishing House, 2002.

22 Chinese Words in *Shuowen Jiezi*

A Probe into the Earliest Word Classification Theory of China[1]

The character *ci* 词 is used as a general term for words in contemporary Chinese. Nevertheless, in the Han Dynasty (202 BCE–220 CE), the character was used in a very different way. The Eastern-Han-Dynasty (25–220) scholar Xu Shen 许慎 (ca. 58–147) used *ci* 词 to refer to certain types of function words in *Shuowen Jiezi* 说文解字 (An Explication of Written Characters). For instance, the character *er* 尔 is explained as a modal particle indicating inevitability (词之必然也),[2] and the character *zhi* 只 is defined as a modal particle indicating that the sentence has been completed (语已词也). Given this, the Han-Dynasty people's understanding and classification of Chinese language components or words is an issue worthy of in-depth discussion.

As to the character *ci* 词, *Shuowen Jiezi* 说文解字 gives the following definition: 词，意内而言外也. There have always been different opinions on the interpretation of this definition. Duan Yucai 段玉裁 (1735–1815) gives his view in his book *Shuowen Jiezi Zhu* 说文解字注 (Notes to *Shuowen Jiezi*): *Yi* 意 or ideas are expressed through speech, and *ci* 词 or words are used to record them in writing; *Yi* 意 refers to meanings, *yan* 言 refers to pronunciations, and *ci* 词 refers to combinations of forms and pronunciations. Xu Shen 许慎 used *ziyi* 字义 to refer to ideas expressed through speech and mentioned the combinations of forms and pronunciation only when discussing written language (意即意内，词即言外，言意而词见，言词而意见。意者文字之义也，言者文字之声也，词者文字形声之合也。凡许之说字义皆意内也，凡许之说形说声皆言外也[3]). Duan Yucai 段玉裁 considered *ci* 词 in *Shuowen Jiezi* as a term referring to all Chinese words, which is a misunderstood view. Besides, there are many other mis-interpreted terms in his viewpoint. First, *yi* 意 and *yi* 义 are two different terms in *Shuowen Jiezi*: the former refers to the grammatical purpose of characters, and the latter, to the meanings of written forms.

For example, when discussing the composition of character *qiu* 裘 (fur garments), the book gives the following two different explanations:

(1) the character is a combination of phonetic component *qiu* 求 (fur garments) and another component *yi* 衣 (clothes); and

(2) the character is a pictograph composed in the same way that character *cui* 衰 (mourning garments of hemp) is built, as the two characters' pictographic small-seal-script forms *qiu* 裘(裘) and *cui* 衰(衰) have similar grammatical functions and

contain the same part *yi* 衣 (garments), which indicate that they belong to the same kind. When discussing the character composition of *tu* 圖 (to plan and contrive), the book also uses the character *yi* 意: 圖，画计难也。从口，从啚。啚，难意也. This sentence can be translated as the following: character *tu* 圖 means "to plan and contrive", consisting of *wei* 口 and *bi* 啚, and *bi* 啚 is included here to indicate difficulties. Evidently, *yi* 意 here refers to a grammatical function instead of being a part of the character's meaning. In *Shuowen Jiezi Judu* 说文解字句读 (Interpretations to *Shuowen Jiezi*), Wang Yun 王筠 (1784–1854) emphasized the difference between *ci* 词 and *yan* 言 and explained 意内言外 as follows: 意内言外者 means that *yi* 意 is not expressed directly. It is indirectly reflected through *ci* 词. Sometimes, *yi* 意 and *yan*言 are unified, such as in *shi* 是 (true) and *fei* 非 (false) when used separately, but this is not the case when they are used together with modal particles, such as *ye* 邪. One potential use of *ci* 词 can be observed in the expression "是邪非邪", which includes the characters *shi* 是 (true) and *fei* 非 (false), but its meaning doesn't concern the literal meaning of either. Instead, the expression is commonly used to describe a state of or ambiguity [意内言外者，谓不直说其意，而于词露之也。是曰是，非曰非，其意如此，其言亦如此也。至于语助之词，则如曰是邪非邪，意不定其为是非，而言故曰是非，加两邪字以为助句之词，而其意见[4]]. This point of view can be supported by the following entries in *Shuowen Jiezi*: "白，此亦自字也。省自者，词言之气，从鼻出，与口相助也" (the character *bai* 白 is a simplified form of *zi* 自, uttered in a nasal sound). The juxtaposition of *ci* 词 and *yan* 言 in this entry proves that they are two different concepts. When explaining the character *zai* 哉 (final exclamatory particle), which is a *ci* 词, *Shuowen Jiezi* explicitly points out that the character does not belong to *yan* 言. In Xu Kai's 徐锴 (920–974) book *Shuowen Jiezi Xizhuan* 说文解字系传 (The Explanation to *Shuowen Jiezi*), 言之外者 is explained as follows: characters that do not belong to *yan* 言 such as 惟、思、曰、兮、斯 are modal particles (直言曰言，又一字曰言，惟、思、曰、兮、斯之类，皆在句之外为助[5]).

According to contemporary language-component-classification standards, the following inclusion can be reached: *Shuowen Jiezi* divides Chinese words into two types, namely *ci* 词 that embodies *yi* 意 (the grammatical function of a character) and *yan* 言 that conveys *yi* 义 (meanings). Terms appearing in both definitions above can be used to explain characters in *Shuowen Jiezi* 说文解字, but they have different connotations. For instance, *sui* 㒸 (to follow) is explained as 从意也 in the book. Although Character 从 means "to follow", the use of *yi* 意 here indicates that character *sui* 㒸 is not a verb but a function word that connects information. Duan Yucai's 段玉裁 *Shuowen Jiezi Zhu* 说文解字注 (Notes to *Shuowen Jiezi*) and *Songben Yupian* 宋本玉篇 (Songben Yupian's Regular-Script Dictionary) all pointed out that character *sui* 遂 (to follow) was originally written as *sui* 㒸: *sui* 㒸 is the original form of *sui* 遂 (随从字当作㒸，后世皆以遂为㒸矣[6]); 㒸，从意也。今作遂也[7] (*sui* 㒸 means "to follow" and is currently written as *sui* 遂). The form *sui* 遂 appeared very early. There is such a sentence in *Zuo Zhuan* 左传 (Zuo's Commentary on the Spring and Autumn Annals): 春，齐侯以诸侯之师侵蔡，蔡溃，遂伐楚. The sentence can be translated as follows: In spring, the Duke of Qi

State led the coalition forces of the states to successfully invade the State of Cai and then attacked the State of Chu). Du Yu 杜预 (222–285) noted that "*sui* 遂 is a conjunction that connects two events before and after (遂，两事之辞也[8])". *Shuowen Jiezi* uses 从意也 to explain this conjunction. This is because, by using the term *yi* 意 instead of *yi* 义, it emphasises that the character belongs to *ci* 词 rather than to *yan* 言. Entries about characters that belong to *yan* 言 are also very common in the book *Shuowen Jiezi*. Here are some relevant examples from the books:

- 嘖: words of savages (野人之言);
- *Tang* 唐: big talk (大言也);
- *Mang* 哤: speech disorder (哤异之言);
- *Hua* 话: good discourse (合会善言也);
- *Xu* 诩: big talk (大言也); and
- *Jian* 譾: talkative (善言也).

These characters explained as *yan* 言 are essentially different from the following characters that are explained as *ci* 词: *zhi* 只 is a modal particle indicating the end of a speech (只,语巳词也); *jie* 皆 means all, which is a qualifier (皆，俱词也); *lu* 鲁 indicates a pause in speech (鲁，钝词也); *zhe* 者 serves as a demonstrative or possessive pronoun, equivalent to that or which (者，别事词也); *ping* 粤 is a modal particle used to express urgency (粤，亟词也); *ning* 宁 is a modal particle used to expressing wishes (宁，愿词也).

What kind of Chinese words does *Shuowen Jiezi* 说文解字 define as *ci* 词? Is the term *ci* 词 equivalent to function words? These issues will be further explained in the following paragraphs.

In Xu Xuan's 徐铉 edition of *Shuowen Jiezi* 说文解字, there are 33 entries that include the term *ci* 词, and relevant sinological research results (as shown below) change the number from 33 to 34.

(1) In Xu Xuan's 徐铉 edition, there is such an entry 诞，词诞也, which is written as 调诞也[9] in *Yuanben Yupian Cnajuan* 原本玉篇残卷 (The Incomplete Original Manuscript of Yupian) and as 调也[10] in *Zhuanli Wanxiang Mingyi* 篆隶万象名义 (Dictionary of Seal- and Official-Script Characters). In *Shuowen Jiezi Yizheng* 说文解字义证 (A Study on Characters from *Shuowen Jiezi*), Gui Fu 桂馥 (1736–1805) points out that 词诞也 (in Xu Xuan's edition of *Shuowen Jiezi*) shall be a mistaken form of 调，譀也.[11] This correction is reasonable because when *Shuowen Jiezi* uses the term *ci* 词 to define a character, the sentence will end with the term 词 instead of beginning with 词. Therefore, the character 调 in *Yuanben Yupian Cnajuan* 原本玉篇残卷 and *Zhuanli Wanxiang Mingyi* 篆隶万象名义 shall be 調, which is explained in *Shouwen Jiezi* as tong 同 (common). This view is accepted in this study.

(2) As to the entry 粤，惊辞 in Xu Xuan's edition of *Shuowen Jiezi*, Duan Yucai 段玉裁,[12] Gui Fu 桂馥, Wang Yun 王筠, and Zhu Junsheng 朱骏声 agreed that the character 辞, which is explained as *song* 讼 (argue) in *Shuowen Jiezi*,

should be changed to 词 after their rigorous textual research. This study also supports this view.

(3) The entry 诶，可恶之辞 in the book is questioned by sinologists. Gui Fu 桂馥 said the following in *Shuowen Jiezi Yizheng* 说文解字义证: "The character 辞 in 可恶之辞 should be 词, and this correction is supported by many documents." ("'可恶之辞'者, 辞, 当为'词', 《广韵》引作'词'。《庄子·达生篇》'公反, 诶诒为病', 《释文》亦引作'词'."[13]) Entries of this format are also found in *Shuowen Jiezi*, such as "䎽, 䒼恶惊词也" and "蠯, 见鬼惊词". The study supports this correction.

Among the 34 entries, including the term *ci* 词, there are nine entries (entries numbered from one to nine) where the term is used to discuss diction, namely the choice and use of words on different occasions.

(1) *Zhu* 祝 is a word used by people who preside over worship ceremonies.
(2) *E* 菩 (grass) is a combination of a phonetic component *wu* 吾 (I/we) and another. Component *cao* 艸 (herbage), and is a word used in an ode of the Chu State: 有菩萧艸 (there is grass).
(3) *Hao* 颢 (white) is a combination of *ye* 页 (page) and *jing* 景 (sunlight). It is a word used in an ode of the Chu State: 天白颢颢 (the sky is white). It also appears in the sentence 南山四颢, 白首人也 (the term Nanshan Si Hao 南山四颢 describes white-headed people).
(4) *Qian* 攐 (to take or capture a city, etc.) is a combination of a phonetic component *han*. 寒 (cold) and another component *shou* 手 (hang). This character was widely used in the southern region of the State of Chu. It appears in an ode of the Chu State: 朝攐批之木兰 (go to pick magnolia in the morning).
(5) *Xu* 嬃 (sister) is a combination of a phonetic component *xu* 须 (facial hair) and another component *nv* 女 (women girls), and this word can also be used to refer to women/girls. There is such a sentence in an ode of the Chu State: 女嬃之蝉媛 (the woman/girl lectured me again and again). Jia Kui 贾逵 (30–101) pointed out that the people of Chu used this word to refer to their elder sisters.
(6) *Xing* 婞 (very) is a combination of a phonetic component *xing* 幸 (meet) and another. Component *nv* 女 (women/girls). There is such a line in an ode of the Chu state: 鲧婞直 (Gun was very stubborn).
(7) *Bi* 弾 (shoot an arrow) is a combination of a phonetic component *bi* 毕 (a hand-net) and another component *gong* 弓 (bow). This word appears in an ode of the Chu State: 弓焉弾日 (弓 shot the sun).
(8) *Si* 祠 (worship events in spring) is a combination of a phonetic component *si* 司 (to take charge of) and another component *shi* 示 (manifest). Worship events referred to as *si* 祠 used animal skins, silk, and precious stones, such as jade, and excluded sacrificial ceremonies.
(9) *Ji* 訊 (collection) is explained as 词之訊矣 (a collection of *ci* 词).

The ninth entry was questioned by Duan Yucai 段玉裁. In *Shuowen Jiezi Zhu* 说文解字注, he pointed out that 词, 当作辞 (the term *ci* 词 in the entry should be replaced with *ci* 辞).¹⁴ In *Shuowen Jiezi Xizhuan* 说文解字系传, Xu Kai 徐锴 (920–974) quotes *Shi Jing* 诗经 (The Book of Songs): "If government decrees are coordinated, the people will be able to live in peace" (臣锴曰：此《诗》云'辞之𦊆矣，民之绎矣'¹⁵). A Qing-Dynasty sinologist named Xu Hao 徐灏 observed in his book *Shuowen Jiezi Zhujian* 说文解字注笺 (Notes to *Shuowen Jiezi*) that *Shuowen Jiezi* tends to use sentences from ancient classics to explain characters (《说文》往往用经句以解字，如《黾部》'蝇'之'营营青蝇'，《男部》'甥'之'谓我舅者吾谓之甥也'¹⁶).

The remaining 25 entries (entries numbered from 10 to 34) containing the term *ci* 词 explain function words in the Chinese language, such as modal particles, auxiliary words, adverbs, conjunctions, and interjections.

(10) *Er* 尔 is a modal particle indicating certainty. Xu Kai's 徐锴 *Shuowen Jiezi Xizhuan* 说文解字系传 explains it as a modal particle and finds examples from *Li* 礼 (Book of Rites): 鼎鼎尔 (it must be great) and 悠悠尔 (they must be worried). (尔词者，言之助也。《礼》曰"鼎鼎尔"、"悠悠尔"，是必然。¹⁷)
(11) *Zeng* 曾 is a modal particle that means "to breathe a sigh of relief". Xu Kai's 徐锴 *Shuowen Jiezi Xizhuan* 说文解字系传 points out that it is used in this way in *Shi Jing* 诗经, or the Book of Songs (《诗》言'曾是掊克'，缓气言之，故曰舒¹⁸).
(12) 只，语已词也。(《说文·只部》) *Zhi* 只 is a modal particle indicating the end of a speech

Wang Yinzhi 王引之 (1766–1834) gives the following explanation in *Jingzhuan Shici* 经传释词 (Explanation of Characters): *Shuowen Jiezi* explains *zhi* 只 as a modal particle indicating the end of a speech, which is supported by many sentences from ancient classics, such as 仲氏任只, 母也天只 and 不谅人只. Wang Yinzhi 王引之 also pointed out that the character *zhi* 只 can be written as *zhi* 轵, such as in 而奚来为轵.¹⁹

(13) *Jie* 皆 means all, which is a qualifier.
(14) *Zhe* 者 serves as a demonstrative or possessive pronoun, equivalent to that or which.

Xu Kai's 徐锴 *Shuowen Jiezi Xizhuan* 说文解字系传 agrees with this view that *zhe* 者 is a qualifier.²⁰ Wang Yinzhi 王引之's *Jingzhuan Shici* 经传释词 (Explanation of Characters) further points out that *zhe* 者 can be used to refer not only to people, but also things.²¹

(15) *Yue* 曰 is a *ci* 词.

Xu Kai's 徐锴 *Shuowen Jiezi Xizhuan* 说文解字系传 adds that the term *ci* 词 means function words or modal particles.²² Duan Yucai's 段玉裁 *Shuowen Jiezi*

Zhu 说文解字注 gives further explanation: *yue* 粤, *yu* 于, *yuan* 爰, and *yue* 曰 are auxiliary words, and they can be used to explain one another.[23]

(16) *Hu* 嚄 is a modal particle that means "exhaling a sigh".
(17) *Nai* 乃 is a modal particle that indicates difficulties in breathing.
(18) *Ping* 粤 is a modal particle used to expressing urgency.

Duan Yucai's *Shuowen Jiezi Zhu* 说文解字注 agrees with this explanation: (粤亦语词也[24]).

(19) *Ning* 宁 is a modal particle used to expressing wishes.

In *Shuowen Jiezi Xizhuan* 说文解字系传, Xu Kai 徐锴 gives an example: when someone uses *ning* 宁 in speech, it is an expression of wish.[25]

(20) *Yue* 粤 is equivalent to *kui* 亏, a modal particle indicating the act of thinking over carefully. It is a combination of *kui* 亏 and *shen* 宷. It often does not serve as a content word, such as in *Zhou Shu* 周书 (The History of the Zhou Dynasty): 粤三日丁亥 (three days later, it was a ding-hai day).

Xu Kai's 徐锴 *Shuowen Jiezi Xizhuan* 说文解字系传 further points out that the character *yue* 粤 used to start the sentence indicates that the speaker carefully and secretly calculated the number of days before uttering the words.[26] Duan Yucai's 段玉裁 *Shuowen Jiezi Zhu* 说文解字注 adds that although both *yue* 粤 and *kui* 亏 are modal particles, *yue* 粤 implies prudence as it features *shen* 宷, which means "detailed" and "learn about".[27]

(21) *Shen* 猌 is a *ci* 词 and equivalent to *kuang* 况, which means "furthermore".

Duan Yucai's 段玉裁 *Shuowen Jiezi Zhu* 说文解字注 agrees with this view and adds that *shen* 猌 is extensively used in *Shang Shu* 尚书 (The Book of Documents), and *kuang* 况 is more frequently used when the book is written.[28]

(22) *Yi* 矣 is a modal particle indicating that the sentence has been completed.

Xu Hao's 徐灏 *Shuowen Jiezi Zhujian* 说文解字注笺 further points out that *yi* 矣 is a modal particle that always appears at the end of a sentence (语词之'矣'恒在句末，故曰语已词[29]).

(23) *Zhi* 知 is a *ci* 词.

This character is often used as a function word instead of a content word, such as in *Shang Shu* 尚书: 知今我初服，宅新邑[30] (Our king has just ascended the throne and settled down in the new capital city). In *Qunjing Pingyi* 群经评议 (Study on Ancient Classics), Yu Yue 俞樾 (1821–1907) agrees with Sun Xingyan's 孙星衍

(1753–1818) point of view that "*zhi* 知 is a function word and observes that in comparison with *shen* 矤 (furthermore) and *yi* 矣 (particle of completed action), *zhi* 知 was more frequently used in ancient times."[31]

(24) *Ji* 㮯 (and) is a conjunction, which consists of a phonetic component *zi* 自 (nose) and another component *yin* 丌 (to stand side by side). It appears in *Yu Shu* 虞书 (The History of the Yu Dynasty) and *Shi Ji* 史记 (Records of the Historian): 㮯咎繇; 淮夷蠙珠㮯鱼. In *Shi Ji Suo Yin* 史记索隐 (Commentaries on Shi Ji), Sima Zhen 司马贞 (679–732) noted that *ji* 㮯 is the archaic form of *ji* 暨, which means "and".[32]

(25) *Yu* 欥 is a conjunction that links two parts together. It is a combination of a phonetic component *yue* 曰 (to say) and another component *qian* 欠 (yawn).

In *Shuowen Jiezi Zhujian* 说文解字注笺, Xu Hao 徐灏 used Dai Zhen's 戴震 (1724–1777) words to illustrate that *yu* 欥 is a conjunction used to link two parts in writing.[33] Wang Yinzhi 王引之 (1766–1834) also discussed this character in Volume 2 of *Jingzhuan Shici* 经传释词: "*Shuowen Jiezi* defines *yu* 欥 as a conjunction, which can be otherwise written as *yu* 聿, *yu* 遹, or *yue* 曰. This character is used to connect two parts instead of being used to start a part in writing. It is different from *sui* 遂, *shu* 述, or *zi* 自. *Shuowen Jiezi*'s interpretation of this character is correct."[34]

(26) 㤅 is a modal particle featuring radical *ji* 旡 (choke on something eaten), which indicates surprise caused by an undesirable sudden change.
(27) 魊 is a modal particle featuring radical *gui* 鬼 (ghost), which indicates surprise caused by some supernatural phenomena.
(28) 兮 is a modal particle featuring radical *xi* 兮 (exclamatory particle), which indicates surprise.
(29) *Xi* 诶 is an exclamation of confirmation featuring radical *yan* 言 (speak).

The following three entries numbered 30 to 32 are special cases. The three Chinese characters described in these three entries are adjectives. They may be barely defined as *ci* 词 because they are usually used to describe qualities and states, and they often involve subjective judgments and assessments.

(30) *Kua* 侉 is an adjective describing someone speaking with an accent, featuring radical *ren* 人 (person).

Wang Yun 王筠 said in *Shuowen Jiezi Judu* 说文解字句读, "Character 憊 is currently written as *bei* 惫 (tired).[35] Zhu Junsheng 朱骏声 (1788–1858) observed in *Shuowen Tongxun Dingsheng* 说文通训定声 (An Explanatory Book of Phonetic Sounds) that this character is a *ci* 词 that means "tired".[36]

(31) *Lu* 鲁 is an adjective meaning "foolish", consisting of a simplified phonetic.

Component *zha* 鲝 (salted fish) and another component *bai* 白 (white). *Lun Yu* 论语 (The Analects) contains such as sentence: 参也鲁 (Zeng Shen is foolish).

In *Zuo Zhuan* 左传 (Zuo's Commentary on the Spring and Autumn Annals), there is a sentence: 鲁人以为敏 (People of the Lu Kingdom believe that he is very clever). Kong Yingda 孔颖达 (574–648) noted that the word 鲁人 in this sentence means foolish people.[37]

(32) 㾓 is an adjective meaning "wise", featuring radical *bai* 白 (white).

Xu Hao's 徐灏 *Shuowen Jiezi Zhujian* 说文解字注笺 explains the character as follows: *zhi* 知 (comprehend) and 㾓, whose simplified official-script form is *zhi* 智 (wisdom), are the same. They were used interchangeably in ancient books. Wang Niansun 王念孙 (1744–1832) explains this characters as "wise".[38]

These adjectives used to express people's subjective judgment and assessments of qualities and states are barely defined as *ci* 词 in *Shuowen Jiezi* 说文解字.

(33) 畴 is a *ci* 词 featuring radical *bai* 白 (white)

Wang Yinzhi 王引之 explained this character in the sixth Volume of *Jingzhuan Shici* 经传释词 (Explanation of Characters) as follows. "There is such an entry in *Erya* 尔雅 (Erya Dictionary): *chou* 畴 is equivalent to *shui* 谁 (who). This usage appears in *Shang Shu* 尚书: 畴咨若时登庸. (Who is good at handling agricultural affairs?) In *Shi Ji* 史记, there is such a sentence: 谁可顺此事. (Who is well versed in handling such affairs?). This character is originally written as 畴 and 畴. *Shuowen Jiezi* 说文解字 points out that 畴 is a function word equivalent to *shui* 谁 (who). This form appears in *Yu Shu* 虞书: 帝曰：畴咨."[39] A Qing-Dynasty scholar named Yan Zhangfu 严章福 questioned the entries containing *ci* 词 in *Shuowen Jiezi* 说文解字 in his book *Shuowen Jiaoyi Yi* 说文校议议 (Discussion on the Proofreading of *Shuowen Jiezi*), and, according to his analysis, the term *ci* 词 in *Shuowen Jiezi* can also be used to refer to pronouns.[40] In the preface of *Guhanyu Xuci* 古汉语虚词 (Function Words in Ancient Chinese Language), Yang Bojun 杨伯峻 (1909–1992) made the following comments: "There is no consensus reached on the division of content words and function words of ancient Chinese language, except for the unified opinions on the classification of nouns and verbs as content words and the classification of prepositions, conjunctions, modal particles, and auxiliary words as function words. The main difference of views lies in the classification of pronouns and adverbs. When I wrote the book *Wenyan Xuci* 文言虚词 (Function Words in Classical Chinese), I defined some pronouns and adverbs, especially demonstratives and interrogatives, as function words. This is difficult to understand for the beginners of classical Chinese."[41]

(34) *Bai* 白, also written as *zi* 自, is uttered in a nasal sound.

The *ci* 词 in the entry is used to explain the character form. It does not give any clues about the classification of the character.

From the above analysis, the following conclusions can be drawn: the term *ci* 词 in *Shuowen Jiezi* 说文解字 can be used to refer to function words, such as modal particles, auxiliary words, conjunctions, etc.; the term can also be used to refer to some content words, such as adverbs, interjections, adjectives, and pronouns. The reason for this phenomenon may be the differences in the classification of words. It is worth noting that the term does not appear in all the explanations of characters that are defined as *ci* 词 in *Shuowen Jiezi* 说文解字. In view of this, it is difficult to examine the detailed connotation of the term. Sometimes, the book also uses *yu* 语 to explain some characters that are defined as *ci* 词 in *Shuowen Jiezi* 说文解字. For instance, there is such an entry in the book: *yu* 吁 is an interjection equivalent to "alas" (吁, 惊语也[42]). Sometimes, the book uses *ci* 词 to explain characters with certain components. The entry 鲁, 钝词也, which means that *lu* 鲁 is an adjective meaning "foolish", is a typical example. Wang Yun 王筠 said in *Shuowen Jiezi Judu* 说文解字句读, "The reason *lu* 鲁 is explained with the character *ci* 词 is probably that it is a character featuring the component *bai* 白." ("孔注《论语》：'鲁, 钝也.' 比加'词'者, 为其从'白'也.")[43] Component *bai* 白 is a simplified form of *zi* 自 (a nasal sound). All the characters containing this component such as *jie* 皆 (all), *lu* 鲁 (foolish), and *zhe* 者 (that/which) are explained with the character *ci* 词. Wang Yun 王筠 annotated another entry, "皆, 俱词也 (*jie* 皆 is a qualifier meaning 'all')": "Character *ju* 俱 means all, and the use of *ci* 词 here indicates that *jie* 皆 is a qualifier. Xu Shen 许慎 (58–147) purposefully arranged 皆 under the radical *bi* 比 (comparison) because this component is easy to understand, as to the explanation of the difficult-to-understand component *bai* 白 (white), he must adopt the term *ci* 词." ("《人部》'俱, 皆也', 不言'词', 是谓其意为俱, 其词为皆也......盖许君之意, 将隶'皆'于《比部》, 则'比'易解, '白'难解, 故不得已入之《白部》而以'词'说之.")[44]

Notes

1 The original Chinese version was published in *Lexicographical Studies* 辞书研究 in 2011 (issue 4).
2 本文《说文解字》引文皆据王贵元《说文解字校笺》, 学林出版社 2002 年版.
   Quotations from *Shuowen Jiezi* in this chapter are proofed versions from *Proofreading Notes to Shuowen Jiezi*, published in 2002 by Academia Press.
3 段玉裁：《说文解字注》, 丁福保《说文解字诂林》(第十册), 第 9003 页, 北京：中华书局, 1988.
   Duan Yucai: *Interpretations to Shuowen Jiezi*, Ding Fubao: *Explanation to Shuowen Jiezi* (Vol. 10), p. 9003, Beijing: Zhonghua Book Company, 1988.
4 王筠：《说文解字句读》, 丁福保《说文解字诂林》(第十册), 第 9004 页, 北京：中华书局, 1988.
   Wang Yun: *Interpretations to Shuowen Jiezi*, Ding Fubao: *Explanation to Shuowen Jiezi* (Vol. 10), p. 9004, Beijing: Zhonghua Book Company, 1988.
5 徐锴：《说文解字系传》, 丁福保《说文解字诂林》(第十册), 第 9001 页, 北京：中华书局, 1988.
   Xu Kai: *The Explanation to Shuowen Jiezi*, Ding Fubao: *Explanation to Shuowen Jiezi* (Vol. 10), p. 9001, Beijing: Zhonghua Book Company, 1988.
6 段玉裁：《说文解字注》, 丁福保《说文解字诂林》(第三册), 第 1964 页, 北京：中华书局, 1988.
   Duan Yucai: *Interpretations to Shuowen Jiezi*, Ding Fubao: *Explanation to Shuowen Jiezi* (Vol. 10), p. 1964, Beijing: Zhonghua Book Company, 1988.

7 顾野王：《宋本玉篇》，第 524 页，北京：中国书店，1983.
   Gu Yewang: *Songben Yupian Regular-Script Dictionary*, p. 524, Beijing: China Bookstore, 1983.
8 阮元：《十三经注疏》，第 1792 页，北京：中华书局，1980.
   Ruan Yuan 阮元 (1764–1849): *Notes and Commentaries to Thirteen Classics Explanatory*, p. 1792, Beijing: Zhonghua Book Company, 1980.
9 顾野王：《原本玉篇残卷》，第 20 页，北京：中华书局，1985.
   Gu Yewang: *The Incomplete Original Manuscript of Yupian*, p. 29, Beijing: Zhonghua Book Company, 1985.
10 空海：《篆隶万象名义》，第 83 页，北京：中华书局，1995.
   Monk Konghai: *Dictionary of Seal- and Official-Script Characters*, p. 83, Beijing: Zhonghua Book Company, 1995.
11 桂馥：《说文解字义证》，丁福保《说文解字诂林》（第四册），第 3081 页，北京：中华书局，1988.
   Gui Fu: *A Study on Characters from Shuowen Jiezi*, Ding Fubao: *Explanation to Shuowen Jiezi* (Vol. 10), p. 3081, Beijing: Zhonghua Book Company, 1988.
12 段玉裁：《说文解字注》，丁福保《说文解字诂林》(第六册)，第 5079 页，北京：中华书局，1988.
   Duan Yucai: *Interpretations to Shuowen Jiezi*, Ding Fubao: *Explanation to Shuowen Jiezi* (Vol. 6), p. 5079, Beijing: Zhonghua Book Company, 1988.
13 桂馥：《说文解字义证》，丁福保《说文解字诂林》（第四册），第 3055 页，北京：中华书局，1988.
   Gui Fu: *A Study on Characters from Shuowen Jiezi*, Ding Fubao: *Explanation to Shuowen Jiezi* (Vol. 4), p. 3055, Beijing: Zhonghua Book Company, 1988.
14 段玉裁：《说文解字注》，丁福保《说文解字诂林》(第四册)，第 2886 页，北京：中华书局，1988.
   Duan Yucai: *Interpretations to Shuowen Jiezi*, Ding Fubao: *Explanation to Shuowen Jiezi* (Vol. 4), p. 2886, Beijing: Zhonghua Book Company, 1988.
15 徐锴：《说文解字系传》，丁福保《说文解字诂林》(第四册)，第 2886 页，北京：中华书局，1988.
   Xu Kai: *The Explanation to Shuowen Jiezi*, Ding Fubao: *Explanation to Shuowen Jiezi* (Vol. 4), p. 2886, Beijing: Zhonghua Book Company, 1988.
16 徐灏：《说文解字注笺》，丁福保《说文解字诂林》(第四册)，第 2886 页，北京：中华书局，1988.
   Xu Hao: *Notes to Shuowen Jiezi*, Ding Fubao: *Explanation to Shuowen Jiezi* (Vol. 4), p. 2886, Beijing: Zhonghua Book Company, 1988.
17 徐锴：《说文解字系传》，丁福保《说文解字诂林》(第三册)，第 1959 页，北京：中华书局，1988.
   Xu Kai: *The Explanation to Shuowen Jiezi*, Ding Fubao: *Explanation to Shuowen Jiezi* (Vol. 3), p. 1959, Beijing: Zhonghua Book Company, 1988.
18 徐锴：《说文解字系传》，丁福保《说文解字诂林》(第三册)，第 1960 页，北京：中华书局，1988.
   Xu Kai: *The Explanation to Shuowen Jiezi*, Ding Fubao: *Explanation to Shuowen Jiezi* (Vol. 3), p. 1960, Beijing: Zhonghua Book Company, 1988.
19 王引之：《经传释词》，第 204 页，长沙：岳麓书社，1984.
   Wang Yinzhi: *Explanation of Characters*, p. 204, Changsha: Yue Lu Book Company, 1984.
20 徐锴：《说文解字系传》丁福保《说文解字诂林》(第五册)，第 3928 页，.北京：中华书局，1988.
   Xu Kai: *The Explanation to Shuowen Jiezi*, Ding Fubao: *Explanation to Shuowen Jiezi* (Vol. 4), p. 3928, Beijing: Zhonghua Book Company, 1988.
21 王引之：《经传释词》，第 195 页，长沙：岳麓书社，1984.
   Wang Yinzhi: *Explanation of Characters*, p. 195, Changsha: Yue Lu Book Company, 1984.

22 徐锴：《说文解字系传》，丁福保《说文解字诂林》(第六册)，第 5036 页，北京：中华书局，1988.
Xu Kai: *The Explanation to Shuowen Jiezi*, Ding Fubao: *Explanation to Shuowen Jiezi* (Vol. 6), p. 5036, Beijing: Zhonghua Book Company, 1988.
23 段玉裁：《说文解字注》，丁福保《说文解字诂林》(第六册)，第 5067 页，北京：中华书局，1988.
Duan Yucai: *Interpretations to Shuowen Jiezi*, Ding Fubao: *Explanation to Shuowen Jiezi* (Vol. 6), p. 506, Beijing: Zhonghua Book Company, 1988.
24 段玉裁：《说文解字注》，丁福保《说文解字诂林》(第六册)，第 5036 页，北京：中华书局，1988.
Duan Yucai: *Notes to Shuowen Jiezi*, Ding Fubao: *Explanation to Shuowen Jiezi* (Vol. 6), p. 5036, Beijing: Zhonghua Book Company, 1988.
25 徐锴：《说文解字系传》，丁福保《说文解字诂林》(第六册)，第 5068 页，北京：中华书局，1988.
Xu Kai: *The Explanation to Shuowen Jiezi*, Ding Fubao: *Explanation to Shuowen Jiezi* (Vol. 6), p. 5068, Beijing: Zhonghua Book Company, 1988.
26 徐锴：《说文解字系传》，丁福保《说文解字》诂林(第六册)，第 5091 页，北京：中华书局，1988.
Xu Kai: *The Explanation to Shuowen Jiezi*, Ding Fubao: *Explanation to Shuowen Jiezi* (Vol. 6), p. 5091, Beijing: Zhonghua Book Company, 1988.
27 段玉裁：《说文解字注》，丁福保《说文解字》诂林(第六册)，第 5091 页，北京：中华书局，1988.
Duan Yucai: *Interpretations to Shuowen Jiezi*, Ding Fubao: *Explanation to Shuowen Jiezi* (Vol. 6), p. 5091, Beijing: Zhonghua Book Company, 1988.
28 段玉裁：《说文解字注》，丁福保《说文解字诂林》(第六册)，第 5496 页，北京：中华书局，1988.
Duan Yucai: *Interpretations to Shuowen Jiezi*, Ding Fubao: *Explanation to Shuowen Jiezi* (Vol. 6), p. 5496, Beijing: Zhonghua Book Company, 1988.
29 徐灏：《说文解字注笺》，丁福保《说文解字诂林》(第六册)，第 5499 页，北京：中华书局，1988.
Xu Hao: *Notes to Shuowen Jiezi*, Ding Fubao: *Explanation to Shuowen Jiezi* (Vol. 6), p. 5499, Beijing: Zhonghua Book Company, 1988.
30 阮元：《十三经注疏》，第 213 页，北京：中华书局，1980.
Ruan Yuan: *Notes and Commentaries to Thirteen Classics Explanatory*, p. 213, Beijing: Zhonghua Book Company, 1980.
31 俞樾：《群经平议》，续修四库全书编撰委员会《续修四库全书》(第 178 册)，第 86 页，上海：上海古籍出版社，2002.
Yu Yue: *Study on Ancient Classics, Sequels to Complete Library of the Four Branches of Literature* (Vol. 178), p. 86, Shanghai: Shanghai Classics Publishing House, 2002.
32 司马迁：《史记》（第一册），第 58 页，北京：中华书局，1982.
Sima Qian: *Records of the Historian* (Vol. 1), p. 58, Beijing: Zhonghua Book Company, 1982.
33 徐灏：《说文解字注笺》，丁福保《说文解字诂林》(第九册)，第 8763 页，北京：中华书局，1988.
Xu Hao: *Notes to Shuowen Jiezi*, Ding Fubao: *Explanation to Shuowen Jiezi* (Vol. 9), p. 8763, Beijing: Zhonghua Book Company, 1988.
34 王引之：《经传释词》，第 30–31 页，长沙：岳麓书社，1984.
Wang Yinzhi: *Explanation of Characters*, pp. 30–31, Changsha: Yue Lu Book Company, 1984.
35 王筠：《说文解字句读》，丁福保《说文解字诂林》(第九册)，第 8175 页，北京：中华书局，1988.
Wang Yun: *Interpretations to Shuowen Jiezi*, Ding Fubao: *Explanation to Shuowen Jiezi* (Vol. 9), p. 8175, Beijing: Zhonghua Book Company, 1988.

36. 朱骏声：《说文通训定声》，丁福保《说文解字诂林》（第九册），第 8175 页，北京：中华书局，1988.
    Zhu Junsheng: *An Explanatory Book of Phonetic Sounds*, Ding Fubao: *Explanation to Shuowen Jiezi* (Vol. 9), p. 8175, Beijing: Zhonghua Book Company, 1988.
37. 阮元：《十三经注疏.》，第 1855 页，北京：中华书局，1980.
    Ruan Yuan: *Notes and Commentaries to Thirteen Classics Explanatory*, p. 1855, Beijing: Zhonghua Book Company, 1980.
38. 徐灏：《说文解字注笺》，丁福保《说文解字诂林》(第五册)，第 3933 页，北京：中华书局，1988.
    Xu Hao: *Notes to Shuowen Jiezi*, Ding Fubao: *Explanation to Shuowen Jiezi* (Vol. 5), p. 3933, Beijing: Zhonghua Book Company, 1988.
39. 王引之：《经传释词》，第 137–138 页，长沙：岳麓书社，1984.
    Wang Yinzhi: *Explanation of Characters*, pp. 137–138, Changsha: Yue Lu Book Company, 1984.
40. 严章福：《说文校议议》，丁福保《说文解字诂林》（第五册），第 3929 页，北京：中华书局，1988.
    Yan Zhangfu: *Discussion on the Proofreading of Shuowen Jiezi*, Ding Fubao: *Explanation to Shuowen Jiezi* (Vol. 5), p. 3929, Beijing: Zhonghua Book Company, 1988.
41. 杨伯峻：《古汉语虚词》，第 1 页，北京：中华书局，1981.
    Yang Bojun: *Function Words in Ancient Chinese Language*, p. 1, Beijing: Zhonghua Book Company, 1981.
42. This may be the origin of the Chinese word "语词", which is used to refer to function words and auxiliary words.
43. 王筠：《说文解字句读》，丁福保《说文解字诂林》(第五册)，第 3926 页，北京：中华书局，1988.
    Wang Yun: *Interpretations to Shuowen Jiezi*, Ding Fubao: *Explanation to Shuowen Jiezi* (Vol. 5), p. 3926, Beijing: Zhonghua Book Company, 1988.
44. 王筠：《说文解字句读》，丁福保《说文解字诂林》(第五册)，第 3925 页，北京：中华书局，1988.
    Wang Yun: *Interpretations to Shuowen Jiezi*, Ding Fubao: *Explanation to Shuowen Jiezi* (Vol. 5), p. 3925, Beijing: Zhonghua Book Company, 1988.

23 *Shuowen Jiezi* and an Exploration of Homologous Characters (Same-Origin Characters)[1]

A group of homologous Chinese characters (same-origin characters) record a group of homologous Chinese words, part of which, directly driven by the derivation of words, can be taken as a sign of the maturity of the differentiated derivation of Chinese monosyllabic words. Therefore, the ligature of Chinese homologous words is always realised by the ligature of homologous characters. *Shuowen Jiezi* 说文解字 (An Explication of Written Characters) stores the original characters of words, and after the exclusion of borrowed characters, the intricate relationship between characters and words in use ceases to exist. Therefore, it is the best material for linking homologous characters. This chapter addresses the issues related to the homologous characters mentioned in *Shuowen Jiezi* 说文解字 (An Explication of Written Characters).

I. Importance of Sense Relations Among Homologous Characters

Homologous characters constitute an age-old topic in traditional philology that has been proposed for a long time, although theoretical progress has been very slow. From the practice of sound training in the Han Dynasty to the Qing's "similar sound leads to meaning interchangeability", the principle of homologous derivation has yet to be thoroughly elaborated, and thus a concrete method for the "fanqie" (interconnection method of fanqie) of homologous characters has never been found.

Historically, the work of linking homologous words always started from sound sameness and sound proximity, looking for those with semantic relevance in a pile of homophones. However, due to the historical pronunciation changes, as well as dialectal and exegetical pronunciation changes, it is impossible to establish a rigorous and comprehensive system of pronunciation and rhyme alone. Although the main phonological system and similar relationships can be developed based on rhyme, phonetic components, and phonological theory, this is far from satisfying the need for long-term historical analysis of meaning evolution relationships. Therefore, many specific inter-word relationships still need to be determined based on their meaning. This was acknowledged and practised by Zhang Taiyan 章太炎 (1869–1936), who wrote *Wenshi Dictionary of Homologous Characters*, a book in which he defined meaning relationships and sound relationships. The standard of sound and rhyme in "Chengyuntu" in *Wenshi Dictionary of Homologous Characters* could not have been a pre-established standard but was perfected in the process of linking word families based on their meanings. Zhang Taiyan was the originator of the study of homologous words and the interconnection of word families on a large scale, and he had a clear understanding of the beginnings and changes of language and writing. Firstly, he introduced the concept of "root" for the first time, arguing that "all words have roots"[2]; secondly, he explained the difference between the root of words and the root of characters, arguing that, in language, it is the name of the state that manifests the earliest, while, in writing, it is the name of the entity that manifests the earliest. He said: "The beginning of language came from one's sensory experiences, and names describing virtues were the most long-standing. However, for written words, the physical descriptions came first, followed by the description of structure."[3] He went on to explain, "The name of a physical description must be the same as the name of virtue while describing its function."[4] This view is very important, since if "reality" is more compatible with "virtue" and "function", then the difference shown between written words "that are visible" and word roots does not affect the original determination of language., i.e., the root of the word and the root of the character can be unified. This is a reflection of the fact that he takes the protoform and quasi-protoform as the root in *Wenshi Dictionary of Homologous Characters*, which is not contradictory to his opposition to the "constrained form" and the unlimited form in the interconnection theory of "fanqie", and is a reflection of "the form and sound category being more mutually supportive".[5] Finally, he believes that the process of language development is the process of mutually deducing between the words of the manifestation of reality and the words of the manifestation of virtue and function. Expressed in the lexical meaning, it's called extension (he calls it "borrowing"), and in the text, it's called derivation, and *Wenshi Dictionary of Homologous Characters* interconnects words along the lines of extension and derivation, that is, the original form of language development. Therefore, he says in his narrative: "to express the meaning of stream of ideas", "one must find its analogs." If we are to link the word families in a downstream manner, we must first establish the root of the language and then trace its development, so he establishes the root of the protoform and quasi-protoform, which share the same components as word roots but are not contradictory. In his *The Origin of the Language*, which preceded *Wenshi Dictionary of Homologous Characters*, he explained the same method of interconnection, saying, "If one establishes the word '*wei* 为 (for)' as a root" and "if one establishes the word '*zha* 乍 (sudden)' as a root," "if one establishes the word '*bian* 辡 (argue)' as a root," etc., it is obvious from such expressions that his method of establishing a root is only a way to facilitate the connection and is not the result of not being able to distinguish between language and writing. Unlike *Wenshi Dictionary of Homologous Character*, *A Dictionary of Word Families*, authored by Wang Li 王力 (1900–1986), who analyses homologous characters entirely from the perspective of planar interconnections, based on the established theoretical premise that homologous characters are those that have similar pronunciation and meaning, those that have similar pronunciation and same meaning, and those that have similar meaning and same pronunciation. Zhang Taiyan traces the origin and follows the stream, making his pursuit a historical study based on meaning; Wang Li, on the other hand, follows the phenomenon of the co-temporal plane formed by the development of the same origin and refers to the meaning within the strictly defined scope of phonology and rhyme. However, in this way, it is difficult to exclude words that have similar pronunciation and same or similar meaning by chance, and it is difficult to reflect the features and laws of homology, which can be said to be the inevitable result of fixing the sound standard rigidly. Although *Wenshi Dictionary of Homologous Characters* is based on the meaning and holds the general direction correctly, there is inevitably arbitrariness in the meaning connection because the essence of the homologous meaning relationship is not completely clear, which is also the reason why "Chengyuntu" is interpreted too broadly.

II. Determining *Yitong* Relations Among Homologous Characters Through Sememe Analysis

The essence of the same-origin sense relation is the sememe relation, characters of the same root and origin share common through-line core semes and related core semes, and the core semes and related core semes come from the common feature of different things that people recognise when naming things.[6]

The core seme is formed by extracting the most universal features of things; thus, its meaning has the nature of adjectives and descriptive verbs. For example:

- *Shuowen Jiezi* explains 鱻 as two fish. Duan Yucai 段玉裁 (1735–1815) notes: "According to *Yi* 易 (The Book of Changes), it means fish that follow one another." Zhu Junsheng's 朱骏声 *Shuowen Tongxun Dingsheng* 说文通训定声 (An Explanatory Book of Phonetic Sounds) explains 鱻 as "going side by side".
- *Liang* 兩 (two), according to *Shuowen Jiezi*, means again. *Yi* 易 (The Book of Changes) says: "High as heavens and earth."
- *Li* 麗 (travel in a group), according to *Shuowen Jiezi*, means to travel, consisting of *lu* 鹿 (deer) and *li* 丽 (beautiful). It's the deer's nature to travel when hungry. *The Book of Rites* notes: "'麗 beautiful leather to serve as

dowry.' Thus, it's beautiful to wear deer skin, hence its ancient derivation." Duan Yucai noted that, *li* 麗 (travel in a group), originally written as "*li* 丽 (beautiful)", means travelling. The component *lu* 鹿 (deer) was added to it later. *Zhou Li* 周礼 (Rites of the Zhou Dynasty) says: set an enclosure for every two horses and a *weishi* (an official title) for every 16 horses. According to its note, *li* 麗 means in pair. The same interpretation could be found in *Li Ji* 礼记 (The Book of Rites), *Zuo Zhuan* 左传 (Zuo's Commentary on The Spring and Autumn Annals), and *Shuowen Jiezi*. *Li* 麗 also means "two things attached to each other. *Yi* 易 (The Book of Changes) says: "*li* 离, also written as 麗. The sun and moon are attached to the sky, and the plants and trees are attached to soil."

- *Liu* 流 (flow), according to *Shuowen Jiezi*, means the flow of water. In *Mengzi* 孟子 (Mencius), *liu* 流 (flow) means to forget to return from upstream to downstream, *lian* 连 (linger) means to forget to return from downstream to upstream, *huang* 荒 (waste) means to hunt tirelessly, and *wang* 亡 (perish) means to drink without restraint. Zhu Junsheng's *Shuowen Tongxun Dingsheng* 说文通训定声 (An Explanatory Book of Phonetic Sounds) cited the following sentence. *Huainanzi* 淮南子 (Master Huainan) says that even the most ordinary men and women are inclined to indulge.

- *Li* 沥 (trickle) means *lu* 漉 (drip) in *Shuowen Jiezi*. It consists of the semantic component *shui* 水 (water) and phonetic component *li* 历 (experience), describing the sound of water dripping down. According to Zhu Junsheng's *Shuowen Tongxun Dingsheng* 说文通训定声 (An Explanatory Book of Phonetic Sounds), under *li* 沥 (trickle), there is "rinsing mouth with the fine flow of the spring", cited from *Siyuanfu*. Ancient meaning: "flow of water."

- *Lou* 漊 (rain that doesn't stop) means unstoppable rain in *Shuowen Jiezi*. It consists of the semantic component *shui* 水 (water), and phonetic component *lou* 娄 (hollow). Duan Yucai noted: rain that falls like silk threads, never-ending. In Zhu Junsheng's *Shuowen Tongxun Dingsheng* 说文通训定声 (An Explanatory Book of Phonetic Sounds), *lou* 漊 means "something that is endless."

- *Lian* 连 (link-/man-pulled carriage), in *Shuowen Jiezi*, means "carried by men". It is a compound-ideograph character consisting of semantic components *chuo* 辵 (walking) and *che* 车 (vehicle). Duan Yucai noted: *lian* 连 comes from the ancient character *nian* 辇 (handcart). The association between man and vehicle is ongoing, hence the derivation of character.

For the sake of clarity, the following is a list of the meaning analysis according to their explanation:

Shuowen Jiezi and an Exploration of Homologous Characters 297

Table 23.1 Meaning Analysis

Character Meaning / Sound / Rhyme	Yu 鱻 (two fish)		Liang 兩 (two)		Li 麗 (travel in a group)		Liu 流 (flow)		Li 沥 (trickle)		Lou 溇 (rain that doesn't stop)		Lian 连 (link/man-pulled carriage)	
	Yi 疑 (doubt)	Yu 鱼 (fish)	Lai 来 (come)	Yang 阳 (south of a hill or north of a river/sun)	Lai 来 (come)	Zhi 支 (limb/branch)	Lai 来 (come)	You 幽 (hidden)	Lai 来 (come)	Xi 锡 (tin)	Lai 来 (come)	Hou 侯 (target/monarch)	Lai 来 (come)	yuan 元 (head)
Su (white silk) Same / Different														
Yu 鱼 (fish)	+	+	–	–	–	–	–	–	–	–	–	–	–	
Shuang 双 (two birds/double)	+	–	–	+	–	–	–	–	–	–	–	–	–	–
Ying 鹰 (eagle/bird)	–	–	–	–	–	+	–	–	–	–	–	–	–	–
Shui 水 (water)	–	–	–	–	–	–	+	+	+	+	+	+	–	–
Yu 雨 (rain)	–	–	–	–	–	–	–	–	–	–	–	+	–	–
Che 车 (vehicle)	–	–	–	–	–	–	–	–	–	–	–	–	+	–
Linked, Interwoven	+	–	+	–	+	+	+	–	+	+	+	+	+	+

Description: + refers to sameness/similarity, − refers to difference

The above seven characters share *lianlv* 连缕 (linked and interwoven) semes in their meaning. *Lianlv* is the common feature of all the characters and is the reason for naming these things, which is the core seme of the descriptive state.

The core semes are the through-line of homologous words, reflecting people's understanding and methodology of an objective division of things, which weaves the existing and future generated word meanings in different categories, like a scale for weighing everything, and gives them different phonetic forms accordingly. The derivational forms of words are broadly divided into two types: derivational and neological. Derivational word creation refers to the creation of word forms for derivational meanings or the creation of new words in the case of phonetic changes in derivational meanings; neological word creation refers to the naming of words for newly emerged things. The connection between original and derived meanings, as well as between derived and derived meanings, is formed by the same correlation of semes, thus the connection of semes between old and new words produced under derived word formation is also expressed. To create a word for something new is to look for a certain feature of the new thing, and then give it a name based on the connection that it has the same feature as the thing reflected by the word, so both forms of word creation have the same intention in terms of sense relations, and both are linked by the core seme.

Core semes play a role mainly in the development of word meanings, while they are generally implicit in the use of words, they mostly appear only occasionally or in the specialized interpretation of word meanings. Therefore, the sameness and difference of core semes should not precede the sameness and difference of meanings (sememes) and their use. For example, according to *Shuowen Jiezi*, *yu* 语 (talk/discuss) means *lun* 论 (discourse). The character consists of two components *yan* 言 (speak) and *wu* 吾 (I/we), the latter also serving as a phonetic component. The sememes of "語" and "论" are the same, but their core semes are different. *Lun* 論 in *Shi Ming* 释名 (Explanations to Names) means *lun* 倫 (human relationships) and implies ethics. *Jingdian Shiwen* 经典释文 (Textual Explanations of Classics and Canons) Vol: 24: "*lun* 論 means *lun* 倫 (human relationships), which is also written as *lun* 輪 (wheel). *Lun* 論 also means reason and sequence." In *Shi Jing* 诗经 (The Book of Songs): "Discuss under drums and bells". Zheng Xuan 郑玄 (127–200) commented, "*lun* 論 means to discuss ethics". Duan Yucai 段玉裁 (1735–1815) noted under the word "*lun* 論 (to discuss)" in his *Shuowen Jiezi Zhu* 说文解字注 (Notes to *Shuowen Jiezi*): "The meaning of 論 comes under *lun* 侖 (to think)". In the section *Ji* 亼 (to assemble), *lun* 侖 means *si* 思 (think). In the Section of *lun* 侖 (to think), *lun* 侖 means *li* 理 (sense). They are not different meanings. For instance, *si* 思 (think), when going under the section of *yu* 玉 (jade), serves as a phonetic component of *sai* 鰓 (bones in a horn). All of which match what Xu proposes. In *Shi Jing* 诗经 (The Book of Songs), where the words follow their reasoning, it is appropriate to call it a theory. Therefore, the words of Confucius' disciples are called "*lun* 论 (discourse) *yu* 语 (talk/discuss)". *Lun* 論 consists of two components *yan* 言 (speak) and *lun*

侖 (to think), the latter also serving as a phonetic component. Other characters that use 侖 as a phonetic component include:

- *Lun* 淪 (ripple), *Shuowen Jiezi*—section of *shui* 水 (water): "small ripples". The character consists of the semantic component *shui* 水 (water) and phonetic component *lun* 侖 (to think). As cited in *Shi Jing* 诗经 (The Book of Songs), the river water is clear with ripples (河水清且淪猗). In *Shi Ming* 释名 (Explanations to Names): Interpretation of *Shui* 水 (water): *Lun* 淪 (ripple) means *lun* 倫 (human relationships). The ripples of water resemble the order of things and reason.
- *Lun* 輪 (wheel), *Shuowen Jiezi*—section of *che* 車 (vehicle): "those with *fu* 輻 (spokes) are called a *lun* 輪 (wheel), and those without *fu* 輻 (spokes) are called a *quan* 軨 (wheel without spokes). The character consists of the semantic component *che* 車 (vehicle), and phonetic component *lun* 侖 (to think)." Duan Yucai notes: "The wheel turns in order, just like reasoning. Pairs of spokes turn to drive, hence it's called wheels."
- *Lun* 綸 (organized silk), *Shuowen Jiezi*—section of *xi* 系 (involve/relate): "scarf made from green silk ribbons. The character consists of the semantic component *xi* 系 (involve/relate), and phonetic component *lun* 侖 (to think)." In *Shi Ming* 释名 (Explanations to Names), *lun* 綸 (organized silk), resembles *lun* 倫 (human relationships) and means order and logic.
- *Lun* 掄 (swing), *Shuowen Jiezi*—section of *shou* 手 (hand): to pick. The character consists of the semantic component *shou* 手 (hand), and phonetic component *lun* 侖 (to think). According to Zhu Junsheng's *Shuowen Tongxun Dingsheng* 说文通训定声 (An Explanatory Book of Phonetic Sounds), *lun* 掄 (swing) was cited in *Guangya* 广雅 (Guangya Dictionary), and it means *guan* 贯 (string). The character is explained in the note as to string in order.
- *Lun* 倫 (human relationships), *Shuowen Jiezi*—section of *ren* 人 (person): "Generation. The character consists of the semantic component *ren* 人 (person), and phonetic component *lun* 侖 (to think)." *Shangshu* 尚书 (Book of Documents) says that the chanting of poetry and playing musical instruments should be well orderly and harmonious. In *Weikong Zhuan* 伪孔传, *lun* 倫 (human relationships) is *li* 理 (sense). When music is harmonious, the order is naturally correct. Note: *lun* 倫 (human relationships) originally referred to the ranking of people in the hierarchy.

As we can see, 論, 淪, 輪, 綸, 掄, and 倫, all use *lun* 侖 as a phonetic component, while sharing a core seme of order and reason. *Lun* 侖 (to think), in *Shuowen Jiezi*—section of *ji* 亼 (to assemble) means to think. The character consists of two components *ji* 亼 (to assemble) and *ce* 册 (book). It was noted by Duan Yucai that all people's thinking must be in accordance with their reasoning. Thus, the characters *lun* 倫 (human relationships) and *lun* 論 (to discuss) all derive meaning from *lun* 侖 (to think). The collection of books into volumes must follow their order and seek its logic. The core seme of "reason and order" therefore originates from "*lun* 侖 (to think)."

Yu 语 (talk/discuss) has its pronunciation derived from *wu* 吾 (I/we), while 吾 has its sound derived from *wu* 五 (five). In *Shuowen Jiezi*, *wu* 五 (five) means five elements. It follows the radical of *er* 二 (two/twice), as *ying* and *yang* meet at midnight between heaven and earth. Other characters that use *wu* 吾 (I/we) as their phonetic component include: *wu* 伍 (army). In *Shuowen Jiezi*, *wu* 伍 (army) means units made of three or five, *yu* 齬 (uneven teeth) means uneven teeth, *yu* 圄 (detain) means to defend, *yu* 敔 (ancient music instrument) means to imprison someone, and *wu* 悟 (disobedient) means to be disobedient. A common core seme of 五, 伍, 齬, 圄, 敔, and 悟 is one of "crossing/converging". *Yu* 语 (talk/discuss), in *Shuowen Jiezi*: Section of *yan* 言 (speak): *yan* 言 is to speak directly, while to discuss is to 语. In *Shi Jing* 诗经 (The Book of Songs), Kong Yingda noted: *yan* 言 is to speak directly; that is, one person speaks to himself; answering doubts is *yu* 语 (talk/discuss), requiring two people to speak to one another. Zheng Xuan noted in *Zhou Li* 周礼 (Rites of the Zhou Dynasty), "*yan* 言 (speak) refers to the speech of the person who starts the conversation, and *yu* 语 (talk/discuss) refers to the speech of the person who replied." Wang Yi 王逸 (89–158) noted in *Chu Ci* 楚辞 (The Odes of Chu) that, "asking questions is 言，answering questions is 语." We can thus see that 语 requires a reciprocal utterance. Its core seme of "cross/converge,"[7] also differs from that of *lun* 論 (to discuss).

There is a corresponding relationship between core semes and phonology, with several phonemes generating a myriad of word pronunciations and a number of core semes running through a myriad of word meanings. Word meanings are given to word pronunciations under the domination of core semes, therefore, there is a direct correspondence between core semes and word pronunciations.

Since the homologous sense relation is one of semes, core semes are derived from the feature of the named thing, so the analysis of lexical feature becomes an important part of the analysis of homologous sense relation, and, in this regard, *Shuowen Jiezi* 说文解字 (An Explication of Written Characters) has a unique value.

III. Clues Provided by *Shuowen Jiezi* for Determining Homologous Characters

Chinese characters are constructed according to the meaning of the word they represent, and the meaning of the word is reflected in the form of the character. Especially in the case of Chinese characters before the Small-Seal Script, each stroke of a character has a certain meaning. Therefore, character form and character meaning can be mutually interpreted, and, especially, character form can provide a strong basis for the examination of character meaning. It is according to this principle that Xu Shen 许慎 (ca. 58–147) used the form to interpret the meaning, to prove the form by the meaning, and to pursue the standard of unity of form and meaning to compile *Shuowen Jiezi*. Hence, *Shuowen Jiezi* is not only a dictionary, but also a theoretical work that embodies certain principles of language and writing, and the author's best intentions of controlling individual words with principles and theories are embedded in its character arrangement and morphological and phonological explanations. Because of this, *Shuowen Jiezi* provides a conducive clue to the exploration of homologous characters in various aspects.

(a) When a Chinese character is used and interpreted as a single character, it is difficult to identify further semes, but when it forms other characters as a component of a character, the implied meaning elements are often revealed, and, in such cases, *Shuowen Jiezi* often features a rationale, providing conditions for the exploration of homologous characters. For example:

- Zeng 曾 (increase), *Shuowen Jiezi*—section of *ba* 八 (eight): "An auxiliary word to express a soothing tone. The character consists of three components *ba* 八 (eight), *yue* 曰 (say), and 囧, the last serving as a phonetic component." In *Shuowen Jiezi*, *hui* 會 (cover/assemble) means to converge. The character consists of the component *ji* 亼 (to assemble) and the simplified form of *zeng* 曾 (increase), which means to benefit.
- In *Shuowen Jiezi*, Zeng 譜 (to add) means to add. The character consists of the semantic component *yan* 言 (speak) and phonetic component *zeng* 曾 (increase).
- In *Shuowen Jiezi*, *ceng* 層 (layer/stack) means two-floored house, consisting of two components *shi* 尸 (to impersonate the dead) and *zeng/ceng* 曾 (increase), with the latter serving as a phonetic component.
- In *Shuowen Jiezi*, zeng 增 (increase/gain) means to gain benefit, consisting of two components *tu* 土 (soil) and *zeng* 曾 (increase), with the latter serving as a phonetic component.
- The rationale *zeng* 曾 means to increase and serves as an ideographic and phonetic component in characters, such as 譜, 層 and 增. Their core semes are all "to increase."

More examples:

- In *Shuowen Jiezi*, *feng* 豐 (abundant) means an abundance of legumes. It is a pictographic character with the component *dou* 豆 (legumes). Another character of the same section is *yan* 豔 (plump), which means good and long, and its component *feng* 豐 (abundant) means big. *He* 盍 (empty container) serves as the character's phonetic component.
- In *Shuowen Jiezi*, feng 寷 (big house) means a big house, consisting of the components *mian* 宀 (roofed room) and *feng* 豐 (abundant), the latter serving as a phonetic component. According to *Yi* 易 (The Book of Changes): "abundance of big house."
- According to the rationale of *feng* 豐 (abundant), it means "big," which also corresponds with the seme of "big house." This shows that the core seme shared by *feng* 豐 (abundant) and *feng* 寷 (big house) is "big."
- In *Shuowen Jiezi*, *lu* 圥 (fungi) means *jun* 菌 (mushroom), ground fungi, grown in the fields, and *ling* 夌 (mount) means to climb and consists of two components, *pu* 夂 (hit lightly) and *lu* 圥 (fungi), which means something tall.

- In *Shuowen Jiezi*, *lu* 坴 (big soil) means large pieces of soil, consisting of two components *tu* 土 (soil) and *lu* 圥 (fungi), the latter serving as a phonetic component. Notes by Duan Yucai said, "*lu* 坴 (big soil) means soil pieces that look big."
- In *Shuowen Jiezi*, *lu* 陸 (land) means high and flat lands. The character consists of two components *fu* 𨸏 (land) and *lu* 坴 (big soil), the latter serving as a phonetic component.

  The rationale behind them is "high/tall", thus we can see that they come from the same origin, with "high" as their core semes.
- According to *Shuowen Jiezi*, *zhi* 至 (arrive) means birds flying to the ground from high up. Its component *yi* 一 (one), which resembles the land being flat, is a pictograph. *Shi* 室 (room) means *shi* 实 (room), consisting of two components *mian* 宀 (roofed room) and *zhi* 至 (arrive). *Zhi* 至 (arrive) refers to where there is a stop.
- According to *Shuowen Jiezi*, *zhi* 窒 (obstruction) means to obstruct, consisting of two components *xue* 穴 (cave) and *zhi* 至 (arrive), the latter serving as a phonetic component.
- According to *Shuowen Jiezi*, *zhi* 庢 (obstacle) means to obstruct, consisting of two components *guang* 广 (wide) and *zhi* 至 (arrive), the latter serving as a phonetic component.
- According to *Shuowen Jiezi*, *zhi* 桎 (restraint) means foot shackles, consisting of two components *mu* 木 (wood) and *zhi* 至 (arrive), the latter serving as a phonetic component.

  From the rationale given about *zhi* 至 (arrive), we can see that 室, 庢 and 桎 all share the common core seme of "*zhi* 止 (toe/end)". They share the same origin.
- According to *Shuowen Jiezi*, *shen* 申 (stretch) means *shen* 神 (gods). In lunar July, the ghosts will appear in form and dynamics, and the officials and ministers will hold the mortar in the evening meal and listen to the gods' orders for the affairs of government. In the section of *da* 大 (big) of *Shuowen Jiezi*, *yan* 奄 (to cover) means to overlay, thus something big that unfolds above to cover the item below. The character consists of two components *da* 大 (big) and *shen* 申 (stretch), which means something that stretches.
- According to *Shuowen Jiezi*, *yin* 敐 (drum instrument) means to hit a small drum to make music. The character consists of two components *shen* 申 (stretch) and *jian* 柬 (to choose), the latter serving as a phonetic component.
- According to *Shuowen Jiezi*, *shen* 㬰 (to stretch/extend) consists of two components *you* 又 (again) and *shen* 㫈, the latter serving as a phonetic component. 㫈 is the archaic form of *shen* 申 (stretch).
- According to *Shuowen Jiezi*, *shen* 呻 (recite/moan) means to recite, consisting of two components *kou* 口 (mouth) and *shen* 申 (stretch), the latter serving as a phonetic component.
- According to *Shuowen Jiezi*, *shen* 紳 (girdle) means a big belt, consisting of two components *xi* 糸 (silk) and *shen* 申 (stretch), the latter serving as a phonetic component.

It was noted by Duan Yucai that, in ancient times, there were leather belts to tie the wear. A wider belt was added later. *Shen* 紳 (girdle) is the girdle that hangs from the big belt. Wang Yuzao 王玉藻 said, "*shen* 紳 (girdle) are made to be three *chi* 尺 (Chinese measure) long." In *Shuowen Tongxun Dingsheng* 说文通训定声 (An Explanatory Book of Phonetic Sounds), it was explained that: "When a big belt ties around the waist, the part that hangs down is an accessory called the *shen* 紳 (girdle)."

From the rationale provided on "*shen* 申 (stretch)", we can tell that 昜, 呻, and 紳 all share the core seme of "*yan* 延 (be on a long journey)."

(ii) *Shuowen Jiezi* includes 1,163 "chong wen" 重文 characters (variant form of a Chinese character), many of which are the same as their proper seal script, being semantic-phonetic characters that simply have different phonetic components. This shows that, two phonetic components may sound the same or similar and may be interchangeable. It is a reliable clue in the inspection of homologous characters.

For instance, in *Shuowen Jiezi*—section of *nei* 內 (inside): "*Pi* 膍 (beef tripe), which is beef stomach, with semantic component *rou* 肉 (flesh), and phonetic component *pi* 毘 (belly button). *Pi* 肶 (beef tripe/bird stomach) and *pi* 膍 (beef tripe) may have a semantic composition *bi* 比 (close to)." *Pi* 膍 (beef tripe) and *pi* 肶 (beef tripe/bird stomach) are variant forms of a Chinese character with different phonetic components. *Pi* 梐 (front of eave), in the *mu* 木 (wood) section of *Shuowen Jiezi*, means *lv* 梠 (eaves), consisting of semantic component *mu* 木 (wood), and phonetic component *pi* 毘 (belly button). *Pi* 毘 (belly button) means "belly button" in *Shuowen Jiezi*—section of *xin* 囟 (top of head). Its component *xin* 囟 (top of head) has a meaning of air going through it. *Bi* 比 (close to) serves as its phonetic component. It is obvious that the meaning of *pi* 毘 (belly button) is not related to *pi* 梐 (front of eave). In *Shuowen Jiezi*, *bi* 比 (close to) means close or density. Two *ren* 人 (person) makes *cong* 从 (follow). Duan Yucai noted: "its original meaning is intimacy, with subsequent meanings of *fu* 俌 (assist), *ji* 及 (overtake), *jiao* 校 (compare), *li* 例 (similar to), *pin* 频 (frequency) . . . which were all derived from it."

In *Shuowen Jiezi*—section of *tu* 土 (soil), *bi* 坒 (connected), means ground below. It consists of the semantic component *tu* 土 (soil), and phonetic component *bi* 比 (close to). This shows that *bi* 比 (close to) has a meaning of "lower", and *pi* 梐 (front of eave) originates from *bi* 比 (close to), thus the two characters have the same origin and are homologous.

In *Shuowen Jiezi*—*yu* 鱼 (fish): "*jing* 鱷 (whale) is a big fish in the ocean. It consists of the semantic component *yu* 鱼 (fish), and phonetic component *jiang* 畺 (border). *Jing* 鲸 (whale), just *jing* 鱷 (whale), may have a semantic component *jing* 京 (artificial mound)."

In *Shuowen Jiezi*—section of *lu* 鹿 (deer): "*jing* 麠 (sambar) means a big deer. It has an ox tail and one horn. The character consists of the semantic component *lu* 鹿 (deer) and phonetic component *jiang* 畺 (border). Thus, *jing* 麏 (sambar) may have a semantic component *jing* 京 (artificial mound)." *Jing* 麏 and *jing* 麠 are variant forms of a Chinese character.

In *Shuowen Jiezi*—section of *jiang* 畕 (border/territory), *Jiang* 畺 (border) means border, consisting of the component *jiang* 畕 (border/territory). *San* 三 (three) shows the borders of its territory. The character *jiang* 疆 (territory) consists of two components *jiang* 畺 (stubborn) and *tu* 土 (soil). The meaning of *jing* 鯨 (whale) and *jing* 麖 (sambar) is not related to *jiang* 畺 (border).

According to *Shuowen Jiezi, jing* 京 (artificial mound) means a mound built by human beings, and the character shapes like the character *gao* 高 (high). Duan Yucai 段玉裁 (1735–1815) noted that "*jing* 京 (artificial mound) means big in *Shigu* 释诂 (Explaining the Old Words). Those are tall are usually big." This way, *jing* 鯨 (whale) refers to big *yu* 鱼 (fish), *jing* 麖 (sambar) refers to big *lu* 鹿 (deer), and they all derive from *jing* 京 (artificial mound) and come from the same origin as *jing* 京 (artificial mound), and *jiang* 畺 (border) is a borrowed component *jing* 京 (artificial mound).

(iii) The core semes are derived from the feature of the thing being named. Each thing has numerous features, and a certain feature is recognised in the naming because it appears to be prominent among the many features of the same thing. Therefore, the core seme derived from this prominent feature will also stand out among the multitude of semes of the lexical meaning. That is why it sometimes appears in the interpretation of word meanings. Xu Shen's interpretation of character meanings differs greatly from that of *Erya* 尔雅 (Erya Dictionary) and others in that he is not satisfied with conceptual generalizations of character meanings, but often intentionally reveals the features of word meanings, which facilitates the identification of its core seme.

Some examples:

- *Tuan* 簨 (round item made of bamboo), in *Shuowen Jiezi*—section of *zhu* 竹 (bamboo), means bamboo utensil. It consists of the semantic component *zhu* 竹 (bamboo), and phonetic component *zhuan* 專 (spindle).
- *Xuan* 楦 (round food trays), in *Shuowen Jiezi*—section of mu 木 (wood), means a desk or table. It consists of the semantic component *mu* 木 (wood) and phonetic component *qiong* 袰 (round/stare).
- *Xuan* 鏇 (round furnace), in *Shuowen Jiezi*—section of *jin* 金 (metal), means a circular furnace. It consists of the semantic component *jin* 金 (metal) and phonetic component *xuan* 旋 (revolve).

Xu Shen did not just explain the above characters as "bamboo utensil," "desk," or "furnace" but added the character "*yuan* 圜 (circle)". *Yuan* 圜, in *Shuowen Jiezi*—section *wei* 囗 (to enclose), means a celestial body. It consists of the semantic component *wei* 囗 (to enclose) and phonetic component *qiong* 袰 (round/stare). In ancient times, there was the concept of the sky being round and the earth being square in form, as cited in works, such as *Chu Ci* 楚辞 (The Odes of Chu) and *Lüshi Chunqiu* 吕氏春秋 (Lü's Commentaries of History). By adding the character "*yuan* 圜 (circle)" in his explanation, Xu Shen meant to depict the circular feature of these objects. As is the case below:

- *Kuan* 梡 (tray for carrying sacrificial meat), in *Shuowen Jiezi*—section *mu* 木 (wood), means a tool made of *hun* 楎 (whole piece of log or unbroken firewood). The character consists of the semantic component *mu* 木 (wood) and phonetic component *wan* 完 (complete).

- *Hun* 棞 (whole piece of log or unbroken firewood), in *Shuowen Jiezi*—section *mu* 木 (wood), means uncut firewood. The character consists of the semantic component *mu* 木 (wood) and phonetic component *hun* 圂 (round pigsty).
- *Tuan* 摶 (roll something into a ball), in *Shuowen Jiezi*—section *shou* 手 (hand), means to roll something into a ball with hand. The character consists of the semantic component *shou* 手 (hand) and phonetic component *zhuan* 專 (spindle).
- *Qun* 囷 (round-shaped storage bin for grain), in *Shuowen Jiezi*—section *wei* 囗 (to enclose), means to store *he* 禾 (standing grain) in *wei* 囗 (to enclose). A round granary is called *qun* 囷, and a square granary is called *jing* 京.
- *Xun* 紃 (round-shaped cord), in *Shuowen Jiezi*—section *xi* 系 (involve/relate), means to tie around. It consists of the semantic component *mi* 糸 (silk) and phonetic component *chuan* 川 (river).
- *Jun* 軍 (army), in *Shuowen Jiezi*—section *che* 車 (vehicle), means to surround. Four thousand people make an army. The character consists of two components *bao* 包 (wrap) and *che* 車 (vehicle).
- *Han* 韓 (fence around the well), in *Shuowen Jiezi*—section *wei* 韋 (tanned leather), means the fence around a well. It consists of the semantic component *wei* 韋, which means to encircle and phonetic component *gan* 倝 (glow of sunrise).
- *Wan* 丸 (pellet), in *Shuowen Jiezi*—section *jiu* 九 (nine), means *yuan* 圓 (circle), something that can be tilted around. It consists of two components *fan* 反 (turn around) and *ze* 仄 (incline).
- *Juan* 𢍯 (rice ball), in *Shuowen Jiezi*—section *gong* 廾 (two hands), means to roll the rice into a ball. It consists of the semantic component *gong* 廾 (two hands) and phonetic component *bian* 釆 (to separate/distinguish).
- *Huan* 豢 (feed), in *Shuowen Jiezi*—section *shi* 豕 (pigs and boars), means to rear pigs with grains. It consists of the semantic component *shi* 豕 (pigs and boars) and phonetic component *juan* 𢍯 (rice ball).
- *Huan* 寏 (courtyard fence), in *Shuowen Jiezi*—section *mian* 宀 (roofed room), means a fence around something. It consists of the semantic component *mian* 宀 (roofed room) and phonetic component of *huan* 奐 (to exchange). *Yuan* 院 (yard) consists of two components *Huan* 寏 (or *fu* 阜 (mound)) and *wan* 完 (whole), the latter serving as a phonetic component.

Based on *Shuowen Jiezi*, we can tell that the above characters all share the core seme of "*zhouyuan* 周圓 (circle)".

- *Yun* 䀏 (blurry vision), in *Shuowen Jiezi*—section *jian* 見 (to see), means dizzy or blurry vision. It consists of the semantic component *xian* 见 (appear) and phonetic component *yuan* 員 (circle).
- *Yun* 賱 (numerous and disorderly), in *Shuowen Jiezi*—section *yuan* 員 (circle), means many items placed in a messy order. It consists of the semantic component *yuan* 員 (circle) and phonetic component *yun* 云 (clouds).

- *Yuan* 员 (number of items/round), in *Shuowen Jiezi*—section *yuan* 员, means number of items. It consists of the semantic component *bei* 贝 (seashell) and phonetic component *wei* 口 (to enclose).
- *Qun* 窘 (cluster), in *Shuowen Jiezi*—section *mian* 宀 (roofed room), means to live in groups. It consists of the semantic component *mian* 宀 (roofed room) and phonetic component *jun* 君 (monarch).
- *Yin* 莽 (grass), in *Shuowen Jiezi*—section *cao* 艸 (herbage), means the appearance of lots of grass. It consists of the semantic component *cao* 艸 (herbage) and phonetic component *yin* 狺 (dog barking).

The characters above all share the core seme of "many".

- *Yun* 啈 (big mouth), in *Shuowen Jiezi*—section *kou* 口 (mouth), means a big mouth. It consists of the semantic component *kou* 口 (mouth) and phonetic component *jun* 軍 (army).
- *Hun* 暉 (big eyes), in *Shuowen Jiezi*—section *mu* 目 (eye), means big and protruding eyes. It consists of the semantic component *mu* 目 (eye) and phonetic component *jun* 軍 (army).
- *Ai* 曖 (ambiguous), in *Shuowen Jiezi*—section *mu* 目 (eye), means big eyes. It consists of the semantic component *mu* 目 (eye) and phonetic component *ai* 愛 (benevolence/love).
- *Huan* 覴 (big view), in *Shuowen Jiezi*—section *jian* 見 (to see), means seeing big. It consists of the semantic component *xian* 见 (appear) and phonetic component *yuan* 爰 (to lead on to).
- *Han* 睅 (big and protruding eyes), in *Shuowen Jiezi*—section *mu* 目 (eye), means big eyes. It consists of the semantic component *mu* 目 (eye) and phonetic component *han* 旱 (drought).
- *Xian* 榍 (big wood), in *Shuowen Jiezi*—section *mu* 木 (wood), means big wood. It consists of the semantic component *mu* 木 (wood) and phonetic component *xian* 閒 (gap).
- *Yun* 頵 (big head), in *Shuowen Jiezi*—section *ye* 頁 (head), means the head is very big. It consists of the semantic component *ye* 頁 (head) and phonetic component *jun* 君 (monarch).
- *Huan* 奄 (exaggerated), in *Shuowen Jiezi*—section *da* 大 (big), means exaggerated largeness. It consists of the semantic component *da* 大 (big) and phonetic component *gen* 亘 (continuous extension).
- *Jun* 菌 (algae), in *Shuowen Jiezi*—section *cao* 艸 (herbage), means a type of algae. It consists of the semantic component of *cao* 艸 (herbage) and phonetic component *jun* 君 (monarch).
- *Fui* 翬 (to fly), in *Shuowen Jiezi*—section *yu* 羽 (feather), means to fly fast. It consists of the semantic component *yu* 羽 (feather) and phonetic component *jun* 軍 (army).
- *Yun* 溳 (big wave), in *Shuowen Jiezi*—section *shui* 水 (water), means big waves in a major river. It consists of the semantic component *shui* 水 (water) and phonetic component *yun* 雲 (cloud).

- *Hun* 混 (torrent), in *Shuowen Jiezi*—section *shui* 水 (water), means abundant flows. It consists of the semantic component *shui* 水 (water) and phonetic component *kun* 昆.
- *Hun* 渾 (surging sounds), in *Shuowen Jiezi*—section *shui* 水 (water), means sounds of torrent flowing. It consists of the semantic component *shui* 水 (water) and phonetic component *jun* 军 (army).
- *Yin* 殷 (music of dance), in *Shuowen Jiezi*—section *yin* 㐆 (to return/conceal), means abundance of music. It consists of two components *yin* 㐆 (to return/conceal) and *shu* 殳 (long pole). According to *Yi* 易 (The Book of Changes): Dedication of a grand ceremony to the Heavenly Emperor.

Thus, the above characters share the core seme of "*da* 大 (big)" or abundance.

- *Yuan* 爰 (to lead on to), in *Shuowen Jiezi*—section *biao* 爪 (an object falling into a fixed place), means to lead. It consists of the two components *biao* 爪 (an object falling into a fixed place) and *yu* 于 (go to).
- *Yuan* 援 (to pull), in *Shuowen Jiezi*—section *shou* 手 (hand), means to pull or lead. It consists of the semantic component *shou* 手 (hand) and phonetic component *yuan* 爰 (to lead on to).
- *Yuan* 媛 (beautiful lady), in *Shuowen Jiezi*—section *nv* 女 (women and girls), means a beautiful lady, someone that people are keen to help. The character consists of the semantic component *nv* 女 (women and girls) and phonetic component *yuan* 爰 (to lead on to). Thus, 爰 also means attraction. As cited in *Shi Jing* 诗经 (The Book of Songs): the nation's most beautiful lady.
- *Yuan* 瑗 (fine jade with a big hole), in *Shuowen Jiezi*—section *yu* 玉 (precious stone), means jade with a big hole, something a monarch holds onto when going up the steps. It consists of the semantic component *yu* 玉 (precious stone) and phonetic component *yuan* 爰 (to lead on to).
- *Yuan* 蝯 (ape), in *Shuowen Jiezi*—section *chong* 虫 (worms and insects), belongs to *yu* 禺 (insect name) and is an animal that is good at climbing. It consists of the semantic component *chong* 虫 (worms and insects), and phonetic component *yuan* 爰 (to lead on to).
- *Yin* 引 (to draw a bow), in *Shuowen Jiezi*—section *gong* 弓 (bow), means to draw a bow. It consists of the two components *gong* 弓 (bow) and *gun* 丨 (through).
- *Yin* 靷 (tether), in *Shuowen Jiezi*—section *ge* 革 (leather), means leading shaft. It consists of the semantic component *ge* 革 (leather) and phonetic component *yin* 引 (to draw a bow).
- *Zen* 紖 (tether), in *Shuowen Jiezi*—section *xi* 系 (involve/relate), means a tether to pull livestock. It consists of the semantic component *mi* 糸 (silk) and phonetic component *yin* 引 (to draw a bow).
- *Qian* 牵 (to pull/hold hands), in *Shuowen Jiezi*—section *niu* 牛 (cattle), means to lead forward. It consists of the semantic component *niu* 牛 (cattle) and phonetic component *xuan* 玄 (black). The character is a pictograph of rope to pull cattle.
- *Yan* 偞 (to raise prices), in *Shuowen Jiezi*—section *ren* 人 (person), means the raise of prices. It consists of the semantic component *niu* 牛 (cattle), and phonetic component *yan* 焉 (a kind of bird).

- *Qian* 乾 (to emerge), in *Shuowen Jiezi*—section *yi* 乙 (the second), means emerging upward. It consists of the semantic component *yi* 乙 (the second), which stands for something that goes upward, and the phonetic component *gan* 倝 (glow of sunrise).
- *Yan* 延 (be on a long journey), in *Shuowen Jiezi*—section *chan* 㢟 (look of walking slowly), means a long walk. It consists of the semantic component *chan* 㢟 (look of walking slowly), and phonetic component *pie* 丿 (go to).
- *Yuan* 遠 (walking), in *Shuowen Jiezi*—section *chuo* 辵 (walking), means the look of walking. It consists of the semantic component *chuo* 辵 (walking), and phonetic component *yuan* 爰 (whirling water).

The characters above all share the core seme of "*qianyan* 前延 (extension)".

- *Yuan* 袁 (long), in *Shuowen Jiezi*—section *yi* 衣 (clothes), means the look of long clothing. It consists of the semantic component *yi* 衣 (clothes) and simplified phonetic component *zhuan* 叀 (sewing device).
- *Chan* 梴 (look of high tree), in *Shuowen Jiezi*—section *mu* 木 (wood), means long or tall wood. It consists of the semantic component *mu* 木 (wood) and phonetic component *yan* 延 (be on a long journey).
- *Shan* 挻 (long), in *Shuowen Jiezi*—section *shou* 手 (hand), means something long. It consists of the semantic components *shou* 手 (hand) and *yan* 延 (be on a long journey), while the latter is also its phonetic component.
- *Yan* 嫣 (tall), in *Shuowen Jiezi*—section *nv* 女 (women and girls), means tall. It consists of the semantic component *nv* 女 (women and girls) and phonetic component *yan* 焉 (a kind of bird).
- *Han* 騿 (long-haired horse), in *Shuowen Jiezi*—section *ma* 馬 (horse), means horses with long hair. It consists of the semantic component *ma* 马 (horse) and phonetic component *gan* 倝 (glow of sunrise).
- *Xuan* 喧 (to cry endlessly), in *Shuowen Jiezi*—section *kou* 口 (mouth), means the nonstop crying of a child in the northeast region of ancient China. It consists of the semantic component *kou* 口 (mouth) and simplified phonetic component *xuan* 宣 (spread all over).
- *Heng* 恒 (permanent), in *Shuowen Jiezi*—section *er* 二 (two/twice), means permanence. It consists of two components *xin* 心 (heart) and *zhou* 舟 (boat), which are placed between the two strokes of *er* 二 (two/twice). *Yan* 駿 (to verity) is the archaic form of *Heng* 恒 (permanent) with *yue* 月 (moon) as its component. Cited in *Shi Jing* 诗经 (The Book of Songs): eternal as the moon.

The above characters all share the core seme of "*jiuchang* 久长 (continuity)."

Based on the phonetic components, other ancient explanations, and historical and cultural backgrounds, it proves that the core semes of "*zhouyuan* 周圜 (circle)", "*duo* 多 (many)", "*da* 大 (big)", "*qianyan* 前延 (extension)", and "*jiuchang* 久长 (continuity)" are relevant core semes.[8]

See the following analysis of phonetic components and core semes.

Shuowen Jiezi and an Exploration of Homologous Characters 309

Table 23.2 Analysis of Phonetic Components and Core Semes

Phonetic Component (Hanyu Pinyin) \ Character \ Core Seme	Yuan (uan/an) houya 喉牙 (throat and teeth sound)	chi 齿 (teeth sound)	she 舌 (tongue sound)	Wen (un houya 喉牙 (throat and teeth sound)	chi 齿 (teeth sound)	Zhen (in/ian) houya 喉牙 (throat and teeth sound)
zhouyuan 周圆 (circle)	xuan 楦 (round food trays), yuan 圆 (circle), kuan 梡 (tray for carrying sacrificial meat), huo 桓 (fence around the well), wan 丸 (pellet), huan 豢 (rice ball), huan 黍 (feed), huan 寏 (courtyard fence)	Xuan 镟 (round furnace)	tuan 筜 (round item made of bamboo), tuan 摶 (roll something into a ball)	hun 梡 (whole piece of log or unbroken firewood), qun 囷 (round-shaped storage bin for grain), jun 军 (army)	xuan 紃 (round-shaped cord)	
duo 多 (many)				yun 暉 (big mouth), hun 瞱 (big eyes), yun 顐 (big head), jun 菌 (algae), hui 翬 (to fly), yun 溁 (big wave), hun 混 (torrent), hun 浑 (surging sounds), yin 殷 (music of dance)		
da 大 (big)	hun 暉 (big eyes), huan 覥 (big view), han 睅 (big and protruding eyes), xian 橺 (big wood), huan 荁 (exaggerated)					
qianyan 前延 (extension)	yuan 妥 (to lead on to), yuan 媛 (to pull), yuan 媛 (beautiful lady), yuan 瑗 (fine jade with a big hole), yuan 猨 (ape), yan 焉 (to raise prices), qian 乾 (to emerge), yan 延 (be on a long journey)					yin 引 (to draw a bow), yin 靷 (tether), zhen 紖 (tether), qian 牵 (to pull/hold hands), yuan 過 (walking)
jiuchang 久长 (continuity)	yuan 袤 (long), chan 梃 (look of high tree), shan 挺 (long), yan 駬 (tall), han 駽 (long-haired horse), xuan 喧 (non-stop crying of a child), neng 恒 (permanent)					

Description: teeth sounds in this table only contains *xie niu* 邪纽 ("xie" Initial Consonant). "*Xie*" and throat and teeth sounds are close consonants, and "*xie*" is also a close consonant of tongue sounds. Therefore, tongue sounds and throat and teeth sounds appear in the same word family.

From the above interpretation of *Shuowen Jiezi*, the Chinese characters that are shaped according to the meaning often have the important features of the word meaning reflected in the character form, while *Shuowen Jiezi* tends to reveal the important features of the word meaning in the interpretation to explain the character form. At the same time, *Shuowen Jiezi* separates its radicals according to the relationship between form and meaning, and the relationship between form and meaning and pronunciation cannot be revealed systematically. However, since *Shuowen Jiezi* is not only a dictionary for explaining the meaning of words, but it also must show the relationship between form and meaning, as well as pronunciation as much as possible.

In the *che* 车 (vehicle) section of *Shuowen Jiezi*, *jun* 军 (army), means *yuan* 圆 (circle), and *wei* 围 (surround). Four thousand people make an army. The character consists of the component *che* 车 (vehicle) and the simplified form of *bao* 包 (enclose). Duan Yucai 段玉裁 (1735–1815) noted, "the character form yields the meaning of 'circle', and the character pronunciation yields the meaning of 'surround'." Duan's note precisely states the features of *Shuowen Jiezi*'s interpretation of the meaning. The characters in the table contain phonetic components, such as *qiong* 睘 (round/stare), *wan* 完 (complete), *zhuan* 專 (spindle), *yuan* 爰 (to lead on to), and *gen* 亘 (continuous extension), and these phonetic components are close in pronunciation and interchangeable in meaning, and the interpretation of the characters' components in *Shuowen Jiezi* is not only refined but also highlights the points of convergence, which is an astonishing unity that would be difficult to achieve if it were not intentional.

Among the previously cited characters, *han* 韓 (fence around the well) consists of the semantic component *wei* 韋, which means to encircle, *yuan* 媛 (beautiful lady) means those who are likely to be helped, *yuan* 瑗 (fine jade with a big hole) means jade with a big hole, something a monarch holds onto when going up the steps, and *yuan* 猨 (ape) means an animal that is good at climbing. The interpretation of the meaning of Chinese characters in other works don't usually involve highlighting the convergence of the characters' components, but *Shuowen Jiezi* does so to reflect the close relationship between characters' forms, meanings, and pronunciations. In the interpretation of the meaning of some characters, *Shuowen Jiezi* even directly presents the phonetic component in the explanation, to show the relationship between form, pronunciation, and meaning.

For example:

- In *Shuowen Jiezi*—section *gu* 骨 (bone), *pian* 骿 means ribs being aligned. It consists of semantic component *gu* 骨 (bone) and phonetic component *bing* 并 (merge).
- In *Shuowen Jiezi*—section *cao* 艸 (herbage), *zhuo* 茁 (thriving grass) means *cao* 艸 (herbage) starts to grow. It consists of the semantic component *cao* 艸 (herbage) and the phonetic component *chu* 出 (out).

- In *Shuowen Jiezi*—section *rou* 肉 (flesh), *hu* 膴 (boneless dry meat) means dried meat without bones. It consists of the semantic component *rou* 肉 (flesh) and phonetic component *wu* 無 (nothing).
- In *Shuowen Jiezi*—section *gu* 骨 (bone), *kuai* 髍 (bone-made accessory for hair) means the use of a bone to comb up hair. It consists of the semantic component *gu* 骨 (bone), and phonetic component *hui* 會 (cover/assemble).
- In *Shuowen Jiezi*—section *yu* 玉 (precious stone), *heng* 珩 means the top gem of the pendants. It consists of the semantic component *yu* 玉 (precious stone) and phonetic composition *xing* 行 (walk).

Of course, *Shuowen Jiezi* sometimes mentions the origin of the name directly in the interpretation, such as in the section *zhu* 竹 (bamboo): "*sheng* 笙 (thirteen-reed-pipe wind instrument), resembling the body of a phoenix, refers to the sound of the first month of a year when things emerge. It consists of the semantic composition *zhu* 竹 (bamboo) and phonetic composition *sheng* 生 (life)." In section *cao* 艸 (herbage), *yu* 芋 (taro with huge leaves and rootstock) consists of the semantic component *cao* 艸 (herbage) and phonetic component *yu* 于 (go to).

The special interpretation system of *Shuowen Jiezi*, which pursues the unity of form and meaning, and the unity of the close relationship between form, pronunciation, and the meaning contained therein is of great significance to the exploration of homologous characters. On the premise of correctly understanding the relationship between the pronunciation and meaning of homologous characters and making full use of *Shuowen Jiezi*, it is believed that a new breakthrough will be made in this time-honoured problem of homologous characters.

Notes

1 The original Chinese version was published in September 1991, on the Collection of Papers of the International Symposium on Xu Shen and *Shuowen Jiezi*, in the first Volume of *Studies of Shuowen Jiezi* (An Explication of Written Characters). It was later edited and published by the Chinese Society in the *Xu Shen Studies*, Henan University Press.
2 《语言缘起说》，见《章氏丛书》.
  The Origin of the Language, see *Works of Zhang Taiyan*.
3 《语言缘起说》，见《章氏丛书》.
  The Origin of the Language, see *Works of Zhang Taiyan*.
4 《语言缘起说》，见《章氏丛书》.
  The Origin of the Language, see *Works of Zhang Taiyan*.
5 《文始·叙》，见《章氏丛书》.
  Wenshi Dictionary of Homologous Characters—Preface, see *Works of Zhang Taiyan*.
6 详见拙著《汉语同源字（词）意义关系研究》，《学术之声》，1989（3）.
  See my work *Sense Relations among Same-Origin Chinese Characters (Words)*, *Academic Voice*, 1989 (3).

7 In his article "The Successive Changes and Explain of the Theory of the Sound Words at Right in Exegetics 右文说在训诂学上之沿革及其推阐", Shen Jianshi talked about the words "Yu 语 (talk/discuss)", "yu 敔 (ancient music instrument)", "yu 圉 (detain)", "wu 悟 (meet)", "yu 啎 (discord)", and so on, and considered that they all have "inverse meaning".
8 详见拙著《汉语同源字（词）意义关系研究》，《学术之声》，1989（3）.
See my work *Sense Relations among Same-Origin Chinese Characters (Words), Academic Voice*, 1989 (3).

Index

Archaic characters 86, 87, 88, 126, 131, 132, 138, 144, 248

bamboo slips 21, 23, 24, 25, 39, 41, 42, 43, 44, 45, 46, 47, 48, 49, 65, 68, 82, 105, 111, 112, 120, 121, 122, 123, 124, 125, 130, 195, 196, 200, 201, 202, 203, 204, 206, 207, 208, 209, 210, 211, 212, 213, 214, 246, 247, 257, 258, 259, 260, 261, 262, 263, 264, 265, 267, 268, 269, 270, 272, 273, 274, 275, 276, 277, 278, 279, 280

bronze inscriptions 2, 3, 4, 9, 10, 18, 26, 35, 38, 41, 48, 52, 53, 57, 61, 69, 74, 75, 76, 77, 79, 81, 82, 83, 84, 88, 89, 111, 112, 132, 153, 193, 196, 198, 202, 218, 248, 251, 258, 273

Chinese characters 1–54, 61, 62, 64, 65, 66, 67, 68, 69, 70, 73, 74, 75, 78, 79, 80, 81, 82, 84, 85, 86, 88, 97, 105, 106, 107, 110, 111, 112, 114, 115, 116, 117, 118, 119, 120, 124, 126–136, 144, 145, 146, 147, 148, 150, 151, 152, 153, 154, 155, 157, 158, 160–182, 184, 185, 186, 187, 188, 189, 190, 193, 198, 200, 201, 205, 206, 210, 219, 223, 230, 240, 241, 244, 248, 252, 253, 254, 266, 272, 273, 280, 287, 293, 300, 310, 311, 312

Chu-State 16, 41, 42, 43, 44, 48, 49, 120, 124, 149, 150, 151, 157, 201, 203, 206, 209, 210, 213, 214, 267, 273, 274, 275, 276, 277, 278, 279, 280

composition system 27, 28, 29, 30, 31, 32, 33, 34, 35, 36, 37, 38, 39, 41, 44, 45, 47, 61, 62, 67, 69, 70, 77, 79, 82, 105, 106, 107, 108, 110, 111, 112, 113, 116, 119, 127, 136, 142, 144, 186, 188, 189, 192, 201, 248

differently structured variants 185–187
differently written variants 185, 187

extended meanings 204, 205, 215, 216, 217, 218, 240, 241, 242, 244

handed-down texts 184
homographs 185, 187, 188, 208
homologous characters 161, 162, 165, 166, 167, 169, 171, 172, 293–312

monomorphemic characters 189, 192, 194
morphemes 29, 30, 188, 189, 192, 193, 194, 195, 197, 198
morphs 28, 29, 186, 187, 188, 197
multicomponent characters 13, 18, 33, 35, 66, 79, 120, 124, 132, 136, 143, 173, 174, 193
multitype modification 12, 13, 14, 15, 18, 21, 39, 101, 154

new-style characters 88, 126, 200

object glyphs 126, 130, 131, 136
official script 1, 2, 9–13, 17, 18, 33, 36–40, 47, 48, 69, 70, 83, 84, 88, 97, 99, 101, 122, 123, 135, 146, 149, 150, 151, 152, 153, 154, 155, 157, 158, 159, 186, 198, 199, 202, 209, 228, 229, 261
oracle-bone script 27, 34, 52, 53, 55, 58, 59, 69, 70, 71, 72, 75, 76, 77, 80, 81, 82, 83, 115, 117, 118, 124, 131,

314   *Index*

133, 134, 136, 186, 190, 192, 196, 202, 215, 218, 241, 248, 251, 253
original meaning 32, 44, 55, 66, 109, 110, 115, 137, 169, 171, 178, 205, 206, 208, 215, 216, 217, 218, 219, 241, 242, 243, 252, 253, 303

palaeography 158
philological 106, 107, 109, 132, 223, 240
phonetic components 7, 8, 11, 32, 33, 64, 65, 73, 88, 127, 128, 133, 134, 137, 139, 141, 143, 144, 148, 163, 173, 175, 179, 180, 202, 203, 277, 293, 303, 308, 309, 310
pictographic 3, 6, 18, 27, 32, 33, 34, 35, 36, 37, 38, 50, 51, 52, 53, 54, 55, 56, 57, 58, 59, 60, 61, 62, 63, 64, 65, 67, 70, 73, 74, 75, 77, 79, 80, 81, 82, 83, 84, 85, 88, 89, 108, 109, 114, 116, 117, 120, 121, 126, 127, 128, 129, 130, 131, 132, 133, 134, 135, 136, 137, 138, 141, 142, 143, 144, 145, 146, 151, 152, 155, 166, 171, 174, 175, 186, 189, 190, 192, 193, 194, 195, 198, 205, 218, 272, 281, 301
poly-morphemic characters 189, 193

radicals 8, 23, 81, 97, 98, 106–125, 134, 173, 174, 188, 230, 237, 249, 256, 310
regular script 1, 2, 6, 7, 8, 9, 10, 11, 12, 13, 15, 16, 17, 18, 19, 20, 21, 22, 23, 24, 25, 37, 100, 115, 153, 154, 198, 199, 201, 202

same-origin Chinese characters 160–172, 311, 312
semantic-compound 50, 51, 58, 61, 65, 66, 67, 77, 79, 80, 82, 83, 128, 131, 174
semantic-phonetic 3, 34, 50, 51, 52, 54, 55, 56, 59, 61, 62, 63, 64, 65, 66, 67, 68, 79, 80, 83, 84, 126, 127, 128, 131, 133, 134, 135, 140, 141, 142, 143, 144, 145, 146, 148, 165, 175, 176, 177, 178, 179, 180, 181, 202, 203, 252, 256, 303
Shuowen Jiezi 12, 17, 18, 40, 47, 51, 52, 54, 55, 57, 58, 59, 60, 62, 63, 64, 65, 66, 67, 68, 82, 83, 84, 85, 106, 107, 109, 114, 115, 117, 123, 127, 128, 131, 132, 133, 135, 137, 138, 140, 142, 143, 146, 155, 156, 157, 160, 162, 163, 164, 166, 167, 168, 169, 170, 171, 187, 188, 190, 192, 193, 194, 196, 197, 198, 202, 204, 205, 206, 207, 208, 211, 213, 214, 218, 223–312
silk manuscripts 9, 10, 13, 14, 15, 16, 17, 18, 19, 20, 21, 22, 23, 24, 25, 47, 49, 90, 130, 149, 150, 151, 157, 183, 184, 187, 190, 191, 192, 193, 194, 195, 196, 197, 198, 199, 200–214, 228, 247, 256, 257, 258, 275
single-component characters 13, 29, 32, 33, 35, 37, 62, 70, 71, 113, 121, 124, 128, 139, 142, 173, 174, 194
stroke system 86–105, 124
structural balance 12, 19, 20, 21, 154
sub-pictographs 1, 3, 4, 6, 7, 11, 37, 38, 66, 67, 83, 120, 130, 174
substitutionary development 22
symbiotic development 22, 23, 25
symbolisation 51, 56, 57, 60, 61, 62, 64, 65, 67, 126–148
systematic transformation 50, 61

unearthed texts 182–199

version 25, 38, 48, 52, 55, 68, 85, 97, 105, 138, 157, 172, 181, 184, 194, 199, 210, 219–239, 255, 256, 258, 259, 265, 266, 267, 270, 271, 272, 280, 289, 311

word classification 281
word symbols 126, 130, 131, 136, 175

Youwen theory 161, 163

For Product Safety Concerns and Information please contact our EU
representative GPSR@taylorandfrancis.com
Taylor & Francis Verlag GmbH, Kaufingerstraße 24, 80331 München, Germany

www.ingramcontent.com/pod-product-compliance
Lightning Source LLC
Chambersburg PA
CBHW070746020526
44116CB00032B/1989